MW00465608

"The Bible clearly reveals the significance of ethnic/national Israel in God's purposes. But history shows that the church has often gotten God's plans for Israel terribly wrong. *Forsaking Israel* is a helpful and much needed book that shows how erroneous views of Israel started and continued. It is rich in historical and theological content but readable for all interested in this issue. While much confusion on Israel has occurred, this work by the faculty of Shepherds Theological Seminary is part of the solution for recovering the biblical view. It is a book I recommend, and I will go back to it over and over again."

Michael J. Vlach, Ph.D., Professor of Theology, The Master's Seminary

"In reading this collection of essays, principally by Larry Pettegrew, Research Professor of Theology at Shepherds Theological Seminary, I am rather deeply impressed by the quality of the scholarship that spans detailed historical research, exegetical acuity, and contextual (sociological) awareness. What is found here is a defense of the premillennial and dispensational reading of Holy Scripture, as well as an argument against a stridently covenantal approach. While disagreement is inevitable, I found this to be the best explanation of recent vintage of the position these authors are attempting to perpetuate. It is my hope that it will lead to a more fruitful dialogue among contrastive approaches to reading the Bible that will prove beneficial to the church regardless of one's interpretative approach to Israel and the Church. I found the work extremely helpful and commend it with enthusiasm."

John D. Hannah, Ph.D., Research Professor of Theological Studies, Distinguished Professor of Historical Theology, Dallas Theological Seminary

"Within the Body of Christ, tremendous debate persists concerning the ongoing calling of Israel within the redemptive plans of God. While many claims that this matter is peripheral to the Gospel, in truth, it is quite central. As history testifies, where Christians stand theologically on this matter directly affects how they relate to Israel and the Jewish people. Having failed miserably so many times through history, the Church cannot afford to repeat its sins of the past. Also at stake is the very character of God. Does the God of the Bible keep His promises or not? Is He faithful or is He not? This important book will contribute greatly toward bringing clarity on this critical subject matter to discerning Christians—particularly at a time in history when the evils of Jew-hatred are once more spreading throughout the world like a satanic cancer. *Forsaking Israel* is a critical book for this hour."

Joel Richardson, *NYT* bestselling author,
author of *When a Jew Rules the World*,
speaker, film-maker, and missions advocate.

"Theology is never done in a vacuum. It emerges over time out of biblical study and a particular historical context. Larry Pettegrew and the faculty of Shepherds Theological Seminary have done an excellent job of tracing the historical-theological background that brought about the emergence of supersessionism in covenant theology. The place of Israel within God's divine plan is a defining question whose answer affects not only eschatology, but almost every other aspect of systematic theology as well. With a scholarly, yet irenic spirit, the authors have capably defended the consistent literal-historical-grammatical hermeneutics of dispensationalism while also tracing the weaknesses and issues inherent in covenant theology. I highly recommend this book to anyone who is seeking to understand how and why replacement theology has emerged with its conclusions regarding Israel and why the more biblically satisfying answer is found in dispensationalism."

Richard P. Bargas, D.Min., Executive Director, IFCA International

FORSAKING ISRAEL

HOW IT HAPPENED AND WHY IT MATTERS

With Contributions By

Shepherds Theological Seminary Faculty

Editor: Larry D. Pettegrew

Foreword: Erwin W. Lutzer

Published by:
Kress Biblical Resources
The Woodlands, Texas
www.kressbiblical.com

Editorial Consultant: Jim Dieffenderfer

ISBN: 978-1-934952-53-5

CONTRIBUTORS

Douglas D. Bookman, PhD
Dr. Bookman is the Professor of Bible Exposition at Shepherds Theological Seminary. Doug has had a long career as a Bible professor in Christian colleges and seminaries, as a pastor, and as a Bible-conference speaker. He is a graduate of Pillsbury Baptist Bible College, Central Baptist Theological Seminary of Minneapolis, and Dallas Theological Seminary. Doug's chapter analyzes the theological differences in worldviews between dispensational premillennialists and non-dispensationalists. He also composed the two appendices.

David L. Burggraff, PhD
Dr. Burggraff is the Professor of Systematic Theology and Chaplain at Shepherds Theological Seminary and serves as the Executive Pastor of Colonial Baptist Church. Dave's long-term Christian ministry includes pastor, professor at Christian colleges and seminaries, and seminary dean and president. He is a graduate of the University of Minnesota, Calvary Baptist Theological Seminary, and Dallas Theological Seminary. One of Dave's specialties is in the study of Augustine's theology. His chapter analyzes Augustine's eschatological conversion from premillennialism to amillennialism.

Stephen D. Davey, STM, DD
Dr. Davey is founder and pastor-teacher of Colonial Baptist Church in Cary, North Carolina. He is also the founder, Professor of Practical Theology, and President of Shepherds Theological Seminary. Stephen is also the Bible teacher on the international radio ministry, Wisdom for the Heart, and an author. He is a graduate of Tennessee Temple University, Detroit Baptist Theological Seminary, and Dallas Theological Seminary. Stephen's chapter is an exposition of Romans 11.

Larry D. Pettegrew, ThD

Dr. Pettegrew is the Dean and Provost, Emeritus, of Shepherds Theological Seminary and the Research Professor of Theology. Larry has served in Christian ministries as a youth director, Christian camp director, author, interim-pastor, and for over fifty years as a professor in Christian colleges and seminaries. He is a graduate of Bob Jones University, Central Baptist Theological Seminary of Minneapolis, and Dallas Theological Seminary. Larry writes the chapter on the early church fathers' acceptance of supersessionism, and three chapters on the rise and development of covenant theology in the Reformation era. He also writes three systematic theology chapters assessing supersessionism, covenant theology, and dispensationalism.

Tim Sigler, PhD

Dr. Sigler is the Dean and Provost of Shepherds Theological Seminary and Professor of Hebrew and Biblical Studies. Tim served the Lord as a pastor and as a Professor of Hebrew and Biblical Studies at Moody Bible Institute of Chicago before coming to Shepherds. Tim hosts study tours throughout the biblical world and serves as the Israel Scholar-in-Residence for CFJ ministries. He also is a published author and maintains an on-going preaching ministry. He is a graduate of Faith Baptist Bible College and Seminary, Grace College and Seminary, and Trinity Evangelical Divinity School. Tim writes the introduction to the book.

With gratitude to the students and alumni of
Shepherds Theological Seminary;
For your confidence in the fulfillment of Scripture—
Confidence that swells with anticipation of Christ's return;
Certainty over inspired pledges made good by Christ's reign;
Assurance that His glory will one day ripple outward from Israel,
Rising and rushing to the ends of the earth.

CONTENTS

FOREWORD

Erwin W. Lutzer

FROM MY HEART TO YOURS

I'm excited about the publication of this book and, in a moment, I will explain why.

Every time I led a tour to Israel, I stood on the Mount of Olives and read from the prophet Zechariah. "On that day his feet shall stand on the Mount of Olives that lies before Jerusalem on the east, and the Mount of Olives shall be split in two from east to west by a very wide valley, so that one half of the Mount shall move northward, and the other half southward" (Zech 14:4).

Then I turn to Acts 1 where we read that after Jesus ascended to heaven from the Mount of Olives, two angels said to the fearful disciples, "Men of Galilee, why do you stand looking into heaven? This Jesus, who was taken up from you into heaven, will come in the same way as you saw him go into heaven" (Acts 1:11).

Although not expressly stated, the implication is not only that Jesus shall return "in like manner," but also that He shall return to the very Mount from which He ascended.

I find it perplexing that some Christians don't believe that Jesus will return to the Mount of Olives; they think we will only meet Him "in the air" or perhaps somewhere else. They interpret the prophecy of Zechariah as theophany—a visible appearance of God but not literally true. One Bible teacher says the passage is symbolic and was fulfilled after Israel returned from exile. He, along with many others, believes that God is finished with Israel as a nation, so there's no reason for Jesus to return to the Mount of Olives.

But could the text be any clearer? "On that day his feet shall stand on the Mount of Olives that lies before Jerusalem on the east." What if God actually wanted us to believe that "His feet shall stand on the Mount of Olives"? As

1

one person put it, "If God didn't mean what He said, why didn't He say what He meant?"

I realize the matter isn't that simple since there are many passages in the Old Testament fulfilled in the New, some of which relate directly to the church. But it also seems clear that there are still many prophecies which apply to Israel as a nation that await future fulfillment.

Now, why am I excited about this book?

First, because I have often wondered why the church for many centuries neglected teaching about the uniqueness of Israel in God's plan. Why didn't the early church fathers and later Augustine, for example, see the teaching about Israel as clearly as we might expect? What biblical hermeneutic blinded them to what seems clear to many of us? I have never read a book that answers these questions—until now.

I have toured the Holocaust Museum in Jerusalem and the Jewish Museum in Berlin. I have wept over the evils done to the Jews throughout the centuries, often at the hands of Christians. I have read Martin Luther's screeds against the Jews and marveled that he who so often spoke the words of God could so callously also speak the words of the devil. These are matters also discussed in this book.

Second, I live and serve with wonderful Christian leaders who adopt some form of "replacement theology"—the idea that the church fulfills the promises made to Israel. Large books are being written in an attempt to show the errors of dispensationalism and the conviction that God still has a future for national Israel. This book responds to these developments with scholarly grace.

Finally, and most importantly for me, this book speaks about Israel's future and why the return of Christ will finally fulfill all the glorious promises about a coming time of peace and the Messiah's rule from Jerusalem. Many mysteries of prophecy will only be understood in the future when we personally experience their fulfillment. This book you hold in your hands will help all of us see the storyline of the Bible's teachings about Israel and what must still come to pass.

The authors of this book are on the faculty of Shepherds Theological Seminary, a school that is committed to mentoring its students and teaching them both academics and practical ministry. The faculty is deeply committed to excellent scholarship but also to having direct input into the life of each student. It has been my privilege to personally get to know some of these faculty members though the ministry of Colonial Baptist Church in Cary, North Carolina, just outside of Raleigh.

Through the leadership of the Senior Pastor, Stephen Davey, the Seminary began in 2003 to train students with deep convictions about the inerrancy of Scripture and its complete sufficiency for doctrine and practice. The faculty mirrors these core beliefs. You can read this book with a sense of confidence that it is written by faithful expositors who seek nothing else but explaining what the Bible teaches to the best of their ability.

As you read this book, you'll be invited to a historical journey about how Israel has been viewed in the context of church history and why it matters. And, hopefully, you will be led to believe that God's promises to Israel have never been rescinded and, perhaps like me, you will wonder why some sincere Christians think otherwise. Eternity will clarify all these matters, but meanwhile God has given us His Word and promises that are sure.

God is speaking:

"I will not violate my covenant or alter the word that went forth from my lips. Once for all I have sworn by my holiness; I will not lie to David. His offspring shall endure forever, his throne as long as the sun before me. Like the moon it shall be established forever, a faithful witness in the skies" (Ps 89:34–37).

Read this book not only to understand Israel's past but its future. Rejoice that God's promises have always been kept in the past and will be fulfilled in the future.

God swore and His promises will come to pass.

Dr. Erwin W. Lutzer
Pastor Emeritus
Moody Church, Chicago

INTRODUCTION

Tim Sigler

Israel is God's chosen nation of blessing throughout Scripture. When the Lord made a covenant with King David promising that one of his descendants would sit on the throne of Israel forever, David rejoiced and exclaimed:

> And who is like your people Israel, the one nation on earth whom God went to redeem to be his people, making himself a name and doing for them great and awesome things.... And you established for yourself your people Israel to be your people forever. And you, O LORD, became their God (2 Sam 7:23-24).

This book is about how the Christian church, down through the centuries, has forsaken Israel, and why this is a biblical and theological mistake.

Indeed, more than just neglecting Israel, it has been suggested that the church's history with the Jewish people has been written in blood and punctuated with violence. Crusades, expulsions, pogroms, and even the Holocaust were perpetrated against the Jewish people by some who claimed biblical grounds for persecuting the Jewish people.

There was nothing extraordinary about Israel, of course, that compelled God to choose her as His covenant nation any more than there was something extraordinary about you and me that caused God to set His love on us. When Moses was preparing Israel to enter the land of Canaan, he made this explicit:

> For you are a people holy to the LORD your God. The LORD your God has chosen you to be a people for his treasured possession, out of all the peoples who are on the face of the earth. It was not because you were more in number than any other people that the LORD set his love on you and chose you, for you were the fewest of all peoples, but it is because the LORD loves you and is keeping the oath that he swore to your fathers (Deut 7:6-8).

Israel became God's covenant nation only because He chose to love her (cf. Ezek 16:1-14).

Much later in Israel's history, the Lord, through the prophet Ezekiel, explained why He would redeem future Israel:

> Therefore say to the house of Israel, "Thus says the LORD God: It is not for your sake, O house of Israel, that I am about to act, but for the sake of my holy name, which you have profaned among the nations to which you came. And I will vindicate the holiness of my great name, which has been profaned among the nations, and which you have profaned among them. And the nations will know that I am the LORD, declares the LORD God, when through you I vindicate my holiness before their eyes" (Ezek 36:22-23).

Ezekiel's prophecy continues with the Lord explaining how He will bring the people of Israel back to the land and put His Spirit within them. But the reason why God is going to bless Israel in this way is so that He can "vindicate the holiness" of His name.

God's program today is primarily focused on the international church. When the nation of Israel rejected her Messiah at His first coming, Jesus declared that He would build His church (Matt 16:18). Consequently, the body of Christ, composed of both Jews and Gentiles on equal footing, has temporarily (for 2000 years now) been the focus of God's redemptive work (Eph 3:1-6). The church is the recipient of the Great Commission, commanded to go into all of the world discipling, baptizing, and teaching the Scriptures. This will continue to be the church's charge "until the fullness of the Gentiles has come in" (Rom 11:25).[1]

However, Paul warned the Gentile believers of his day to avoid prideful attitudes toward unbelieving Jewish people (Rom 11:19-24), exemplified great compassion toward his fellow Jewish kinsmen according to the flesh (Rom 9:1-5), and sought their salvation (Rom 10:1). Israel is still in God's plan.

In fact, though the Bible is about our holy, loving, and faithful God, in a secondary sense, the Bible is about Israel. Even a proper account of the life and ministry of Jesus of Nazareth must acknowledge His messianic qualifications including the fact that He was born a descendant of Abraham, of the tribe of

---

[1] We are not arguing in this book that Christians in the church age are supposed to support secular Israel in every political decision that her leaders make. The nation of Israel today is still under God's judgment for not accepting Jesus as her Messiah. We *are* arguing that the Scriptures are clear that God has not forsaken the nation of Israel.

Judah, the Son of David, born in Bethlehem, and was called the King of the Jews. He came, not to Tokyo, New York, London, or Paris, but to Jerusalem where He died, was buried and rose again. He promised His disciples that He would return to the Mount of Olives in Jerusalem to set up His messianic kingdom (Matt 24:26). When He returns, He will sit upon the throne of his father, David. After the end-time judgments, He will create the new heavens and the new earth and will bring the New Jerusalem down from heaven. And from this New Jerusalem, He will rule the earth. On this, the Scripture is clear.

Yet, many believers are unaware or unaffected by the fact that they believe in a Jewish Messiah who came from and is returning to the land and people of Israel. Israel is a nice story that has concluded, they seem to think. They happily read verses like John 1:11-12 as if the final word on the Jewish people is that God has used them for His purpose but is now done with them: "He came to his own, and his own people did not receive him. But to all who did receive him, who believed in his name, he gave the right to become children of God." End of story.

Well, not so fast! Upon closer examination of God's redemptive plan, there is not only a past for the people of Israel but a future as well. Though both the Old Testament prophets and the New Testament apostles declare this truth in multiple places, Romans 9-11 may be the clearest, most intentional, and complete treatment of God's redemptive plan available to us in Scripture. Romans 9 speaks of Israel's *past election*. The selection of Israel as the people through whom God would bring salvation is all part of His plan. Romans 10 tells of Israel's *present rejection and assures us that the current* lack of interest in the gospel among the majority of Jewish people is consistent with Israel's history in biblical times. Romans 11 explains the nature of Israel's *future reception and encourages us that* her rejection is only temporary.[2] Far from being finished with Israel, God has a plan to bring His salvation full circle—from Jerusalem, Judea, Samaria, to the uttermost parts of the earth, and back to Israel again (Acts 1:8; Zech 14; Isa 41; Joel 3).

How can Christians miss this fact? How can it be possible for a person to be a Christian for many years and not know anything about Israel, the Jewish people, and God's covenant promises to Abraham, Isaac, and Jacob? Could it be that the systems of theology and approaches to Scripture taught in many churches today have found a way to read Israel out of the Bible? From beginning

---

[2] See Chapter 11 for a complete exposition of Romans 11.

to end, the Bible is telling the story of God's redemptive plan—a story about how God purposed to bless all the families of the earth *through Israel*.

Indeed, in that future day when the Lord "will extend his hand yet a second time to recover the remnant that remains of his people" (Isa 11:11), the glorious salvation of the Lord will also encompass the other nations of the world. Isaiah prophecies, "In that day Israel will be the third with Egypt and Assyria, a blessing in the midst of the earth, whom the Lord of hosts has blessed, saying, 'Blessed be Egypt my people, and Assyria the work of my hands, and Israel my inheritance'" (Isa 19:24-25). Redeemed Israel will be at the center of a worldwide revival. God is providentially, step by step, bringing His plan with Israel and the nations to fruition.

Our study thus answers two questions: (1) How is it that Israel has become so forsaken in the history of the church? and (2) Why does forsaking Israel matter biblically and theologically? With a mastery of the subject matter, the faculty of Shepherds Theological Seminary will guide readers through the history of how the Christian church has been forsaking Israel from the time of the church fathers, to Augustine, and the Reformation, and then provide biblical and theological reasons to explain why forsaking Israel is so contrary to the message of the Bible itself. They will describe the historical debates, define the theological terms, unpack the hermeneutical principles behind the debates, and assess three important theological systems which determine how interpreters address the question of Israel: dispensationalism, supersessionism, and covenantalism.

Our desire is to honor the Lord and His Word. Our prayer is that you, our reader, will be encouraged by understanding better the faithfulness of God, both to Israel, and to you. "For great is his steadfast love toward us, and the faithfulness of the Lord endures forever. Praise the Lord!" (Ps 117:2).

FORSAKING ISRAEL

Part One: *How It Happened*

1

THE CURIOUS CASE OF THE CHURCH FATHERS AND ISRAEL

Larry D. Pettegrew

The leaders of the Christian church who lived immediately after the death of the apostles were faced with tough theological questions. How should we understand and explain the mystery of Jesus Christ? How can He be both God and man? And how should we explain the complex nature of God as He is revealed in Scripture? How can He be one and yet three? The Fathers of the Church thought deeply about such questions, preached, wrote, prayed, and convened councils. God used these men to clarify the foundational doctrines of Christianity.

There were other questions to answer that were not as foundational but would nonetheless impact the church down through the centuries. Two of these questions were closely related: How should we understand the future of Israel now that she has rejected her Messiah? And what should we do with the Old Testament?

In answering the first question about the future of Israel, there were some reasons to think that the church had permanently replaced the nation. After all, Israel had been led by her religious leaders to kill her Messiah. On the other hand, there were evidences in Scripture that the nation of Israel did have a future. God had formalized with Israel what seemed to be an irrevocable covenant—a one-sided grace contract (Gen 15). God promised Abraham that his descendants would be as many as the stars in the heaven, that they would have an eternal ownership of a section of land in the Middle East, and that through Abraham God would bless the nations of the world. The Old Testament

11

prophets reiterated numerous times that there would indeed be a future age for Israel with Messiah ruling the world from Jerusalem (Isa 2; Ezek 36 ff.; Zech 13-14). Furthermore, in the New Testament, the Apostle Paul declared that "a partial hardening has come upon Israel, until the fullness of the Gentiles has come in. And in this way all Israel will be saved, as it is written, 'The Deliverer will come from Zion, he will banish ungodliness from Jacob'; 'and this will be my covenant with them when I take away their sins'" (Rom 11:25-27).

The early Fathers of the Church had three options concerning the role of the Old Testament now that the New Covenant document had be completed. They could agree with the heretics that the Old Testament was not inspired, that it revealed a wicked god, and that the church should totally and finally discard it. Or they might decide that they should keep the Old Testament, but reinterpret it through the paradigm of the New Testament. This would make the nation of Israel less significant in God's plan for the future. Or, these early theologians could decide that though the New Testament was God's final revelation for the faith and practice of the church, the promises to Israel in the Old Testament had not been revoked, but had actually been reaffirmed by the New Testament Apostles. If so, a redeemed Israel led by her Messiah would one day be the political and religious center of the world.

In this chapter, therefore, we are answering three questions: (1) Did the early church fathers believe in a future kingdom that would be established on earth by Christ after His return? In other words, were the early church fathers premillennialists? (2) If the early church fathers were premillennialists, did they teach that the kingdom of Christ would focus on the nation of Israel (dispensational premillennialism)[1] or on the church (historic premillennialism)?[2] (3)

---

[1] Dispensational premillennialism is based on God's irrevocable promises to Israel in the Abrahamic, Davidic, and New Covenants, Old Testament prophecies, and important New Testament passages. These promises will be fulfilled with Israel after the Second Coming of Jesus Christ. Messiah will rule the world from an earthly Jerusalem in a wonderful era of peace between Israel and the Gentile nations. The city of Jerusalem will be the center of religion and government for one thousand years, and God's glory will be displayed on the earth as in no other time in history. After this millennium, God will remake the heavens and the earth, and then the second stage of God's kingdom will begin and last forever. Concerning the rapture of the church, most dispensationalists believe that God will rapture the church out of the world before the seven-year Tribulation begins (i.e., pretribulationism). During the Tribulation, God will begin to bring Israel back to Himself.

[2] Historic premillennialists usually agree that God made covenants with Israel in the Old Testament promising her that Messiah would one day set up a kingdom with Israel at the center. But tragically, Israel forfeited these promises when, instead of accepting Christ as her Messiah, she crucified Him. Consequently, historical premillennialists teach that God permanently transferred the promises of the covenants from Israel to the church. The church, being a multi-national organism, in this view, is a step-up from the one nation of Israel, and thus the church permanently "superseded" Israel. If there is a large conversion of Jews in the future, they will be added to the church. But national Israel is no longer a part of God's plan. Most historic premillennialists teach that the church will go through the Tribulation (posttribulationism).

If the early church fathers did not believe that Israel would be the center of God's plan for the future, why not? In other words, why did they decide that the promises to Israel had been redirected to a mostly Gentile church? These questions form the essence of the curious case of the church fathers and Israel.

THE CHURCH FATHERS AND ESCHATOLOGY

The study of the church fathers is called "Patristics." The Fathers were pastors, bishops, and theologians who lived from the time of the completion of the canon of the Scriptures up to about A.D. 600, or some would say a little longer. Some church historians divide the period of the Fathers into the Ante-Nicene Fathers (before the Council of Nicaea in 325), and Post-Nicene Fathers. Others have classified the Fathers as Apostolic Fathers, the earliest group of Fathers that theoretically could have been alive when one or more of the apostles were living; Apologetical Fathers, who wrote defenses of Christianity against pagans and state officials; and Polemical Fathers, who attacked the heretical groups such as the Gnostics. Some of the Fathers were Greek-speaking from the Eastern part of the Roman Empire, and some lived in the Western part of the empire and spoke Latin. Most of this chapter interacts with the Ante-Nicene Fathers from both the East and the West. Our time period then is from about A.D. 96, when Clement of Rome wrote a letter to a church at Corinth, until the middle of the third century—a total of about 150 years after the death of the last Apostle.

The Ordinariness of the Church Fathers

However much we may respect the church fathers, especially those that suffered horrendous persecution and martyrdom, they were not on the same theological level as the Apostles of Christ. They were not borne along by the Holy Spirit like the Apostles were, as is obvious from the Fathers' many disagreements with each other. Most of them changed their minds about various aspects of theology—even as we do sometimes. Augustine, for example, was a premillennialist in his early career, but later became an amillennialist.[3] The contradictions between the Fathers were so obvious that Abelard, a twelfth century philosopher, wrote a book, *Sic et Non*, (*Yes and No*) to demonstrate the biblical and theological inconsistencies and contradictions among the church fathers.[4]

---

[3] Augustine, *The City of God* 20.7, NPNF, first series, 426. See our next chapter for the story of how this came to pass.

[4] Peter Abelard, *Yes and No*, trans. Priscilla Throop (Charlotte, VT: Medieval MS, 2007).

The church fathers also brought errors into Christian theology. Within one hundred years of the death of the last Apostle, some were teaching false doctrines such as baptismal regeneration, the ransom theory of the atonement, salvation only through the organizational church, legalism, and asceticism and celibacy as a means of sanctification.[5]

Moreover, there are research problems for modern day scholars who study the church fathers. In the words of one patristic scholar, "Reading the church fathers is difficult. Simply to pick up Irenaeus' treatise *Against Heresies* and read invites confusion and boredom if one does not know the point of the many digressions."[6] Some patristic literature is still not translated out of the Greek or Latin. In many cases, the ancient manuscripts are fragmentary, and some copies disagree with other copies. Some scholars, in fact, do textual criticism on the extant copies trying to determine the correct reading of a passage in a Father's sermon or book.[7]

Beyond these problems, the historical and cultural context of the Fathers is so different from ours that we can easily err by trying to find a short, snapshot statement from them about any one specific topic. One paragraph in "The Shepherd of Hermas," for example, could easily persuade us, if we were not observant of the context, that Hermas believed in the pretribulational rapture of the church. Hermas writes,

> You have escaped from great tribulation on account of your faith, and because you did not doubt in the presence of such a beast. Go, therefore, and tell the elect of the Lord His mighty deeds, and say to them that this beast is a type of the great tribulation that is coming. If then you prepare yourselves, and repent with all your heart, and turn to the Lord, it will be possible for you to escape it.[8]

---

[5] For a discussion of the doctrinal deviations in the church fathers, see Ken Guindon, *History Is Not Enough!* (n. p.: Xulon Press, 2007).

[6] John J. O'Keefe and R. R. Reno, *Sanctified Vision* (Baltimore: Johns Hopkins University Press, 2005), 1.

[7] See, for example, Kenneth B. Steinhauser and Scott Dermer, ed., *The Use of Textual Criticism for the Interpretation of Patristic Texts* (Lewiston, NY: Edwin Mellen Press, 2013). This book contains seventeen case studies. Chapter Sixteen as a specific example, is written by Scott Dermer and entitled, "*Vellet* or *Vellent*? A Textual Variant in Augustine's *Enchiridion*," 479-510.

[8] "Shepherd of Hermas," V.4.2., in *The Apostolic Fathers*, ed. J. B. Lightfoot (London: Macmillan Co.; reprint, Grand Rapids: Baker Book House, n.d.,), 180.

"The Shepherd of Hermas" is a sort of allegorical novel, so it is even more difficult to discern distinct doctrinal ideas from it than it is from other more doctrinal patristic documents. At first look, Hermas seems to be saying that it will be possible to "escape" the "great tribulation." But the speaker in this section is actually the church herself who is encouraging Hermas for going through a personal trial, symbolized by the beast. What the personified "church" means when she speaks of the "great tribulation" is also not clear. Thus, the church fathers were ordinary Christians in many ways who did not write any inspired, inerrant documents. But this begs our questions.

The Millennial Theology of the Early Church Fathers

What then, did the early church fathers teach about a future millennial kingdom? Most of the later Fathers, beginning with Origen (d. 254), were amillennialists—the belief that there would not be a future one-thousand-year rule of Christ on the earth after the Second Coming of Christ. But what about the Fathers who lived before the time of Origen? Were they premillennialists?

The Early Fathers Were Premillennialists

The best interpretation of the eschatology of the early church Fathers concludes that most were indeed premillennialists.[9] According to some scholars, at least

---

[9] Despite overwhelming evidence that most of the early church fathers were premillennialists, some do in fact argue for different interpretations of the early fathers' eschatology. Charles Hill, for example, argues mainly from silence, that some of the early fathers were amillennialists, believing "in an eschatological return of Christ and his kingdom to earth for a final judgment of the quick and the dead, ushering in the ultimate and eternal state of salvation or ruin for humanity, with no intervening, earthly, golden age. This alternative to chiliasm may be distinguished as 'orthodox' non-chiliasm or amillennialism" (Charles Hill, *Regnum Caelorum*, 2nd ed. [Grand Rapids: Eerdmans, 2001], 6). Others have presented the view that the early fathers were preterists (Gary DeMar and Francis X. Gumerlock, *The Early Church and the End of the World* (Powder Springs, GA: American Vision, 2006). Preterism is the system that teaches that all, or almost all, of prophecy has already been fulfilled. Usually preterists use Matthew 24:34 ("Truly, I say to you, this generation will not pass away until all these things take place") as the basis for saying that all of prophecy had to be completed within the generation that was living in the time of Jesus Christ. We will analyze the Olivet Discourse and this passage in chapter ten. Still others have argued that premillennialism was dominant in only one part of the empire (George Lyons, "Eschatology in the Early Church," in *The Second Coming: A Wesleyan Approach to the Doctrine of Last Things*, ed. H. Ray Dunning [Kansas City, Mo: Beacon Hill, 1995]). These views have been shown to my satisfaction to be without merit by the historical research of such theologians as Charles Hauser and Donald Fairbairn (see Donald Fairbairn, "Contemporary Millennial/Tribulational Debates: Whose Side Was the Early Church On?" in *A Case for Historic Premillennialism*, ed. Craig L. Blomberg and Sung Wook Chung [Grand Rapids: Baker Academic, 2009], 107-113. Although Fairbairn's defense of premillennialism in the early church is excellent, his critique of pretribulationism in his next section is curious. In this section of his chapter, Fairbairn presents a three-point polemic against pretribulationism in the early church fathers. I have no problem agreeing with his first and third arguments. First, he argues, they didn't have the same hermeneutic as do modern day pretribulationists, a conclusion with which pretribulationists today would happily concur. In fact, one of the main reasons that the New Testament teaching on pretribulationism was lost in the Fathers was their disappointing hermeneutical system. His third argument is that the early Fathers didn't show any awareness of a two-part return of Christ. This can also be granted, though Fairbairn's

fifteen of the better-known early Fathers were premillennialists.[10] One of the most honest[11] and complete studies of the early Fathers that demonstrates this was written by Charles Hauser in a doctoral dissertation back in the middle of the twentieth century. Seventeen of the early church fathers are analyzed in the study. Hauser concludes his analysis as follows:

> Down through the Church Fathers considered in this paper runs a central core of teaching. Although it may vary slightly from one writer to another, it remains essentially the same. This is true until the time of Origen. These men believed that what they taught had come to them from the New Testament times through the disciples of Apostles.... The core of this teaching ... was the following: a future time of tribulation with the rise of the Antichrist followed by the second advent of Christ; at the same time the resurrection of the righteous took place which prepared them for entrance into the kingdom; the kingdom of Christ on earth then was established which would last for a thousand years; this would be followed by the universal resurrection and judgment. The different writers elaborated on various aspects of these points as their inclinations led them. However, these remain the basic points of the eschatology of the early Church Fathers.[12]

In brief, the early church fathers believed that there would be a future time of tribulation that would be followed by Second Coming of Christ, the resurrection of believers, and the establishment of a one-thousand-year kingdom of

posttribulationism also has a two-part return. For most modern-day posttribulationists, the two-stage return happens in rapid succession at the end of the Tribulation rather than being separated by at least seven years as pretribulationists teach. But his second argument is problematic. Fairbairn says, "Modern dispensationalism shies away from asserting that God would allow his people to suffer severely, and this attitude is part of the reason for affirming a pretribulational rapture of the church" (122). Fairbairn admits that this is not the view of every dispensationalist, but, he writes, "It is fair to argue that dispensationalism as a whole is undergirded by the assumption that God will protect his people from excessive suffering" (123). I personally don't know any pretribulationists who would argue this as a top-five reason for pretribulationism; and "undergirded" is too strong of a term. Pretribulationists resent the implication that we are pretribulationists because we don't want to suffer. It is not a good argument. If Fairbairn had said that one of the main reasons for the dispensational pretribulational belief is the doctrine of imminency—that pretribulationists believe that they might see Jesus Christ today—he would have been far more accurate.

[10] H. Wayne House, "Premillennialism in the Ante-Nicene Church," *Bibliotheca Sacra* 169 (July-September, 2012):273.

[11] I say "honest" because Hauser, a dispensational premillennialist, concludes that the eschatology of the early fathers is different from his own eschatological view. The chapters in Hauser's dissertation are devoted to key eschatological topics: "The Great Tribulation"; "The Antichrist"; "The Second Advent of Christ"; "The Resurrection"; and "The Kingdom." Each chapter is divided chronologically into three epochs: "The Fathers from A.D. 96 to A.D. 150"; "The Fathers from A.D.150 to A.D. 200"; and "The Fathers from A.D. 200 to A.D.250."

[12] Charles August Hauser, Jr., "The Eschatology of the Early Church Fathers" (Th.D. diss., Grace Theological Seminary, May, 1961), 251.

Christ on earth. They did not give evidence, as we will see, of believing that the nation of Israel would be the center of that kingdom.

The following somewhat well-known passages from the writings of some of the early fathers demonstrate their premillennialism.

Papias

Papias (d. 150?) was apparently a pastor in Hierapolis, a city located in modern day Turkey. He was a friend of the martyred Polycarp who in turn was a disciple of the Apostle John. Papias was the author of *Exposition of the Lord's Oracles* which may have been five volumes containing stories and teachings about Christ that he had gathered over the years from first generation Christians. Only fragments of his work have been preserved, and these are found in *Ecclesiastical History*, written by Eusebius of Caesarea, the "Father of Church History" (d. 339). Eusebius, although an enemy of premillennialism, cites Papias as writing that "after the resurrection of the dead there will be a thousand-year period when the kingdom of Christ will be established on this earth in material form."[13] Eusebius comments, "I suppose that he got these notions by misunderstanding the apostolic accounts, not realizing that they had used mystic and symbolic language.... Due to him, however, many church writers after him held the same opinion, relying on his early date: Irenaeus, for example, and many others who adopted the same views."[14]

Irenaeus

Irenaeus (d. 200) was born in Asia Minor, possibly Smyrna, and is therefore a representative of the theology of Asia Minor, which is known as being based generally on a more literal method of hermeneutics. Irenaeus was later sent to France as a missionary and was appointed the Bishop of Lyons. He devoted his life to the study and refutation of false doctrine—more from the perspective of a pastor than a philosopher. Toward the end of his life he wrote his major five books *Against Heresies*. Several passages in Book Five teach premillennialism. Irenaeus outlines the end events as follows:

---

[13] *Eusebius—The Church History: A New Translation with Commentary*, trans. Paul L. Maier (Grand Rapids: Kregel), 129. Cf. Eusebius, *The Church History of Eusebius* trans Arthur Cushman McGiffert, 3.39.12, NPF, Second Series, 1.3:172.

[14] Ibid.

But when this Antichrist shall have devastated all things in this world, he will reign for three years and six months, and sit in the temple at Jerusalem; and then the Lord will come from heaven in the clouds, in the glory of the Father, sending this man and those who follow him into the lake of fire; but bringing in for the righteous the times of the kingdom, that is, the rest, the hallowed seventh day; and restoring to Abraham the promised inheritance, in which kingdom the Lord declared, that "many coming from the east and from the west should sit down with Abraham, Isaac, and Jacob."[15]

Irenaeus' statement captures some key features of premillennialism: the antichrist rules the last three and one-half years of the Tribulation; the Second Coming occurs at the end of the Tribulation; the antichrist and his followers are sent to the lake of fire; and Christ's kingdom is established.

Irenaeus also argues that if we "shall endeavor to allegorize prophecies …, they shall not be found consistent with themselves in all points…."[16] Quoting Isaiah 65:21, Irenaeus comments, "For all these and other words were unquestionably spoken in reference to the resurrection of the just, which takes place after the coming of Antichrist, and the destruction of all nations under his rule; in the times of which resurrection the righteous shall reign in the earth…."[17] He continues,

All these things being such as they are, cannot be understood in reference to supercelestial matters; 'for God,' it is said, 'will sow to the whole earth that is under heaven thy glory.' But in the times of the kingdom, the earth has been called again by Christ to its pristine condition, and Jerusalem rebuilt after the pattern of the Jerusalem above.[18]

For Irenaeus, the Old Testament prophets taught that after the judgment on the Antichrist and the nations loyal to him, there would be the resurrection of

---

[15] Irenaeus, *Against Heresies* 5.30.4, ANF, 1:560. Chapters 25-36 (553-67) are a primer on premillennialism.

[16] Ibid., 5.35.1, ANF 1:565.

[17] Ibid.

[18] Ibid. When we read these confident defenses of premillennialism in Irenaeus, as well as his meticulous apologetics against heresies, we may be tempted to look to him as a representative of evangelical orthodoxy. But, despite many doctrinal areas in which we can respect him, there are serious problems in his theology. Irenaeus may be the earliest of the Fathers to promote Mariology as well as apostolic succession as an unbroken chain in the Roman church. He is designated a saint in both the Roman Catholic and Eastern Orthodox churches.

the righteous, and the righteous would rule with Christ on the earth, before the eternal state. These are standard key features of premillennialism.

Justin Martyr

Justin Martyr (d. 165), in his early life, had been a wandering philosopher in search of truth. He tried out Stoicism, Platonism, and Pythagorean numerical philosophy before he was converted to Christianity. In his *Dialogue with Trypho*, Justin writes: "Moreover, a man among us named John, one of Christ's Apostles, received a revelation and foretold that the followers of Christ would dwell in Jerusalem for a thousand years, and that afterwards the universal and, in short, everlasting resurrection and judgment would take place."[19] There may be other Christians who do not believe in a millennial kingdom here on earth, Justin admits. "But I and every other completely orthodox Christian feel certain that there will be a resurrection of the flesh, followed by a thousand years in the rebuilt, embellished and enlarged city of Jerusalem, as was announced by the Prophets Ezekiel, Isaiah and others."[20]

Tertullian

Tertullian (d. ca. 225), born in Carthage, North Africa, is a representative of the Western branch of the church. He practiced law, and after his conversion in about 180 turned his rhetorical abilities to the defense of Christianity. He apparently became a presbyter in the Carthage church, but converted to Montanism after he decided that the Carthage church was too lax in Christian living. He also was a premillennialist. In his apologetic work, *Against Marcion*, he writes,

> But we do confess that a kingdom is promised to us upon the earth, although before heaven, only in another state of existence, inasmuch as it will be after the resurrection for a thousand years in the divinely-built city of Jerusalem 'let down from heaven.... After its thousand years are over, within which period is completed the resurrection of the saints, who rise sooner or later according to their deserts there will ensue the destruction of the world and the conflagration of all things at the judgment.[21]

---

[19] Justin Martyr, *Dialogue with Trypho* 81, ANF 1:240.

[20] Ibid., 80.

[21] Tertullian, *Against Marcion* 3, 25, ANF 3:342.

Even though most present-day premillennialists wouldn't describe the millennium quite this way, Tertullian is clearly a premillennialist like Papias, Irenaeus, Justin, and several others. So, the answer to the first question we are asking is, "Yes, the early church fathers were premillennialists."[22]

The Early Fathers Were Historic Premillennialists

But did they believe that Israel would be the focus of the future Tribulation and millennial kingdom, or did they think that it would be the church? That is, were they dispensational premillennialists or were they historic premillennialists? Dispensational premillennialists believe that the church will be raptured out of the world before the Tribulation begins, and thus Israel will be the focus of the end-time events. There were elements of what we would describe today as "dispensational premillennialism" in the Fathers' teaching, such as the doctrines of imminency and dispensations. Clement of Rome could have been a pretribulationist, perhaps, but he says nothing that would prove or disprove it.[23] Irenaeus could have believed in pretribulationism because in all of his discussions about the Tribulation he does not say that the church will be there.[24] Moreover, it is unclear to me as to whom he believes will be the focus of the kingdom—Israel or the church. Most of the early church fathers, however, did teach that the church would be in the Tribulation, and were thus historic premillennialists. Hippolytus, for example, a student of Irenaeus and one of the most important theologians of the third century taught that the woman in Revelation 12 who is being persecuted by the Antichrist in the Tribulation, is the church—not Israel.[25] For the Fathers like Hippolytus, the church had permanently replaced the nation of Israel (i.e., replacement theology, that is, supersessionism, or

---

[22] Since we have a limited amount of information about the eschatology of some of the early church fathers, it is possible that some of them were not premillennialists. But we don't have any evidence of that.

[23] Clement does evidence premillennialism saying that the Apostles in their post-resurrection ministries, "went forth with the glad tidings that the kingdom of God should come" (Clement, "First Epistle to the Corinthians," 42, in J. B. Lightfoot, *The Apostolic Fathers*, 31). He also taught the imminency of the return of Christ: "Of a truth, soon and suddenly shall His will be accomplished, as the Scriptures also bear witness, saying, 'speedily will he come, and will not tarry;' and 'The Lord shall suddenly come to His temple, even the Holy One, for whom ye look'" (23).

[24] Some of the earliest church fathers such as Polycarp, Ignatius, and Clement of Rome, except for their commitment to the resurrection of the body and a coming kingdom, wrote very little about specific eschatological details, so it is impossible to know their precise views.

[25] Hippolytus, *Christ and Antichrist* 61, ANF 5:217.

fulfillment theology).[26] There would be a future world-wide kingdom, these premillennialists said, but the church, not the nation of Israel, would be the nucleus of this kingdom. So, the promises to Israel of a glorious future kingdom following a Tribulation era were no longer valid for Israel. As Hauser, a committed pretribulationist, acknowledges, "The Church Fathers believed that the Church would be on earth during the tribulation period. This is seen in the earliest writers and there is nothing in the other writers to contradict this."[27]

So, the answer to our second question is that though the early church fathers were premillennialists, they were historic premillennialists, not dispensational premillennialists. They believed that the church had permanently replaced Israel, that the church would be in the Tribulation, that the rapture of the church would occur after the Tribulation (i.e., posttribulationism), and that the church would be the focus of the millennial kingdom.

THE EARLY CHURCH FATHERS AND ISRAEL

To come to the point of this chapter, why is this the case? Why did the church fathers, especially the early fathers who believed in premillennialism, conclude that the church had permanently superseded Israel? The answer to this question is found in several intertwining issues, most of which focus in some way on the Jew-Gentile relationship.

Social Background to the Jew-Gentile Problems

In addition to the Biblical and theological issues which we are only able to survey here, there are social issues that impacted the early Jew-Gentile problem. For example, Israel had three military disasters in the first and second century. The first was the Jewish revolt in A.D. 70 where the Roman legions destroyed Jerusalem and the Temple and killed thousands of Jews. Most twenty-first century historians of this period do not believe that this was a decisive point of

---

[26] For a biblical and theological response to supersessionism, see Michael J. Vlach, *Has the Church Replaced Israel?* (Nashville: B&H Academic, 2010). Some whom we are identifying as replacement theologians do not believe that "replacement" or "supersessionism" describes their system. Instead, "fulfillment" theology better fits their view since they believe that the promises to Israel are now fulfilled (not replaced or superseded) in the church. The result is nearly the same, regardless of how one states it. The millennial kingdom will center on the church rather than Israel.

[27] Hauser, "The Eschatology of the Early Church Fathers," 234. Though there are some differences of detail between the posttribulational premillennialism of the church fathers and the twenty-first century adherents of posttribulationism, their systems are fundamentally the same. This is the reason that contemporary posttribulational premillennialists often refer to themselves as "historic premillennialists."

division between Jews and Gentiles. James Dunn writes that "talk of a clear-cut or final parting of the ways at 70 C. E. is distinctly premature."[28]

The second Jewish rebellion, the Kitos War (115-117) was a disorganized revolt that spread throughout the empire to Egypt, Cyprus, Mesopotamia, and Judea itself. The Jewish rebels were able at first to defeat the depleted Roman forces in some of these territories, but eventually the Roman armies overran them.

The third rebellion was the Bar Kokhba revolt that began in 132. Simon Bar Kokhba, the commander of the revolt, was a messianic figure who took the name "Prince," and promised to restore national independence to Israel. The Jews thus had a choice between two Messianic figures: Jesus and Simon.[29] By the end of the revolt, almost 600,000 Jews had been killed in battle and thousands more had died of hunger and disease. The emperor made plans to build a new Roman city, *Aelia Capitolina*, on the site of the ruble of Jerusalem and forbade any Jews to enter it. According to some historians, the failure of Gentile Christians to aid the Jews in this last revolt was a significant exacerbation to the Jew-Gentile problem. A few years after this war, the Fathers begin to argue that the church is new Israel.

The Centrality of the Jew-Gentile Problem

In the theological world today, the Jew-Gentile problem impacts more than just eschatology. It is also central to contemporary soteriological debates between conservative Reformed theologians and the representatives of the New Perspective on Paul. This debate is beyond the scope of our study, but it is important to point out how it intertwines with eschatological issues. The traditional interpretation of many of the church fathers, as well as the Protestant leaders of the Reformation, is supersessionism. Historians such as Adolf von Harnack and other nineteenth century historians promoted this view.

The Contemporary "Parting of the Ways" Solution

After the Holocaust and World War II, a milder and more ecumenical interpretation of the "parting of the ways" between the Jews and early Christians gained popularity among some scholars. In fact, the term, "parting of the ways," has become a common description for this view that emphasizes good

---

[28] James D. G. Dunn, *The Parting of the Ways*, 2nd ed. (London: SCM Press, 2005), 311.

[29] Ibid., 317-19.

in both religions. Andrew Jacobs explains that "the 'parting of the ways' is a clear yet benign metaphor that allows each religion to maintain a robust history and a common genealogy, just connected enough to justify ongoing, friendly relations, but not so connected that the distinctive tradition of each religion becomes too blurred. This amicable model, however, rests on several contestable presuppositions." [30]

The "parting of the ways" interpretation requires a "new perspective on Paul," and tries to soften the church fathers' clash with the Jews. In some more extreme forms, it even suggests that the writings of the church fathers against the Jews were basically symbolical and not necessarily based on historical events. So Justin, for example, created Trypho the Jew in his work, *Dialogue with Trypho*, in order to dramatize through dialogue the superiority of Christianity over Judaism. The hope of this softened parting of the ways is that it will lead to a better ecumenical relationship between Christians and Jews. Many modern-day historians, however, argue that the Fathers' writings tell the truth about the bad relationship of Jews and Christians.[31]

The Biblical Source of the Jewish Gentile Problem

It is easy to forget that the mission of Jesus the Messiah was restricted in his early ministry to Jews. Jesus was a Jew, his followers were Jews, and the earliest mission of the Apostles after the death and resurrection of Christ focused on the Jews. Moreover, much of Christ's teaching "would have been unintelligible if addressed to Gentiles.... The men to whom Jesus spoke knew the Law, the Prophets, and the Psalms, and followed the Tradition."[32]

When the Jewish religious leaders steered the nation into rejecting Christ and His kingdom, Jesus promised that He would build His church (Matt 16:18). The church was subsequently formed on the Day of Pentecost with "Jews living in Jerusalem, devout men from every nation under heaven" (Acts 2:5) and Jewish proselytes (v. 10) being the nucleus of this new body. But the Jewish-Gentile problem is highlighted in the following chapters of Acts when two other ethnic people groups were added in to the church. In Acts 8, believing

---

[30] Andrew S. Jacobs, "Jews and Christians," *The Oxford Handbook of Early Christian Studies*, ed. Susan Ashbrook Harvey and David G. Hunter (New York: Oxford University Press, 2008), 170.

[31] Ibid., 270-72. See further, Dunn, *The Parting of the Ways*, for a development of this approach to the Jewish problem.

[32] F. J. Foakes-Jackson, *The Rise of Gentile Christianity* (New York: George H. Doran Co., 1927), 38.

Samaritans were brought into the church by the Holy Spirit through Peter and John. In Acts 10, the Gentiles were added in.

The Gentile Problem

At first, the Jew-Gentile problem was more of a Gentile problem. The entrance of the Gentiles into the church was a puzzle to the Christian Jews in Jerusalem who had formed the nucleus of the church on the Day of Pentecost. They were not upset about the Gentiles being saved because the Old Testament talked about the salvation of Gentiles. But they were confused over the fact that the Gentiles were added into the body of Christ in the same way that they, as believing Jews, had been brought into the church. It didn't seem to match with what they expected from the Old Testament's teaching about a coming kingdom. The Jewish Christians no doubt thought that the Gentiles who wanted to join the New Covenant church should go to Jerusalem and participate in some sort of proselyte ceremony as was required in the past. But Peter explained to his Jewish friends who were questioning him about his ministry with the Gentile, Cornelius:

> "As I began to speak, the Holy Spirit fell on them just as on us at the beginning. … If then God gave the same gift to them as he gave to us when we believed in the Lord Jesus Christ, who was I that I could stand in God's way?" When they heard these things they fell silent. And they glorified God, saying, "Then to the Gentiles also God has granted repentance that leads to life" (Acts 11:16-18).

Peter explained to the Jews that the Holy Spirit fell on these Gentiles just as He had fallen on the Jews on the Day of Pentecost, and that information satisfied the Jerusalem Jews.

The Jewish-Gentile problem was not answered once and for all here in Acts 11, however. The first major church council was held to deal with the details of having Jews and Gentiles together on equal footing in the body of Christ (Acts 15). The specific controversy centered on whether "those converted to Christianity from outside of Judaism needed also to become Jews as well."[33] Jewish Christians were clearly in control at this council.

---

[33] Stanley E. Porter and Brook W. R. Pearson, "Ancient Understandings of the Christian-Jewish Split," ed. Stanley E. Porter and Brook W. R. Pearson, *Christian-Jewish Relations through the Centuries* (New York: T & T Clark International, 2004), 41.

The Jewish Problem

But before too many years had passed in the Christian era, a clear majority of Christians was Gentile.[34] So the issue became less of a Gentile problem and more of a Jewish problem. Understanding the Jewish problem in the apostolic and patristic era is made more complicated by the fact that there were different kinds of Jews. Even basic terms such as "Jews" and "Judaism" "were also in some state of flux." [35] Moreover, there were different kinds of Jews, culturally speaking: Palestinian Jews that spoke Aramaic, Greek-speaking Jews or Hellenists, Jewish proselytes, and apostate Jews like the Samaritans. In addition, there were the Jews at Qumran, and, of course, Christian Jews. Thus, the various kinds of Jews were often in debate among themselves in the patristic era.

Jews Against Jews

Both the Old and New Testaments are filled with strong denunciation of Jews by Jews—and for good reasons. The ancient kings of Israel and Judah neglected their godly responsibilities and often led the nation to worship other gods. The priests failed to perform their religious duties, and the people often disregarded Yahweh and His Law. From the beginning of the nation, Moses, Joshua, Samuel, and the other prophets condemned both the northern and southern kingdoms, calling them to repent. If it were not for the fact that God had made an irrevocable covenant with the nation, Israel would no doubt have been destroyed like many other ancient nations.

If anything, the condemnation of Israel—especially of her religious leaders—became even more severe in the New Testament. They led the nation to reject the kingdom of God that Christ presented. The climax to the struggle between Christ and these leaders is described in Matthew 12. When Jesus healed a man with a withered hand on the Sabbath, the Pharisees "conspired" how they could "destroy" Christ (Matt 12:14). Christ continued healing, and when He healed a demon-possessed man who was blind and mute, the people were "amazed," and wondered if this were indeed the Son of David, the Messiah (v. 23). The Pharisees, to head off any kind of a ground-swell, gave their interpretation of the miracle: "It is only by Beelzebul, the prince of demons, that this

---

[34] Origen, writing in the middle of the third century, says that there were less than 144,000 (cf. Rev 7:4) Jewish Christians at that time (Origen, *Commentary on John* 1.2, ANF 9:298).

[35] Dunn, *Parting of the Ways*, 189.

man cast out demons" (v. 24). The Pharisees had proposed this defense before, and now it became in effect their official evaluation of Jesus. He was not the Messiah. He was a demon-inspired magician.

Jesus responded with several reasons why this could not be true and pronounced a curse on this "brood of vipers" (v. 34). "Whoever speaks a word against the Son of Man will be forgiven," He said, "but whoever speaks against the Holy Spirit will not be forgiven, either in this age or in the age to come" (v. 32). The hardened Pharisees had committed the so-called "unpardonable sin" by not only rejecting Christ in His incarnational ministry, but also by declaring that Jesus was demon-inspired rather than Holy Spirit-inspired. After Christ pronounced the unpardonable sin on this generation, He no longer publicly presented His kingdom except at His prophesied triumphal entry (Zech 9:9).

The pathos of this struggle between Jesus and the leaders of Israel is vividly portrayed in Matthew 23. After Christ pronounces eight devastating "woes" on the Scribes and Pharisees for their hypocrisy, He concludes with a lament and prophecy:

> O Jerusalem, Jerusalem, the city that kills the prophets and stones those who are sent to it! How often would I have gathered your children together as a hen gathers her brood under her wings, and you were not willing! See, your house is left to you desolate. For I tell you, you will not see me again, until you say, "Blessed is he who comes in the name of the Lord" (Matt 23:37-39).

In the midst of these prophecies of judgment on that generation, however, He promises to give the kingdom to a later generation of Jews "producing its fruits" (Matt 21:43).[36]

After Pentecost and the beginning of the church, there is some fluctuation in the Apostles' references to the Jews. Christian Jews struggled with "the Jews," as Luke calls them in his early history of the church. Some of Luke's references to the Jews—those that became Christian Jews— are positive, and a few of his descriptions are both positive and negative: "Now these Jews were more noble than those in Thessalonica; they received the word with all eagerness, examining

---

[36] Matthew 21:43 is regularly misinterpreted as Jesus assigning the kingdom to the church. But there is nothing in the context that would imply this. Christ's teaching is all about the wickedness of that generation of Jews. He is specifically condemning the "chief priests and Pharisees" who "perceived that he was speaking about them" (v. 45). As we have noted previously, the Old Testament prophets show that there will be a later generation of Jews that will accept the Messiah. They will be the "people producing its fruits."

the Scriptures daily to see if these things were so" (Acts 17:11). But many of Luke's references to the Jews are critical (Acts 9:22, 23; 12:3; 13:45, 50; 14:2, 4, 19; 16:3; 17:5, et. al.). The Jews killed Stephen (Acts 6 and 7), and a Jew named Saul (later Paul) "approved of his execution ... [and] was ravaging the church, and entering house after house, he dragged off men and women and committed them to prison" (Acts 8:1, 3). After Paul's conversion, the Jews, "having persuaded the crowds ... stoned Paul and dragged him out of the city, supposing that he was dead" (Acts 14:19).

The Apostle Paul, a Jew who is sometimes "credited with being the chiefest factor in bringing about the final rupture between the church and the synagogue,"[37] also wrote discourses against those Jews who tried to maintain Jewish Law-keeping in Christianity. His belief was that "no one is a Jew who is merely one outwardly, nor is circumcision outward and physical. But a Jew is one inwardly, and circumcision is a matter of the heart, by the Spirit, not by the letter. His praise is not from man but from God" (Rom 2:28-29; cf. Gal 6:16). Throughout these discourses, "Paul may have been disowning the Judaism in which he had been brought up (Gal 1:13-14), but he did so self-consciously as an Israelite—that is, as one who sought to maintain and promote the true character of Israel's election."[38]

Paul also made it clear that there was a future for the nation of Israel (Rom 9-11). In fact, Paul's "heart's desire and prayer to God" for the people of Israel was "that they may be saved" (Rom 10:1). In one of the most passionate expressions in Scripture, Paul states,

> I am speaking the truth in Christ—I am not lying; my conscience bears me witness in the Holy Spirit—that I have great sorrow and unceasing anguish in my heart. For I could wish that I myself were accursed and cut off from Christ for the sake of my brothers, my kinsmen according to the flesh. They are Israelites, and to them belong the adoption, the glory, the covenants, the giving of the law, the worship, and the promises. To them belong the patriarchs, and from their race, according to the flesh, is the Christ, who is God over all, blessed forever. Amen (Rom 9:1-5).

Moreover, in the conclusion of his denunciation of the Jewish legalists in Galatia, Paul praises the believing Gentiles and "the Israel of God" (Gal 6:16),

---

[37] Foakes-Jackson, *Rise of Gentile Christianity*, 84.

[38] Dunn, *Parting of the Ways*, 196.

a title not for the church but for true, godly Israelites whom he differentiated from the "Judaizers." There were true Jews and false Jews, in Paul's theology.

But many of the Jews despised Paul. One of the most striking events in the early history of the church is found in Acts 21-22 when Paul went to the Temple in Jerusalem. The "Jews from Asia … stirred up the whole crowd and laid hands on him, crying out, 'Men of Israel, help! This is the man who is teaching everyone everywhere against the people and the law and this place'" (Acts 21:27-28). When Paul gave his defense and told the story of his conversion, the Jewish crowd was quiet until Paul mentioned the Lord's commission to him to take the gospel to the Gentiles. Luke records, "Up to this word they listened to him. Then they raised their voices and said, 'Away with such a fellow from the earth! For he should not be allowed to live'" (Acts 22:22). Seemingly even the mention of the word "Gentile" nearly brought on a riot.

Paul's Letter to the Galatians as well as the Letter to the Hebrews make significant contributions to improving the Jewish problem. Paul wrote Galatians to warn Christians about the semi-Christian Judaizers who had added elements of the Old Covenant into their theology, contrary to the decision of the Council of Jerusalem.

The Letter to the Hebrews is written to warn Christian Jews about the dangers of relapsing into Judaism. The writer builds the case that New Covenant Christianity is better than Old Covenant Judaism because Jesus is superior to the Old Testament prophets who spoke for God many times and in many ways (Heb 1:1). Moreover, since the Old Covenant was passing away, if they forsook the New Covenant, there would be nothing left for them. In the Old Testament, those who set aside the Mosaic Law were subject to capital punishment. "How much worse punishment," the writer asks, "will be deserved by the one who has trampled underfoot the Son of God, and has profaned the blood of the covenant by which he was sanctified, and has outraged the Spirit of grace?" (Heb 10:29). Christian Jewish Apostles thus were often compelled to warn the first-century church about apostate Jewish Christians.

Gentiles Against Jews

Perhaps we shouldn't be surprised, therefore, to discover that the church fathers were also critical of the "Jews." Occasionally there is a word of kindness from the Fathers that accompanies a harsh reproach. Justin Martyr writes, "Even when your city is captured and your land ravaged, you do not repent. Rather, you dare to utter curses on Him and all who believe in Him. Nevertheless, we do not hate you."[39] And again, "You curse in your synagogues all those who are called from Him Christians. ... And in addition to all this, we pray for you that Christ may have mercy upon you."[40] But these semi-kind statements are rare and seem to be said in the context of criticism. So, they hardly soften the antagonism. "It is rare," writes Andrew Jacobs, "to find an early Christian text that does not speak about Jews and Judaism, and usually in a highly charged (though multifaceted) manner."[41]

The church fathers, however, are not primarily criticizing Christian Jews. We don't know much about how the Christian Jews reacted during the early patristic era other than that the early fathers thought that some of the Christian Jews had kept too much of their Judaism. Ignatius, in his letter to the Magnesians (ca. 110), reflects the New Testament Letter to the Hebrews, admonishing the Magnesians, some of whom seem to have been Jewish, "Be not seduced by strange doctrines nor by antiquated fables which are profitless. For if even unto this day we live after the manner of Judaism, we avow that we have not received grace."[42] But we don't know how the Christian Jews responded to these kinds of admonitions from the Fathers. Marcel Simon writes, "As far as Jewish Christians are concerned, we are hampered by the total lack of documentary evidence. We possess no document that may with certainty be ascribed to this party and giving information about their reactions."[43] So, when we begin to study the Jew-Gentile problem in the second and third centuries, the focus is almost entirely on Jews who had not become Christians.

The Fathers Were Gentiles

The church fathers continued the New Testament authors' arguments against the non-Christian Jews in at least a couple of areas: (1) The superiority of the New Covenant over the Old; and (2) the Jewish guilt for rejecting and crucifying Christ. But now, instead of Jews debating Jews, Gentiles were debating the Jews. To some degree, at least, the Fathers seem to have forgotten the context

---

[39] Justin Martyr, *Dialogue with Trypho* 108, ANF 1:253.

[40] Ibid., 96, ANF 1:247.

[41] Jacobs, "Jews and Christians," 172.

[42] Ignatius, "Epistle to the Magnesians" 8.1, in *Apostolic Fathers*, ed. Lightfoot, 70. Ignatius has a similar comment in his "Letter to the Philadelphians."

[43] Marcel Simon, *Versus Israel*, trans. H. McKeating (Portland: The Litman Library of Jewish Civilization, 1986), 65.

of the New Testament anti-Jewish talk, interpreting it as "opposition to Jews in general, rather than for what it was, an in-house debate." Interpreting the New Testament debates as anti-Judaism, writes H. Wayne House, "should be seen as preposterous in view of the fact that all of the authors (except Luke) were Jews and that our *Lord* was a Jew."[44] The Jews' debates among themselves in the New Testament, though often highly theological, were in some ways intramural. But another dimension had been added to the struggle of Christians with Jews. Because most of the church fathers were Gentiles,[45] their reproach of the Jews became, not only theological, but also an ethnic and cultural issue.

Whether intended or not, some of the Fathers' statements give the impression of being anti-Jewish.[46] Hippolytus (d. 235), a premillennialist disciple of Irenaeus, wrote *The Expository Treatise Against Jews,* most of which is lost to us. His view of the church being essentially Gentile is evidenced when he argues that when Christ on the cross said, "Father forgive them," He was forgiving "the Gentiles, because it is the time for favor with Gentiles."[47] Tertullian (d. 220) writes that, in contrast to Abraham's willingness to sacrifice his son, Isaac, it behooved Christ "to be made a sacrifice *on behalf of all Gentiles.*"[48] Even though Hippolytus, and Tertullian were premillennialists, the permanent replacement of the nation of Israel by a Gentile church is certainly implied in these kinds of statements. The later Fathers, either historic premillennialists or amillennialists, repeat and emphasize these same sentiments.[49]

---

[44] House, 89. See also David L. Allen, "The Identity of Luke and the Jewish Background of Luke-Acts," in *Lucan Authorship of Hebrews*, NAC Studies in Bible and Theology, vol. 8, series editor E. Ray Clendenen (Nashville: B & H Academic, 2010), 261-323. Allen argues that Luke was a Jew.

[45] One possible exception may be Melito of Sardis (d. ca. 190) who probably was a Jew. There may have been other lesser known Jewish bishops who qualify as church fathers. Melito was apparently a premillennialist, but he is very critical of the Jews who rejected Christ. See Alistair Stewart-Sykes, in his introduction to Melito of Sardis, *On Pascha* (Crestwood, NY: St. Vladimir's Seminary Press, 2000), 3. See pp. 56-65 for Melito's poetic attack on unbelieving Israel.

[46] The New Testament teaches that we are living in the "times of the Gentiles" (Luke 21:24), a phrase describing Gentile political dominion over Israel that began in Old Testament history. The Apostle Paul says that "a partial hardening has come upon Israel, *until* the fullness of the Gentiles has come in" (Rom 11:25). But when the fullness of the Gentiles has come in, Israel will be judged and restored to a central place in God's plan. When Paul asks, "Has God rejected his people?" He answers his own question, "May it never be!" (Rom 11:1). In the meantime, the church is composed of Jews and Gentiles in one body on equal footing.

[47] Hippolytus, *The Expository Treatise Against Jews* 3, ANF 5:220.

[48] Tertullian, *An Answer to the Jews* 13, ANF 3:171, (emphasis added).

[49] Origen, the amillennialist, writes, "And we say with confidence that they [the Jews] will never be restored to their former condition. For they committed a crime of the most unhallowed kind, in conspiring against the Saviour of the human race" (Origen, *Contra Celsum* 4.22, ANF 4:506). Simon comments, "This was henceforth to be the unshakable opinion of the whole of the early church" (Simon, *Versus Israel*, 68).

God Had Disowned Israel

What the Fathers were teaching about God's permanent replacement of Israel with the Gentile church ran counter to what the New Testament teaches. In the theology of the New Testament writers, "the Jews have not entirely forfeited their election."[50] Paul strongly warned the Gentiles that though they, as wild branches, had been grafted in to God's covenant program with Israel, they were not to be arrogant. Paul writes,

> Now I am speaking to you Gentiles. Inasmuch then as I am an apostle to the Gentiles, I magnify my ministry in order somehow to make my fellow Jews jealous, and thus save some of them. For if their rejection means the reconciliation of the world, what will their acceptance mean but life from the dead? If the dough offered as firstfruits is holy, so is the whole lump, and if the root is holy, so are the branches. But if some of the branches were broken off, and you, although a wild olive shoot, were grafted in among the others and now share in the nourishing root of the olive tree, do not be arrogant toward the branches. If you are, remember it is not you who support the root, but the root that supports you. Then you will say, "Branches were broken off so that I might be grafted in." That is true. They were broken off because of their unbelief, but you stand fast through faith. So do not become proud, but fear. For if God did not spare the natural branches, neither will he spare you (Rom 11:13-21).[51]

The "gifts and the calling of God" with Israel are "irrevocable" (Rom 11:29).

But a future conversion of the nation of Israel was not the message of the Fathers. In their opinion, Israel had been removed from God's covenant program permanently. The Epistle of Barnabas (A.D.120), which was not written by the Jewish Barnabas of the New Testament and is somewhat over the top in comparison to some of the other Fathers, vigorously emphasizes that Israel has been left behind forever with the formation of the church. After demonstrating that God has voided sacrifices, the Mosaic Law, circumcision, the Sabbath, the Temple (all of which agrees with the Book of Hebrews), he takes his anti-Judaism to new heights and urges the readers of his epistle "not to liken yourselves to certain persons who pile up sin upon sin, saying that our covenant remains

---

[50] Jeremy Cohen, *Living Letters of the Law* (Los Angeles: University of California Press, 1999), 8. At the time of the writing of this book, Cohen was the Professor of Medieval Jewish History at Tel Aviv University.

[51] For an exposition of Romans 11, see chapter 11.

to them also. Ours it is; but they lost it in this way for ever, when Moses had just received it."[52]

Clearly, Barnabas is a change from the New Testament authors. The thesis of the Letter to the Hebrews is that Jesus Christ and the New Covenant is far "better" than Moses and the Old Covenant. The thesis of Barnabas is that the Old Testament was always intended to be taken allegorically, but the Jew, led astray by an "evil angel" had erroneously understood it literally, ignorantly trying to follow an absurd system of laws and sacrifices.[53] No New Testament author teaches anything like this permanent replacement of Israel.

A clear signal that the Fathers are thinking as supersessionists occurs in Justin Martyr's "Dialogue with Trypho," written about 160. Justin, a premillennialist, takes up a crucial issue in this document as to whether Israel is Israel or the church is Israel. He quotes Isaiah 19:24 ff. and applies it to the church. "'What, then?' says Trypho; 'are you Israel?' and speaks He such things of you?"[54] Justin's extended reply is essentially "yes, the church is Israel."

Justin's claim is the first time in church history that a father argues specifically that the Church is a new Israel. It is obviously "a symptom of the developing take-over by Christians of the prerogatives and privileges of Jews," writes Peter Richardson. "Initially there is hesitancy about this transposition: but a growing recognition of the necessity to appropriate titles and attributes ensures a complete transfer."[55] Richardson observes that for Justin, "Christians are a *genos* which has superseded the Jewish race, and this demands a complete taking over of the name 'Israel.'... By the middle of the second century the Church in its apologetic has effected a total transposition."[56] These early premillennialist Fathers believed in a coming one-thousand-year kingdom. But they had concluded that the Gentile church had superseded the nation of Israel.

---

[52] "The Epistle of Barnabas," 4, in *Apostolic Fathers*, ed. Lightfoot, 139. See his premillennialism, 182.

[53] Ibid., 9, in *Apostolic Fathers*, ed. Lightfoot, 145.

[54] Justin Martyr, *Dialogue with Trypho* 81:261.

[55] Peter Richardson, *Israel in the Apostolic Church*, Society for New Testament Studies, Monograph Series 10 (New York: Cambridge University Press, 1969), 1. Richardson's book, the result of his doctoral dissertation, is a major contribution to unfolding the Jewish problem in the early church.

[56] Ibid., 11-12.

The Puzzle of the Old Testament

The church fathers' commitment to supersessionism resulted in a distinct way of interpreting the Old Testament prophets. Justin, for example, claims that when Malachi prophesies about a future time when the nations will offer incense to the Lord's name, "he speaks of those Gentiles, namely us, who in every place offer sacrifices to Him, i.e., the bread of the Eucharist and the cup of the Eucharist, affirming both that we glorify His name, and that you profane [it]."[57]

Such reinterpretations of the Old Testament demonstrate that the church fathers were confused about the role of the Old Testament for Christians. The Fathers knew that there were two extreme views about the Scriptures. In one extreme, the heretic Marcion denied that there was any value at all in the Old Testament for Christians. He also claimed that the God of the Old Testament was not the true God. Marcion was wrong, said the Fathers.

On the other extreme, the Jews denied that the New Testament was a revelation from God, and the Fathers knew that the Jews were wrong. So, the orthodox Fathers were in the middle of this debate. They firmly believed that both the Old Testament and the New Testament were inspired and authoritative documents. "But having taken this stand," writes Simon, "the Church found that formidable difficulties were involved in maintaining it."[58] The New Testament documents were quickly becoming more available, and the Fathers knew how to use them. But the real problem was, how should Christians make use of the Old Testament?

An Apologetical Solution

The church fathers' answer to this question solved another issue that they were facing. One of the criticisms of early Christians was that they were the new kids on the block. Greek philosophy stretched back into previous centuries as did Judaism. So, if Christianity is such a good religion and philosophy, asked the philosophers and the Jews, why did it just now show up? As Simon writes, "The problem for Christians was that they believed the Church had superseded Israel. But Israel was still there, employing the OT. How could the Church claim that the OT belonged to them?"[59]

---

[57] Justin Martyr, *Dialogue with Trypho* 81:141.

[58] Simon, *Versus Israel*, 71.

[59] Ibid., 72.

For the Fathers, moreover, it would seem that if the Old Testament were still a valid revelation of God, it would prove that Israel was more ancient than the newcomer, Christianity. So, to convince either the philosophers or the Jews of the legitimacy of Christianity, the Fathers had to insist that the Church had existed from all eternity. To prove this, the Fathers taught that the Old Testament was not a Jewish document, but it was a Christian document. The author of Second Clement writes,

> Wherefore, brethren, if we do the will of God our Father, we shall be of the first Church, which is spiritual, which was created before the sun and the moon. ... And I do not suppose that you are ignorant that the living Church is "the body of Christ"; for the Scripture says, "God made man male and female." The male is Christ, the female is the Church. And the Books [Old Testament] and the Apostles plainly declare that the Church exists not now for the first time, but has been from the beginning.[60]

Thus, for Clement, Eve is a type of the church, and the church is as ancient as the human race.

In the apocalyptic novel, "The Shepherd of Hermas," Hermas receives a vision of an aged woman who interacts with him and gives him a document to copy. In a later vision, a young man appears to explain the previous vision of the old lady. He explains that the old lady is the church. Hermas responds, "Why then is she aged?" The messenger replies, "Because ... she was created before all things; therefore is she aged; and for her sake the world was framed."[61] The antiquity of the church was a common apologetic employed by the church fathers. For them, the Old Testament relates the history of the preexistent church, and Israel was only a "coarse outer shell for the spiritual reality within." [62]

A Hermeneutical Solution

It would take some hermeneutical gymnastics, however, to show that the Old Testament was in reality a Christian document. But this did not seem to deter

---

[60] "Second Clement," 14, in *Apostolic Fathers*, ed. Lightfoot, 49. "Second Clement" is probably the earliest Christian sermon, after the Apostles, which exists. It was preached perhaps around 130. Although it goes by the name of Clement, it has no relationship to the letter that Clement of Rome wrote to Corinth in about A. D. 95.

[61] "Shepherd of Hermas," V. 2.4.

[62] Simon, *Versus Israel*, 79.

the Fathers. The aforementioned Barnabas was the first and most daring of the Fathers to take a try at it. According to Barnabas, the Old Testament prohibition against eating pork really means that we are to separate ourselves from people who are like pigs.[63] Others of the early Fathers, though not employing gross allegorical interpretation, employed extensive typological interpretation to find the church in the Old Testament. Justin, for example, taught that the twelve bells on the robe of the high priest in Old Testament Israel were "a symbol of the twelve apostles who depend on the power of Christ, the eternal Priest."[64]

Melito of Sardis, in his meditation *On Pascha*, explains how typological interpretation was supposed to work. Typology begins with a "first draft," he writes, or a "preliminary sketch" (meaning Israel). But when the finished copy or the thing that was sketched comes into existence, "then the type is destroyed." Melito elaborates,

> But when the church arose and the Gospel came to be, the type, depleted, gave up meaning to the truth: and the law, fulfilled, gave up meaning to the Gospel. In the same way that the type is depleted, conceding the image to what is intrinsically real, and the analogy is brought to completion through the elucidation of interpretation, so the law is fulfilled by the elucidation of the Gospel, and the people is depleted by the arising of the church, and the model is dissolved by the appearance of the Lord. And today those things of value are worthless, since the things of true worth have been revealed.[65]

In other words, Israel was just a type or "preliminary sketch" of the real—the church. The type, moreover, has been permanently eliminated.

In the prophetic sections of the Old Testament, the church fathers regularly interpreted the great blessing sections for a future Israel as referring to the church. At the same time, they didn't apply the judgment sections of the prophecies to the church. These still referred to Israel. Tertullian, for example, quotes a series of verses on judgment from Isaiah and comments, "Since, therefore, the Jews were predicated as destined to suffer these calamities on Christ's account, and we see they have suffered them, and see them sent into

---

[63] "Barnabas," 10, in *Apostolic Fathers*, ed. Lightfoot, 146.

[64] Justin Martyr, *Dialogue with Trypho* 81: 215. Obviously, the twelve bells represent the twelve tribes of Israel.

[65] Melito of Sardis, *On Pascha*, 42-43.

dispersion."[66] When he comments on a blessing passage such as Isaiah 2:2-3 that describes nations flowing in the house of the God of Jacob, Tertullian explains, "not of *Esau*, the former Son, but of *Jacob*, the second that is, of our 'people' whose 'mount' is Christ."[67]

Tertullian is a premillennialist, to be sure.[68] But the millennial kingdom is not about Israel. Tertullian explains, "As for the restoration of Judea, however, which even the Jews themselves, induced by the names of places and countries, hope for just as it is described, it would be tedious to state at length how the figurative interpretation is spiritually applicable to Christ and His church, and to the character and fruits thereof."[69] For Tertullian, therefore, there will be a thousand-year period on earth, with the resurrection of the just before it begins, and the resurrection of the unjust afterwards. But this kingdom is for the church, not for Israel.[70] He supports his opinion by a "spiritual" interpretation of the Old Testament prophecies.[71] Cohen concludes that for the early church fathers, "God had therefore disowned the Jews, annulled their ritual law, and transferred their inheritance to the church, which now constituted the only true Israel, not a recently arrived impostor."[72]

A Philosophical Solution

Another cause for the use of "spiritual interpretation" of the Old Testament was Platonism and Neoplatonism. Platonism in one form or another elevated

---

[66] Tertullian, *An Answer to the Jews* 13:171.

[67] Ibid., 154.

[68] Tertullian, *Against Marcion* 25:342.

[69] Ibid.

[70] An additional factor for further investigation is the role of the Septuagint in the Jewish question. Origen seems to be the first major Father to understand Hebrew. But the fact that Christians used the LXX was another evidence to the Jews that Gentile Christians had taken over the Jewish Old Testament.

[71] The Fathers in the Alexandrian school followed Origen's hermeneutical approach in employing typological interpretation for the Book of Revelation—if they interpreted it at all. Eusebius tells how Dionysius of Alexandria (d. 264) convinced some church leaders in Egypt to give up their belief in premillennialism, even though he was "greatly impressed by the soundness, sincerity, logic, and intelligence of the brethren." Eusebius references Dionysius' *On Promises* where Dionysius writes about the Book of Revelation, "I, however, would not dare reject the book, since many brethren hold it in esteem, but since my intellect cannot judge it properly, I hold that its interpretation is a wondrous mystery. I do not understand it, but I suspect that the words have a deeper meaning that they are too high for my comprehension. I do not reject what I have failed to understand but am rather puzzled that I failed to understand" (Dionysius, in Eusebius, *Church History* 7.24-25:271-72.). Cf. NPF, Second Series, 1.7:24-25;1.8:309. See further Augustine's tortured interpretation of Revelation 20 in *The City of God*, 20, 7-17, NPF, 2, 426-37.

[72] Cohen, *Living Letters of the Law*, 11.

the spiritual realm to a point where a physical material kingdom on this earth was unbelievable. According to the history of philosophy specialists, the form of Platonism that was dominant between 80 B.C. and A.D. 220 was Middle Platonism. Middle Platonism was then gradually replaced in the third century by Neoplatonism.[73] Both forms of Platonism were based on metaphysical dualism. Cowan and Spiegel explain,

> For Plato there were two worlds or levels of reality. There is the imperfect, changing world of particular things.... This world for Plato, could not be ultimately real nor could it provide any basis for the unity of things.... This led Plato to conclude that there must be another realm, a non-physical or spiritual reality that grounded the unity of things in the material world. Things in this spiritual realm are perfect, immutable, and eternal.[74]

This explanation of Platonism sounds similar to Melito's explanation of how to interpret the Bible. For Melito, this meant that the church, the spiritual reality, had replaced Israel, the physical entity. Eventually this hermeneutical methodology based on Platonic metaphysical dualism led the later Fathers to teach that the kingdom promised in Scripture was not a real, material (though spiritual) kingdom, but a spiritual kingdom without a material dimension.

Still, the idea of a physical, material kingdom did not disappear overnight. There was a "surprisingly large [body of Christians] at the end of the second century, who continued to believe in the imminent coming of the Kingdom of God in a quite literal sense."[75] But, continues Dennis Minns,

> Half a century later, partly in consequence of the growing influence of Platonism within Christian theology, the "spiritual interpretation" of the coming of the Kingdom had triumphed, and the views on the Kingdom of Irenaeus and other like-minded theologians were derided as naïve or outlandish. ... For these theologians, in the starkest contrast to Irenaeus, what really mattered was the spiritual

---

[73] Colin Brown, *Christianity and Western Thought*, vol. 1 (Downers Grove, IL: Intervarsity Press, 1990), 84.

[74] Steven B. Cowan and James S. Spiegel, *The Love of Wisdom* (Nashville: B&H Academic, 2009), 154.

[75] Denis Minns, *Irenaeus* (New York: T & T Clark International, 2010), 140. Minns is a Dominican friar who at one time was a member of the Theology Faculty of Oxford University.

dimension in the human being: the spirit or the soul.... But as God is spiritual, it is only the spiritual dimension that can be concerned in this salvation.[76]

Neoplatonism therefore impacted the theology of the church fathers in several areas. In hermeneutics, it led the Fathers to spiritualize the Old Testament. Spiritualization of the Old Testament led naturally to the rejection of a future for Israel. Neoplatonism also gave the Fathers a philosophical foundation for teaching that true reality could be found in the spiritual dimension. So, the kingdom must be spiritual, and not a physical kingdom on earth. And thus, eventually the future physical kingdom of premillennialism would be replaced with the present spiritual kingdom of amillennialism.

CONCLUSION

Our goal in this chapter was to answer three questions: (1) Were the early church fathers premillennialists? The answer to this question is "yes." Those who wrote on the topic of eschatology up until the middle of the third century taught the premillennial return of Christ. (2) Did the early church fathers believe that Israel would be the nucleus of the coming kingdom (dispensational premillennialism)? The answer to this question is "No. They believed that the church would be the nucleus (historic premillennialism). Jews could be saved as a part of the church. But, according to the Fathers, at no time in the future would Israel have a national revival, repent of her sins, accept Jesus as Messiah, live in her land, and become the center of the kingdom of God on earth. These promises would go unfulfilled to Israel. Instead, many of these prophecies about a glorious future would be fulfilled with the church. (3) Why and how did the church fathers become historic premillennialists? To answer this question, we surveyed several intertwining issues that guided the Fathers to reject the future importance of the nation of Israel in the kingdom. It involved the Jew-Gentile problem, the puzzle of the Old Testament, hermeneutics, and Neoplatonism

Dispensational premillennialists have often argued that inadequate hermeneutics is the main reason for the rejection of pretribulational premillennialism. But is this the case with the Fathers? Or, was it the Jewish problem—the Gentile church fathers' assessment of the Jews? Of course, both hermeneutics and the Jewish problem were important issues. But we could argue historically that the

---

[76] Ibid., 140-141.

church fathers' disregard of Israel led to their spiritualization of the prophecies of the Old Testament, rather than the other way around. Peter Richardson, in his analysis of the Fathers' interpretation of the Old Testament, gives a cautious vote for the Jewish problem being the primary driving force for the acceptance of supersessionism. Using one church father as an example, he writes, "There is insufficient evidence for certainty, but it is likely that the formative factor is the author's attitude to Judaism, and then (consciously or subconsciously) his hermeneutical principle would follow."[77]

---

[77] Richardson, *Israel in the Apostolic Church*, 30.

2

AUGUSTINE: FROM THE "NOT YET" TO THE "ALREADY"

David L. Burggraff

"Lord, will you at this time restore the kingdom to Israel?"
— Apostles, *Acts* 1:6

"Perhaps whoever will read my works in the order in which they were written will discover how I made progress while writing them."
— Augustine, *Retractationes*, prol. 3[1]

INTRODUCTION

It was a simple question. Or so it seemed to the Apostles. After all, the resurrected Jesus had been appearing to them during the past forty days and speaking about the kingdom of God (Acts 1:3).[2] Although Jesus had been teaching

---

[1] Augustine, *Retractationes*, prol. 3, trans. Mary Inez Bogan, *Saint Augustine: The Retractions*, FC 60:5.

[2] Following Christ's resurrection and prior to the ascension, He made numerous bodily appearances to believers which are recorded in the Gospels. On such occasions He talked with them (Luke 24:13-32; John 20:19-21:14), ate with them (Luke 24:41-43), and instructed them (Matt 28:16-20; John 21:15-25), thus demonstrating the reality of his physical resurrection. On the appearances, Darrell Bock, *Acts* (Grand Rapids: Baker Academic, 2007), 55, notes that "the idea is not that Jesus was continuously with them for forty days but that he appeared at intervals within that period as the appearances in the Gospels indicate."

His speaking to them of things pertaining to the kingdom of God was additional proof that the risen Christ was the same person who was now continuing his same teaching. The content of this post-resurrection teaching on the kingdom is not recorded here, but it is reflected in the teaching of the apostles in Acts and in the Epistles. No doubt the teaching included such matters as the harmonization of a suffering Messiah with a coming, glorious kingdom. Additionally, His teaching must have included the Messianic significance of many Old Testament passages (for example, Acts 1:16, 20; 2:16-36; 3:18-26).

41

the disciples about His kingdom throughout His ministry (Matt 4:17), the disciples were still puzzled: "Will you at this time restore the kingdom to Israel?" It seems obvious from the Apostles' question that they were asking about the kingdom which the Jews looked for Messiah to establish (Isa 9:6-7; 11:10-12). Now that He was alive again, having just demonstrated His power to overcome death itself, surely the *time* to restore the Jewish kingdom ("kingdom *to Israel*") on earth in all its glory must be close at hand. Their question was simply one of *timing*.

Jesus refused to answer their question, not in respect of the matter itself, but only in respect of the time inquired after. Christ's answer did not say that there would be no literal physical kingdom on earth. He merely said that the time of establishment would not now be revealed to them. The reason the apostles must not concern themselves with pinpointing the inaugurating of Israel's restored kingdom, Christ pointed out, was that they had a new task to perform. They were soon to be Christ's witnesses once the empowering of the Holy Spirit occurred and the new international church began. And the apostles were content with Christ's answer and instructions to them.[3]

---

[3] Since Luke tells us in Acts 1:3 that the resurrected Christ tutored the disciples for forty days on the kingdom of God, it is unreasonable to suggest that they would adopt some other teaching immediately after the Ascension. There must be a real continuity between what follows in the apostles' teaching on the kingdom and what Jesus Himself taught. It is also evident that Jesus' answer to their question, His last words to them before His Ascension, failed in changing the disciples' understanding of the kingdom. Peter again brings up the question of the future kingdom for Israel in his sermon recorded in Acts 3. Addressing the absence of Jesus now, he says that the Christ must be in heaven until "the period of restoration of all things about which God spoke by the mouth of his holy prophets from ancient time" (Acts 3:21). The clear reference to the Old Testament hope of Israel's restoration shows again the correctness of the initial question of Acts 1:6 and the force of Jesus' answer then. As Jesus' answer concerned not the nature of the hope but its timing, so Peter now is explaining the new timing of the hope, not a radical reformulation of its nature. He and his Jewish brethren are still looking forward to the fulfillment of the ancient prophetic voice in Israel. God's kingdom for Israel was not yet there; it remained a hope for the future. (See further, Darrell Bock "The Kingdom of God in New Testament Theology," in David W. Baker, ed., *Looking into the Future: Evangelical Studies in Eschatology* [Grand Rapids: Baker Academic, 2001], 45-46.)

The other mentions of the kingdom in the New Testament also assert that the kingdom is something of the future. The kingdom is something to be inherited (1 Cor 6:9-10; 15:50; Gal 5:21; Eph 5:5; Col 1:12-13; Jas 2:5; see also 1 Cor 4:8-13; Acts 14:22; 2 Tim 4:18). See further, Michael Vlach, *He Will Reign Forever* (Silverton, OR: Lampion) for a complete Biblical study of the Kingdom.

On the other hand, it is doubtful that the disciples' instruction on the kingdom of God only concerned eschatological matters. In light of Luke's consistent use in Acts of *basileia tou theou* for a summary of the whole Christian proclamation, it is evident that while the kingdom surely did include matters of eschatology, it also summarized the whole Christian message about "Jesus as the Christ." See Acts 8:12; 19:8; 28:23, 31, and especially 20:24, 25 where Paul's declaration to the elders of Ephesus that he went about preaching the kingdom of God (v. 25) is parallel to the thought that he solemnly testified to them "of the gospel of the grace of God."

Thus, it seems the NT writers assert that there is some real manifestation of the promised kingdom now in the presence and work of the Holy Spirit; and there is a future hope for the kingdom to come in its fullness, a fullness that would accord with the Old Testament hope of Israel. (For the tension between the "already" and the "not yet," see the Lord's parable about the mysteries of the kingdom in Matthew 13—the "already," and His parable in Luke 19:11-27—the "not yet").

The apostles would give themselves to Christ's command of "disciple-making" (Matt 28:19-20); they would spread the Christ's gospel and establish Christ's church (Eph 1:20-23; 4:7-16). All the while, the coming of Christ and His kingdom remained a future hope—a hope the apostles apparently understood would involve *Israel*, and a hope they believed was *imminent*: *"Surely I am coming soon." Amen. Come, Lord Jesus!* (Rev 22:20). However, the Lord did not return during the apostolic era, and the kingdom was not restored to Israel—tragically, the nation of Israel would experience quite the opposite. The Christians living in the first four centuries of the church did not experience the Second Coming and the kingdom either. In fact, they suffered persecution, not triumph! And like the apostles before them, they now had questions about the kingdom of Christ.

In those early years, the church fathers would attempt to address questions relating to the eschatological hope found in the Scriptures and held by the New Testament church. But it would be one church father, Augustine of Hippo, who would explain the kingdom and its timing that would have the greatest impact on Christianity's understanding of the kingdom and its constituents for centuries to come. As Jonathan Hill observes:

> Augustine of Hippo is unquestionably one of the greatest theologians of all time. His influence over Western thought—religious and otherwise—is total; he remains inescapable even over 15 centuries after his death. He has been hailed as the first medieval, or even the first modern man; and his greatest works rank with the timeless literature of the ages ... It is little exaggeration to say that the whole history of the Western Church for the last 1,500 years is the story of Augustine's influence.[4]

In the Preface to the *Retractationes*, Augustine himself, as he reflected over his writings near the end of his life, signaled to his interpreters how he might be understood: "Perhaps whoever will read my works in the order in which they were written will discover how I made progress while writing them."[5] Augustine's suggestion to his interpreters has not gone unnoticed. Augustinian

---

[4] Jonathan Hill, *The History of Christian Thought* (Downers Grove: InterVarsity Press, 2003), 78, 91.

[5] It is essential to read Augustine with a sense of the chronology of his writing, even though chronology alone is not a sufficient guide to his developing ideas. Context is required, too, since he thought freshly in response to fresh challenges. Yet Augustine's development is something very much more than simple change of mind. There is, as it were, a slow accretion of new layers to his thought. At points of new departure, he will reorganize the way he approaches a question, while still carrying forward the observations and conclusions that he has made at earlier stages.

scholar R. A. Markus astutely observes that "the one thing that has emerged from almost all serious studies of Augustine in the last fifty years is that whatever can be said about almost any aspect of his thought is unlikely to be true over the whole span of his career as a writer and thinker ... Augustine changed his mind about many things."[6]

One of the significant changes in Augustine's thinking occurred in his understanding of the kingdom. The impact of that change is felt to this day. It is this eschatological change in Augustine's thinking that is the focus of this chapter.[7] I will seek to demonstrate the development in Augustine's thinking that would ultimately lead him to put forth an interpretation of Revelation 20, found in his *City of God,* that would be the basis for amillennialism and postmillennialism. In short, Augustine's doctrine of the kingdom changed from "not yet" to "already."

GETTING ACQUAINTED WITH AUGUSTINE

Augustine Aurelius (A.D. 354-430)—better known to us as Augustine—is the hinge figure between the end of the early church and the beginning of the Middle Ages. Augustine was born in a small city not far from Carthage in North Africa. His family was middle class, his father a nonbeliever, his mother (Monica) was a Christian. Early on, Augustine was trained in rhetoric; he would become a teacher of literature, oratory, and philosophy. At the age of thirty-two, in a garden in Milan, Augustine was convicted by a passage in Paul's Letter to the Romans: "Let us live honorably ... not in debauchery and licentiousness ..." (Rom 13:13-14 NRSV). He came under the influence of Ambrose, the bishop of Milan, whose clear, reasoned teaching convinced Augustine of the truth of Christianity. Ambrose baptized Augustine and his son on Easter Sunday 387. In the year 396, at the age of forty-two, Augustine became bishop of Hippo, the modern-day city of Annaba in Algeria.

---

[6] R. A. Markus, "Saint Augustine's Views on the Just War," in *The Church and War,* ed. W. J. Sheils (London: Basil Blackwell, 1983), 2. Markus further notes, 2: "More crucially important than the explicit changes of view on particular matters, recorded or, for that matter passed over in silence there, are the shifts of perspective which are not and cannot be recorded, which, sometimes, give a different twist even to statements which Augustine saw no reason to revise." Markus went on to suggest that there *are* two such changes, or shifts, as Markus calls them, that occurred in Augustine's intellectual perspective over the course of his career. These shifts occurred at the core of Augustine's thinking, and Markus argued that these shifts must be reckoned with when trying to understand Augustine's views.

[7] For a discussion regarding the importance of understanding the distinctions between amillennialism and premillennialism, see Robert L. Saucy, *The Case for Progressive Dispensationalism: The Interface Between Dispensational & Non-Dispensational Theology* (Grand Rapids: Zondervan, 1993), 264-296, especially 271-274. See also Matt Waymeyer, *Amillennialism and the Age to Come: A Premillennial Critique of the Two-Age Model* (The Woodland, TX: Kress, 2016).

Augustine's Key Theological Battles

Augustine waged and won three battles while bishop of Hippo. First, against the *Manichaeans*.[8] Since he had led some of his friends to that religion, he now felt a responsibility to refute the teachings he had supported earlier. Many of these early works dealt with the authority of Scripture, the origin of evil, and free will. Second, against the *Donatists*.[9] It is in trying to deal with the Donatist issue that Augustine developed much of his theory for the justification of war. Third, against the *Pelagians*.[10] It was against the Pelagians that Augustine wrote some of his most important theological works.

Augustine's Works

Augustine's writings are voluminous and influenced almost every sphere of Western theology.[11] He wrote hundreds of treatises, letters, and commentaries.[12] His classic work, *On the Trinity*, is probably the best-known work on that subject. Among his most widely read works are his *Confessions of St. Augustine*

---

[8] Followers of Mani, an eclectic Persian prophet, who believed there were two deities, one good and one evil. Augustine said that there was one God, who was good and all-powerful, and that evil did not come from God but from the misuse of free will. Many of Augustine's first writings were attempts to refute the Manichaeans.

[9] Named for Donatus, the bishop of Carthage, who believed the validity of the ordinances depended on the personal purity and holiness of the priests who administered them. Augustine said the ordinances are effective *ex opera operato* ("by the act itself"). That is, any rite of the church does not depend on the moral virtue of the person administering it.

[10] Named after Pelagius, a British monk who lived in Rome, who believed that men and women were not born sinful and that they could, through the exercise of their wills, live sinless lives ("salvation by merit"). Augustine said that sin, because of the "fall" of Adam and Eve, is now part of the human condition (Augustine wrote that we are all part of the same "lump"). According to Augustine, the power of sin is such that it takes hold of our will, and as long as we are under its sway we cannot move our will to be rid of it. Only the power of God's grace can free us.

[11] Augustine's battles and extensive writings shaped the thinking and theology of the church with regard to the doctrine of *original sin*, based on Paul's statement that "sin came into the world through one man" (Rom 5:12); God's unmerited *grace*, which came to Augustine, as it had to Paul; *predestination*, the (controversial) doctrine that God foreordains all things, including the election of some and not others for salvation; the equality of the "persons" of the *Trinity*; and the *church* as the channel of God's grace. With respect to later Calvinism, Augustine is significant, for in the writings of Augustine one finds all five points of Calvinism including Total Depravity, Absolute Predestination, Particular Redemption, Irresistible Grace, and Perseverance of the Saints. It is not possible, however, to tell from Augustine's writings that he believed in single or double predestination. George S. Faber, *The Primitive Doctrine of Election* (San Bernadino, CA: Ulan Press, 2012, reprint), 75-88, 93, argues that Augustine's teaching on this subject was original. He was criticized as being an innovator by his contemporaries including Prosper and Hilary (two writers from Gaul). Calvin often appeals to Augustine's authority.

[12] Cf. Jonathan P. Yates, "The Doctrine of the Future in Augustine," in *Eschatology*, ed. D. Jeffrey Bingham and Glenn R. Kreider (Grand Rapids: Kregel, 2016), 300. Yates writes that "we know more about Augustine's life and have more words from Augustine's pen than we know or have from any other figure in the premodern period." He further notes that "Scholars have reckoned that … we possess approximately 5.5 million of his own words." This is only Augustine's extant works; it is certain that many of his works, and perhaps thousands of his sermons, have been lost. To put that in perspective, Yates tells us that we have available to us today *nine times more* material from Augustine than we have from William Shakespeare.

(397-400) and his *City of God* (Latin: *De Civitate Dei*; hereafter *De Civ. D.*, or *DCD*).[13] *Confessions* is Augustine's account of his own spiritual quest, which is usually considered the first Christian spiritual autobiography. The *City of God* may be Augustine's most important work, written in response to the fall of Rome to the Visigoths.[14] It is in his *City of God*, as we will see, that Augustine discusses his (new) understanding of the Millennium.

Augustine's great achievement in the *City of God* was to state the Christian worldview in a theological and philosophical system that cohered as a unified whole and formed the basis for the thinking and philosophizing of subsequent centuries down to Aquinas and beyond. A man of his time, he did this in the context of current philosophical thought, some of which, such as Manichaeism and skepticism, he rejected, but some of which he used. In particular he was influenced by Plato and Neoplatonism and found no problem in using their insights to help defend and clarify the Christian worldview.

Even though, next to Paul, Augustine did more to shape Christian thinking and theology than any other human being, interestingly, he never wrote a systematic theology "in the way we understand that now." Gerald Bray explains,

> This was not because he never got round to it, because systematic theologies were unknown in his time. The first person to write anything resembling one was John of Damascus (d. 749), who wrote in Greek. No Latin writer attempted anything similar until Peter Lombard (ca. 1090-1160) composed his famous *Sentences*, which became the textbook of the medieval schools and did much to popularize Augustine's teaching, from which Peter made copious extracts. From then until the widespread dissemination of printed editions of Augustine's writings in the sixteenth century, Peter Lombard was the gateway through which most students learned about him, and so Augustine acquired a reputation as a systematic theologian without having been one![15]

---

[13] Augustine, *The City of God*, Nicene and Post-Nicene Fathers, vol. 2, ed. Philip Schaff (Grand Rapids: Eerdmans, 1979).

[14] Some people blamed the Christians, arguing that Rome fell in 410 because its people had neglected the native gods. So Augustine responded by defending and explaining God's plan and working in history. Since Cain and Abel there have been two cities in the world: The City of God (the faithful) and the City of Man (pagan society). Though they intertwine, God will see that the City of God, the church, will endure through eternity.

[15] Gerald Bray, *Augustine on the Christian Life* (Wheaton: Crossway, 2015), 34-35. See also Jonathan Yates, "The Doctrine of the Future in Augustine," 303: "Augustine was not a systematic theologian; that is, he never attempted to account for all the major doctrines of Christianity within one framework. On the contrary, Augustine was first and foremost a pastor, a priest, and a bishop, who often wrote in order to think and to help others understand what to confess. Moreover, much of what he wrote was in response to a particular question that had been posed to him or an issue that had arisen either inside or outside the life and faith of the church."

Augustine's Theological Development: Three Distinct Periods

Scholars now recognize that Augustine's intellectual career divides into three distinct periods. His thought would remain essentially unchanged during the first period from 386 to about 395. A continuity in Augustine's interests and basic assumptions would extend through a second period from 396 until about 410, the third period extending from 410 until his death.[16]

First Period

From the time of his conversion to Christianity in 386 to his ordination as Bishop of Hippo in 395, Augustine wrote several dialogues. The main theme of Augustine's first dialogues is the quest for wisdom. In the dialogues, Augustine centers his attention primarily on the individual Christian thinker, yet there are several points at which he works out his ideas on society which become significant for his later development.[17]

But also of significance, it appears that doctrinal development was taking place in these early years as Augustine progressed from expressing himself in Neoplatonic language and categories to that of the language of Paul and the Scriptures.[18] What prompts the changes during this period? At least one decisive event occurs in the shaping of both Augustine's ecclesiastical career and his theological development, namely his ordination to the priesthood in Hippo Regius in 391. Ordination forced him into the turbulent milieu of African Christianity where the Christian life was at least as much a matter of violent ecclesiastical partisanship as it was of philosophic approach to divine truth.[19] In short, Augustine's ordination compelled him to depart the Christianity of the

---

[16] Eugene TeSelle, *Augustine the Theologian* (New York: Herder and Herder, 1970), 185. See also Peter Brown, *Augustine of Hippo* (Berkeley, CA: University of California Press, 1969), 146-48; R. A. Markus, "Saint Augustine's Views on the Just War," 6.

[17] F. C. Cranz, "The Development of Augustine's Ideas on Society before the Donatist Controversy," *Augustine a Collection of Essays*, ed. R.A. Markus (NY: Doubleday, 1950), 258.

[18] TeSelle, *Augustine the Theologian*, 156, writes: "A sudden surge of interest in the epistles of Paul becomes apparent about 394." He now begins to think in different "terms," according to TeSelle, 158. See the entire section from 156-65.

[19] The Latin, Catholic church to which Augustine belonged was and remained a minority in North Africa; Donatists were in the majority and enjoyed local support of the populace. Since both groups shared a Latin Christian religious culture, and often both groups had a social connection through intermarriage and property relations, they were forced to work and live among each other. However, strong partisanship existed between them. Augustine wrote and spoke against the Donatists, especially the Circumcellion group. On the Donatists in North Africa, see Paula Fredriksen, "Tyconius and Augustine on the Apocalypse," in *The Apocalypse in the Middle Ages*, ed. Richard K. Emmerson and Bernard McGinn (Ithaca, NY: Cornell Univ. Press, 1992), 21-24. Fredrickson notes that "An uncomplicated millenarianism figured prominently in this culture."

philosophic elite and to enter the Christianity of the North African crowd. It is noteworthy that Augustine's reaction to the transition was first, to turn to the study of Scripture.[20] Babcock states:

> Feeling desperately unprepared, Augustine turned to an old project with a new and urgent purpose. Even before his ordination, he had planned to set aside a period of leisure for the study of scripture. Now he wrote to Valerius, his bishop, to request an immediate leave of absence so that he could study scripture precisely in order to equip himself for the priestly ministry. He wanted, to paraphrase his own expressions, to learn how to minister to others, not seeking what might be useful to himself but what would serve the many and bring them to salvation. In short, he recognized that his new status and new duties imposed a new reading of the Biblical record.[21]

By 396, the influence of his reading Paul's works, especially the Epistle to the Romans, can be seen in this move from his largely Neoplatonic view of salvation by knowledge and the good life, to salvation by God's grace—a growing emphasis upon grace and love, and a lessening emphasis on human ability to do good. This will profoundly affect Augustine's entire worldview.

Second Period

In 395, Augustine was consecrated Bishop of Hippo. On August 24th 410, the Gothic army, led by Alaric, entered Rome. The two events mark off a period that coincides with the middle period in Augustine's life, marked by profound changes in his thought.

A consequence of Augustine's rediscovery of Paul is that his views in social thought now undergo change. He came gradually to envision a new and unclassical attitude towards society and therefore towards the character of Christian participation in society.[22] Through his study of Paul, Augustine came to recognize that in a sense the world is unavoidable, that is, its temptations cannot be

---

[20] Augustine, *Ep.* 21, written shortly after his ordination, is a request to his bishop for time to study the Scriptures so that he might learn how to perform his clerical duties or, at least, how to live the Christian life *inter manus iniquorum* (*Ep.* 21. 4). Augustine's new interest in Scripture is clearly correlated with his move from one milieu to another. See Peter Brown, *Augustine of Hippo*, 139-41.

[21] Wm. Babcock, "Augustine and Tyconius: A Study in the Latin Appropriation of Paul," *Studia Patristica* 17 (1978): 1209.

[22] John Rist, *Augustine* (Cambridge: Cambridge Univ. Press, 1994), 203-4.

avoided and merely substituted by withdrawal. Augustine began to see that the world had to be recognized as a place where the Christian and the non-Christian must meet, where God's Word must be worked out. It therefore became necessary to understand the structures of secular society and what relationship they have to the Christian life.

During this period Augustine will compose his autobiographical *Confessions*. Cranz writes that the *Confessions* are "the most important statement of Augustine's general position, and they also provide the most significant elaboration of his new ideas on society" in this middle period of Augustine's life.[23]

Third Period

Shortly after the turn of the century, and especially by 413,[24] Augustine evidences a second upheaval in his intellectual perspective,[25] thus beginning a third and final phase of his thought. TeSelle writes of Augustine during this period:

> We now come to another clearly delineated period in Augustine's thought, marked off by the rise of fresh interests—the undertaking of the apologetic task of writing about the destiny of the Roman Empire and simultaneously the polemical task of evaluating classical civilization in all its aspects; the use of the theme of two cities as the overarching principle for organizing and interpreting the entire historical process ... and the defense and elaboration of his earlier convictions about sin and grace.... These years mark the climax of Augustine's theological career. For the first time he can truly be called a "systematic theologian."[26]

---

[23] Cranz, "The Development of Augustine's Ideas on Society before the Donatist Controversy," 287.

[24] TeSelle has carefully observed the various changes that have occurred in Augustine's life. "A decisive change in Augustine's career as a theologian occurred at this point, about the year 406. ... Now he turned against some of the most characteristic doctrines of the Platonists and looked to the writers of the Church. ... The years between 407 and 410 are very nearly unknown territory in Augustine's intellectual life. He was at work on the Genesis commentary, and he was busy trying to bring the controversy with the Donatists to a close with a decisive victory for the Catholic Church and its friends in the Imperial court. But aside from that we know little of his activities. The *Retractationes* mention no major writings, and scholars who have tried dating the extant sermons have been unable to place many of them in these years. Perhaps it was a time of intellectual reorganization, if not disorientation, and those with a flair for psychology might find it significant that in 410 Augustine's health failed and he spent some time resting at a villa near Hippo (*Ep.* 98.8; 109.3; 118.34). While he was there he received word of the sack of Rome. A period spent in relative isolation had ended in exhaustion; a new period full of stimulation from the broader world had begun, and it would lead to full maturation of Augustine's theology," Eugene TeSelle, *Augustine the Theologian*, 130.

[25] Evidences will appear in Augustine, *De Trinitate* (books 1-4 written A.D. 400-406; books 5-7, 9-12 were written A.D. 413-416), and especially *De Civ. D.* (*The City of God*), A.D. 413-426.

[26] TeSelle, *Augustine the Theologian*, 267.

Likewise, R. A. Markus considers that changes in Augustine's language are especially significant regarding this third phase of Augustine's life: "In the *City of God*, and especially in its last books, Augustine turned his back on the mirage of the 'Christian Empire' of the Theodosian dynasty, and on the assumptions about God's hand in human affairs which had sustained it."[27] "He is, for instance, very much less ready to speak of a Christian Empire, or of the conversion of *regna* to Christianity."[28] By this time, Augustine's eschatological viewpoints had changed, especially in his understanding of Revelation 20:1-6. He develops and explains his new view in his magnum opus *City of God* (written from ca A.D. 413 to ca. 426).

THE CITY OF GOD: AUGUSTINE'S AMILLENNIALISM EXPRESSED

In 410 Rome was sacked by barbarians. Rome's pagans charged that the sack of Rome by Alaric was divine retribution by Jove for the empire's adoption of Christianity. This charge was not easily dismissed, even by the faithful, for it was plausible to think that an event of such catastrophic proportions must be the work of God. To accept the idea that God would permit the earthly bastion of Christianity to be raped by pagans was not consistent with commonly held beliefs about the omniscient, omnipotent, and omni-beneficent nature of the Christian God. Many of the faithful, faced with explaining God's actions, concluded that the demise of the empire signaled the onset of the eschatological promise. Indeed, the eternal empire, the *pax romana* that had endured for centuries, seemed to be ending.

Late fourth-century North African Christians, as Christians elsewhere, continued to look forward to the approaching kingdom on earth.[29] The years of Augustine's episcopacy coincided with a stream of apocalyptic due dates and events,[30] both

---

[27] R.A. Markus, "Saint Augustine's Views on the Just War," 9.

[28] R.A. Markus, *Saeculum: History and Society in the Theology of St. Augustine* (Cambridge: Cambridge University Press, 1970; repr., 1988), 38.

[29] Paula Fredriksen, "Tyconius and Augustine on the Apocalypse," 23.

[30] The due date for the approaching kingdom (worked out two centuries earlier by Julius Africanus, and affirmed a century later by his compatriot Lactantius) was drawing near: in 397, the bishop Hilarianus reiterated that the year 6000 since the Creation was a scant century off. See the chronological calculations of Julius Africanus, *Fragments of the Five Books of the Chronography of Julius Africanus*, ANF 6:130-38). Lactantius states, ca. 313, that "the entire expectation or length of time left seems no greater than 200 years" (Lactantius, *Divine Institutiones* 7.25, ANF 7:220.

within Africa and beyond.[31] Of these, Alaric's invasion of Rome was by far the most dramatic. "Behold from Adam all the years have passed," some Christians exclaimed, "and behold, the 6000 years are completed ... and now comes the day of judgment."[32] The pious noted prodigies and watched for signs of the End.

For example, spurred by a recent solar eclipse that had coincided with great drought and an earthquake, the bishop of Salona, Hesychius, inquired whether the faithful might now rejoice, as the evangelist Luke had urged, "for redemption is at hand" (Luke 21:28). Hesychius, further, based his case on a fundamentally optimistic reading of recent Roman history.[33] Since the emperors had become Christians, he urged, most of the signs of the approaching *parousia* predicted in the gospels had been accomplished, and the gospel had been preached throughout the whole world (Matt 24:14). Against such sentiments, Augustine argued tirelessly.[34]

The Two Cities

The significant work that would propel Augustine's viewpoint of amillennialism to the masses would be his magisterial *The City of God.* Consisting altogether of twenty-two books, Augustine's *De Civitate Dei* (*The City of God*) was his most substantial work and a vital source for his mature theology. The *De Civitate Dei* is meant to provide an explanation for the barbarian successes—an explanation especially needed because of Ambrose's admonition that earlier barbarian successes were due to the pagan nature of the empire.[35] Augustine set out to

---

[31] An alternative Christian chronology that had named 400 as the year 6000 since Creation "coincided closely with a series of independent eschatological traditions in which computists variously added some 350, 365, or 400 years to Christ's birth or death in order to discover the end of the interim period between the First Coming and the Parousia. In the period between 350 *Annus Incarnationis* and 400 *Annus Passionis*, then, a series of target dates for the Parousia fell due, coming most densely in the final years of the 4th century" (Fredrickson Landes, "Apocalyptic Expectations," 155). See ibid., nn. 68-70a, for abundant citations to primary documents. For Augustine's own discussion of such phenomena and calculations, see his correspondence with Hesychius, *Ep.* 197-99, and *De Civ. D.* 20-22; cf. his earlier discussion of the pagan prophecy that the church would end 365 after the Crucifixion (ibid., 18.53.2); his sermon on the fall of Rome in 410 (*CC* 46.249-62) and his *De excidio urbis, Ennarationes in Psalmos* 89.

[32] Augustine, *Serm.* 113.8 (*PL* 38.576).

[33] The account of Heychius is found in Fredriksen, "Tyconius and Augustine on the Apocalypse," 22.

[34] For instance, Augustine, *Ep.* 198.

[35] Gerald Bray notes, "Augustine was always concerned to win the pagan world for Christ, and in pursuit of that aim he wrote a number of evangelistic treatises designed to expound Christianity to unbelievers and to overcome their opposition to its teachings. By far the most important composition in this category is his massive twenty-two volume work *City of God*, which is one of the most important books in world literature. ... In the course of expounding his theme, Augustine ranged over just about every subject imaginable, and there are frequent digressions dealing with subjects that occurred to him in the course of writing and that he thought were of sufficient interest to warrant special comment" (*Augustine on the Christian Life*), 35.

demonstrate that this event was a punishment for Rome's paganism and not the result (as the pagans claimed) of the emperor's adoption of Christianity. To achieve this demonstration, he attempted to expose several key "pagan" notions (e.g. fate) and to ridicule the whole idea that the pagan gods had, in any way, protected Rome from her enemies. In contrast to this, Augustine elaborated the concept of the heavenly city, founded and ruled alone by God revealed in Jesus Christ. He later described it as follows:

> The first five books refute those who attribute prosperity and adversity to the cult of the gods or to the prohibition of this cult. The next five are against those who hold that ills are never wanting to men, but that worship of the gods helps towards the future life after death. The second part of the work contains twelve books. The first four describe the birth of the two cities, one of God, the other of this world. The second four continue their story, and the third four depict their final destiny.[36]

Augustine started the work in 413, when he was in his late fifties, but did not finish it until 426, at the age of seventy-four, three years before his death.[37]

The Identification of the Two Cities

Augustine's thinking on questions of the Christian and this world (society, politics) rested firmly on his faith in the reality and transcendence of God. For him, God is both the source and center of human existence.[38] Therefore, Augustine insisted that a human being's most important decision is the choice between turning toward and turning away from God. The relationship of each human being to God is one's primary relationship; all other choices and relationships are secondary for Augustine.

---

[36] Augustine, *Retr.* 2.43.2.

[37] The first ten books, containing his polemical reply to the pagans and doubters, were finished quickly, probably by 415. The second part took longer: the four books dealing with the origin of the two cities were written perhaps between 415 and 418; the four books dealing with the course of the two cities through history, between 419 and 421; and the four dealing with the destiny of the two cities, between 421 and 426. For discussion on the date(s) of composition of the various books, see Charles Kannengiesser, *Handbook of Patristic Exegesis: The Bible in Ancient Christianity* (Leiden, Boston: Brill, 2004), 1179-1181.

[38] See, for example, *De Civ. D.* 11.10; 12.2; 12.26; 14.13; 15.22; *Soliloquies* 1.1.1-1.2.7; *Conf.* 1.2; 1.20; 3.6; 4.16. See also Figgis, *The Political Aspects of S. Augustine's "City of God,"* 39; Etienne Gilson, *God and Philosophy* (New Haven, CT: Yale University Press, 1941), 60-63; Frederick van der Meer, *Augustine the Bishop* (New York: Sheed and Ward, 1961), 28; Herbert A. Deane, *The Political and Social Ideas of St. Augustine*, 13; and Eugene Portalie, *A Guide to the Thought of St. Augustine* (Chicago: Regnery, 1960), 127, 128, 307.

Those human beings who turn toward God compose a "city," what Augustine called the *civitas Dei*, or "city of God," while those who turn away, centering their attention on the created world, compose the *civitas terrena*, or "earthly city."[39] These two "cities" of ultimate human allegiance result from "two loves," one "a love of God carried even to the point of contempt of self," and the other "a love of self carried even to the point of contempt for God." Members of the one live "spiritually," the city existing "in the hope placed in God," while those of the other live "carnally," the city existing only "in the things of this world."[40]

The two "cities" are not actual, or at least tangible, cities. They exist, as Augustine said, "mystically" (*mystice*), that is, "allegorically." Although God already knows their content, they will become actual cities only at the end of time, when "justice is turned into judgement." Then, each city will be assembled. Members of the city of God, their bodies resurrected, will be given eternal life and perfect freedom in communion with God and each other; members of the other city will suffer eternal death and punishment absent from God. Then that city will immediately cease to exist, "for when it is condemned to final punishment, it will no longer be a city." At present, however, one can only say that there are two loves and that two loves imply two cities. It is interesting to note that Augustine gives us a good amount of detail about the City of God, but he does not define it himself. That has not prevented many scholars from offering a definition, while others stop short

---

[39] Augustine, *De Civ. D.* 11.1; 14.1. As many scholars have pointed out, the symbolism of the two cities is not original with Augustine. The idea of two cities, one heavenly or of God, the other earthly, has origins as far back as Cicero (*De Legibus* 1.23) and Paul (Phil 3:20: Eph 2:19); and the name "City of God" comes from Ps 87:3. There is a more immediate source for Augustine's conception: he probably got it from Tyconius, the Donatist. See Brown, *Augustine of Hippo*, 314; Christopher Dawson, "St. Augustine and His Age," in *A Monument to St. Augustine*, compiled by Thomas F. Burns (New York: The Dial Press, 1930), 48, 58; Geoffrey Willis, *St. Augustine and the Donatist Controversy* (London: S.P.C.K., 1950), 139-40; W. H. C. Frend, *The Donatist Church: A Movement of Protest in Roman North Africa*, 2nd ed. (New York: Oxford, 1985), 315-17; Christopher Kirwan, *Augustine* (New York: Routledge, 1989), 220; and Figgis, *The Political Aspects of S. Augustine's "City of God,"* 46.

[40] Ibid., 14.28; 14.1; 15.21. For Augustine, "the most glorious city of God, the city that knows and worships one God" ("the God of gods"), unquestionably surpasses the earthly city, whose citizens "give preference to their own gods," whose hearts, as Herbert Deanne says, "are fixed only on material goods and earthly enjoyments." Since God, as creator, is the highest good, the various elements of God's creation are by definition of the lower order. So a city whose members attach themselves primarily to God is vastly superior to one whose members attach themselves primarily to some part of the created world, and its honors, power, and wealth. On this see, *De Civ. D.* 10.25; 11.1; Deane, *The Political and Social Ideas of St. Augustine*, 15, 30. See also *Ep.* 138.2.14; *De Civ. D.* 5.17; *Conf.* 12.15; Stanley Windass, *Christianity versus Violence: A Social and Historical Study of War and Christianity* (London: Sheed and Ward, 1964), 25-26; and Etienne Gilson, *The Christian Philosophy of Saint Augustine* (New York: Knopf, 1960), 175.

of a simple identification.[41] However, it hardly seems that Augustine would have left his readers with an ambiguous understanding of the city of God. Cranz says as much:

> St. Augustine devotes a work of twenty-two books to the defense of the city of God, and in his other writings he often assumes his readers to be familiar with this heavenly city of which they are members. It is consequently surprising that scholars have found his account of it ambiguous and that they have been so little able to reach agreement as to just what the city of God is. ... [Augustine] tells us a great deal about it, but he does not define it. In part, this is because the concept is familiar and traditional. More significantly, it is because the city of God, like grace, is for him so immediately bound up with the Christian experience that it hardly admits of definition. Augustine perhaps comes closest to direct communication with his audience when he simply speaks of the city in the first person plural.[42]

In sum, Cranz says "the fundamental thesis of De Civitate Dei [is] that there are in the final analysis not more than two cities."[43]

---

[41] Some scholars have answered the question by deemphasizing the allegorical nature of the two cities and identifying them more directly with existing human institutions. The city of God is thus manifest in the visible church and the earthly city in the visible state. See, for example, Norman H. Baynes, "The Political Ideas of St. Augustine's De Civitate Dei," in Norman H. Baynes, Byzantine Studies and Other Essays (London: University of London, 1955), 302, 304; Barker, xxxi; F. Edward Cranz, "De Civitate Dei, 15, 2, and Augustine's Idea of the Christian Society," Speculum 25 (April 1950): 219. On the other hand, several scholars stop short of a simple identification, but instead have spoken of the church and state as "manifestations," or "organs," or "representatives" of the two cities. See, for example, Dawson, "St. Augustine and His Age," 61, 72; Rex Martin, "The Two Cities in Augustine's Political Philosophy," Journal of the History of Ideas 33 (April 1972): 200.

[42] Cranz, "Christian Society," 215. He elsewhere notes that: "Augustine in presenting the ideas of De Civitate Dei, XV, 2, refers to the specifically Christian society either as city of God or as heavenly kingdom or as ecclesia. Such usage shows that the three concepts are to some extent interchangeable. Furthermore, Augustine on occasion explicitly equates them. In the De Civitate Dei, for example, he speaks of the philosophers 'against whom we are defending the city of God, that is His ecclesia'; he refers to the many prophecies 'concerning Christ and the kingdom of heaven, which is the city of God'; and he declares 'Therefore even now the ecclesia is the kingdom of Christ and the kingdom of heaven.' Such equations are regularly introduced parenthetically, but this is no justification for denying that Augustine uses all three terms to refer to the same society. He has no reason to labor the point with an audience which already felt themselves members of that society," 219. Cranz recognizes that such equation is not generally accepted: "Modern scholars have not in general accepted these statements of Augustine at their face value but have instead set up distinctions such as that between the 'church' and the city of God. Additional proof, however, that such distinctions are not Augustinian may be found in the fact that Augustine himself expresses his basic generalizations about the Christian society in all three terminologies."

[43] Ibid., 218. He argues that in De Civitate Dei, the main outlines of Augustine's social thought appear in a "city terminology," but that Augustine can elsewhere state them in terms of other key concepts, such as the doctrine of two kingdoms, and the earthly Jerusalem can be explained not only as the prophecy of the city of God but also as a prophecy of the ecclesia. He writes: "The best illustration of a parallel to De Civ. D., xv, 2, in the terminology of kingdom is found in the Enarratio in Psalmum 119, where Augustine again discusses Isaac and Ishmael and again uses Galatians as his authority. 'The old testament is from God, and the new testament is from God, as both Isaac and Ishmael were sons of Abraham. But Ishmael pertains to the earthly kingdom and Isaac to the celestial kingdom. ... As symbols (in figura) they are understood

What implications does the metaphor of two cities have? The primary implication, which Augustine proceeded to draw out in detail, is this: the *saeculum*, the world of space and time, the world as it appears to human senses, the world in which the two cities intermingle, is clearly of secondary importance.[44] The ultimate allegiance of each human being, that is, the city to which one truly belongs, is most important. The *saeculum* will "pass away"; the destiny of every human being lies in eternity, either life and happiness for eternity or death and suffering for eternity. The *saeculum* is merely a way station, a temporary phase in the working out of human destiny. While they are in the *saeculum*, human beings, as potential members of the heavenly city, live as "aliens" (*peregrini*); their true citizenship, potentially at least, lies in a city beyond the world. What happens in the world is significant, of course, but it is not *most* significant.[45]

Augustine's Theological Adjustment

There is strong agreement among New Testament scholars as to the strong eschatological element in early Christianity. Gager describes early Christianity as a millenarian movement and stresses its apocalyptic expectations and separatist ethic.[46] But with time, things changed.

The growing realization in the early days of the church that the last days were not immediately at hand implied an increasingly less radical separation from the world at large, or else it implied a revised understanding of what was meant by the expectation of a new form of life in a new age. In the early church, both adjustments were made: the majority of Christians taking the former track, a minority, the monastics and separatists, the latter. This dual adjustment supports the eschatological interpretation of the early church, and it helps conceive of what may have happened in the development of Christian attitudes toward society and the Christians role in it (the world of

spiritually, just as the earthly Jerusalem was a shadow of the heavenly kingdom and as the earthly kingdom was a shadow of the kingdom of heaven'."

[44] For an elaboration on Augustine's understanding of the term see Markus, *Saeculum*. See also Peter Brown, *Religion and Society in the Age of Saint Augustine* (London: Faber, 1971), 37.

[45] See Augustine, *De Civ. D.* 5.17; 19.17; *Serm.* 40.7-8. See also Dawson, "St. Augustine and His Age," 38, 48; Peter Brown, *Augustine of Hippo* (Berkeley, CA: University of California Press, 1969), 210, 324; and Roland Bainton, *Christian Attitudes toward War Peace: A Historical Survey and Critical Re-evaluation* (Nashville: Abingdon Press, 1960), 95.

[46] John Gager, *Kingdom and Community: The Social World of Early Christianity* (Englewood Cliffs, NJ: Prentice Hall, 1975), 20-57. See also Robert G. Clouse, introduction to *The Meaning of the Millennium: Four Views*, ed. Robert G. Clouse (Downers Grove, IL: InterVarsity, 1977), 9, where he asserts: "During the first three centuries of the Christian era, premillennialism appears to have been the dominant eschatological interpretation."

"this age").[47] Johnson argues that since both the mass of Christians and their leadership were prepared to accept what developed under Constantine and his successors—and not only to accept it passively, but to work at advancing it—suggests that something was happening in the church's attitudes toward life in the world during the early centuries.[48] Augustine would further that attitude; Augustine's eschatological developments would play a significant role in the development of the church's participation in the affairs of state and society. Johnson has suggested that there was an eschatological basis to Augustine's thoughts on social involvement.[49] Augustine's change in his eschatology—his new understanding of the "kingdom"—would become foundational to that attitude.

AUGUSTINE'S ESCHATOLOGY

According to Augustine's eschatology,[50] the world is destined to persist through six ages between the creation and the final judgment of Christ.[51] Five of these ages, each lasting 1,000 years, were complete at the time of Christ's birth; the sixth, which is also spoken of as a Millennium but may even be of a different length,[52] was in progress when Augustine wrote. The termination of this sixth age is described in the last three books of the *City of God*, 20-22.

---

[47] The social-political context, after the conversion of the empire in the early fourth century, was vastly different from that of the New Testament or the earliest church. By this time, the institutional stability of the church-state structure had replaced the fervent hope of most Christians for a quick end to the world as we know it and a transformation of believers' fortunes through the millennial kingdom. See Philip Schaff, *History of the Christian Church*, vol. 2, *Ante-Nicene Christianity from the Death of John the Apostle to Constantine the Great, A.D. 100-325*, 5th ed. (New York: Scribner's Sons, 1889; repr., Peabody, MA: Hendrickson, 1996), 619, writes: "The millennial reign, instead of being anxiously waited and prayed for, began to be dated either from the first appearance of Christ, or from the conversion of Constantine and the downfall of paganism, and to be regarded as realized in the glory of the dominant imperial state-church."

[48] James T. Johnson, *The Quest for Peace* (Princeton, NJ: Princeton University Press, 1987), 17. This all leads to what Johnson describes as a "gradual consolidation of a positive moral acceptance of participation in affairs of state, including military service and war." I use war here as an example since it demonstrates the dramatic shift in Christians' attitudes toward war (and society) in just two centuries, especially by the time of Ambrose and Augustine.

[49] Ibid., 14-17.

[50] It is helpful to note that Augustine's *City of God* basically divides into two parts, the first of which (books 1-10) seeks to "refute the enemies of the city of God" (*De Civ. D.* 18.1) by demonstrating the vices and failures of pagan empires, and especially of the existing empire whose chief city had recently succumbed to its first barbarian conqueror. The second part belongs to the genre of apocalypse. Augustine prefaces his description of future events by an account of the creation, and a survey of world history. See Brown, *Augustine of Hippo*, ch. 26; Kirwan, *Augustine*, 221.

[51] E.g. Augustine *De Genesi contra Manichaeos* 1.23.35-24.42; Augustine *De Catechizandis. Rudibus* 22.39; *De Civ. D.* 22.30.5; see Kirwan, *Augustine*, 221.

[52] At one point Augustine even envisages 600,000 years, see *De Civ. D.* 12.13.

The Present Age in *The City of God:*
Augustine's Eschatology and Rev 20

Augustine describes the present age as the conflict between the City of God and the City of Satan, or the conflict between the church and the world. This was viewed as moving on to the ultimate triumph of the church to be climaxed by a tremendous struggle in which the church would be apparently defeated, only to consummate in a tremendous triumph in the second coming of Christ to earth.

Drawing mainly on Revelation 20, Augustine maintains that when the end arrives, the devil, who is now bound and sealed in an abyss, will be released for a period of three and a half years, during which time he will persecute the church; this will be a time of terror and chaos. Next, Christ will come to judge both the living and the dead. The judgment will proceed as in Matthew 25:31-46. Then fire will consume the whole earth, except for human bodies. The bodies of the dead are re-formed from their scattered materials, and together with the bodies of all the living, transmuted to become incorruptible. After the destruction of the earth a new heaven and a new earth are created.

Augustine asserts that the present age of conflict is the Millennium and argues that many Christians misunderstand Revelation 20:1-6 by thinking that the first resurrection is physical and that the thousand years will be a form of Sabbath rest for the people of God. He, like Origen (ca. 185-254) before him, now rejects chiliasm that he previously held because of the sensuous nature of the delights it offers. Augustine writes:

> This notion would be in some degree tolerable if it were believed that in that Sabbath some delights of a spiritual character were to be available for the saints because of the presence of the Lord. I also entertained this notion at one time. But in fact, those people assert that those who have risen again will spend their rest in the most unrestrained material feasts.[53]

The admission by him that he once was a chiliast and his use of the phrase "unrestrained material feasts" seems to suggest that the problem for Augustine, in his mind, is not premillennialism per se, but a perverse version of it. Augustine now views (pre)millennialism as an overly extravagant event that turns the kingdom

---

[53] Augustine, *De Civ. D.* 20:7.

into an occasion for the exercise of gluttony and other lusts.[54] Thus, on trivial grounds, at least as he explains it, Augustine abandons the literal interpretation of Revelation 20.

As an alternative to chiliasm, Augustine offers a view of Revelation 20:1-6 in which the thousand years (Millennium) represent the last period of history, the present church age, during which Satan is prevented from controlling believers. As a consequence of interpreting the Millennium as this present age, Augustine interprets the binding of Satan to be in effect in this present age as well. After concluding that the binding of Satan is synonymous with the victory of Christ in His first advent, Augustine draws the conclusion that the "first resurrection" of Revelation 20:5 is the spiritual birth of believers—the passing of a person from spiritual death to life, or what we have come to call conversion. All those who partake in the first resurrection are those who, during the entire course of the church age (the thousand years), have been converted to Christ.[55] They now reign with Christ. Those who reign with Christ are the ones who do as He commands, and thus believers themselves constitute the kingdom. Those who do not come to life until the end of the thousand years are unbelievers, for they have not "come to life" during the church age. They are the ones who will be resurrected to judgement at the end of history.[56]

And after the judgement? What sort of life will the saints lead then, or in other words, what will they do (Augustine asks the question in 22.29)? Life in heaven, he answers, will be not so much action as rest and leisure. The saints will live in the peace of God; there will also be time for praising God. There will be no flattery, no wrongs, and no envy. Life in heaven will be one long holiday, *sabbatum non habens vesparum*.[57]

---

[54] Donald Fairbairn, "Contemporary Millennial/Tribulational Debates: Whose Side Was the Early Church On?" in Craig L. Blomberg and Sung Wook Chung, eds., *A Case for Historic Premillennialism* (Grand Rapids: Baker Academic, 2009), 116. See also *Ep.* 29.11, where Augustine expressed that he was regularly annoyed to distraction by the "carnal sousing" of the faithful at feasts honoring the dead, when they would dance, feast, and get splendidly drunk. He complained that these were pagan corruptions brought into the church with the influx of forced converts after 399. Furthermore, in the abandon of the faithful in their drinking and feasting at the shrine of their saints, one gets a glimpse of the ancient Christian hopes of these church members for life after the *prima resurrectio* (first resurrection), an affirmation for them that when the kingdom came they would experience such feasting, life would be full of joy, and labors would cease. For more discussion, see Peter Brown, *Augustine of Hippo*, 206, 217-220, 229.

[55] Fairbairn, "Contemporary Millennial/Tribulational Debates" in Blomberg and Chung, eds, *A Case for Historic Premillennialism*, 116.

[56] Augustine, *De Civ. D.* 20:9.

[57] Ibid., 22.30.

It is central to Augustine's conception of heaven that there will be no government in it, no *imperium*. Saints will not need to keep themselves in order, not to be kept in order by a governing body of other saints, nor by God. The peace of the heavenly city, he says, "is a completely ordered and completely concordant fellowship in the enjoyment of God and of one another in God."[58] In that consummation the state will wither away.

Augustine's Eschatological Change: History's Influencer Had Been Influenced

A closer look at several features of Augustine's understanding of the reign of Christ, and the meaning of the thousand years, evidences the influence of a contemporary theologian on Augustine's theological development. In *City of God*, Book XX, Chapters 6-11, dealing with Revelation 20:1-6, it is apparent that Tyconius the Donatist influenced Augustine's thinking.[59] Similar terminology, explanations, and scriptural citations support this claim.[60]

Tyconius, a Donatist lay theologian, was one of the most incisive thinkers of the African church in the seventies and eighties of the fourth century. But Tyconius appears not to have been widely known in his time outside North Africa.[61] He was hardly a prolific author. He is known to have written four

---

[58] Ibid., 19.13.

[59] Markus, *Saeculum*, notes: "There was a fundamental insight behind Augustine's theology of the two cities which he had undoubtedly learnt from Tyconius.... The Body of Christ had 'two parts', or the one Body, the Church, could be seen simultaneously as holy and wicked. This was the insight for which Augustine above all praised Tyconius.... But Tyconius was the first to have elaborated a theology of the Church's holiness as *eschatological* [italics mine].... This was the foundation on which Augustine built his theology of the 'two cities'," 116-17.

[60] Augustine, *De Civ. D.* 20.6-11, echoes the concerns, the arguments, and the scriptural citations of the *Book of Rules* of Tyconius, especially on the "two resurrections" and the "thousand years."

[61] Paul B. Harvey, Jr., "Approaching the Apocalypse: Augustine, Tyconius, and John's Revelation," *Augustinian Studies* 30:2 (1999) 133. See also, Paula Fredriksen [Landes], "Tyconius and the End of the World," *Revue des etudes Augustiniennes* 28 (1982):74-75, writes of Tyconius: "Rejected by his own party, refusing the Catholics, he appears in the perspective of history a solitary, lonely figure." See further, D. F. Wright, "Tyconius," *The New International Dictionary of the Christian Church*, ed. J. D. Douglas (Grand Rapids: Zondervan, 1975) 989. Little is known of Tyconius. He was probably a native of Africa and a layman. He died about the year 390, and his main writings would date between 370-380. The most lucid account of his work is found in Gennadius' *De viris illustribus*, 18, ed. E. C. Richardson, in Texte und Untersuchungen 14.1 (in English, see NPNF, 1952) 285-402, where we learn Tyconius was a Donatist, well-educated, and ecclesiastical writer, and a scriptural commentator. From Augustine we learn of Tyconius' conflicts with the Donatist bishop of Carthage, Parmenian, in the late seventies. About 385, Parmenian summoned a Council and Tyconius was excommunicated. (See Augustine's *Contra Epistolam Parmeniani*, I 1.1; also *Ep* 93.44.) The facts of the conflict are known; of the background, nothing has survived. For more on the Donatist-Catholic conflict, see Frend, *The Donatist Church*, 114, 174, 202-205.

books,[62] but his reputation rests upon the two books that survived him, a commentary on the Apocalypse, now lost, and his *Book of Rules*, the first treatise written on biblical hermeneutics in the Latin West.[63] The lost Apocalypse commentary has been undergoing reconstruction from quotations of it in the works of medieval exegetes.[64] Tyconius' *Book of Rules* has remained intact, but it has not found prestige on its own. "But Augustine has spoken for him. The Catholic bishop's [Augustine's] instinct for finding valuable resources had led him to the Donatist layman."[65]

Augustine was intrigued by the thought of the Donatist writer, and summarized the seven rules of Tyconius in his own *De Doctrina Christiana*.[66] Through the overwhelming popularity of Augustine's summary of the seven

---

[62] On Tyconius himself, see Gennadius, *De viris illustribus*. See also, Harvey, "Approaching the Apocalypse," 151. Harvey attaches an updated English translation of Gennadius as an appendix to his article (Appendix 2). Harvey writes of Tyconius: "He wrote too late to be included in Jerome's *De viris illustribus*, although by the time Jerome came to revise Victorinus' commentary on the Apocalypse, he had learned to exploit Tyconius. Gennadius' continuation of Jerome's *De viris illustribus*, however, includes an entry (chapter 18) on Tyconius, where we read that the Donatist scholar explained the entire Apocalypse and interpreted all the imagery in Revelation not in a carnal, but a spiritual sense."

[63] Pamela Bright, *The Book of Rules of Tyconius* (Notre Dame, Indiana: U of ND Press, 1988), 2.

[64] Kenneth Steinhauser, *The Apocalypse Commentary of Tyconius: A History of Its Reception and Influence* (Frankfurt: Peter Lang, 1987).

[65] Paula Fredriksen [Landes], "*Tyconius and the End of the World,*" 75. She says of Tyconius: "[T]hrough his admirer Augustine, Tyconius inadvertently formulated an ecclesiology that worked to undermine the theological foundations of his own church. But ultimately his adoptive party treated him better than his own. Assuming his exegesis, it shunned him as a heretic, until, eventually, all but one of his works were lost. What remained was Tyconius' "exegetical revolution," his thorough-going de-eschatologizing both of apocalyptic texts and of political events. It helped to liberate Augustine from the earlier millenarian framework of most Christian thought, and provided him with the key to a more profound understanding of Paul. More generally, it freed Western Christianity from the apocalyptic traditions of its own past, so that it could settle into its new post-Constantinian position in the world and, as it were, in history," 74.

[66] Augustine, *De Doctrina Christiana* III, 30-37, *PL* 34:15-121. (Or see NPNF, p. 568). Was Tyconius' *Book of Rules* written to provide exegetes guidelines for the interpretation of obscure or difficult passages of Scripture? Apparently Augustine thought so. In the mid 390's Augustine was drawing up a program for the study and interpretation of Scripture that he would call *De Doctrina Christiana*. In 396 he broke off his work well into the third book of *DDC*. Augustine did not resume this work until 427, by concluding the third book and adding a fourth on the style of homiletics. It is in finishing the third book which concludes his study of exegetical method in *DDC* that Augustine explains and comments on the *Book of Rules* of Tyconius. He writes that Tyconius "wrote a book which he called the *Book of Rules* because in it he laid down seven rules, which are, as it were, keys to open the secrets of Scripture.... Now these rules as expounded by their author, do indeed, when carefully considered, afford considerable assistance in penetrating the secrets of the sacred writings." (Taken from *On Christian Doctrine*, in NPNF, 568). Jean-Marc Vercruysse, "Tyconius' Hermeneutics" in Tarmo Toom (editor), *Patristic Theories of Biblical Interpretation: The Latin Fathers* (New York: Cambridge University Press, 2016) writes: "Augustine presented Tyconius' hermeneutics in a simplified form and for educational purposes, ... The stature and the moral authority of the bishop of Hippo were such that his abridged version of the *Liber regularum* saved its author from being forgotten and disappearing from the scene. However, it also prevented, for a long time, the readers—even the well-informed ones—from considering Tyconius' original version of the *Liber regularum* ... In fact, in the subsequent ecclesiastical literature, the *Liber regularum* was most widely known and assessed in the form that Augustine gave to it and not in the original form in which Tyconius wrote it. It was not until the second half of the twentieth century that people started considering the original version again" (42-43).

rules in the *De Doctrina Christiana*, the *Book of Rules* itself was relegated to the status of an unread classic.[67] Ironically, it is the contention today that Tyconius may have been misunderstood by Augustine—that Tyconius was not offering to write a textbook, or "rule" book, or even proposing seven steps or methods for proper exegesis. Nonetheless, Augustine assumed it was such, and employed it as such in his approach to Revelation.[68] It is interesting to note that Augustine, though he may not have understood Tyconius' purpose and logic behind the "rules," appreciated and adopted Tyconius' typological method. When applying Tyconius' method to the Scriptures, especially to Revelation, Augustine arrived at the same conclusions.[69]

By applying a "spiritual" interpretation to the text, Tyconius had repeatedly discovered that the Johannine Apocalypse refers above all to the church, both in its ideal form and as it has already begun to be. In Scripture, present and future are always mysteriously intermingled for Tyconius. What is significant both eschatologically and ecclesiologically is that Augustine arrived at Tyconius' conclusion (Rule V of Tyconius *Book of Rules*) that the "thousand years" in

---

[67] F. C. Burkitt, *The Book of Rules of Tyconius (Liber Regularum)* (Cambridge: Univ Press, 1894; repr., 1967) vi. Burkitt writes: "Therefore it is not unlikely that the fame of the book in the Middle ages and its preservation to the present time is entirely due to S. Augustine. It was his recommendation, rather than the intrinsic merit of the work of a Donatist, that secured the respect of Latin Christendom."

[68] Tyconius says in the prologue of *Liber Regularum* that his exegetical principles are *mystical* rules ("sunt enim quaedam regulae mysticae") which enable spiritual understanding – in contrast to the usual allegorical style of the day. (It is interesting to note that Augustine thought Tyconius not as successful in his endeavor as he thought he was, *DDC*, 3, xxx, 42.) In his carefully crafted preamble to the *Book of Rules*, Tyconius tells us that he intended to write a book to introduce the reader to the logic of seven "mystical rules" which obscured the "treasures of truth" from some people. He referred to his exegetical "rules" as *mysticae*. If the logic of these rules were understood, then the reader would be led along "paths of light" through the "immense forest of prophecy." (For Tyconius a "prophetic" text was not just the oracle of a prophet of Israel, but any text, Old or New Testament, that calls a sinner to repentance by warning of the coming death and destruction that awaits those that are separated from the love of God.) Thus, according to Charles Kannengiesser, *A Conflict of Christian Hermeneutics*, the "mystic rules" were "a coherent pattern which would structure scripture itself, in other words a system of revelatory procedures," 6. This is a notable contrast to the purpose that Augustine had assumed. It is Bright's analyses that "Augustine's interpretation of the *Book of Rules* obscured for future generations of exegetes the very purpose and logic of Tyconius' *Book of Rules*" (Bright, "Tyconius and His Interpreters: A Study of the Epitomes of the *Book of Rules*," Kannengiesser, *A Conflict of Christian Hermeneutics*, 24). Augustine seems to identify "book" and "rules" and "keys" with the idea of methods. He thus seems to have understood, or used, the *Book of Rules* as a textbook or "rule" book for exegesis. It is Bright's thesis that Tyconius is not offering seven rules (steps or methods) for exegesis (Ref. *The Book of Rules of Tyconius: Its Purpose and Inner Logic*. C. Kannengiesser further develops Bright's thesis). It should especially be noted that Augustine's understanding of Tyconius purpose has since influenced readers of Tyconius *Book of Rules*. This became the understood purpose behind Tyconius' work even as recently as Burkitt in his critical edition.

[69] But Augustine's reliance on Tyconius was more profound and independent than the simple reiteration on Tyconius' exegetic strategies might imply. It appears that Augustine's long meditation on Paul begun already in the 390s, when he had first encountered Tyconius, would ultimately lead Augustine to formulate his own ideas on time and history—which would then radically alter the terms in which he would be able to discuss traditional Christian millenarianism. By the time of the sack of Rome in 410, Augustine was ready to start his exposition of God's work in world history—and he would spend over a decade writing his *City of God* to explain this new worldview.

Revelation 20:6 are not to be interpreted literally. The "thousand years" speak of this "whole intervening time" referring to the present church age. "Therefore the church even now is the kingdom of Christ, and the kingdom of heaven. Accordingly, even now His saints reign with Him."[70] Like Tyconius, the use of an apocalyptic image no longer indicates an "apocalyptic" message for Augustine. Using what he understood to be Tyconius' rules of exegesis, Augustine's exegetical methods were so affected that the result was a reshaping of Augustine's theology, particularly in eschatology. Bonner states:

> Augustine's thought has therefore developed since his early days as a scriptural exegete.... There seems to be little doubt that a major influence in producing this development in Augustine's thought was his study of the Donatist writer Tyconius. ... The effect of Tyconius' work was to produce a type of exegesis which avoided crude literalism on the one hand and overstrained allegory on the other. Thus Tyconius rejected the old materialistic notion of a literal thousand-year reign of Christ with the saints after the first resurrection (Rev 20:4-6), regarding ... the reign of the saints as the reign of the Church in the world to the end of time. It seems that he was instrumental in converting Augustine to his view.[71]

Without totally abandoning the allegorical method, which was popular during the fourth century, Tyconius initiated a radically new development based on a typology of the text.

This resulted in several achievements for his exegesis of Revelation. First, the typological method enabled Tyconius to integrate the Old Testament with the New. Therefore, the two Testaments could be interpreted in relationship to one another without recourse to primitive allegory while still preserving their essential unity. Second, the typological method enabled Tyconius to apply the Scriptures to his contemporary historical situation; he could be relevant. Third, the typological method enabled Tyconius to solve an acute theological question—millenarianism. According to Tyconius one need not posit a future thousand-year reign of Christ on earth in a strict sense because a part may stand for the whole or vice versa. In this way Tyconius put an end to millenarian teaching

---

[70] NPNF 2:430.

[71] Gerald Bonner, "Augustine as Biblical Scholar," in *The Cambridge History of the* Bible, edited by P. R. Ackroyd and C. F. Evans (New York: Cambridge University Press, repr., 1989), 554-55.

by interpreting numbers in a spiritual way.[72] "As far as we know, Tyconius was among the first who rejected chiliasm."[73]

The vivid eschatological images of persecution, the double resurrection in Rev 20:1-6, the man of sin, the sea giving up its dead—these he also thoroughly de-eschatologizes, seeing in them not prophecies of the End but symbolic descriptions of the present.[74] Tyconius thus *reversed* the values of the old categories which had for so long served millenarian speculation—he essentially "de-eschatologized" the long-assumed prophetic text.[75]

Employing Tyconius' exegetical reasoning of de-eschatologizing the apocalyptic texts, Augustine freed himself from the earlier millenarian framework. He would now go on to sketch out in detail his resultant *ecclesiological* interpretation of Rev 20:1-6.

The Two Resurrections

What is Augustine's interpretation of the first and second resurrections? Augustine explains:

> There are two regenerations, of which I have already made mention,—the one according to faith, and which takes place in the present life by means of baptism; the other according to the flesh, and which shall be accomplished in its incorruption and immortality by means of the great and final judgment,—so are there also two resurrections,—the one the first and spiritual resurrection, which has place in this life, and preserves us from coming into the second death; the other the second,

---

[72] Tyconius' method is described in his Rule V: Times. He describes two different methods of interpreting biblical "times." The first is "synecdoche," the part for the whole, or the whole for the part. For example, Tyconius deals with the problem of computing three days between the crucifixion and the resurrection of Christ whereby a part of a day counts as a whole day. His second method concerns "legitimate" numbers. Here he explains that the duration of time is symbolic rather than quantitative. There are certain favored numbers for time in Scripture. As such, forty "days" or "years," seven "days" or "years," multiples of ten, especially a thousand "years," are times that are to be interpreted not quantitatively but as referring to the "whole time" of God's work of salvation. So, for Tyconius, "whole time" is the time of the church; of particular significance to the millenarian debate is his insistence on the spiritual interpretation of the number one thousand, which is the "whole time" of the first resurrection—that is, the "resurrection" of sinful humanity through baptism in the church. For discussion, see Bright, *Book of Rules*, 76-79.

[73] Jean-Marc Vercruysse, "Tyconius' Hermeneutics," 40. He adds: "The bipartite church is a place of conflict in which Christ and the devil spiritually clash with each other through their respective members ... For him, the biblical message remains acute in all times. The ultimate fight will be preceded by a thousand-year-long period, which ... is to be understood as a symbolic time reference. It designates the period between the passion of Christ and the outbreak of the final persecution, that is, the present time" (40).

[74] On the double resurrection and reign of the saints, see Gennadius, NPNF 2:389.

[75] P. Fredrickson [Landes], "Tyconius and the End of the World," 72.

which does not occur now, but in the end of the world, and which is of the body, not of the soul.[76]

Thus, the first resurrection, "which now is ... regards not the body, but the soul."[77] In this first resurrection "a transition from death to life is made in this present time."[78] The first resurrection is the conversion experience.

The Thousand Years

Augustine then begins his discussion on Revelation 20:1-6 in *De Civ. D.* 20.7. He notes:

> The evangelist John has spoken of these two resurrections in the book which is called the Apocalypse, ... some Christians ... construe the passage into ridiculous fancies. For the Apostle John says ... "And I saw an angel come down from heaven ... Blessed and holy is he that hath part in the first resurrection: on such the second death hath no power; but they shall be priests of God and of Christ, and shall reign with Him a thousand years."[79]

After quoting Revelation 20:1-6, Augustine, as noted previously, comments that he had once held to a literal understanding but has since accepted a different interpretation (i.e., Tyconius'). He writes:

> Those who, on the strength of this passage, have suspected that the first resurrection is future and bodily, have been moved, among other things, specially by the number of a thousand years,... I myself, too, once held this opinion.... such assertions can be believed only by the carnal. They who do believe them are called by the spiritual Chiliasts, which we may literally reproduce by the name Millenarians. It were a tedious process to refute these opinions point by point: we prefer proceeding to show how that passage of Scripture should be understood.[80]

---

[76] Augustine, NPNF 2:426.

[77] Robert Saucy discusses the Augustinian interpretation of the two resurrections and demonstrates the inconsistencies in Augustine's exegesis. See his discussion on this and several other weaknesses of Augustine's exegesis of Rev 20:4-6 in Robert Saucy, *The Case for Progressive Dispensationalism*, 274-292.

[78] Augustine, NPNF 2:425 (i.e., referring to what is commonly understood today as one's salvation experience).

[79] Ibid., 426.

[80] Ibid.

He then explains the meaning of the "thousand years" as the duration of history.

> Now the thousand years may be understood in two ways, so far as occurs to me:
> either because these things happen in the sixth thousand of years or sixth millennium
> ... to be followed by a Sabbath ... so that, speaking of a part under the name of the
> whole, he [John] calls the last part of the millennium—the part, that is, which had
> yet to expire before the end of the world—a thousand years; or he used the thousand
> years as an equivalent for the whole duration of this world, employing the number
> of perfection to mark the fullness of time. For a thousand is the cube of ten. For ten
> times ten makes a hundred.... Besides, if a hundred is sometimes used for totality, ...
> how much greater reason is a thousand put for totality?[81]

This is Augustine's understanding of how Tyconius' fifth rule applies.

Augustine solves the problem of a thousand years by either using synecdoche ("The figure synecdoche either puts the part for the whole, or the whole
for the part."[82]), or by using "legitimate" numbers ("[W]hich Holy Scripture
more highly favors, such as seven, or ten, or twelve, or any of the other numbers which the diligent reader of Scripture soon comes to know. Now numbers
of this sort are often put for time universal."[83]). In utilizing Tyconius' rules,
albeit improperly understood, Augustine arrived at Tyconius' conclusion that
the "thousand years" in Revelation 20:6 are not to be interpreted literally.

Thus, Augustine would explicitly say in *De Civ. D.* 20.9 *that the "thousand
years" denotes not literally one thousand years but "the period beginning with Christ's
first coming" and includes all the years of the Christian era, no matter how long it
will last.* This would mean that, for Augustine, the Millennium is "an allegorical representation of the historical church in its present state,"[84]—though the
church is not yet the perfect kingdom of God since *the church presently, as a
mixed body (a "bi-partite" body; the term used by Tyconius and Augustine), contains
both the elect and non-elect.*

---

[81] Ibid.

[82] He is explaining Tyconius' fifth rule. Augustine, *On Christian Doctrine*, trans. J. F. Shaw, NPNF, vol. 2 (Grand Rapids: Eerdmans, 1956), 571.

[83] Augustine, NPNF, 2:426.

[84] K. Pollman, "Molding the Present: Apocalyptic as Hermeneutics in *City of God* 21-22," in *History, Apocalypse, and the Secular Imagination: New Essays on Augustine's City of God*, ed. M. Vessy, K. Pollman, and A. Fitzgerald (Bowling Green, OH: Philosophy Document Center, 1999), 168.

The Reign of the Saints

After a lengthy discussion on the thousand years and the binding and loosing of the devil in chapters 7 and 8 of Book 20, Augustine deals with the meaning of the reign of the saints with Christ for a thousand years. He comments, "But while the devil is bound, the saints reign with Christ during the same thousand years, understood in the same way, that is, of the time of His first coming."[85] Again, Augustine does not view this as a future, literal thousand years. He sees the "thousand years" as referring to this present time.[86] Obviously, the nation of Israel plays no positive role in Augustine's kingdom theology.

> The Church could not now be called His kingdom or the kingdom of heaven unless His saints were even now reigning with Him,... the Church even now is the kingdom of Christ, and the kingdom of heaven. Accordingly, *even now His saints reign with Him,... in this whole intervening time called a thousand years.*[87]

For Augustine, the reign of Christ has two aspects: in the present, through His saints/church; and in the future at the second advent when He comes in manifest glory to judge.[88]

Augustine understands the present reign of Christ in a threefold way: in the believer, through the government of the church, and with the departed saints. It is necessary to observe his explanation of the present reign (kingdom) of Christ by a lengthy citation. The church in time is a *regnum militiae*, a church struggling against the forces of evil both outside and inside her own ranks. Augustine continues,

> Therefore the Church even now is the kingdom of Christ, and the kingdom of heaven. Accordingly, even now His saints reign with Him,... For they reign with Him who do what the apostle says, "If ye be risen with Christ, mind the things which are above, where Christ sitteth at the right hand of God." [Col 3:1,2] ...

---

[85] Augustine, NPNF 2:429.

[86] Gennadius, in his survey of ecclesiastical writing at the end of the fifth century, said of Tyconius: "He (Tyconius) doubts that there will be a reign of the righteous on the earth for a thousand years after the resurrection, or that there will be two resurrections of the dead in the flesh, one of the righteous and the other of the unrighteous." See, *De Viris Inlustribus* 389.

[87] Augustine, NPNF 2:430-31 (italics mine). "Whole time" is a Tyconian expression applying the intervening thousand years to the church age.

[88] The similarity to Tyconius' explanation of Rule 1 is most apparent here..

Of such persons he also says that their conversation is in heaven. [Phil 3:20] In fine, they reign with Him who are so in His kingdom that they themselves are His kingdom.... It is then of this kingdom militant,... that the Apocalypse speaks ... For, after saying that the devil is bound a thousand years and is afterwards loosed for a short season, it goes on to give a sketch of what the Church does or of what is done in the Church in those days, in the words, "And I saw seats and them that sat upon them, and judgment was given." It is not to be supposed that this refers to the last judgment, but to the seats of the rulers and to the rulers themselves by whom the Church is now governed. And no better interpretation of judgment being given can be produced than that which we have in the words, "What ye bind on earth shall be bound in heaven; and what ye loose on earth shall be loosed in heaven." [Matt 18:18] Whence the apostle says, "What have I to do with judging them that are without? do not ye judge them that are within?" [1 Cor 5:12] "And the souls," says John, "of those who were slain for the testimony of Jesus and for the word of God,"—understanding what he afterwards says, "reigned with Christ a thousand years," [Rev 20:4]—that is, the souls of the martyrs not yet restored to their bodies.... Therefore, while these thousand years run on, their souls reign with Him, though not as yet in conjunction with their bodies.... The Church then, begins its reign with Christ now in the living and in the dead. For, as the apostle says, "Christ died that He might be Lord both of the living and of the dead" [Rom 14:9].[89]

So, the church now is the kingdom of heaven. Believers dead and alive are in the kingdom, ruling with Christ.

It was with the aid of Tyconius' eschatology that Augustine could speak of the church now, in the interim, as not what it will be at the end. For Augustine, the church is always caught up in the tension of what it is and what it will be. Thus Markus comments that the "simple fact remains that in [Augustine's] vocabulary the Church was the City of God, even though it certainly numbered citizens of the earthly city among its members while on its earthly pilgrimage among the wicked."[90]

---

[89] Augustine, NPNF 2:430-31.

[90] Markus, *Saeculum*, 120-21.

The Resulting Interpretations

In summary, the following are the main points which Augustine makes (similarly made by Tyconius) in his interpretation of Revelation 20:

1. The Millennium is the present church age and does not necessarily last only one thousand years.

2. The figure 1000 years (vv. 2 ,3, 4, 5, 6, 7) indicates that this time period is not the future rule of eternity, but the finite rule of the church-age.

3. The now-present millennial rule of Christ and the church, the kingdom, will last until the end of the age.

4. Christ sits at the right hand of power and rules in favor of the saints.

5. Satan is bound (vv. 2-3) during the entire church age, from the birth of Christ to the *Parousia*.

6. Being "bound" (v. 3) means that he cannot deceive the nations (the international church) during the church age.

7. At the end of the church age, Satan will be loosed to test the church (vv. 3, 7).

8. "Thrones" (v. 4) are within the church, which exercises a judicial office on its twelve-fold apostolic basis.

9. The "souls" of the righteous dead (v. 4) are those who die with Christ in present afflictions during the church age.

10. Since these "souls" are reigning with Christ during the present church age and before the resurrection, their rule is over a spiritual kingdom, sharing in the reign of Christ and those who are still alive.

11. Those who have a part in this kingdom do not bear the mark of the beast (v. 4), but rather the divine image and likeness—the "image" in the body and the "likeness" in the soul.

12. The first resurrection (vv. 4-6) is a spiritual resurrection of the soul—from the spiritual death of sin to the spiritual life of righteousness, i.e., being born again in baptism.

13. The second resurrection (v. 5) is a literal bodily resurrection which is still future.

14. Those who are forgiven are the priests of God (v.6) who participate in His present kingdom rule.

Obviously, everything that Augustine wrote about the Millennium was church centered. Augustine had no room in his theology for a restoration of Israel to her land,[91] with her Messiah ruling from Jerusalem for a thousand years.[92]

The last two books of Augustine's *De Civitate Dei*, XXI and XXII, deal with hell and heaven, the final destinies of all humans. The aged Augustine, in his seventies by then, receives from Scripture itself "an over-streaming inspiration for depicting afterlife"—he ties scripture verse after verse together, giving him a final opportunity in "this immense work" (*ingentis huius operis* xxx, 5) to celebrate the fulfillment of God's salvific work on earth.[93] He then speaks of that new creation:

> Wherefore it may very well be, and it is thoroughly credible, that we shall in the future world see the material forms of the new heavens and the new earth in such a way that we shall most distinctly recognize God everywhere present and governing all things, material as well as spiritual, and shall see Him, not as we understand

---

[91] Because of Augustine's theological stature, his eschatological/ecclesiological shift will impact later Christian theology relative to the church's (and society's) attitude toward Jews as well as it's understanding of a future for Israel. See especially Michael J. Vlach, "Rejection Then Hope: The Church's Doctrine of Israel in the Patristic Era" in *The Master's Seminary Journal* 19/1 (Spring 2008): 51-70. Vlach states: "As the Patristic Era's most influential theologian, Augustine (354-430) contributed to the view that the church was now Israel. As James Carroll points out, Augustine's attitude toward the Jews was rooted in 'assumptions of supersessionism.' According to Cardinal Carlo Maria Martini, Augustine introduced a 'negative element into judgment on the Jews.' He did so by advancing the 'theory of substitution' whereby the New Israel of the church became a substitute of ancient Israel." In line with supersessionist theology, Augustine explicitly stated that the title 'Israel' belonged to the Christian church: "For if we hold with a firm heart the grace of God which has been given us, we are Israel, the seed of Abraham. . . . Let therefore no Christian consider himself alien to the name of Israel.' He [Augustine] also said, 'The Christian people then is rather Israel.' He impacted later Christian theology heavily in taking this position" (58). For further study on Augustine's impact on attitudes toward Jews and Israel see: Paula Fredriksen, *Augustine and the Jews: A Christian Defense of Jews and Judaism* (New Haven: Yale Univ. Press, 2010); Stephen R. Haynes, *Reluctant Witnesses: Jews and the Christian Imagination* (Louisville, KY: Westminster John Knox Press, 1995), 25-63; Jeremy Cohen, *Living Letters of the Law: Ideas of the Jew in Medieval Christianity* (Los Angeles: University of California Press, 1999), especially 1-72 on Augustine; Marcel Dubois, "Jews, Judaism and Israel in the Theology of Saint Augustine: How He Links the Jewish People and the Land of Zion" in *Immanuel* 22/23 (1989): 162-214; and Adriann H. Bredero, *Christendom and Christianity in the Middle Ages* (Grand Rapids: Eerdmans, 1986), 53-78.

[92] According to Augustine's new theological position, might Israel and her hopes of a kingdom be forsaken? What about the restoration of Israel in the New Testament? Does it not appear that the teaching of Christ and the expectation of the apostles anticipated the fulfillment of the prophecies relative to Israel's kingdom (Acts 1:6-8; and Romans 11:26, where we read a specific declaration that Israel will be restored)? John Walvoord, *The Millennial Kingdom* (Grand Rapids: Zondervan, 1959) writes: "Amillenarians who follow Augustine usually spiritualize the restoration of Israel as meaning merely the growth and progress of the church" (184). For an informed discussion, see Jared Compton and Andrew Naselli, eds., *Three Views on Israel and the Church: Perspectives on Romans 9-11* (Grand Rapids: Kregel, 2018).

[93] Charles Kannengiesser, "Augustine of Hippo" in *Handbook of Patristic Exegesis*, 1181.

the invisible things of God, by the things which are made, ... but by means of the bodies we shall wear and which we shall see wherever we turn our eyes.[94]

Eternity, therefore, will be a glorious celebration God's presence, governing both the spiritual and the material.

ONE MAN'S CHANGE WILL BECOME MANY MEN'S KINGDOM

Augustine's influence was and is immense. His definitions of Christian doctrines and his exploration of philosophical ideas and their relationship to Christianity have been foundational down to the present day. Until Aquinas, no Christian thinker came anywhere near him in significance. Augustinian scholar Sir Henry Chadwick labeled Augustine as "the greatest single mind and influence in Christian history."[95] The consensus among scholars, adds Jonathan Yates, is that Augustine may be "the single most important and influential post-biblical Christian theologian in the western tradition."[96] Brian Daley, in regard to the theme of this chapter, states, "Without a doubt the theologian who has most influenced the development of Latin eschatology, as indeed all Latin theology, [is] Augustine of Hippo."[97]

Augustine, early in his career was a millenarian, that is, a premillennialist, believing that the first resurrection, as described in Revelation 20:1-6, would be bodily and that the sabbatical rest of the saints after this resurrection would last for a thousand years.[98] His eschatology at that time was similar to the early

---

[94] Augustine, *De Civ. D. 22.29.*

[95] Henry Chadwick, "Augustine," *A Dictionary of Biblical Interpretation*, ed. R.J. Coggins and J. L. Houlden (London: SCM Press, 1990).

[96] Cf. Jonathan P. Yates, "The Doctrine of the Future in Augustine," 299-300. Yates also comments on Augustine's literary output: "To this should be added that we know more about Augustine's life and have more words from Augustine's pen than we know or have from any other figure of the premodern period."

[97] Brian E. Daley, *The Hope of the Early Church: A Handbook of Patristic Eschatology* Cambridge: Cambridge University Press, 1991), 131.

[98] Still, Augustine later insists, he had held even then that the saints' delights would be of a spiritual character, unlike "those people" who asserted that the raised would "spend their rest in the most unrestrained material feasts, in which there will be so much to eat and drink that those supplies will break the bounds not only of moderation, but also of credibility"—a fair description of the prophecy of superabundance preserved in ancient Christian tradition and actively anticipated in the *laetitiae* observed by Catholic and Donatist alike. See *De Civ. Dei* (*The City of God*) 20.7.1; see also, Georges Folliet, "La typologie du *sabbat* chez Saint Augustin: Son interprétation millénariste entre 386 et 400," *Revue des Études Augustiniennes* 2 (1956): 371-90.

church fathers' historic premillennialism. His later theory of the Millennium and Christ's rule, doubtlessly influenced by the Donatist, Tyconius, was understood in a three-fold way: "It comprises at the same time the conquest of lusts by the believer, the government of the church by its office-bearers, and the blessed state of the departed saints, especially of the martyrs."[99] As Gerald Bray observes, "Augustine was what would now be called 'amillenarian' because he rejected the literal interpretation of the thousand-year reign of Christ that was common in his day."[100] Not only did he reject a literal one-thousand year kingdom on the earth after the Second Coming, he, like the church fathers before him, erased national Israel from prophecy.

So influential has been Augustine's view of the reign of the church saints and the thousand years in Revelation 20:1-6 that he is recognized today as "the father of the amillennial view."[101] His view would become the prevailing doctrine of the western (Roman Catholic, Latin) church, and it was adopted with variations by most of the Protestant Reformers.[102] To this day, his viewpoint is the basis of amillennialism, which has dominated the Christian church until well into the modern period.[103]

---

[99] D. H. Kromminga, *The Millennium in the Church* (Grand Rapids: Eerdmans, 1945), 111.

[100] Gerald Bray, *Augustine on the Christian Life*, 35. He adds: "Instead, he believed that Revelation was an allegory of the conflict between good and evil and not a prophecy that would be worked out in human history more or less recorded in the biblical text. Many movements have tried to revive a purely *historical* reading of Revelation, but many churches have adopted the Augustinian position on the matter, and it is now the one which, broadly speaking commands the assent of most academic theologians" (35-36).

[101] Kromminga, *The Millennium in the Church*, 259. But Augustine is not just associated with amillennialism—he is also seminal in the development of postmillennialism. See David S. Dockery, "The Doctrine of the Future: Millennialism in Contemporary Evangelical Theology," in *Eschatology: Biblical, Historical, and Practical Approaches*, ed. D. Jeffrey Bingham and Glenn R. Kreider (Grand Rapids: Kregel, 2016), 451. Dockery writes: "The interpretation of Revelation 20 that developed into postmillennialism has its roots in the great Christian thinker Augustine. According to this view, the age of the church flows into the millennial kingdom."

[102] Walvoord, *The Millennial Kingdom*, 47-48. I reference this older book by Walvoord as a demonstration of the fact that scholars have long characterized Augustine as the *fons et origo* of amillennialism.

[103] Walvoord, *The Millennial Kingdom*, writes: "Because of the weight of Augustine in other major issues of theology where he was in the main correct, Augustine became the model of the Protestant Reformers who accepted his amillennialism along with his other teachings. It is quite clear from the literature of the Reformation that the millennial issue was never handled fairly or given any considered study. The basic issues of the Reformation involved the right of private interpretation of the Scriptures, the individual priesthood of all believers, the doctrine of justification by faith, and similar truths. It was natural for the emphasis to rest in this area, and for eschatology as found in the Roman Church to be corrected only in denial of purgatory and other teachings which were regarded as inventions.... Because amillennialism was adopted by the Reformers, it achieved a quality of orthodoxy to which its modern adherents can point with pride. They can rightly claim many worthy scholars in the succession from the Reformation to modern times such as Calvin, Luther, Melanchthon, and in modern times, Warfield, Vos, Kuyper, Machen, and Berkhof. If one follows traditional Reformed theology in many other respects, it is natural to accept its amillennialism. The weight of organized Christianity has largely been on the side of amillennialism" (60-61). Such has been the influence of Augustine

Augustine's final message to the world in his *magnum opus*, expresses his joy at completing his mission: "I think I have now, by God's help, discharged my obligation in writing this large work. Let those who think I have said too little, or those who think I have said too much, forgive me; and let those who think I said just enough, join me in giving thanks to God. Amen."[104] Perhaps he was wondering if his masterwork would make an impact. If he only knew!

---

[104] Augustine, *De Civ. D.* 22.30

3

ISRAEL AND THE DARK SIDE
OF THE REFORMATION

Larry D. Pettegrew

After Augustine, theology was essentially static for over one thousand years. The Roman Catholic Church of the Middle Ages perpetuated Augustine's method of interpretation of Scripture and his doctrine of the "kingdom already." The riches of the Roman Catholic Church, as exhibited by the magnificent church buildings, fulfilled the Old Testament prophecies about Israel's glorious future (Isa 35 and 60, for examples). God now intended that the church, not future redeemed Israel, would be rich and powerful.

When the Reformation began, God used the Reformers to restore biblical soteriology to the teaching of their churches through a new emphasis on the Solae: Sola Scriptura, Sola Gratia, Sola Fide, Solus Christus, and Soli Deo Gloria.[1] Salvation, the Reformers taught, comes by grace through faith, not by sacramental works. Justification is a one-time act of God whereby on the basis of the death, burial, and resurrection of Jesus Christ, God declares a repentant guilty sinner not guilty. These truths constitute the bright side of the Reformation that we honor.

But there is also a dark side to the Reformation. In the next three chapters, we will survey two ways whereby the Reformers continued to forsake Israel: (1) anti-Semitism; and (2) covenant theology.

---

[1] These five terms were all used by Reformers, but not yet listed together.

MARTIN LUTHER AND ISRAEL

The Reformers retained the state-church philosophy and through it perse-cuted those Christians like the Anabaptists who disagreed with them. The Reformation Protestants, both the Lutheran and Reformed, were also commit-ted to supersessionism and amillennialism. Israel had been replaced, so there would be no millennial kingdom on earth following the Second Coming of Christ, they taught. Sadly, some of the Reformers were not only supersession-ists. They were anti-Semitic.

Martin Luther was an out-spoken anti-Semite. Luther scholars have shown that in the early years of his ministry, Luther held out hope that many Jews would be converted and join the Reformation. He wrote, "Although the vast majority of them are hardened, yet there are always some, however few, that are converted to Christ and believe in Him….We ought, therefore, not to treat the Jews in so unkindly a spirit, for there are future Christians among them, and they are turning every day."[2]

But the later Luther changed his mind. He is somewhat infamous for his little book, *On the Jews and Their Lies* that he wrote to respond to a pro-Jewish treatise that had been sent to one of his Christian friends. Luther claims that his goal was (1) not to quarrel; (2) not to learn how they interpret Scripture (because he already knew that); and (3) not too try to convert them, "for that is impossible."[3] His goal, instead, was to go on record as an opponent of the Jews and to warn Christians of the dangers of Judaism.

The Religious and Social Context

Luther's analysis of the Jews is hostile, full of sarcasm and mean language. There is no excuse for his militant attack, but we do need to keep in mind the religious and social context of Luther's day. Luther lived his life in a state-church which had been the standard civil/religious organization in Europe for over 1200 years. Before the Reformation, only Roman Catholicism was allowed in the Holy Roman Empire of which Saxony, Luther's state of residence, was a part. When Luther began his Protestant Reformation, he had to contend not only with the Roman Catholic Church, which considered him a heretic, but also with the

---

[2] Martin Luther, *The Magnificat*, Luther's Works, 21 (St. Louis: Concordia, 1956), 354-55.

[3] Martin Luther, *On the Jews and Their Lies*, tans. Martin Bertram, ed. Franklin Sherman, Luther's Works, vol. 47 (Philadelphia: The Christian in Society, IV; repr., 1971, originally published in 1543), 137.

Holy Roman Empire, that, after the Diet of Worms in 1521, considered him an outlaw. State and church were united, and toleration of other religions was looked upon as theological compromise and disloyalty to the government.

Saxony became Lutheran during the Reformation. But that only meant that Lutheranism was the official religion there instead of Roman Catholicism. So Luther believed like almost every other Christian (other than the Anabaptists) that there should be a state-church and that only one religion could be recognized. Luther not only said harsh things about the Jews, he also said harsh things about the Anabaptists and the Roman Catholics—and even other non-Lutheran Reformers like Ulrich Zwingli. Moreover, Roman Catholics and other non-Lutheran Reformers like Zwingli said harsh things about any religion different from them.

We also need to keep in mind that the Judaism that Luther attacked in *On the Jews and Their Lies* was a Rabbinic Judaism similar to the Judaism that had crucified Jesus Christ. Jesus Himself pronounced "woes" on the generation that, led by the religious hierarchy, rejected Him. The sin of that generation of Jews, Jesus said, would "not be forgiven, either in this age or in the age to come" (Matt 12:32). And if Luther is correct in his assessment of the Jews with whom he was familiar, they were antagonistic to the Christians.

The Essence of Luther's Arguments

Luther organizes *On the Jews and Their Lies* into thirteen brief sections. His approach is to choose some of their claims and demonstrate that they are unbiblical. He argues against their "boast of nobility," that they were descendants from the Patriarchs of Israel. He criticizes the Jews' reliance on circumcision, and concludes: "Therefore be on your guard against the Jews, knowing that wherever they have their synagogues, nothing is found but a den of devils in which sheer self-glory, conceit, lies, blasphemy, and defaming of God and men are practiced most maliciously."[4]

Much of the book is dedicated specifically to refuting the Jews' claim that another Messiah would yet come. Luther takes the position that all of the seventy weeks of Daniel were fulfilled with the destruction of Jerusalem in A.D. 70. Thus, "the Messiah must have come before the destruction of Jerusalem while something of those seventy weeks still remained.... this the

---

[4] Ibid., 172.

Jews cannot refute."[5] The Jews, Luther asserts, "have done nothing these fourteen hundred years but take any verse which we Christians apply to our Messiah and violate it, tear it to bits, crucify it, and twist it in order to give it a different nose and mask. They deal with it as their fathers dealt with our Lord Christ on Good Friday."[6]

The most troubling part of Luther's discourse comes near the end of his book in which he gives seven words of advice to the government officials and pastors as to how to deal with the Jews. These are (1) Set "fire to their synagogues or schools"; (2) Destroy their houses; (3) Take away their prayer books and Talmudic writings; (4) Forbid the rabbis to teach; (5) Abolish safe-conduct on the highways for Jews; (6) Prohibit them to make money through usury; (7) Make the young Jews do physical labor.[7]

It doesn't seem that the Lutheran princes followed most of Luther's anti-Semitic advice. Modern Lutheran denominations have expressed their regrets about Luther's vicious counsel. But the Reformation Lutherans were militant supersessionists.

COVENANT THEOLOGY AND ISRAEL

There were other ways in which Israel was forsaken during the Reformation. Only a few years after Martin Luther nailed his ninety-five theses to the door of the Castle Church in Wittenberg, Germany, a different kind of Protestantism called Reformed theology was born. Though there is much in Reformed theology to be appreciated, Reformed theologians retained the state-church and supersessionism. But they also began to reformulate, step by step, supersessionism into a theological system that eventually became known as covenant theology. In covenant theology, supersessionism was codified, and Israel was in effect covered over by three theological covenants.

It is not as though no one had ever recognized the importance of covenants in Scripture. But, as Lyle Bierma notes, "it was only in sixteenth- and seventeenth-century Reformed Protestantism that the covenant concept came to be viewed as the thread that wove together the entire message of Scripture."[8]

---

[5] Ibid., 230.

[6] Ibid., 238.

[7] Ibid., 268-76.

[8] Lyle D. Bierma, *German Calvinism in the Confessional Age, The Covenant Theology of Caspar Olevianus* (Grand Rapids: Baker, 1996), 11.

Covenantalists did not emphasize the biblical covenants like the Abrahamic or New Covenants, but their system was based on theological covenants: the covenant of grace, the covenant of works, and the covenant of redemption.

The covenant of grace, according to Berkhof, "may be defined as that gracious agreement between the offended God and the offending but elect sinner, in which God promises salvation through faith in Christ, and the sinner accepts this believingly, promising a life of faith and obedience."[9] Most covenantalists also add or imply that the covenant is made with the believer "and his seed." This means that infants are in some way included in this covenant, though it does not mean that the infants are automatically Christians.

The second covenant for covenant theology is the covenant of works, an agreement in the Garden of Eden between God and Adam wherein God promises life for perfect obedience and death for disobedience. *The Westminster Shorter Catechism*, 1647, asserts, "When God had created man, he entered into a covenant of life with him, upon condition of perfect obedience: forbidding him to eat of the tree of knowledge of good and evil, upon pain of death."[10] It has gone by other names such the Edenic covenant, the covenant of nature, the covenant of creation, and the covenant of law. The preferred traditional name, though, is the covenant of works.

The third covenant of covenant theology is the covenant of redemption. In the covenant of redemption, God the Father and God the Son entered a pact or covenant in eternity past. In this pact, (1) the Father gives the Son as the redeemer and head of the elect. In response, (2) the Son offers Himself to the Father as a perfect vicarious sacrifice. (3) The Holy Spirit, who is not an actual partner in this pact, agrees to administer the plan of salvation. In Louis Berkhof's words, "The covenant of redemption may be defined as *the agreement between the Father, giving the Son as Head and Redeemer of the elect, and the Son, voluntarily taking the place of those whom the Father had given Him*."[11] The Holy Spirit is "the applier."[12] Berkhof adds that the plan of salvation "can only be the result of a voluntary agreement among the persons of the Trinity

---

[9] Louis Berkhof, *Systematic Theology* (Grand Rapids: Eerdmans, 1959), 277.

[10] "The Westminster Shorter Catechism, 1647," in *Creeds of Christendom*, vol. 3, ed. Philip Schaff (Grand Rapids: Baker; repr. 1977), 678.

[11] Berkhof, *Systematic Theology*, 271, (emphasis his).

[12] Ibid., 266.

so that their internal relations assume the form of covenant life."[13] Mark Jones adds, "Christ's death would be meaningless apart from a covenantal agreement between the Father and the Son in eternity, commonly known as the covenant of redemption (*pactum salutis*)."[14]

These three covenants are not explicitly set out in Scripture in one or two specific passages, and some covenant theologians readily admit this. Carl R. Trueman, for example, writes, "... the covenant of works was not developed simply by exegeting Genesis 1 and 2; it arose more out of reflection on the Pauline epistles than on the creation account, still less the ambiguous Hosea 6:7."[15] In the rest of this chapter we will survey four important Reformed theologians who can be considered founders of covenant theology.[16]

Ulrich Zwingli

The early development of a systematized covenant theology occurred in the German-Swiss context,[17] and Ulrich Zwingli (1484-1531) was the founder. Bierma writes, "Since the pioneer research of von Korff early in this [twentieth] century, historians of theology have almost without exception looked to the Swiss reformer Ulrich Zwingli ... as the founder of Reformed covenant theology."[18] Zwingli's view of the covenants was not complex, and he did not develop a system. Nevertheless, his use of a theological covenant of grace is the best place to begin this survey.

In his early adult life, Zwingli, like Erasmus of Rotterdam (1469-1536), was a humanist who hoped to raise the ethical standards of society by using the insights of the ancient classics. He received a Master of Arts from the University of Basel in 1506 and became so proficient in Greek that he memorized the

---

[13] Ibid.

[14] Mark Jones, *Antinomianism, Reformed Theology's Unwelcome Guest* (Phillipsburg, NJ: Presbyterian and Reformed, 2013), 63.

[15] Carl R. Trueman, "Atonement and the Covenant of Redemption," chapter eight in *From Heaven He Came and Sought Her*, ed. David Gibson and Jonathan Gibson (Wheaton, IL: Crossway, 2013), 216.

[16] Obviously, there are more than four important theologians in the early history of covenant theology. Others that should be researched for a full picture include Johannes Oecolampadius (1482-1531), Caspar Olevianus (1536-87), and Dudley Fenner (1558-87), to name a few. Peter Lillback points out that before Zwingli began to emphasize a theological covenant in his debate with the Anabaptists, Johannes Oecolampadius had discussed the covenant concept in his commentary on Isaiah. See Peter A. Lillback, *The Binding of God* (Grand Rapids: Baker, 2001), 83.

[17] "Reformed covenant theology began in the German-Swiss Reformed thought," (Bierma, *German Calvinism in the Confessional Age*), 81.

[18] Ibid., 31.

Pauline epistles in Greek. He was successively a village priest, a chaplain in the Swiss army, and a priest in an abbey. While a pastor in Einsiedeln (1516-1518), Zwingli abandoned the humanist goals and began to study Scripture more from a Protestant perspective.

Zwingli's Reformation

It is easy to forget how early Zwingli's reforming ministry began. As the chief pastor of the Great Minster Church in Zurich, Switzerland,[19] Zwingli had already been preaching and teaching Reformation ideas when in 1520 he made it official by relinquishing his papal pension. Then in 1522, he resigned his position as priest at the church, and was immediately hired by the city council to continue his ministry as their preacher.

Zwingli conducted two debates with representatives of the Roman Catholic Church. The first debate, in January of 1523, was a debate over Zwingli's Reformation teachings as they appear in his *Sixty-Seven Articles*. The city council declared that Zwingli had won the debate and stated that Zwingli should keep on preaching God's Word to the city. The second debate occurred in October 1523, in which Zwingli took up the issues of images in church and the use of the mass. Even though Zwingli believed that these Roman Catholic practices were unbiblical, he agreed to the wishes of the city council not to abandon these practices immediately. So, the mass continued to be performed for a couple more years. In the meantime, Zwingli "was at least publicly disposed to hold that the Mass might well be a proper representation of Christ's unique, historic, and atoning sacrifice."[20] Though Zwingli continued to preach the sole authority of Scripture, "in practice he followed the wishes of the council, thus virtually committing the implementation of reform of the church to the civil government."[21]

Zwingli's first steps toward a developed covenant theology came as a result of a division between him and his supporters. Early in his reform, Zwingli had included some strong personalities in his "theological think-tank," including Conrad Grebel and Felix Mantz. George Blaurock, who would later be the first person in the Reformation to be "rebaptized," described Zwingli, Grebel, and

---

[19] Zurich was one of thirteen cantons, or city-states, that made up the Swiss Confederation, which in turn was a part of the Holy Roman Empire. The cantons were culturally French, Italian, or German. Zurich was culturally German.

[20] George Huntston Williams, *The Radical Reformation*, 3rd edition (Kirksville, MO: Truman State University Press, 2000), 187.

[21] Ibid.

Mantz as "much experienced and men learned in the German, Latin, Greek, and also the Hebrew, languages…."[22] Grebel and Mantz were devastated by Zwingli's compromise with the city council over the continuation of the mass.

The disagreement between Zwingli and these associates was more complicated than just the continuation of the mass for a couple more years, however. The foundational issue was the nature of the church. Zwingli wanted to move his reformation slowly to maintain the enthusiastic support of the city council. In other words, Zwingli's vision for Zurich, and ultimately all of Switzerland, was for it to become a "reformed 'Israel'"—that is, a Reformed state-church.[23] "It is also evident," writes Peter Lillback, "that Zwingli was working with the notion of a national reformation, rather than a separatist reformation. His initial reforms … were built on the parallel of Israel and Zurich as national entities."[24] Grebel and Mantz, however, were envisioning an independent church made up of Christians who had been regenerated by the Holy Spirit. For Grebel and Mantz, this would also include believer's baptism.

In their deliberations together, Zwingli, Grebel, and Mantz had first agreed that "infant baptism is no baptism."[25] Grebel and Mantz believed that if this were true, then "one must and should be correctly baptized according to the Christian ordinance and institution of the Lord, since Christ himself says that whoever believes and is baptized will be saved."[26] Zwingli, however, "did not wish this and asserted that an uprising would break out," and that would cost them the support of the state.[27]

Grebel, Mantz, and others individually submitted plans to Zwingli that would redo the Zurich church with a regenerated baptized membership that would abandon the mass and partake of the Lord's Supper as the Apostle Paul explained its observance in his first letter to the Corinthians. With no encouragement from Zwingli, these "Brethren in Christ," as they called themselves, began to hold teaching conventicles in the areas around Zurich with the result

[22] George Blaurock, "The Beginnings of the Anabaptist Reformation Reminiscences of George Blaurock," in *Spiritual and Anabaptist Writers*, ed. George H. Williams and Angel M. Mergal (Philadelphia: Westminster Press, 1957), 42.

[23] Williams, *Radical Reformation*, 212.

[24] Peter A. Lillback, *The Binding of God*, 89.

[25] Ibid. In his later books, Zwingli admits that he had "conceded to the desires of certain [i.e., the Anabaptists] through our idleness or blindness …" (Ulrich Zwingli, *Selected Works of Huldreich Zwingli*, ed. Samuel Macauley Jackson, trans. Lawrence A. McLouth, Henry Preble, and George W. Gilmore [Philadelphia: University of Pennsylvania, 1901], 123.)

[26] Ibid.

[27] Ibid.

that some parents began to withhold baptism from their babies.[28] In the meantime, during December 1524 and early January 1525, Grebel, Mantz, and George Blaurock, a former priest who had joined the cause, again presented Zwingli with what they thought were biblical reasons (as well as plans as to how it would work) for a primitive regenerated church. But by then, the two sides had hardened their positions so that no compromise was possible.

On January 21, 1525, there was an event that could be considered "the most revolutionary act of the Reformation."[29] Grebel, Mantz, and Blaurock, apparently overcome with discouragement, began to pray that God would enable them to do His will. Blaurock arose and asked Grebel to baptize him. He then kneeled and Grebel baptized him, apparently by pouring water over his head. When Grebel, Mantz, and the others in the gathering also asked to be baptized, Blaurock baptized all of them.[30] In the following weeks, many others in the areas surrounding Zurich were rebaptized and became "Anabaptists," a name that none of them wanted.

Zwingli's Covenant

Zwingli had been forced to devote a great deal of time to the subject of baptism during 1523-1525 with the result that his view of baptism changed from tacit agreement with Grebel and Mantz to militant opposition to their views. Perhaps we can grant that Zwingli was an honest and courageous man "so that his change of view should be accepted as sincere and not as ... hypocritical."[31] But Zwingli became a vicious opponent of the Anabaptists, describing them in his apologetical works as full of "untaught audacity," "monsters of deceit," "wolf in sheep's clothing," and "hypocrites."[32] In line with the long history of state-church persecution of dissenters, Zwingli eagerly pursued a vigorous suppression of the Anabaptists.[33] He and other state-church authorities drowned

---

[28] See Williams' narration of the story, *Radical Reformation*, 188-89.

[29] William R. Estep, *The Anabaptist Story*, 3rd ed. (Grand Rapids: Eerdmans, 1996), 14.

[30] Williams' narration of the events includes a primary source document that records the reminiscences of George Blaurock, *Radical Reformation*, 216-217.

[31] Samuel Macauley Jackson was an early twentieth century editor of Zwingli's *Selected Works*, noted above.

[32] See for example, Zwingli's "Refutation of the Tricks of the Baptists," in Zwingli, *Selected Works*, 127,

[33] For a study of state-church persecution of dissenters throughout church history, see Leonard Verduin, *The Reformers and Their Stepchildren* (Grand Rapids: Eerdmans, 1964). See pages 38-39 for his discussion of Zwingli and the Anabaptists.

and beheaded the Anabaptists, burned them at the stake, and confiscated their property.

But the theological plot had also thickened. The concept of the covenant had become a powerful tool in Zwingli's apologetic arsenal against the Anabaptists. Zwingli did not believe, like the Roman Catholics, that infant baptism removed original sin from the infants. He also did not believe, like the Lutherans, that infant baptism somehow justified them before God. But he did conclude that infant baptism placed the infant into the covenant. Zwingli apparently believed in a theological covenant from his early days as a Reformer. But his debates with the Anabaptists led him to emphasize the unity of the Old and New Testament—so that infant baptism replaced circumcision. Lillback agrees, "It must be admitted, then, that the struggle with the Anabaptists did cause the Reformed to begin to use the covenant concept of unity of Old and New Testament to bolster their argument for infant baptism."[34]

In Zwingli's theology, there was only one covenant—period. Zwingli writes, "God therefore made no other covenant with the miserable race of man than that he had already conceived before man was formed. One and the same testament has always been in force."[35] What about passages like Hebrews 8 that plainly says that the New Covenant replaces the Old Covenant, we might ask. Or what about the discussions of the New Covenant in Galatians 4-5 and 2 Corinthians 3? Zwingli argued that the "two covenants are spoken of, not that they are two diverse covenants, for this would necessitate not only two diverse people, but also two gods." For Zwingli,

> Paul speaks of two testaments, but the one he calls a testament by a misuse of language, when he wishes them to be understood who, although they were under that one eternal covenant and testament.... Paul therefore called the way of these a testament, not that it was a true testament, but by a copying or imitation of those who so named it.[36]

Apparently, when Paul writes about a new covenant, it was "a misuse of language."

Yes, Zwingli admitted, there are a few advancements in the covenant after the death of Christ. Christ had actually come, believers go to heaven rather than

---

[34] Lillback, *The Binding of God*, 95.

[35] Zwingli, *Selected Works*, 234.

[36] Ibid., 228-29. The following citations are from Zwingli's *Selected Works*.

the bosom of Abraham, Christ's death replaced the sacrificial system, and many nations replaced the one nation.[37] But even with these differences, there is only one covenant. The covenant that was originally made with Adam was renewed with Noah. Then with Abraham "he renewed the covenant he had compacted with Adam…. And as the sign of this covenant, he ordered circumcision" (234). "Therefore the same covenant which he entered into with Israel, he has in these latter days entered into with us, that we may be one people with them, one church, and may have one covenant" (227).

Zwingli was, of course, a supersessionist. Since there is only one covenant, the Jews were the people of God in the Old Testament; but "now when we who are Gentiles are God's people and the Jews are cut off, there is only one people of God, not two" (227). He adds, "For we are put in their place after they have been cut off, not in some place next to them" (228). So Zwingli does not entertain the idea that Israel has a national future.[38]

But to return to the point, how does the one covenant theology prove infant baptism? According to Zwingli, we know that in the Old Testament, infants "are members of one and the same body of God's covenant people … [because] circumcision, the sign of the covenant, is given to them" (222). "Hebrew infants were sealed with circumcision, the sign of the covenant; they were therefore under the covenant" (223). So if there is only one covenant, the conclusion for Zwingli is obvious:

The children of Christians are no less sons of God than the parents, just as in the Old Testament. Hence, since they are sons of God, who will forbid their baptism? Circumcision among the ancients (so far as it was sacramental) was the same as baptism with us. As that was given to infants so ought baptism with us. As that was given to infants so ought baptism to be administered to infants.[39]

Since Jewish male infants were circumcised in the Old Testament to enter the covenant, so Gentile infants in the church should be baptized.

---

[37] Ibid., 234.

[38] Interestingly, the Anabaptists were supersessionists as well, though they did not connect circumcision with infant baptism. Karl Barth observes, "The Anabaptists in Switzerland and elsewhere liked to describe themselves as 'covenant-members,' and their believers' baptism as a covenant, the sign of the true covenant, the covenant of grace …" (Karl Barth, Church Dogmatics, IV.1, "The Doctrine of Reconciliation," ed. G. W. Bromiley and T. F. Torrance (Peabody, MA: Hendrickson Publishers, 2010), (par. 57), 56.

[39] Zwingli, Selected Works, 139.

It doesn't seem to matter to Zwingli that infants cannot understand any of the gospel. In the Old Testament, the male babies who could not understand were circumcised and had the sign of the covenant and were therefore children of the covenant. The same is true of infants who are baptized. Parents should think of their children as elect, but if an infant grows to maturity and does not accept the Gospel, then he was not elect.[40] But, argues Zwingli, in the Old Testament both the elect babies (Jacob) and the non-elect babies (Esau) were circumcised. All children of believers, therefore, should be baptized, even if some of them eventually give evidence of not being elect.[41]

For Zwingli, it is all about continuity throughout biblical revelation. There is one covenant, one church, one people of God, one law. Zwingli writes, "They are not then diverse or two churches, not two peoples. They are indeed, two in name, but unless they were made the same people in one spirit they are not the people of God" (231). Zwingli's one covenant appears to have the same characteristics of that which covenantalists came to call the "covenant of grace."

Zwingli's Death

Zwingli, as a representative of "new Israel" Zurich, was extensively involved in European politics in the latter part of the 1520's. His desire to see all Swiss cantons become Reformed was not fulfilled, though about half of the cantons did follow Zurich's lead. Several of the cantons remained Roman Catholic. Consequently, there were two Wars of Kappel between the Roman Catholic and Reformed cantons. The first War of Kappel in 1529 did not really get started before diplomacy halted it. The result of the negotiations was favorable to the Reformed forces.

In 1531 the second War of Kappel was initiated when Zwingli's Christian Civil Union applied a food blockade on the Roman Catholic cantons. The Roman Catholics in turn declared war on Zurich. On October 11, 1531, an army of 7000 Roman Catholic soldiers approached Zurich. Zurich had little time to prepare and was not supported by the other Reformed cantons. Thus, when the 2000-3000 Zurichers met the Roman Catholics, the battle lasted only a few minutes. Five hundred Zurichers, including twenty-four pastors,

---

[40] For an interesting and helpful discussion of this ambiguity in covenant theology, see E. Brooks Holifield, *The Covenant Sealed: The Development of Puritan Sacramental Theology in Old and New England, 1570-1720* (New Haven: Yale University Press, 1974), 27-73.

[41] Zwingli, *Selected Works*, 237-47.

and Zwingli himself, who was only forty-seven years old, were slaughtered. The victorious Roman Catholic army found Zwingli's body and burned it.

So, was there covenant theology at the time of Zwingli's death? Zwingli had laid a foundation for systematize covenant theology. But it would be premature to conclude that covenant theology had actually been born. Zwingli's covenantalism was only embryonic.

Heinrich Bullinger

Heinrich Bullinger (1504-1575), a supporter of Zwingli and a pastor in nearby Bremgarten, was forced to flee to Zurich after his town was made Roman Catholic—a result of the Second Peace of Kappel. In December of 1531, he was declared the successor to Zwingli at the Great Minster Church in Zurich, and he led the Reformation there until his death. He had earned a Master of Arts degree at the University of Cologne and was a powerful speaker and author of dozens of books and tracts. He married a former nun and was a loving father of eleven. All of his sons went into the ministry. By all accounts, Bullinger is one of the most underrated leaders of the Reformation.

Bullinger was generally irenic—but not with the Anabaptists. Like his predecessor, Bullinger was concerned with the Anabaptist menace that was confronting the Reformed church. He calls them names, like "mad-headed Anabaptists,"[42] and thought that they should be subject to the death penalty. His confrontations with the Anabaptists led Bullinger to write an important book about the covenant. McCoy and Baker state, "It was within the context of this continuing debate about church, state, and Christian discipline that Bullinger wrote *The One and Eternal Testament or Covenant of God,* apparently in October and November of 1533."[43] To put this into historical context, this was about two years before Calvin published his first edition of the *Institutes of the Christian Religion.*

---

[42] Henry Bullinger, *The Decades of Henry Bullinger,* trans. H. I., and ed. Thomas Harding (Cambridge: The University Press, 1850), "Third Decade," 20.

[43] Charles S. McCoy and J. Wayne Baker, *Fountainhead of Federalism, Heinrich Bullinger and the Covenantal Tradition* (Louisville: Westminster/John Knox Press, 1991), 19. McCoy and Baker include an English translation of Bullinger's small book in their book.

Key Covenantal Terms

Bullinger's book is basically Zwinglian, "though somewhat more carefully developed and complete than that of his mentor."[44] Early in this book, Bullinger explains and exegetes some of the key covenantal terms. Covenant theology is sometimes called federal theology, he explains, because "federal" is a translation of the Latin, "*foedus*," which means covenant. He adds,

> *Diatheke*, a Greek word for covenant, "in the singular means 'a pact,' 'an agreement,' 'a promise,' that is, in Greek '*epaggelia*'.... Finally, '*diatheke*,' or '*diathekai*' in the plural, means 'pact' and also 'covenant' (*foedus*), to which the Hebrew word *berith* most closely corresponds. *Berith* is derived from *barah*, that is, 'he made a pact,' 'he entered into a covenant.'[45]

A "covenant," Bullinger continues, "is properly made between enemies when ending a war. Though it puts proposals for harmony and fellowship, yet it is still entered into solemnly, and with special ceremonies and conditions."[46]

Just One Covenant

Although somewhat more willing to admit that there are two biblical covenants, the Old and the New, Bullinger, much like Zwingli, thought in terms of just "one covenant ... from Adam to the end of the world."[47] Even the title of his work, *The One and Eternal Testament or Covenant of God*, emphasizes this. He taught that the one covenant began with Adam, then was renewed with Abraham and believing Israel, and then confirmed and fulfilled in Christ—much as Zwingli taught.

So covenant theology with Bullinger was still in its embryonic stage. There is only one covenant, and his understanding of the one covenant, like Zwingli's, is comparable to what eventually became known as the covenant of grace in covenant theology. Lillback explains, "Bullinger does not discuss the prefall relationship of God and Adam. There is no word of a covenant of works

---

[44] Bierma, *German Calvinism in the Confessional Age*, 35.

[45] Heinrich Bullinger, "One and Eternal Testament," in *Fountainhead of Federalism*, 102-03.

[46] Ibid., 103.

[47] McCoy and Baker, *Fountainhead of Federalism*, 22. Bullinger does speak of the "new covenant," but it is at best only an updated old covenant.

or a covenant of creation…. There is no idea of a pre-temporal covenant of redemption."[48]

Because there is only one overarching covenant, Bullinger has no hesitation in interchanging "Israel" and "church" in the Old Testament. The New Testament interprets the Old Testament, so the Old Testament prophets were prophesying about the church. "How clearly," he exclaims, "they speak about the seed of Abraham, about Christ and his blessing, about the kingdom and its whole mystery, and about the calling of the Gentiles, and the glory of the church."[49] He writes about "the church or kingdom of Judah,"[50] as though they were the same. To be found in the Old Testament is "the Jewish church."[51] And he writes about "the sacraments of the old church [being] circumcision and the Passover."[52] Bullinger declares,

> The sacraments also of the ancient Jews are flatly abrogated, and in their places are substituted new sacraments, which are given to the people of the New Covenant. Instead of circumcision is baptism appointed. Instead of the Pascal Lamb is the Lord's Supper ordained, which by another name is called the Eucharist, or as thanksgiving.[53]

Bullinger, like Zwingli, does admit that the "church of Christians" does have some advantages over those who lived before Christ came and died. We have better sacraments, "the shadows have been dispersed by the bright light of the gospel and … the typological foreshadowings have been fulfilled…. God has made our church superior to the church of our dead fathers before the coming of Christ…."[54]

---

[48] Lillback, *The Binding of God*, 113.

[49] Bullinger, *One and Eternal Testament*, 115. Dispensational premillennialists do not think that the Old Testament prophets knew anything about the "glory of the church." They teach that the church was a secret in the Old Testament, as Paul explains in Ephesians 3 and Colossians 1. Paul defines the church in Ephesians 3 as Jew and Gentile together in one spiritual body on equal footing. There is no place in the Old Testament where this unique organism is explained or prophesied. For dispensationalists, the glory of the church that Bullinger is speaking about is actually about the glory of the nation of Israel in the future kingdom.

[50] Bullinger, *Decades*, Third Decade, 10.

[51] Ibid., 72.

[52] Ibid., 217.

[53] Ibid., 269.

[54] McCoy and Baker, *Fountainhead of Federalism*, 9.

Christianity as Ancient

Like the church fathers, Bullinger taught that the church was superior to other religions because it was the oldest of all religions. Christianity is before Judaism—even long before Judaism. He asserts,

> Now the Jewish religion, which I understand to be defined in time by circumcision and laws, is also ancient, seeing that it began partly in the time of Abraham and partly in the time of Moses. But the Christian religion is older by far than such things. For Abraham is declared justified in the sacred Scripture before he was circumcised. There are also those prior to Abraham—Noah, Enoch, Seth, Abel, Adam—who pleased God through faith without circumcision.[55]

Apparently, all believers in the God of Scripture from the beginning of time were Christians and members of the Christian church. He excludes the Roman Catholic Church from Christianity, asserting that it is "scarcely older than Islam." Some form of Protestant Christianity, therefore, was the real Christianity, and Christianity in the form of Protestantism was in fact the oldest of all religions.

The Covenant as Centerpiece

In the end, Bullinger's contribution to the development of covenant theology was mainly in his attempt to tie all doctrines into the one theological covenant. Zwingli had used the covenant idea as a weapon against the Anabaptists. Bullinger, however, made the covenant the centerpiece of his theology. It was the greatest evidence of God's grace and mercy to sinners. He exclaimed,

> I do not know whether humans are capable either of conceiving this mystery fully or conveying how praiseworthy it is. For what greater deed than this has ever been heard of in the world, that the eternal power and majesty, the immortal all-knowing God, the creator of the universe, in whom all things consist, by whom all things exist, and through whom all things are preserved, joined himself in covenant with miserable mortals corrupted by sin.[56]

---

[55] Bullinger, "One and Eternal Testament," in *Fountainhead of Federalism,* 134-35.

[56] Ibid., 105.

Zwingli believed that if we wished to summarize the entirety of Scripture, all we would need to do is to describe the covenant:

> The entire sum of piety consists in these very brief main points of the covenant. Indeed, it is evident that nothing else was handed down to the saints of all ages, throughout the entire Scripture, other than what is included in these main points of the covenant, although each point is set forth more profusely and more clearly in the succession of times.[57]

The Old Testament prophets, Zwingli declares, speak of "the glory of the church," and have essentially "woven together not only prophecy but also a history of past events."[58] Then Jesus Christ "explained and confirmed in a marvelous and living way that eternal covenant of God made with the human race."[59] Likewise the apostles agree with the Old Testament prophets so that "everything in sacred Scripture is directed to that testament or covenant as to a most certain target."[60]

Bullinger's Impact

We can hardly overestimate the impact of Bullinger's writings, especially of *The One and Eternal Testament or Covenant of God*. In the estimation of McCoy and Baker, "it is the first work that organizes the understanding of God, creation, humanity, human history and society around the covenant. It must be regarded therefore as the point of origin or the fountain head of federalism as it has increasingly come to permeate the world in the four and one-half centuries since its publication."[61] Whether it is the point of origin or not, the centrality of the one covenant in Bullinger's theology is a significant step forward in the development of covenant theology. Bullinger also influenced later contributors to covenant theology. Many came to Zurich to study under him. Also Bullinger's many writings spread his influence throughout the Reformed churches of Germany, Switzerland, the Netherlands, Scotland, Ireland, England, and New England.

---

[57] Ibid., 114.

[58] Ibid., 115.

[59] Ibid.

[60] Ibid., 117.

[61] McCoy and Baker, *Fountainhead of Federalism*, 9.

So, is there systematized covenant theology now? Probably not. Essentially what Zwingli and Bullinger developed was supersessionism with an emphasis on one theological covenant. They used this covenant as a polemical weapon, and Bullinger made it the center of his theology. This theological covenant encompassed both the Old and New Testaments into one covenant and would eventually be known as the covenant of grace. In spite of the foundational work of these Zurich reformers, the details and implications of the covenant were not yet filled in, and there were two other covenants yet to be specified.

John Calvin

A significant "elephant in the room" is John Calvin's role in the development of covenant theology. Few historians would deny that John Calvin (1509-1564) was the greatest Protestant theologian of the Reformation era. His *Institutes of the Christian Religion* is the most important of the theological works published in the sixteenth century; and Calvin published commentaries on almost every book of the Bible. So how does he fit into this survey of the founders of embryonic covenant theology?

Calvin's Relationship to Covenant Theology

Actually, it is tempting to bypass John Calvin in our survey. The historical theologians who specialize in sixteenth and seventeenth centuries theology cannot seem to come to an agreement about Calvin. Peter A. Lillback, who has written an important and helpful book on Calvin and covenant theology, surveys four views as to Calvin's relationship to covenant theology. One view (referencing Charles Ryrie[62]) declares that covenant theology is absent from Calvin's theology; another view asserts that Calvin developed an incomplete form of covenant theology; another view states that Calvin's theology is in tension with a fully developed covenant theology; and still another view claims that Calvin developed an extensive, if incomplete, covenant theology.[63]

Calvin mentions a "covenant of grace" a few times—somewhat informally—but he doesn't write about the other two covenants of systematized covenant theology. In some ways, say McCoy and Baker, "Calvin's idea of 'covenant'

---

[62] Charles Ryrie, *Dispensationalism* (Chicago: Moody Press, 2007), 215.

[63] Lillback, *The Binding of God*, 13-26. Lillback's book is written to show that Calvin taught covenant theology, if only in an incomplete form.

was hardly different from Augustine's notion of the unity of faith in the Old and New Testaments.... But Augustine was not a covenant theologian."[64] In fact, for McCoy and Baker, "The differences between Bullinger and Calvin formed the basis for the two alternative, though related, strands within the Reformed tradition—Federalism and Calvinism."[65] There may be some truth to this bifurcation. But the trend among modern Reformed historical theologians is to minimize the differences between Bullinger and Calvin.

Another major problem in deciding whether Calvin (or anyone else) is a covenant theologian is defining covenant theology.[66] Lillback, for example, believes that Calvin taught covenant theology, if only in an incomplete system. He chooses a definition of covenant theology that he borrows from Jürgen Moltmann that helps his case: "One defines covenant theology as a theological method which utilizes the biblical theme of the covenant as the key idea for (a) the designation of the relationship of God and man, and (b) the presentation of the continuity of redemptive history in the Old and New Testaments."[67] Using this definition as a paradigm, Lillback believes that Calvin can be shown to be an early covenant theologian.

At the end of his study, however, Lillback concludes that "Calvin is not the initiator of covenant theology, since this honor must really fall to Zwingli. He is not the designer of the first paradigm of covenant thought, since this distinction falls to Bullinger." Moreover, "we must, of course, stop short of calling Calvin a federalist."[68] But Lillback doesn't mean by this that Calvin was unimportant in the history of covenant theology. He goes on to assert that "covenant theology owes its existence in various ways to Calvin."[69] Why is this so?

---

[64] McCoy and Baker, *Fountainhead of Federalism*, 23.

[65] Ibid., 24.

[66] Lillback admits, "Thus, Calvin may or may not be a covenant theologian depending upon one's definition" (*Binding of God*, 28).

[67] Ibid., 27. Lillback adds, "In this study, Moltmann's definition will be accepted." The quotation is Lillback's translation from Moltmann's *Federal theologiae*, 190. But dispensationalists could describe themselves with this definition if they were allowed to define the key terms. Dispensationalists believe that the biblical covenants (Abrahamic, Mosaic, Davidic, New) indeed form the structure for divine revelation. And they certainly believe that all people throughout biblical history are redeemed by grace through faith on the basis of the shed blood of Christ.

[68] Ibid., 311.

[69] Ibid.

Calvin's Integration of Covenant Themes

It is so because Calvin is much more comprehensive in his systematic theology than was Zwingli or Bullinger. He systematizes the continuity of the events of salvation history, including the various biblical covenants (i.e., Abraham, New), the Mosaic Law, the sacraments, and the replacement of Israel by the church.

Defining the Covenant

Calvin employs the word, "covenant" (Latin, *foedus*) and related words over 270 times in his *Institutes of the Christian Religion*. According to those who count, "his most frequent phrases are "God's covenant," "My covenant," "His covenant," "Lord's covenant," and "covenant of God."[70] As noted above, the term, "covenant of grace," in an informal sense is found in a couple of places: "… the Lord does not examine for merits the works of those whom he has received into the covenant of grace."[71] And, "… until the advent of Christ the Lord set apart one nation within which to confine the covenant of his grace."[72] Obviously, the concept of the covenant is important to Calvin's theology. The covenant is an act of a sovereign and holy God who lovingly and graciously condescends to come into union with helpless and sinful creatures. Once the transcendent Lord makes a covenant with a creature, He binds Himself to that creature. Thus, the basic idea of a covenant in Calvin's thinking is a binding of God.

Unifying the Biblical Covenants

Calvin's covenant ties all of the biblical covenants together and makes them essentially one. There is a covenant before Abraham in Calvin's mind, but still, "in a very real sense, the covenant's formal establishment was with Abraham in the words of Genesis 17."[73] Then, Moses was sent to renew the Abrahamic covenant.[74] Thus, all of the biblical covenants are essentially statements of the one theological covenant. This includes the New Covenant after Christ. Calvin

---

[70] See Lillback, *Binding of God*, 134-37, and Andrew A. Woolsey, *Unity and Continuity in Covenantal Thought* (Grand Rapids: Reformation Heritage, 2012), 255.

[71] John Calvin, *Institutes of the Christian Religion*, ed. John T. McNeill, trans. Ford Lewis Battles (Philadelphia: Westminster Press), III. XVII. 15.

[72] Ibid., II. XI. 11.

[73] Lillback, *Binding of God*, 144.

[74] Calvin, *Institutes*, II. VII. 1.

insists that "the covenant made with all the patriarchs is so much like ours in substance and reality that the two are actually one and the same. Yet they differ in the mode of dispensation."[75]

The differences between the covenant before Christ and the covenant after Christ are superficial, in other words. The Old Covenant required ceremonies that were temporary, to be sure. It was "wrapped up in the shadowy and ineffectual observance of ceremonies and delivered to the Jews; it was temporary because it remained, as it were, in suspense until it might rest upon a firm and substantial confirmation." With the death of Christ, these Old Testament ceremonies had to be abrogated "to give place to Christ, the Sponsor and Mediator of a better covenant.[76] Nonetheless, the Old Testament believers "had and knew Christ as Mediator, through whom they were joined to God."[77] The one covenant, for Calvin, comprehends all of the history of salvation.

Unifying the Law of God

The law of God, in a narrower sense, also comprehends all the history of salvation. The unchangeable law of God begins as natural law in the Garden of Eden. Calvin defines natural law as "that apprehension of the conscience which distinguishes sufficiently between just and unjust, and which deprives men of the excuse of ignorance, while it proves them guilty by their own testimony."[78] This law is essentially the same as the Mosaic Law and the law to which mankind after Christ is responsible. "Now we can clearly see," says Calvin, "that all men adopted by God into the company of his people since the beginning of the world were covenanted to him by the same law and by the bond of the same doctrine as obtains among us."[79] Thus, to come back to his point, "the gospel did not supplant the entire law as to bring forward a different way of salvation. Rather it confirmed and satisfied whatever the law had promised and gave substance to the shadows.[80] This view of the law still prevails in covenant theology.

---

[75] Ibid., II. X. 2.

[76] Ibid., II. XI. 4.

[77] Ibid., II. X. 2. Contrary to the covenant system, dispensationalists believe that the new covenant is a different covenant from the old covenant, not just an updated old covenant (Jer 31:31-32).

[78] Ibid., II. II. 22.

[79] Ibid., II. X. 1.

[80] Ibid., II. IX. 4.

Unifying the Covenant and Predestination

One of the issues in evaluating Calvin's connection to covenant theology is the relationship of predestination with the covenant. In simple terms the question is, if predestination is the unifying feature of Calvin's theology, how does the covenant fit into that paradigm? Calvin's answer is that there are two parts in the covenant. As with much of covenant theology, the model is God's covenant with Israel. The nation of Israel was the covenant nation, but within Israel there were obviously non-elect people. So, Calvin argues, "We must add a second, more limited degree of election, or one in which God's more special grace was evident, that is, when from the same race of Abraham God rejected some but showed that he kept others among his sons by cherishing them in the church." Calvin brings as examples Ishmael, Esau, and Saul. Though "the condition had been laid down that they should faithfully keep God's covenant," they "faithlessly violated" it.[81]

This model is then applied to the church of the New Testament. The church therefore does not require regenerated membership. Many in the covenant are non-elect. As Lillback summarizes, for Calvin "the covenant community is hence a combination of the elect and the non-elect in terms of special election. Nevertheless, all who are generally elect are also in the covenant."[82] Some in the covenant enter the covenant through birth to covenant parents by means of infant baptism. Others enter it through a hypocritical faith and will eventually apostatize and be cut off. And still others in the covenant are indeed the elect of God. Thus, in Calvin's interpretation of the covenant, a person in the covenant is not necessarily regenerated. In this way Calvin merges the doctrines of predestination and covenant.

Unifying the Sacraments

Calvin, like Zwingli and Bullinger, believes that the sacraments were essentially the same in the Old and New Testaments. How could they not be since they exist under the control of one over-arching theological covenant? So, infant baptism replaces circumcision, the communion service replaces the Passover. Calvin states,

---

[81] Ibid., III. 21. 6. One of the features of the new covenant is that everyone in it is regenerate (Jer 31:33-34). This was not true of everyone who lived under the old covenant.

[82] Lillback, *Binding of God*, 217.

For circumcision was for the Jews their first entry into the church because it was a token to them by which they were assured of adoption as the people and household of God, and they in turn professed to enlist in God's service. In like manner, we also are consecrated to God through baptism, to be reckoned as his people and in turn we swear fealty to him. By this it appears incontrovertible that baptism has taken the place of circumcision to fulfill the same office among us.[83]

The sacraments did not save anyone, as the Roman Catholics and Lutherans may have taught. They are tokens and seals of the covenant and serve as a means of assurance to God's people that they are indeed in covenant relationship with God. But of course, this could only be a tentative assurance since many who had received infant baptism and were in the covenant were not elect.

We can understand how imperative it was for the early covenantalists to battle those, like the Anabaptists, who rejected infant baptism. Calvin calls the Anabaptists "mad beasts" who "ceaselessly assail this holy institution of God."[84] As Lillback says, "If infant baptism is to be overturned, then the continuity of the Old and New Covenants must be denied."[85] Systematic covenant theology would then disintegrate all at once like the "one-hoss shay" of Oliver Wendell Holmes' parody.

Calvin's Covenantalism

Some features of covenantalism are missing in Calvin's theology. We do not discover a covenant of works in his writings though some of his discussion about the events in the Garden of Eden certainly do not contradict the later federal theologians who identified, named, and developed the implications of such a covenant. Calvin does not speak of the covenant of redemption, but some think that Calvin's discussion of the decrees of God led later theologians to develop this covenant. Calvin's theology, therefore, is not fully organized covenant theology. Willem van Asselt concludes, "At most, one could maintain that Calvin taught nothing that explicitly contradicted or denied the federal system. However, a direct line running from Calvin to the later federal theologians can

---

[83] Ibid., IV.XVI.4.

[84] Calvin, *Institutes*, IV. XVI. 10.

[85] Lillback, *Binding of God*, 147.

certainly not be proved."[86] On the other hand, we can agree with Woolsey who states, "Calvin took up all the points raised by Oecolampadius, Zwingli, and Bullinger, and expounded and applied them in considerably more detail than his predecessors had ever done."[87]

So, do we have covenant theology by the time of the deaths of Calvin (1564) or Bullinger (1575)? Not really—at least not in these two Reformers' theology. At this time, the process of reformulating supersessionism can still be described as unborn embryonic covenant theology. But by the end of the sixteenth century, a new piece of the puzzle will have been placed on the table and covenant theology will be born. The articulation of a second covenant, the prelapsarian (i.e., pre-fall) 'covenant of works' is "the key identifying feature of the federal theology."[88] The name of the covenant is significant because "the name covenant of works … highlights the means whereby Adam was going to earn eternal life; it was by his works that eternal life was to be achieved."[89] The covenant of works is a sine qua non of covenant theology because, as we will see, covenant theologians believe that it continues to exist until the Second Coming of Christ.

Zacharias Ursinus

Most of us are not familiar with Zacharias Ursinus (1534-1583).[90] Nevertheless, he made an important impact on the formulation of the covenant of works in about 1562. He was born in Breslau, a city in the Hapsburg Empire at the time, but which is in Poland today. In his early life, he was a Lutheran, a student of Melanchthon at Wittenberg. In 1560, he moved to Zurich and studied under Peter Martyr, and thereafter became a German Reformed theologian. He was a Professor of Dogmatics at the University of Heidelberg from 1562 to 1568. When the University of Heidelberg became Lutheran, he moved and became a Professor of Dogmatics in the Reformed school in Neustadt an der Hardt. He

---

[86] Willem J. van Asselt, *The Federal Theology of Johannes Cocceius*, trans. Raymond A. Blacketer (Boston: Brill, 2001), 327.

[87] Woolsey, *Unity and Continuity*, 336.

[88] David A. Weir, *The Origins of the Federal Theology in Sixteenth-Century Reformation Thought* (Oxford: Clarendon Press, 1990), vii.

[89] Michael Brown and Zach Keele, *Sacred Bond, Covenant Theology Explored* (Grandville, MI: Reformed Fellowship, 2012), 46.

[90] "Ursinus" is the Latin word for a bear. Interestingly there is a liberal arts college near Philadelphia named Ursinus College, founded in 1869. And of course, the mascot is a bear.

is best known for his primary role in the production of the *Heidelberg Catechism* in 1563. But he wrote many other theological works during his lifetime, the two most important for our purposes being his *Commentary on the Heidelberg Catechism* and the "Larger (Major) Catechism."[91]

The Covenant of Grace

We are not surprised by anything we read in Ursinus' *Commentary on the Heidelberg Catechism*. His theology reflects the literature of his time when Reformed theologians were reformulating supersessionism into covenant theology. He discusses the concept of the covenant at length and defines the covenant of grace that God makes with us as two sided:

> [The covenant is] a mutual promise and agreement between God and men, in which God gives assurance to men that he will be merciful to them, remit their sins, grant unto them a new righteousness, the Holy Spirit, and eternal life by and for the sake of his Son, our mediator. And, on the other side, men bind themselves to God in this covenant that they will exercise repentance and faith, or that they will receive with a true faith this great benefit which God offers, and render such obedience as will be acceptable to him.[92]

Both God and man commit to specific obligations when they enter into covenant.

Ursinus, like the other covenant theologians, believed that the covenant system solves many of the problems of discontinuity in Scripture. Clearly there are at least two biblical covenants—the Old or Mosaic covenant and the New Covenant. But assimilating these two biblical covenants into the one theological covenant of grace minimizes the discontinuity and maintains the continuity of salvation throughout all biblical revelation. The consequences of such continuity are broad and comprehensive. There is only one covenant mediator, for example. Although we might think that Moses was the mediator of the Old Covenant (John 1:17; Heb 8:6), "he was a Mediator only as a type of Christ, who was even then already Mediator, but is now the only Mediator without any type."[93]

---

[91] Zacharias Ursinus, *The Commentary of Zacharias Ursinus on the Heidelberg Catechism*," trans. G. W. Willard (n.p., Forgotten Books, n.d., but the original Latin book was first published in 1564).

[92] Ursinus, *Commentary*, 97. Ursinus makes much out of the spiritual and practical value of the covenant bringing comfort and assurance to the believer that he is indeed a son of God ("Of True Christian Comfort," 17-20).

[93] Ibid., 99.

The church, moreover, parallels the doctrine of salvation and has existed from the beginning of salvation history.[94] Ursinus states, "That there is but one church of all times, from the beginning to the end of the world, there can be no reasonable doubt; for it is manifest that the church has always existed, even before the time of Abraham."[95] Abraham and Melchizedek were members of the church, he explains, because they worshipped the one true God. Any redeemed person was and is a member of the church. Like the third century church father, Cyprian, Ursinus asserts, "Out of the church there is no salvation."[96]

This oneness also includes the sacraments in the same way they did with Zwingli, Bullinger, and Calvin. The Lord's Supper replaces the Passover, and "baptism occupies the place of circumcision in the New Testament and has the same value that circumcision had in the Old Testament,"[97] placing infants into the covenant. Female babies in the Old Testament were in some way "included in the circumcision of the males; because God spared their weaker sex. It was sufficient for them that they were born of circumcised parents."[98] In the New Testament, even the baptism of John "was the same in substance with Christian baptism."[99] So all who are baptized, including "children of Christians, as well as adults, belong to the covenant and church of God."[100]

Ursinus' explanations betray the tension that the doctrine of infant baptism has for covenant theologians. Baptism does not in itself save a person any more than circumcision in the Old Testament saved a Jewish boy. It is only a seal of the covenant. Yet Ursinus sometimes comes close to saying that baptism does save. Through baptism, he writes, "Christ testifies to the faithful ... the forgiveness of all their sins, the giving of the Holy Spirit, and engrafting into

---

[94] Dispensationalists, in contrast, teach that the church is a new covenant organism that began on the Day of Pentecost. People are saved in the same way as they were in the Old Testament, so the differences between Old and New Testament believers are essentially ecclesiological and pneumatological rather than soteriological.

[95] Ursinus, *Commentary*, 290.

[96] Ibid., 2.

[97] Ibid., 367. Ursinus declares that one of the meanings of the Greek word for baptism is "to sprinkle." The mode, however, "is a matter of no importance, as washing may be performed either by dipping or sprinkling" (357).

[98] Ibid., 374.

[99] Ibid., 359.

[100] Ibid., 366. Ursinus, like the other sixteenth-century founders of covenant theology, asserted that the doctrines of the Anabaptists, had "without doubt, been hatched by the devil and are detestable heresies which they have fabricated from various errors and blasphemies" (368).

the church and his own body."[101] Christ baptizes a person "by the hand of his ministers just as he speaks through them."[102] Ursinus knew, however, that some infants who had been baptized and were therefore in the covenant and in the church later denied God and gave clear evidence that they had never been redeemed through Christ. He thus had to live with the tension of covenantalism that baptism places a person into the covenant and the church, affirms their forgiveness of sins and engrafting into the body of Christ—but yet, baptism is not a certain testimony to these facts.

It may be unnecessary to point out that Ursinus did not believe that there was a future for the nation of Israel. In his theology, Old Testament Israel laid the foundation for the Gentile church. But the Old Testament "types and shadows" continue only in the sense that "the things signified thereby, which are spiritual ... will continue forever in the church, even though the types and signs themselves be abolished by Christ."[103] Ursinus did not modify the developing Reformed tradition about a covenant of grace. And he maintained the doctrine of supersessionism, that the church had replaced Israel.

The Covenant of Works

But Ursinus began to write about a second covenant which he called the "covenant of nature" and the "covenant of creation." This is the theological covenant that eventually came to be known as the "covenant of works" in Reformed covenant theology. This pre-fall covenant is derived from God's command to Adam in the Garden: "And the LORD God commanded the man, saying, 'You may surely eat of every tree of the garden, but of the tree of the knowledge of good and evil you shall not eat, for in the day that you eat of it you shall surely die'" (Gen 2:16-17).

Interestingly, it appears that Roman Catholic theologians were some of the first to place Adam in covenant with God. J. V. Fesko points out that in 1541, the Dominican theologian, Ambrogio Catharinus (d. 1553), a major apologist for the Roman Catholic doctrine of salvation at the Council of Trent, stated that God was in a covenant with Adam "from the beginning." [104] Cartharinus'

---

[101] Ibid., 371.

[102] Ibid., 372. This means that those who are not called to the "ecclesiastical ministry," "and especially women, ought not to take upon themselves the right and authority to baptize" (373).

[103] Ibid., 494.

[104] J. V. Fesko, *Death in Adam, Life in Christ* (Geanies, Fearn, Ross-shire, UK: Christian Focus, 2016), 72-73.

doctrine of a covenant between God and Adam predated the development of this doctrine in Reformed circles by about forty years.

Even in Reformed circles, Ursinus may not have been the first theologian to think about a covenant in the Garden;[105] but he was the first to specifically write about it. Historians have observed that there were two stages in the acceptance of the covenant of works. The first stage was its proposal in 1562 by Ursinus. The second stage occurred from 1584 to 1590 when the covenant of works became "commonplace" in Reformed theology. David Weir explains, "Since the prelapsarian covenant idea is novel for the sixteenth century, one can clearly trace this second stage in four theologians who, in various ways, had connections with Ursinus and the Reformed Church of the Palatinate: Caspar Olevianus, Thomas Cartwright, Dudley Fenner, and Franciscus Junius."[106]

The "Larger Catechism," in which Ursinus teaches this second covenant, was written in 1562, though it was not published for wide distribution until 1584, a year after Ursinus' death. Between 1584, when his "Larger Catechism" was published, and 1590, others of his students and friends, especially Dudley Fenner (1558-1587), began to expound this covenant. Fenner published his *Sacra Theologia* in 1585 and was probably the first theologian to use the specific term, "covenant of works" (instead of "covenant of nature" or "covenant of creation") in a theological work.[107] After 1590, "the covenant idea blossoms all over Europe, and it is impossible to keep track of the manifold uses and conceptions of the covenant motif."[108]

Ursinus introduces this second covenant as a part of the answer to the question about the difference between the law and gospel:

Q. 36: What is the difference between the law and gospel?

---

[105] Andrew Woolsey thinks that the idea of a pre-fall covenant was already present in Reformed thought before Ursinus (cf. Calvin's *Commentary* on Ezekiel 20:11). Woolsey does agree that Ursinus "is to be credited with coining the terms *foedus creationis* and *foedus naturale* in speaking of sinless Adam's relationship with God ..." (Woolsey, *Unity and Continuity*, 409). Lyle D. Bierma agrees that "Ursinus was the first to explain the *foedus gratiae* ... in relation to a second covenant, a *foedus naturale* (Bierma, *German Calvinism in the Confessional Age*, 58). McCoy and Baker also agree, "Ursinus apparently was the first of the Federal theologians to formulate explicitly the notion of a covenant of nature that God made with the human race" (McCoy and Baker, *Fountainhead of Federalism*, 202.)

[106] Weir, *Origins of the Federal Theology*, vii-viii.

[107] Woolsey, *Unity and Continuity*, 443.

[108] Weir, *Origins of the Federal Theology*, 115.

A. The law contains the natural covenant, established by God with humanity in creation, that is, it is known by humanity by nature, it requires our perfect obedience to God, and it promises eternal life to those who keep it and threatens eternal punishment to those who do not. The gospel, however, contains the covenant of grace, that is, although it exists, it is not known at all by nature; it shows us the fulfillment in Christ of the righteousness that the law requires and the restoration in us of that righteousness by Christ's Spirit; and it promises eternal life freely because of Christ to those who believe in him.[109]

For Ursinus, the covenant of works can be delineated as follows:

1. It is called the "natural covenant" because it is known by humanity by nature (later called "the covenant of works").

2. After the Fall of Adam and Eve into sin, the covenant of works continued to exist in the form of law, eventually located in the Mosaic Law. Ursinus begins his answer in his catechism: "The law contains the natural covenant."

3. The covenant of works "requires perfect obedience to God."

4. The covenant of works "promises eternal life to those who keep it."

5. The covenant of works "threatens eternal punishment to those who do not" keep it.

6. "The righteousness that the law" (i.e., the covenant of works) requires is fulfilled by Christ because He perfectly kept the Mosaic Law (i.e., the covenant of works).

7. The righteousness that Christ earned in keeping the Law (i.e., the covenant of works) is restored in those that believe "by Christ's Spirit."

The role of works in one's salvation is emphasized more in the context of the covenant of works than in embryonic covenant theology. This is curious because there is not much in God's command to Adam and Eve about works. Especially surprising is Ursinus' belief that the covenant of works did not end at the Fall, but instead was incorporated in law, eventually the Mosaic Law (and as

---

[109] Zacharias Ursinus, "Larger Catechism," in Lyle Bierma, et. al., *An Introduction to the Heidelberg Catechism* (Grand Rapids: Baker Academic, 2005), 168. Both his Larger and Smaller Catechism are quoted in full in this work (141-223).

we will see, in the Law of Christ as well). Thus, even after Adam disobeyed the covenant of works and had to depend on the covenant of grace, the covenant of works was still binding on the human race.

The covenant of works thus becomes perpetual. The only difference is that "before the fall it was effectual through Adam's obedience, whereas after the fall it was effectual only though Christ's obedience on behalf of the people."[110] This leads to the doctrine of active obedience of Christ: (1) Christ kept perfectly the covenant of works which was first known by Adam by nature since it was engraved on his heart, but then found its expression in the Decalogue. (2) In so doing Christ became the federal head of believers so that His law-keeping righteousness is imputed to their account. We will analyze the theological implications of the covenant of works in a later chapter.

As for a sacrament attached to the covenant of works, it was the tree of life. The Old Covenant sacraments of circumcision and Passover replace the sacrament of the tree of life. Then with the coming of the New Covenant, infant baptism and the Lord's Supper replace circumcision and Passover in the covenant system.

CONCLUSION

So, do we now have covenant theology? Yes. At least by 1590 a "covenant of nature," alias "covenant of creation," alias "covenant of works," was becoming well-known in Reformed circles. With the combination of the covenant of works with the covenant of grace, the system of covenant theology was created. Ursinus' contemporaries and successors worked on the implications of the covenant of works for soteriology in the following years, and by the beginning of the seventeenth century, a covenant theology with two covenants was widespread throughout the Reformed world. Embryonic covenant theology had been born and become nascent covenant theology—alive and well. The church's supersessionism over Israel had been reformulated into a theological system.

---

110 Woolsey, *Unity and Continuity*, 284.

4

SOVEREIGN ELECTION
AND ISRAEL

Larry D. Pettegrew

The responsibility for systematizing the theological nuggets of gold that the first-generation Reformers mined out of Scripture became the happy obligation of their theological heirs, many of whom were professors in academic institutions. The successors of Luther, Zwingli, and Calvin also had the task of protecting their theology from alternative theological worldviews. For the Reformed, losing political and theological ground to the Lutherans or Roman Catholics was a serious threat to the movement. The very existence of Reformed covenant theology "demanded an academically respectable method for articulating its positive content and the differences with Rome and among fellow Protestants."[1]

Though the development of covenant theology was a major task, at the same time, the precise definition and role of the doctrine of God's sovereign election became a key topic on the agenda of the Reformed theologians. In this chapter we are analyzing the debates over the doctrine of election.

We also have a secondary goal. We might think that the predestinarian agenda would include a discussion of God's sovereign choice of Israel. After all, the Apostle Paul asserts that God has not rejected Israel whom he foreknew (Rom 11:2). Calvinists often use this verse to demonstrate that "foreknowledge" means "foreordination" in some Scriptures. Saying that someone is foreknown

---

[1] Kenneth D. Stanglin and Thomas H. McCall, *Jacob Arminius, Theologian of Grace* (New York: Oxford University Press, 2012), 15.

is to say that he is one of the elect. But Paul's declaration here concerns the eternal election of the nation of Israel. What the Scriptures say about the election of individuals would seem to apply to the election of God's chosen nation. But this issue was mostly overlooked in the debates of the sixteenth and seventeenth centuries, and consequently, also in the Reformed creeds. Thus, we will briefly explain the necessity of correlating the election of individuals with the election of a covenant nation.

THE AGE OF PROTESTANT ORTHODOXY

The "Age of Protestant Orthodoxy," as it has often been called, extended from the death of Calvin in 1564-1700.[2] This era is sometimes also described as the Age of Protestant Scholasticism. But "orthodoxy" and "scholasticism" are not synonyms. "'Scholasticism' refers to a method and must not be confused with particular content. 'Orthodoxy,' in contrast, refers to a particular period in history, tied to particular content, and has nothing to say about method."[3] The discussions and debates in the age of Protestant orthodoxy, moreover, involved theologians in several countries. Whether they lived in Switzerland, Holland, Germany, England, or New England, they could all read and write Latin, and could interact with each other on the most intricate of theological issues.

So, what should we think of this age of Orthodoxy? [4] Roger Olson explains a common, somewhat negative interpretation:

---

[2] See Richard A. Muller, *After Calvin, Studies in the Development of a Theological Tradition* (New York: Oxford University Press, 2003), 4-5, for the different stages in this era. Some of the Age of Orthodoxy overlaps with the Reformation era because a good historical case can be made that the Reformation era extended to the Peace of Westphalia in 1648.

[3] Willem J. van Asselt and Pieter L. Rouwendal, "Introduction: What is Reformed Scholasticism?" in *Introduction to Reformed Scholasticism*, trans. Albert Gootjes (Grand Rapids: Reformation Heritage Books, 2011), 8.

[4] The extensive amount of published literature on every topic that we contemplate in this and the next two chapters is almost overwhelming. In the words of Carl R. Trueman, "The last two decades have seen nothing short of a renaissance of interest in the theological world of late sixteenth and seventeenth centuries" (Carl R. Trueman, "Foreword" to Jonathan D. Moore, *English Hypothetical Universalism* [Grand Rapids: Eerdmans, 2007], ix). See, for example, the eighty-six pages of bibliography in Andrew A. Woolsey, *Unity and Continuity in Covenantal Thought* (Grand Rapids: Reformation Heritage Books, 2012), 553-639. Woolsey also has two helpful chapters on the historiography of covenantal thought in *Unity and Continuity*. Or see the extensive bibliography in Charles S. McCoy and J. Wayne Baker, *Fountainhead of Federalism, Heinrich Bullinger and the Covenantal Tradition* (Louisville: Westminster/John Knox, 1991), 149-70. Or, to see the extensive literature available as employed in journal articles, see Lynne Courter Boughton, "Supralapsarianism and the Role of Metaphysics in Sixteenth-Century Reformed Theology," *Westminster Theological Journal* 48 (1986): 63-96, and the sources used in her article. Also, see Mark R. Shaw, "William Perkins and the New Pelagians: Another Look at the Cambridge Predestination Controversy of the 1590's," *Westminster Theological Journal* 58 (1996): 267-301.

Although the major first-generation Protestant Reformers such as Luther, Zwingli, and Calvin reacted against scholasticism and scholastic theology, their immediate followers fell back into a kind of scholastic thinking that placed a great deal more emphasis on philosophy and logic and sought to use these to construct highly coherent systems of Protestant doctrine. This tendency of post-Reformation Protestant thinkers has earned them the dubious label of "Protestant scholastics," and their theology is often vaguely characterized as Protestant scholasticism. What many of them tried to do was discover and carve into stone a rigid Protestant orthodoxy that could repel all heresy, including attacks by skeptics and Roman Catholic critics.[5]

True enough, for the scholastic theologians, logic became more important in the explanation and defense of theology so that theology was sometimes presented as syllogistic deductions based on known axioms.

We should not, however, overemphasize the differences between the first-generation Reformers and the scholastic Reformed theologians. Richard A. Muller, an important scholar of the post-Reformation era, has warned us not to think that the Reformed theologians who followed Calvin focused exclusively on dogmatic theology: "Rather ... than producing only a single form (i.e., a dogmatic one) of exegetical work, the Protestant orthodoxy must be recognized as producing highly varied and diverse exegetical works and commentaries, ranging from text-critical essays, to textual annotations, theological annotations, linguistic commentaries, and, indeed all manner of permutations and combinations of these several types of effort."[6]

Saying that in the defense of theology logic became more important also does not mean that the post-Reformation theologians abandoned Scripture as their authority and wandered off into natural theology.[7] The "scholastics" of the

---

[5] Roger E. Olson, *The Story of Christian Theology* (Downers Grove, IL: InterVarsity, 1999), 455.

[6] Muller, *After Calvin*, 85. Muller's thesis is that there is more continuity between the first-generation Reformers and the seventeenth-century Reformed theologians than has often been recognized. Still, Muller is not denying the distinctive characteristics of the scholastic era. In another of his works, Muller writes:

After the Reformation, in the period extending roughly from 1565 to 1700, Protestantism faced the crisis of being forced to defend its nascent theology against attack from the highly sophisticated and carefully articulated vantage point of Roman Catholic scholastic theology. It faced the problem of institutionalization—of passing from its beginnings as a protest movement within the Catholic Church to its destiny as a self-sufficient ecclesiastical establishment with its own distinct academic, confessional, and dogmatic needs. It also faced, together with the Roman Catholic Church, the twin challenges of modern philosophical rationalism and the dawn of modern science (Richard A. Muller, *God, Creation, and Providence in the Thought of Jacob Arminius* [Grand Rapids: Baker: 1991], 3).

[7] See Boughton, "Supralapsarianism and the Role of Metaphysics," especially 78-9.

late Reformation and post-Reformation eras did not even want to be identified as "scholastics." The Lutheran "scholastic" theologian, J. A. Quenstedt, for
example, differentiated his theology from pre-Reformation scholasticism:

> Of the scholastics, whose total theology is nothing else than a mixture of theol-
> ogy and philosophy or, by the judgment of Erasmus, a two-formed discipline put
> together by a kind of mixture of divine oracles and philosophic reasonings, like
> a kind of centaur. For in the highest mysteries of faith the scholastics draw their
> conclusions from logical, physical, and metaphysical principles, with statements of
> Scripture disregarded or touched with a light hand.[8]

Clearly, the "scholasticism" of the late Reformation era was different from the
scholasticism of the Middle Ages, having been refined through the Renaissance
and early Reformation eras.[9]

In its bare essence, "scholasticism" means "school," i.e., "academic method."
It is a neutral word, not necessarily implying something troublesome. According
to van Asselt and Rouwendal, "Reformed Scholasticism (1) refers to the academic theology of the schools (2) practiced in the period of orthodoxy, (3)
using scholastic method in the exposition of doctrine and (4) in content, is
bound to the Reformed confessions."[10]

The Age of Orthodoxy, when all is said and done, was a vitally important
age. As Muller observes, "without the establishment and successful defense of
this confessional orthodoxy in the Reformed churches, the reform efforts of
Bucer, Zwingli, Calvin, Bullinger and their contemporaries would probably
have registered in the pages of Western history as an evanescent movement
long ago vanished from the face of the earth rather than as the foundation of an
institutional form of Christianity."[11]

---

[8] J. A. Quenstedt, *The Nature and Character of Theology: An Introduction to the Thought of J. A. Quenstedt from Theologia Didactico-Polemica Sive Systema Theologicum*, edited, translated, and abridged by Luther Poellot (St. Louis: Concordia, 1986), 161. According to Poellot, the full 1696 published book "consists of 4 parts, 48 chapters, 2,073 large pages ... and weighs 11 pounds and 2 ounces." *The Nature and Character of Theology* is only a translation of Quenstedt's first part of his massive work.

[9] See Muller's chapter, "Scholasticism and Orthodoxy in the Reformed Tradition," *After Calvin*, 25-46.

[10] van Asselt and Rouwendal, "What is Reformed Scholasticism?" 9. Lutheran scholasticism can be explained in the same way, only that it was loyal to the Reformation Lutheran creeds.

[11] Ibid., 46. For a study of Lutheran Orthodoxy, see Robert Preus, *The Theology of Post-Reformation Lutheranism*, 2 vols (St. Louis: Concordia, 1972).

Defenses of Key Doctrines

Furthermore, the scholastic theologians of the Post-Reformation era produced weighty apologetics for doctrines that many of us hold dear. Quenstedt, for example, wrote a powerful defense of the doctrine of inerrancy of Scripture.[12] The plenary and verbal inspiration of Scripture leads naturally to its inerrancy, he taught. If the Holy Spirit of truth moved the biblical authors, "it follows that they could under no condition make mistakes in their writing, and no falsification, no error, no danger of error, no untruth existed or could exist in their preaching or writing" (1,77).

Inspiration extends to the autographs, but also to the copies if "they were faithfully transcribed from them [autographs] so that not only the sense but also the words were exactly the same" (I, 206). Scripture is also self-authenticating (1 Thes 2:13) and does not need the Roman church to guarantee its authority. It is the operation of the Holy Spirit by which "we clearly perceive in our hearts the majesty and holiness and truth of the word" (1.88.92-93).[13]

Reformed scholastic theologians, like Lutheran scholastics, also defended the inerrancy of Scripture in the original writings. Francis Turretin (1623-1687) is well-known in theological circles for his systematic theology book, *Institutio theologiae elencticae*. Locus 2 of this book is dedicated to a thorough study of the doctrine of Scripture, including a detailed defense of inerrancy.[14]

Perplexities of High Calvinism

The most intense debate among the Reformed theologians in the Age of Orthodoxy centered particularly on the election of some humans to eternal happiness and the reprobation of other humans to eternal damnation. No doubt "there were many conundrums which Calvin, and all the first reformers for that matter, had not answered in sufficient detail. He had left too many loopholes, too many openings for Papist disputants to thrust in embarrassing questions."[15]

---

[12] Geoffrey W. Bromiley, *Historical Theology, An Introduction* (Grand Rapids: Eerdmans, 1978), 318-24, has a helpful discussion of Quenstedt's systematic theology.

[13] Ibid., 320-23. The quotations are from Bromiley's translation and analysis of Quenstedt's *Theologia Didactico-Polemica Sive Systema Theologicum*.

[14] *The Doctrine of Scripture*, Locus 2 of the *Institutio theologiae elencticae*, has been edited and translated by John W. Beardslee III, and published by Baker, 1981.

[15] Perry Miller, "The Marrow of Puritan Divinity," chapter 3 in *Errand into the Wilderness* (Cambridge, Mass: Belknap Press, 1956; repr. New York: Harper and Row, 1964), 50.

Theodore Beza (1519-1605), the successor to John Calvin and head of the University of Geneva, took up this matter and constructed a detailed, logically air-tight system eventually known as supralapsarianism to defend High Calvinism.[16] Although Calvin had not formulated supralapsarianism in his theological works, he may have been comfortable with its teachings. According to one historian, in 1555, about nine years before Calvin died, Beza informed Calvin of his supralapsarianism, and Calvin "expressed no objections."[17]

For Beza and supralapsarianism, the decrees of election and reprobation logically precede the decree of creation.[18] God, in effect, decrees to create two classes of human beings: the elect and the reprobate. One class of people is born from all eternity reprobate, some of which are cut off as infants, but others are allowed to come to maturity and receive "a more sharp judgment."[19] Sin, except possibly Adam's sin, therefore, is not the cause for one's reprobation. God is.[20] The non-elect do not even know that they are non-elect. The Spirit of God reveals election to an individual, but reprobation "is ever hidden from man, except it be disclosed by God, contrary to the common course of things."[21]

Not all scholastic Reformed theologians accepted the order of the decrees displayed in supralapsarianism. Likely, more Reformed theologians held to the infralapsarianism of Bullinger and others. Even among the theologians at the Synod of Dort there was a variety of opinions on the order of the decrees as well as on limited atonement and reprobation.[22] Carl Trueman adds that even "terms such as 'Calvinism,' 'Arminianism,' 'supralapsarianism,' 'infralapsarianism,' and the like have been shown to be broad labels that can often hide important differences and nuances within the theological world of the

---

[16] Philip Melanchthon (1497-1660), the successor to Martin Luther, also taught supralapsarianism. See Boughton, "Supralapsarianism and the Role of Metaphysics," 74-5.

[17] Ibid., 80. Boughton interprets this incident as Beza correctly understanding Calvin's theology.

[18] "Lapsus" = the fall of Adam and Eve. "Supra" = above. "Infra" = follows. The order of the decrees, in my opinion, is not helpful in understanding Scripture or systematic theology. It is helpful in clarifying historical theology—what people were thinking theologically at a certain time in history.

[19] Theodore Beza, *A Brief Declaration of the Chiefe Poyntes of the Christian Religion*, n. p., available at www.covenanter.org/Beza/besas-table.html. See Greg Allison's explanation, *Historical Theology* (Grand Rapids: Zondervan, 2011), 466-67.

[20] Moore, has a good discussion of William Perkins' view of reprobation: *English Hypothetical Universalism*, 30ff.

[21] Beza, *A Brief Declaration of the Chiefe Poyntes of the Christian Religion*, n.p.

[22] Muller, *After Calvin*, 87.

time ... and even the great church confessions of the period embraced a spectrum of opinion."[23]

It is clear, however, that both supralapsarianism and infralapsarianism imply limited atonement because the decree to elect comes logically before the decree to provide salvation. So, Christ's atonement is divinely intended only for the elect. The order of the decrees can be charted as follows:

Infralapsarianism	Supralapsarianism
1. Decree to create all human beings	1. Decree to elect some to be saved and to reprobate all others to just condemnation
2. Decree to permit the Fall	2. Decree to create the elect and the non-elect
3. Decree to elect some, and reprobate others to just condemnation	3. Decree to permit the Fall
4. Decree to provide salvation for the elect	4. Decree to provide salvation for the elect
5. Decree to call the elect to salvation	5. Decree to call the elect to salvation

Supralapsarianism and infralapsarianism with their attendant charts were obviously useful tools for the Reformed theologians to explain and defend God's sovereign plan of election.[24] The logic was impeccable. But in its teachings, Reformed theologians, pastors, and lay people were being asked to "contemplate, with steady, unblinking resolution, the absolute, incomprehensible, and transcendent sovereignty of God; ... to stare fixedly and without relief into

---

[23] Trueman, "Foreword" to Jonathan D. Moore, *English Hypothetical Universalism*, ix.

[24] More than one theologian put his mind to drawing a chart that would show the logical details of supralapsarianism. See, for example William Perkins, *A Golden Chain* (Cambridge: John Legate, 1597; edited by Greg Fox, Puritan Reprints, 2010). We are told that the order of the decrees is logical and not chronological. But it is difficult for human beings to think this way about the decrees since the explanations often use words like "before" and "after."

the very center of the blazing sun of glory."[25] Some Reformed (and Lutheran) theologians, consequently, devised ways to soften the rigid scholastic doctrine of the sovereignty of God.

ATTEMPTS AT SOFTENING SCHOLASTIC CALVINISM

The soul-burdening question that many Reformed Christians were compelled to ask was, "How can I know for sure that I am one of the elect and guaranteed to go to heaven?" John Bunyan, for example, the Independent Reformed preacher and author of the well-known *Pilgrim's Progress*, also published the book, *Grace Abounding to the Chief of Sinners*, in which he details the steps to his own conversion and assurance. Bunyan describes his struggles to know whether he was elect or not:

> Firstly, to speak concerning my questioning whether or not I was elected. I found at this time that though I was burning with desire to find the way to heaven and glory, and though nothing could distract me from this, the question of election so offended and discouraged me that I felt, especially at times, as if its force and powers had taken away the very strength of my body. This scripture, "It is not of him who wills, nor of him who runs, but of God who shows mercy" (Rom 9:16) also seemed to trample upon all my desires.... Therefore, these questions remained with me: "How can you tell that you are elected? And what if you are not? What then? O Lord," I thought, "indeed, what if I am not?" "It may be that you are not," said the tempter. "It may be so indeed," I thought. "Why then," said Satan, "you may as well leave it and strive no more; for if, indeed, you are not elected and chosen of God, there is no hope of your being saved."[26]

If God were as sovereign as High Calvinism was teaching, what level of assurance could a Christian have that God had chosen him? And who knows, some thought, if it might even be possible that a powerful, sovereign God could arbitrarily change his mind about the salvation of a soul. What, or who, could

[25] Miller, "The Marrow of Puritan Divinity," 51. See also Peter J. Thuesen, *Predestination, The American Career of a Contentious Doctrine* (New York: Oxford, 2009). Thuesen has an interesting discussion of some of the personal and emotional struggles that the American Puritans had with the doctrine of election in his chapter, "The Agony and the Ecstasy," 22-72.

[26] John Bunyan, *Grace Abounding to the Chief of Sinners* (Auburn, MA: Evangelical Press, 2000, originally published in 1666), 43-44.

make God keep His promises? And how does a human being, elect before the foundation of the world, become a born-again Christian in earth-time existence? Does God just zap him? Or are there steps that an elect sinner must take to be redeemed. If there are steps to be taken, what are they?

The Reformed theologians were well-aware of these questions and gave answers that defended High Calvinism. But some among the Reform suggested doctrinal modifications to make the Reformed theology more palatable.

Softening the Doctrine of Predestination

The most public and well-known of the debates about the nature of election occurred in the Netherlands and focused on James Arminius (1559-1609). Aminius, like his successor, Simon Episcopius, and later Arminians like John Wesley, was a covenant theologian. He had no place in his theology for a future Messianic kingdom here on earth after the Second Coming of Christ.[27] Thus we might think that one does not have to be a Calvinist in order to be a covenant theologian.

Some Reformation specialists, however, argue that Arminius was a Calvinist, or more accurately, a Reformed theologian. The argument occurs because many often misevaluate Arminius' theology. Robert Picirilli, a contemporary evangelical Arminian, correctly observes, "More than one Calvinist, on carefully studying Arminius, has found that he was not 'Arminian' after all—at least not as that view is often understood. Both while he was alive, and ever since, Arminius has been unfairly accused of sentiments that were not his."[28]

Nevertheless, this still begs the question as to whether Arminius can properly be called a Reformed theologian. Carl Bangs, who wrote a classic study on Arminius, has argued that Arminius was a Reformed theologian.[29] Richard Muller, on the other hand, has argued that he was not, but he admits, "The answer is quite complex. Arminius certainly understood himself as Reformed— and his appointment both to the pastorate in Amsterdam and to the faculty at

---

[27] See Richard A. Muller, "The Federal Motif in Seventeenth Century Arminian Theology," *Dutch Review of Church History* 62, No. 1 (1982): 102-122.

[28] Robert E. Picirilli, "Foreword" to *Arminius Speaks*, ed. John D. Wagner (Eugene, OR: Wipf & Stock, 2011), xi. From all indications, moreover, Arminius was an outstanding Christian. Petrus Bertius, a friend of Arminius, gave a wonderful testimony to the kind of Christian life that Arminius lived at Arminius' funeral when he said, "In Holland there was a man: those who knew him could not adequately esteem him; those who did not esteem him, never adequately knew him."

[29] Carl Bangs, *Arminius, A Study in the Dutch Reformation* (Grand Rapids: Francis Asbury Press, 1985). Also see Carl Bangs, "Arminius and the Reformation," *Church History*, 30:2 (June, 1961), 155-170.

Leiden indicates a similar assumption on the part of fellow clergy, professors, and university curators."[30]

Arminius also claimed that he had signed and agreed with the Belgic Confession, one of the foundational Confessions of the Reformed faith in the Netherlands, written in 1561. Article sixteen on the doctrine of election is mild, so we can understand how Arminius could agree with the statement but disagree with its interpretation by other Reformed theologians. The statement reads,

> We believe that all the posterity of Adam being thus fallen into perdition and ruin, by the sin of our first parents, God then did manifest himself such as he is; that is to say, merciful and just: Merciful, since he delivers and preserves from this perdition all, whom he, in his eternal and unchangeable counsel of mere goodness, hath elected in Christ Jesus our Lord, without any respect to their works: Just, in leaving others in the fall and perdition wherein they have involved themselves.[31]

Apparently, Arminius could agree that there is an eternal election "in Christ Jesus," though, as we will see, he would have interpreted this statement as conditional election. God, through His omniscience, knows those who will in the course of time choose of their own free will to place their faith and trust in Jesus Christ for their salvation. On the basis of this divine foreknowledge, God elects these individuals "before the foundation of the world."

A closer look at Arminius' theology demonstrates that, even before the dogmatic conclusions of the Synod of Dort (which was held after Arminius' death), Arminius was not in agreement with the theological decisions of at least three earlier regional, but important, synods. Also, his interpretation of the Belgic Confession of Faith and the Heidelberg Catechism, Questions 20 and 54, was clearly in disagreement with the interpretation of the major author of the catechism, Zacharias Ursinus, whom we have studied already.[32] Yes, Arminius agreed with the standard Reformed views on the nature of theology, the authority of Scripture, the person of Jesus Christ, justification, the church,

---

[30] Richard Muller, "Arminius and the Reformed Tradition," *Westminster Theological Journal* 70.1 (2008): 19. Also see Muller's book on Arminius: *Creation and Providence in the Thought of Jacob Arminius* (Grand Rapids: Baker, 1991), 30. Also see Erf Dekker, "Was Arminius a Molinist?" *Sixteenth Century Journal* XXVII/2 (1996): 337-351.

[31] *Belgic Confession of Faith*, Article 16.

[32] Muller, "Arminius and the Reformed Tradition," 33. See also, Zacharias Ursinus, *The Commentary of Zacharias Ursinus on the Heidelberg Catechism*, trans. G. W. Williard (1851), reprinted by Forgotten Books, n.p., n.d.).

and the evils of the papacy."[33] But his dislike of the standard Reformed view of predestination means that at a key point, Arminius was not a Reformed theologian. "A few key differences," write Stanglin and McCall, "created a ripple effect throughout his theology. Recognizing these differences allows for a greater appreciation than is sometimes expressed for Arminius as a significant thinker and a contributor to the history of theology."[34] Still, the point is that Arminius, try as he might to fit his views into the creedal statements, was not a true Reformed theologian.

The Theology of James Arminius

In a social context and ecclesiastical relationship, however, Arminius was a part of the Reformed Church. "He ministered in the Reformed Church and taught in its seminary, subscribed to its confessional statements, and at the time of his death was officially in good standing with the Reformed Church."[35] As a member of the Reformed church in these ways, he set about to soften what he considered to be unbiblical ideas in Reformed soteriology.

The Doctrine of Man

Reformed theologians teach that all human beings are born into the world totally depraved and guilty because of Adam's sin. The Belgic Confession, with which Arminius had agreed, expresses original sin and total depravity specifically:

> We believe that, through the disobedience of Adam, original sin is extended to all mankind; which is a corruption of the whole nature and a hereditary disease, where-with infants themselves are infected even in their mother's womb, and which produceth in man all sorts of sin, being in him as a root thereof; and therefore is so vile and abominable in the sight of God that it is sufficient to condemn all mankind.[36]

Total depravity does not mean that a person is as bad as he could be or that he cannot do anything good through God's common grace. It does mean that

---

[33] Muller, "Arminius and the Reformed Tradition," 40.

[34] Stanglin and McCall, *Jacob Arminius*, 202.

[35] Ibid., 201.

[36] *Belgic Confession of Faith*, Article 15. Also see Ursinus, *Commentary on the Heidelberg Catechism*, 39-44.

before salvation every part of a person's being is corrupt. His mind is depraved (Titus 1:15), his emotions are corrupt (Rom 1:26-27), his will is corrupt (Jer 13:23) and his entire moral nature is polluted (Jer 17:9).

Arminius' teaching on total depravity, perhaps surprisingly, agrees with the Reformed view. In the section of his "Public Disputation" dealing with "The Free Will of Man and Its Powers," Arminius argues that an unsaved person is, in fact, totally depraved: "In this state, the free will of man towards the true good is not only wounded, maimed, infirm, bent, and weakened; but it is also imprisoned, destroyed, and lost. And its powers are not only debilitated and useless unless they are assisted by grace, but it has no powers whatever except such as are excited by Divine grace.[37]

A confirmed Calvinist would have to look hard to find something with which to disagree in this statement. Arminius adds that "nothing can be spoken more truly concerning man in this state, than that he is altogether dead in sin (Eph 2:1; Rom 3:10-19)."[38] Specifically, "the mind of man, in this state, is dark, destitute of saving knowledge of God, and according to the Apostle, incapable of those things which belong to the Spirit of God" (1 Cor 2:14).[39] For Arminius, such depravity also implies a doctrine of total inability. The will "is not free to do good, unless it be made free by the Son through His Spirit."[40] Clearly, there is nothing "softening" in this part of Arminius' doctrine of man.

The Doctrine of Grace

The softening of depravity, however, comes in Arminius' doctrine of grace. The standard Reformed doctrine of grace asserts that God has provided common grace that includes a general call to salvation, and efficacious grace that includes a special call only to the elect.[41] Common grace and the general call to salvation do not result in the salvation of anyone without efficacious grace and the special call.

Arminius, however, taught prevenient grace. Prevenient grace, sometimes called preventing grace, or sufficient grace, is an action of the Holy Spirit that

---

[37] Arminius, "Public Disputation," in *Arminius Speaks*, 3.

[38] Ibid., 5.

[39] Ibid.

[40] Ibid., 4.

[41] Ursinus, *Commentary on the Heidelberg Catechism*, 56.

neutralizes inherited depravity and corruption in all people.[42] Prevenient grace, according to Arminius, restores all sinners to a condition where they have sufficient ability to respond to the Gospel call. This essentially nullifies the doctrine of total depravity and inability by making it hypothetical. Prevenient grace thus paved the path for Arminius' softening of the Reformed doctrine of predestination.

The Doctrine of Predestination

Zacharias Ursinus defined predestination in the *Heidelberg Catechism* as most Reformed theologians would:

> The two parts of predestination are embraced in election and reprobation. Election is the eternal and unchangeable decree of God, by which he has graciously decreed to convert some to Christ, to preserve them in the faith, and repentance, and through him to bestow upon them eternal life. Reprobation is the eternal, and unchangeable purpose of God, whereby he has decreed in his most just judgement to leave some in their sins, to punish them with blindness, and to condemn them eternally, not being made partakers of Christ, and his benefits.[43]

This is unconditional election, which, for the Reformed, was not based on God's looking down the halls of time and seeing that someone would believe if given a chance. Ursinus adds, "Our faith, or holiness, therefore, which was foreseen is not the cause, but the effect of our election in Christ."[44] "The efficient and moving cause of predestination is the good pleasure of God."[45]

In Arminius' view, however, strict predestination was a new doctrine not taught in the creeds of the early church nor in the earlier Protestant confessions. It attacked God's wisdom, justice and goodness, he said, because it pictures God as willing evil to His creatures. Strict predestination also abuses mankind, compromising his being created in the image and likeness of God with free will. Even the doctrine of creation is undermined because God creates what is

---

[42] The term, "preventive" grace," come from the old English word that meant "precede." An example of this is found in the King James Version translation of 1 Thessalonians 4:15: "We which are alive and remain until the coming of the Lord will not prevent them which are asleep."

[43] Ursinus, *Commentary on the Heidelberg Catechism,* 297.

[44] Ibid., 299.

[45] Ibid., 297.

reprobate, and supralapsarianism makes God the author of sin. Moreover, since Jesus is not involved in this decree, strict predestination cannot be the foundation of election.[46]

Arminius also argues that the decree of unconditional election and reprobation has distressing practical consequences. It encourages Christian ministers to be lazy and negligent and implies that God will save some people whether they seek for Him or not. It takes away a desire for a Christian to do good works and even "extinguishes the zeal for prayer."[47]

Instead, for Arminius, the decrees of God regarding salvation proceed through four steps. First, God decreed "to appoint His Son, Jesus Christ, as Mediator, Redeemer, Savior, Priest and King."[48] Second, God decreed to accept for salvation those who repent and believe in Christ, but to reject into eternal condemnation all the impenitent and unbelievers. Third, God decreed to provide the means by which a sinner is convicted of his sins and brought to a point of faith. Fourth, God made His decisions about whom to elect and whom to reprobate on the basis of His foreknowledge, "by which he knew from all eternity those individuals who would through his preventing grace, believe, and, through his subsequent grace would persevere ...; and, by which foreknowledge, he likewise knew those who would not believe and persevere."[49] This doctrine is known as "conditional election" because God's choices are conditioned on the free will decisions of human beings that God knows will be made in earth time.

The Rejection of Arminius' Theology

Arminius died from tuberculosis on October 19, 1609, at about the age of fifty. He was survived by his wife of about forty years of age and nine children. He had been involved in many debates with Reformed theologians and the debates did not subside after his death. Simon Episcopius assumed the leadership of the Arminian pastors and theologians.

Since the Reformed faith was the state church of Holland, the States of Holland invited the Arminians to present an analysis of the Reformed Confession

---

[46] Arminius, "A Declaration of the Sentiments of James Arminius," Part 1, in *Arminius Speaks*, 36-47. See also, James Arminius, *The Works of James Arminius* (3 vols.), translated by James and William Nichols (Nashville: Randall House, 2007, reprinted from the London Edition), I: 621-45.

[47] Arminius, "A Declaration of the Sentiments of James Arminius," Part 1, in *Arminius Speaks*, 47-49.

[48] Ibid., 63.

[49] Arminius, "A Declaration of the Sentiments of James Arminius," Part 2, in *Arminius Speaks*, 64.

and Catechism. The Arminian document was known as the "Remonstrance of 1610" and was signed by more than forty ministers. They proposed five points summarized as follows:

1. God's decree of election and reprobation are conditional based on foreseen faith.

2. Christ died for all people, "yet so that no one actually enjoys the forgiveness of sins except the believer."

3. Regeneration by the Holy Spirit is necessary to salvation.

4. Grace is resistible.

5. The perseverance of believers in the faith cannot be positively affirmed or denied. [50]

Eventually, the debate between the Arminian Remonstrants and the Calvinist Counter-Remonstrants climaxed at the Synod of Dort, held at Dordrecht, 1618-1619. The Remonstrants were not seated at the synod but were treated as accused heretics. The Counter-Remonstrants presented their five-point summary as follows:

1. The decrees of election and reprobation are absolute and unconditional (unconditional election).

2. Although Christ's death is sufficient to expiate the sins of the whole world, God eternally intended the atonement to be applied only to the elect (usually limited atonement).

3. The total inability of mankind to respond to the Gospel necessitates the regenerating work of the Holy Spirit (total inability—regeneration logically precedes faith).

4. God's call is effectual, and hence His grace is irresistible (irresistible grace).

5. Those who are elected and called will respond to the Gospel and cannot lose their salvation (perseverance of the saints). [51]

---

[50] "The Remonstrance," in *The Creeds of Christendom*, vol. I, ed. Philip Schaff (New York: Harper and Brothers; repr., Grand Rapids: Baker, 1977), 516-17.

[51] Ibid., 517-23

The Counter-Remonstrants doctrinal presentation easily won the day, and the Arminian theology was condemned. The Arminians were forbidden to preach, some were imprisoned, and many had to leave the country. Eventually the Arminians formed themselves into a separate denomination known as the Remonstrant Brotherhood, or the Remonstrant Reformed Church.

So, what should we conclude? Did Arminius succeed in softening the doctrine of predestination? The answer is "no" and "yes." No, he failed in the seventeenth century to soften the doctrine of predestination in the Dutch Reformed Church. Yes, Arminius (perhaps along with theologians in the Anabaptist tradition) blazed a trail for seventeenth-century Anglicans such as Bishop Laud (1573-1645), the General Baptists and The New Connection General Baptists in England, as well as John Wesley and the Methodists in the eighteenth century. Eventually Arminian theology spread almost world-wide. Few people in the history of the church have had the honor of having their names attached to a wide-spread theological system.

Softening the Doctrine of the Atonement

The doctrine of the extent of the atonement was another potentially dividing issue at the Synod of Dort. In broad terms, the question was, Did Christ die for the entire world (unlimited or general atonement)—the Arminian view? Or did He die only for the elect (limited or particular or definite atonement)—the Reformed view? Or perhaps there was a third or fourth middle explanation.

John Calvin's Perspective

John Calvin, who died fifty-four years before the Synod of Dort, did not speak explicitly to the issue of the extent of the atonement, and theologians have eagerly debated what Calvin's view was. There are at least two issues that complicate the question. One is that there are clearly universalistic statements in Scripture about the extent of the atonement (1 Tim 2:6) and at the same time particularistic statements about Christ loving the church and giving himself up (only?) for her (Eph 5:25). Calvin speaks to the impact of both Biblical concepts in his commentaries. So, as one Calvin specialist points out, "It is possible to assemble a collection of sentences where Calvin writes in universal terms about Christ being the Savior of the world and of his dying for all men and women, and a second collection of sentences which go the other way, which stress the particularistic focused scope of Christ's atonement."[52]

The second complicating issue is that the first-generation of Reformers had not specifically structured limited atonement into a distinct doctrine. In other words, had we asked John Calvin whether or not he believed in limited atonement, we might have had to explain specifically what we meant by "limited atonement." Calvin no doubt knew of the explanation of the twelfth century Roman Catholic scholastic theologian, Peter Lombard, that Christ offered himself for all as far as the sufficiency of the price is concerned, but, as far as efficacy is concerned, for the elect only.[53] Philip Schaff quotes Calvin as saying, Christ died *"sufficienter pro omnibus, efficaciter pro electis."*[54] But this statement itself has more than one interpretation. Since we cannot ask Calvin about his view, and since "he did not avow it in express terms, but neither did he deny it,"[55] we are compelled to deduce his understanding of the extent of the atonement from the rest of his theology, and thus the difficulty of answering the question.

The Remonstrant (Arminian) Doctrine of the Atonement

Regardless of Calvin's view, the international gathering of theologians at the Synod of Dort (1618) rejected the Remonstrant (Arminian) view that stated that "Jesus Christ, the Saviour of the world, died for all men and for every man, so that he has obtained for them all, by his death on the cross, redemption and the forgiveness of sins; yet that no one actually enjoys this forgiveness of sins except the believer...."[56] It is difficult to know exactly what "sufficient for all" meant to the Arminian theologians. Did it mean "effective for all, unless a person rejects it"?

---

[52] Paul Helm, "Calvin, Indefinite Language, and Definite Atonement," in *From Heaven He Came and Sought Her*, 99. This book contains seven excellent historical essays about definite atonement.

[53] Peter Lombard was Bishop of Paris and the author of the standard theology text of that era, *Four Books of Sentences.*

[54] "The Canons of Dort," in *The Creeds of Christendom*, vol. I, ed. Philip Schaff (New York: Harper and Brothers; repr., Grand Rapids: Baker, 1977), 518.

[55] Helm, "Calvin, Indefinite Language, and Definite Atonement," 98. Helm, for example, concludes that Calvin did believe in what later was called definite (or limited or particular) atonement (119). Others have concluded that Calvin's doctrine of soteriology and methodology of studying theology did not lead to definite atonement. This is the view, for example, of Brian G. Armstrong, *Calvinism and the Amyraut Heresy* (Madison, WI: The University of Wisconsin Press, 1969). Armstrong writes, "it would seem that the position is untenable which holds that Calvin teaches Christ died for the elect only" (138, n. 58).

[56] *The Five Arminian Articles*, Article II.

The Counter-Remonstrants Reformed apparently understood this to be the Arminian view, that Christ's death was sufficient for all, was intended for all, and was realized for all in some sense. The atonement, therefore, paid for the sins of all people. Lee Gatiss writes, "This takes the first part of the Lombardian formula ('sufficient for all, effective for the elect') but pushes it further. Not only was the cross sufficient but it was also effective in paying for each and every person, and indeed was designed by God to do so."[57]

These followers of Arminius did not mean by this that everyone went to heaven (though some later distant followers of Arminius became universalists). They meant that though Christ's death had paid for everyone's sins, unless a sinner believed, he would squander that payment for his sins. Some followers of this Arminian doctrine have logically concluded that repentance is not necessary since a person's sins were already paid for. Unbelief becomes the "unpardonable sin" and is the only real reason anyone goes to hell. Combining this view of the atonement with the Arminians' denial of unconditional election made this view completely unacceptable to the Counter-Remonstrants at Dort. They rejected those who teach that God "has been minded to apply to all equally the benefits gained by the death of Christ; but that, while some obtain the pardon of sin and eternal life, and others do not, this difference depends on their own free will, which joins itself to the grace that is offered without exception...."[58]

The Counter-Remonstrant (Calvinist) Statement of the Atonement

The Reformed Counter-Remonstrants at the Synod of Dort dealt extensively with the atonement of Christ as "the only and most perfect sacrifice and satisfaction for sin."[59] The so-called "five points of Calvinism" began (in a different arrangement of the points at Dort than which we might be familiar) in point number one with an affirmation and explanation of unconditional election. Point number two expounded the "The Death of Christ, and the Redemption of Men Thereby." In their explanation of the atonement, the Dort theologians declared:

---

[57] Lee Gatiss, "The Synod of Dort and Definite Atonement," in *From Heaven He Came and Sought Her*, 149

[58] See *Canons* of Dort, "Rejection of Errors," Second Head, Paragraph 6. This statement is also a rejection of the Arminian doctrine of sufficient grace. See also Paragraph 1 and Paragraph 5.

[59] *Canons of Dort*, Second Head, Article 3.

> For this was the sovereign counsel and most gracious will and purpose of God the Father that the quickening and saving efficacy of the most precious death of His Son should extend to all the elect, for bestowing upon them alone the gift of justifying faith, thereby to bring them infallibly to salvation; that is, it was the will of God that Christ by the blood of the cross, whereby He confirmed the New Covenant, should effectually redeem out of every people, tribe, nation, and language, all those, and those only, who were from eternity chosen to salvation and given Him by the Father.[60]

At first glance this declaration may look like limited or particular atonement and no doubt could be interpreted as such. But the question is, does this statement affirm *only* limited atonement? Or could it be interpreted in another way?

Though these Counter-Remonstrants declared that "the quickening and saving efficacy of the most precious death of His Son should extend to all the elect," and that the atonement should "effectually redeem ... those only, who were from eternity chosen to salvation," the declaration is somewhat curious because it could have been stated more strongly than it was. Every non-Arminian at Dort could agree that "saving *efficacy*" extended only to the elect. But the question, "Is Christ's death hypothetically *available* for every person, elect and non-elect?" was not specifically answered. Indeed, a person who did not believe in particular redemption, as it is almost always understood, could agree with this article because it clarifies only the *application* of the atonement, *not the availability* of it.

In another part of their explanation of the atonement, the Dort Counter-Remonstrants explained that "the death of the Son of God ... is of infinite worth and value, abundantly sufficient to expiate the sins of the whole world."[61] Thus the atonement was "sufficient for all, but efficient only for the elect." The Dort theologians further took pains to explain that "the promise of the gospel is that whosoever believes in Christ crucified shall not perish, but have eternal life," and that "the command to repent and believe, ought to be declared and published to all nations, and to all persons promiscuously and without distinction, to whom God out of His good pleasure sends the gospel."[62] Actually, many "four-point Calvinists" can agree with Dort's statements on the extent of the

---

[60] Ibid., Second Head, Article 8.

[61] Ibid., Second Head, Article 3.

[62] Ibid., Second Head, Article 5.

atonement. Lee Gatiss suggests, "Perhaps, then, others who take a less 'strict,' non-Genevan view on this issue may also lay claim, historically speaking, to all five petals of the TULIP (though not in the oversimplified way this is sometimes defined)."[63]

Hypothetical Universalism at the Synod of Dort

A third, moderating view, was promoted behind the scenes, especially by some of the British delegates to Dort.[64] When the Synod of Dort was held, King James I (1566-1625) had been on the throne for about fifteen years. James chose six delegates to attend the international conference at Dort and gave them nine points of instruction. In summary, James told the English delegates (1) To brush up on Latin so that they could speak with clarity at the Synod; (2) that they should discuss the theological questions among themselves; (3) that they should discuss a matter among themselves if some new question came up before speaking to it; (4) that they should advise the theologians at Dort not to speak to these hard questions with the common people in their churches; (5) that they should not promote any new doctrine; (6) that they should try to conform to other Reformed churches; (7) that they should try to moderate between mean-spirited debates; (8) that they remember to glorify God and keep in touch with the King through the English Ambassador; (9) that they should carry themselves with moderation and discretion.[65]

The impact of the English delegates was felt most strongly at Dort in the discussion of the extent of the atonement. The Arminian view had been dismissed, but the English delegates, especially John Davenant (1572-1641) argued for a view between Arminianism and limited atonement, a "sophisticated form of what is now known as Hypothetical Universalism."[66] Davenant, who was later to become the Lord Bishop of Salisbury, insisted that the doctrine

---

[63] Lee Gatiss, "The Synod of Dort and Definite Atonement," 163.

[64] One nineteenth century historian commented that "it was owing to the influence of the English divines that its sanctions were not given to the monstrous doctrine of Supralapsarian" (Robert Southey, in Morris Fuller, *The Life, Letters and Writings of John Davenant* [London: Methuen & Co., 1897], 109).

[65] Ibid., 74-6. Morris Fuller lived in the second half of the nineteenth century and was a descendent of the well-known church historian, Thomas Fuller (1608-1661). Morris Fuller quotes Thomas Fuller often in the biography of Davenant.

[66] Gatiss, "The Synod of Dort and Definite Atonement," 155. See further the extensive study by Moore, *English Hypothetical Universalism*. The subtitle, "John Preston and the Softening of Reformed Theology," illustrates the softening of scholastic Calvinism that this chapter is describing. Moore discusses John Davenant's Hypothetical Universalism in detail, 187-213.

of a general redemption, different from the Arminian doctrine, "be admitted into the decrees or else withdraw from the Synod." Morris Fuller, Davenant's biographer adds, "However, the doctrine of Redemption as a blessing to be universally proposed and offered to all men, was so little relished by the Synod of Dort, that it is clear, nothing but the threatened loss of the English deputies induced its assertion."[67] Davenant was so committed to his view of the atonement that he said that he would sooner cut off his hand than to change his view. This is one of the main reasons why Dort's declaration on the atonement was not stated in a way that only those who believed in particular redemption could agree to it. Fuller opines, however, that the British delegates' "labours in softening the synodal decrees ... had rendered them objects of suspicion to many in the synod."[68]

So, if it were not Arminianism, what was the view that John Davenant promoted at Dort? As Gatiss pointed out above, it was Hypothetical Universalism, the teaching that "sufficient for all" means that God "desires all people to be saved" (1 Tim 2:4) and makes it possible in the universal provisions of the atonement of Christ for that to occur. There is even a sense in which the atonement may be at work through the Holy Spirit in hearts of the non-elect in preparing them for salvation, though in the end these will reject the Gospel."[69] So the atonement of Christ is available for every human being.

But still, Hypothetical Universalism is also founded on the decrees of unconditional election and reprobation. Like all delegates, Davenant was committed to Dort's statement of unconditional election. Samuel Ward, one of the British delegates to Dort, in a letter to Archbishop Ussher, noted that "On the 23rd April 1619, the Canons were signed by all members of the Synod. Arminians were pronounced heretics, schismatics, teachers of false doctrine."[70] For Davenant and some of the other English signers of the Dort Canons, therefore, Hypothetical Universalism combines a doctrine of universal provisions of the atonement with unconditional election.

Davenant illustrated hypothetical universalism in this way:

---

[67] Fuller, *Life, Letters and Writings of John Davenant*, 88.

[68] Ibid., 90.

[69] Moore, *English Hypothetical Universalism*, 191. We will discuss the doctrine of preparation in the next chapter.

[70] Quoted in Moore, *English Hypothetical Universalism*, 91.

Suppose that all the inhabitants of a certain city labored under some epidemic and moral disease; that the king sent to them an eminent physician furnished with a most efficacious medicine, and caused it to be publicly proclaimed, that all should be cured who were willing to make use of this medicine. Doubtless we might truly say of this king, that he so loved that city, as to send to his own most skillful physician to it; that all who were willing to attend to his advice, and take his medicine, should not die, but recover their former health. But if any should object that this physician was sent only to those who should follow *his* prescriptions, and that this medicine was applicable by the appointment of the king only to those who were willing to take it, he would in reality not only make the beneficence of the king appear less illustrious but affirm what was evidently false. For medical assistance was offered to all, without any previous condition on the part of the person sent, or of the sick; healing medicine applicable to all, without exception, was provided. The willingness to receive the physician and take the medicine had no connexion with the intention of the sovereign in sending the medical assistance, but with the certain restoration to health.[71]

Thus, the medicine of the atonement is available to all and intended for all.

On the other hand, the sons of Adam are totally depraved and therefore unable to respond to the offer of the Gospel. Indeed, the result of sinners' rejection of Christ's provision of salvation when it was available for them makes them "more unjust towards Christ,"[72] so that they are under a greater condemnation. But God, in His amazing grace, takes another action. "But lest the Blood of the Son of God should flow, and through the fault of the human will … that no one should enjoy the benefit of it, God resolved with Himself a more deep and secret counsel, and determined of His mere and special ministry to give to some persons the ability and will to fulfill the aforesaid condition of faith."[73] Hypothetical Universalism therefore asserts that the preacher can say to "any individual," "God so loved thee, that he gave his only begotten Son, that if thou shouldest believe in him, thou shalt not perish but have everlasting life."[74] But it also asserts the doctrine of unconditional election is necessary for any to benefit from the atonement.

[71] Quoted in Fuller, *Life, Letters and Writings of John Davenant*, 232.

[72] John Davenant, "On the Death of Christ" (1627), quoted in Fuller, *Life, Letters and Writings of John Davenant*, 235.

[73] Ibid., 234.

[74] John Davenant, "A Dissertation," II:344, quoted in Moore, *English Hypothetical Universalism*, 201.

There were other seventeenth-century English theologians who held to a similar soteriology. James Ussher (1581-1656), the Bishop of Armagh, and John Preston (1587–1628) an Anglican clergyman (with some Puritan leanings) and master of Emmanuel College, Cambridge, "embraced a remarkable similar system of theology with regard to predestination, the death of Christ, and the call of the gospel...."[75] Both Ussher and Preston, like Davenant, employed the illustration of the medicine that was available to all, but made effective only to those who accepted it.[76] Clearly, there was more diversity at Dort among the Counter-Remonstrant theologians than what we sometimes think. Some of this diversity led to a softening of High Calvinism.

French Amyraldism

The French Reformed version of Hypothetical Universalism is often called Amyraldism after its most influential proponent, Moise Amyraut (1596-1664). The Reformed Church in France only had a brief time when its pastors and professors were free to meet and discuss theological matters. Toleration for the French Reformed Church began in 1598 when Henry IV issued the Edict of Nantes. Though most of France was Roman Catholic, the Edict granted the Protestants the right to co-exist. When Louis XIV revoked the Edict in 1685, most of the leading Protestants were forced to leave France or be imprisoned or worse. Thus, the debates over Hypothetical Universalism in France were a part of the theological scene from the 1620's until the Revocation of the Edict of Nantes and focused especially on the Reformed academy at Saumur.

The first important theologian at Saumur to teach a form of Hypothetical Universalism and to raise concerns among some of the French Reformed theologians was a Scottish theologian, John Cameron (1579-1625).[77] Cameron

---

[75] Moore discusses Bishop Ussher's Hypothetical Universalism, *English Hypothetical Universalism*, 175-86.

[76] Preston and Ussher both quoted a disciple of Augustine, Prosper of Aquitaine (c. 390-c.455), who used this illustration. Interestingly, the medicine illustration parallels the story in Numbers 21:4-9 of the bronze serpent, and then later employed by Jesus Christ in John 3:14 to explain His substitutionary atonement.

[77] Cameron was born in Glasgow, received his college education at Glasgow where he taught Greek, and then relocated to France where he taught at the Collège de Bergerac and the Protestant Academy of Sedan (1602-1603). He also did further study at Paris and Geneva, and then at Heidelberg where he defended his thesis on the divine covenants. From 1618-1621 or 1622, he taught at the Academy of Saumur back in France until Louis XIII repealed the right of foreigners to teach theology. In 1622-1623, he served as a professor of theology at Glasgow under the appointment of King James I. He returned to France the next year resuming his professorship at Saumur after Louis changed his mind, and then moved to the academy at Montauban in 1624. He was beaten and killed in a riot in 1625. See Richard Muller, "Divine Covenants, Absolute and Conditional: John Cameron and the Early Orthodox Development of Reformed Covenant Theology," *Mid-America Journal of Theology* 17 (2006):13. See his footnotes for further sources. Muller says that it was a riot against Protestants (14), and

believed that the decree to redeem the world in Christ is first universal and available for every person. Potentially, God has redeemed every human being in the world. This decree is followed by the decree to give faith to the elect; a third decree which renders sinners capable of believing; and a fourth decree that "is to save those who believe."[78] Cameron knew that the decrees are one in God. But God had explicated His decree in steps to help us who live in time understand them.[79] Though criticized and occasionally charged with heresy because of emphasis on the universal availability of the atonement, Cameron's theology was judged orthodox and within the guidelines of the Synod of Dort. Richard Muller, after an extensive, detailed study of Cameron's covenant system, concludes that the views of Cameron and his followers at Saumur were not heretical and, "like it or not, were consciously framed to stand within the confessionalism of the Canons of Dort."[80]

The most important student and follower of John Cameron was Moise Amyraut. The theological system that he developed is often called Amyraldism after an English translation of his name. Amyraut was born in 1596 in Bourgueil, France, not far from Saumur where he would minister most of his life. He was preparing for a career in law when a pastor encouraged him to think about the ministry. After reading through John Calvin's *Institutes of the Christian Religion*, Amyraut, with the reluctant agreement of his father, arrived at the Reformed Academy of Saumur at about the same time as did John Cameron. Later, in 1633, Amyraut was appointed to the Chair of Theology at Saumur and served there until his death in 1664. He is described as a somewhat cosmopolitan person who was a friend of the governor of Saumur, visited and interacted with Cardinal Richelieu, and who could represent the Reformed faith with distinction to the nobility.[81]

Armstrong suggests that it was a riot conducted by Protestants against royalists (Brian G. Armstrong, *Calvinism and the Amyraut Heresy*, 70).

[78] John Cameron, Letter of Dec., 1610, *Opera*, 531, quoted in Armstrong, *Calvinism and the Amyraut Heresy*, 58.

[79] Armstrong, *Calvinism and the Amyraut Heresy*, 58.

[80] Richard Muller, "Divine Covenants, Absolute and Conditional," 36.

[81] Armstrong, *Calvinism and the Amyraut Heresy*, 72. In 1634, Amyraut published *Brief Traitté de la Predestination et de ses principales dependances* (*Short Treatise on Predestination*), followed in the succeeding months by two other works defending his main thesis, *Six Sermons*, and *Eschantillon de la Doctrine de Calvin Touchant la Predestination*, "the latter being an argument for his faithfulness to John Calvin." Amyraut wrote his *Brief Traitté* in order to explain the doctrine to a gentleman that he had met who was shocked and horrified by predestination. Amyraut thus emphasizes God's grace and mercy.

Though he taught the standard doctrine of predestination, Amyraut presented a doctrine of two different kinds of decrees in God, somewhat like Cameron. One kind was conditional and required a response from humans. God conditionally decreed to make the atoning benefits of Christ's death available to all if they would believe. Christ died equally for all mankind. In the second kind of decree, God unconditionally decreed some matters based on His sovereign pleasure. Therefore, God decrees that the elect willingly and not begrudgingly will come to Christ based on the preaching of the Gospel and the internal, efficacious drawing by the Holy Spirit.[82]

Amyraut's ideas, however, ignited a firestorm in the French Reformed camp. A heresy trial to deal with Amyraut's theology (as well as Cameron's) was held in 1637 at the national Synod of Alençon. Four points of Amyraut's theology were analyzed: (1) the order of the decrees; (2) the sending of Jesus Christ for all universally; (3) the universality and sufficiency of the grace presented to all; (4) original sin and moral and natural ability.[83] In the end, the council required Amyraut to make a few adjustments in the way that he explained his beliefs such as not to teach that Christ died for all equally because that was confusing to some people. But other than these minor corrections, Amyraut was judged to be orthodox and was honorably dismissed.

After his death, the Swiss Reformed Church in their Formula Consensus Helvetica (1675) rejected Amyraut's softer interpretations of John Calvin's theology as well as the declarations on the atonement at the Synod of Dort. The Swiss theologians declared that Amyraut's teachings "and all other similar teachings are in no way insignificant deviations from the proper teaching concerning divine election; because the Scriptures do not extend unto all and each God's purpose of showing mercy to man, but restrict it to the elect alone, the reprobate being excluded even by name, as Esau, whom God hated with an eternal hatred (Rom 9:11).[84]

On the other hand, as Amar Djaballah observes,

---

[82] Amar Djaballah, "Controversy on Universal Grace," in *From Heaven He Came and Sought Her*, 186. Djaballah is explaining chapter eleven of the *Brief Traitté*.

[83] Armstrong, *Calvinism and the Amyraut Heresy*, 91.

[84] Canon five, "Formula Consensus Helvetica." Amyraut believed that to say that Christ did not in any way die for the reprobate would be to give them an excuse when they stood at the judgment seat.

We should remember that Amyraut wrote as a professor of theology in a confessional Reformed academy and that he was cleared of accusations of heresy by a national synod and allowed to teach theology until his death. ... [He] should be studied as a member of the Reformed theological community with whom one may differ, not as an adversary to silence.[85]

For our twenty-first century theological situation, the question is whether "Hypothetical Universalists today are as careful to avoid the slippery slope of Arminianism as the British at Dort were, and whether the Reformed are as willing now as they were at Dort to tolerate a certain amount of diversity within their robust internal debates" (163).[86]

It is good to be reminded, having surveyed these intense doctrinal debates over election, eternal security, and the extent of the atonement, that the scholastic theologians were godly men, concerned about the spiritual welfare of their people, defining theology as "living blessedly forever," and writing books on how to live out the Christian faith as a truly redeemed Christian. In other words, they were not the hard-bitten, cold, philosophers that they are sometimes made out to be.[87] Most of these theologians who identified with Reformed theology—of whatever shade—no doubt believed that they were simply trying to teach the inspired Word.[88]

GOD'S SOVEREIGN ELECTION OF ISRAEL

Perhaps it would not be fair to expect that the Reformed theologians would include a section in their creeds about the future conversion and regathering of Israel to her land. We know that there was an increasing number of Reformed

---

[85] Djaballah, "Controversy on Universal Grace," 167.

[86] Gatiss, "The Synod of Dort and Definite Atonement," 163.

[87] As we have learned from observing the Reformed leaders' antagonism toward the Anabaptists, it would not have been pleasant for those of us whose church tradition is baptistic to exist in some of these Reformed and Lutheran state-church environments.

[88] Amyraut claimed that this was his goal: "No, my brethren, when on the one hand the Word of God will teach me that He has reprobated some and consigned them to eternal punishment, and that on the other hand this same Word will teach me that God wills all men to be saved, that He goes before them and calls them with a lively voice ... although my reason found there some things which seemed to be in conflict, although whatever effort that I exert I am not able to harmonize or reconcile them, still I will not fail to hold these two doctrines as true. Nor will I undertake to resolve the opposition of these two wills of God which seem so repugnant. Either God will someday give us greater illumination of His Spirit, or at least in the appearance of His Son He will manifest all things. However, I will keep what He has revealed to me, and I will not permit that the presumption ... of my reason do any injury to His unspeakable grace toward men." (Amyraut, *Six Sermons*, quoted in Armstrong, *Calvinism and the Amyraut Heresy*, 184.)

theologians who believed this. As William Watson has demonstrated, "It was not until the Reformation and the publication of the Geneva Bible (1557) and subsequently the King James Bible (1611) in England that Christians began to read those Jewish Scriptures for themselves. In doing so, they began to believe once again the promises God had made to the Jews."[89] But the Reformed theologians were on a mission. They needed to publish creeds and books that could serve as apologetics against the Lutherans and Roman Catholics. God's sovereign election of Israel was not a part of that debate.

The election of national Israel, nevertheless, parallels individual election in significant ways. At the beginning of the history of Israel, Abram was minding his own business in Ur of the Chaldees while worshipping a pagan god. When God sovereignly chose Abraham and called him out of his land, He promised to make Abraham the father of a great nation, and make his name great, and bless him, and to bless those who bless him, and curse those who dishonor him (Gen 12:2-3). In the English text, God repeats several times, "I will."

Later in Israel's history, God explains why He chose Israel:

> The LORD your God has chosen you to be a people for his treasured possession, out of all the peoples who are on the face of the earth. It was not because you were more in number than any other people that the LORD set his love on you and chose you, for you were the fewest of all peoples, but it is because the LORD loves you and is keeping the oath that he swore to your fathers, that the LORD has brought you out with a mighty hand and redeemed you from the house of slavery, from the hand of Pharaoh king of Egypt (Deut 7:6-8).

God did not choose Israel to be His covenant people for any quality that He found in them. Rather, He loved them because He loved them. This is unconditional election.

The terms for God's sovereign election are also used for both individuals and corporate Israel. Elect individuals are "chosen" (Rom 16:13; Col 3:12; 1 Thess 1:4); Israel is a "chosen" nation (Deut 7:6, et. al.). God "foreknows" men and women to salvation (Rom 8:29); God "foreknew" Israel (Rom 11:2).

---

[89] William C. Watson, *Dispensationalism Before Darby* (Silverton, OR: Lampion, 2015), 13. This book is an important history of the many theologians in England and other Protestant nations who taught and wrote about the future conversion of Israel and her return to the land.

Likewise, in Romans 8-9, Paul explains God's election of national Israel in parallel with His election of individuals to salvation.

God, furthermore, preserves the nation of Israel even as he does a redeemed Christian. The Old Testament is saturated with the prophets' teaching that though God will judge Israel, He will ultimately bring her back to Himself (see Ezek 37-39; Zech 12-14, for examples). In the New Testament, likewise, Paul proclaims that "God has not rejected His people whom He foreknew" (Rom 11:2). Israel's preservation as God's elect nation is just as sure as our election to eternal life.

CONCLUSION

Theologians in the scholastic era had a different responsibility from the pioneer Reformers such as Martin Luther and Ulrich Zwingli. Many of the scholastics served on the faculties of universities where they had the opportunity and duty, they thought, to focus their academic energies on systematizing their theology in intricate detail. The rise of covenant theology was an important part of this endeavor, and so was the determination to produce an air-tight logical doctrine of salvation that featured predestination and unconditional election. At the same time, there were also a counter-efforts from within Reformed Christianity to modify and soften these doctrines, particularly by those who became known as Arminians, Hypothetical Universalists, and Amyraldists. Though it should have been apparent that the election and preservation of a person to salvation was parallel with the election and preservation of Israel as God's elect nation, the Reformation documents excluded Israel from eschatology.

5

COVENANTALISM: READING ISRAEL OUT OF THE BIBLICAL COVENANTS

Larry D. Pettegrew

Scholastic Calvinism described a stern deity who seemed to some to be sovereignly unrestrained in His relationship with mankind. As we saw in the previous chapter, Arminians, Hypothetical Universalists, and Amyraldists developed possible ways to soften the doctrines of unconditional election and limited atonement. Depending on one's perspective, such attempts were or were not necessary, and were or were not successful. In this chapter we survey two more modifications in seventeenth-century Reformed covenant theology that focused on man's role in the plan of salvation and consequently lessened the concerns about unconditional election. The first adjustment spotlighted the doctrine of conversion and focused on the process of how God prepares a depraved sinner, dead in trespasses and sins, to repent and believe in Jesus Christ as his Savior and Lord. The second adjustment centered on the addition of a third theological covenant to covenant theology. Though both of these tweaks suggest a friendlier and less mysterious picture of God, neither should be understood as departing from the theological canons of the Synod of Dort or the Reformed creeds.

THE PREPARATION FOR CONVERSION

If a human being is totally depraved and dead in trespasses and sins, how does an elect sinner come to the place where he or she accepts the Gospel? Richard Muller, tongue in cheek, describes hyper-Calvinists' view of "God's electing grace as an unmediated bolt from the blue. No one knows where it may strike and no one can find any assurance either through participation in the life of God's covenanting people or on grounds of belief or conduct that he or she will be or, indeed, is now numbered among the elect."[1] Since God is all-powerful, the Holy Spirit could sovereignly and irresistibly "sweep aside such obstacles and bring the sinner immediately to faith, but that is not the Spirit's usual or ordinary way."[2] So, what is the Spirit's usual way?

The Underlying Theology of Preparation

The answer to this question falls under the heading of what has often been called, "preparation" for salvation. In scholastic Reformed theology, preparation involved both God's part and man's part. God's part was His calling of the sinner to Himself. Reformed theologians taught that there is a general, outward call that goes out to the whole world, as when Jesus said, "Come to me, all who labor and are heavy laden, and I will give you rest" (Matt 11:28). According to seventeenth century Reformed theologian Herman Witsius, "The external call is in some measure published by the words of nature, but more fully by that of supernatural revelation without which every word of nature would be insufficient and ineffectual."[3] The general call is thus composed of general revelation and the proclamation, in one way or another, of the gospel message.

---

[1] Richard A. Muller, "How many Points?" *Calvin Theological Journal* 28:2 (November 1993), 428. To be clear, Muller is himself a Reformed theologian. Muller argues in this article that one cannot legitimately describe himself as "Reformed," unless he believes in all of doctrines taught in the historic creeds such as "the baptism of infants, the identification of sacraments as means of grace, and the unity of the one covenant of grace from Abraham to the eschaton … that the church is both visible and invisible—that it is a covenant people of God identified not by externalized indication of the work of God in individuals, such as adult conversion experiences but by the preaching of the word of God and the right administration of the sacraments." He also adds belief in amillennialism as a requirement for being able to call oneself "Reformed" (427). If this claim be true, Baptists cannot call themselves "Reformed."

[2] Joel E. Beeke and Paul M. Smalley, *Prepared by Grace, for Grace: The Puritans on God's Way of Leading Sinners to Christ* (Grand Rapids: Reformation Heritage Books, 2013), 9. This book is an excellent resource and provides excellent guidance in understanding how the Reformed theologians, particularly the Puritans, understood the doctrine of preparation of a sinner for salvation. Beeke and Smalley chose not to use the terms "preparationism" or "preparationist" because they believe that these terms imply an emphasis on free will, which the sixteenth-century Reformed theologians did not want to emphasize. So they use the term "preparation," "prepared," and "prepares," as in *God* "prepares" the sinner for salvation (4); thus the title of the book, *Prepared by Grace for Grace.*

[3] Herman Witsius, *The Economy of the Covenants Between God and Man* (London: R. Baynes, 1822; original Latin version, 1677; repr., Kingsburg, CA: den Dulk, Christian Foundation, 1990), 176.), III.V.VII:345-46.

The Inner Call

There is also a special, inner efficacious call from the Holy Spirit in which He works in an effective way with the elect sinner, not only enabling him or her to respond to the message of the gospel, but also making it certain that he or she will respond. In Jesus' words, "All that the Father gives me will come to me, and whoever comes to me I will never cast out" (John 6:37); and "No one can come to me unless the Father who sent me draws him. And I will raise him up on the last day" (John 6:44). Witsius explains, "The internal call comes from the power of the Holy Spirit working inwardly on the heart, and without this, every external revealed word though objectively very sufficient, … yet is subjectively ineffective."[4] God's revelation of the gospel in the Scriptures, in other words, is objectively sufficient to bring a sinner to Christ. But for the Scriptures to accomplish salvation, the Holy Spirit must make them effective through the inner, special call. Thus, "those whom he predestined he also called, and those whom he called he also justified" (Rom 8:30). Preparation for salvation is consequently under the sovereign control of God in Reformed thought.

Gracious Predispositions

Man's part is described in Scripture as conversion and involves the sinner repenting of his sin and believing the gospel. But even in conversion, the Holy Spirit is sovereignly involved. As Beeke and Smalley say, "Thus preparation is not our hearts opening themselves by our own power to let the Spirit enter, but rather, the Spirit opening our hearts by His power so that He may come in."[5]

As a kind of preface to the efficacious call whereby the sinner is brought to regeneration, therefore, the Holy Spirit generates gracious predispositions such as fear, sorrow, regret, humility, and shame in the elect sinner, softening and convicting him of his need of a Savior and leading him to repent and believe. The English Puritan Thomas Watson adds,

> Before this effectual call, a humbling work passes upon the soul. A man is convinced of sin, he sees he is a sinner and nothing but a sinner; the fallow ground of his heart is broken up. Jer iv.3. As the husband-man breaks the clods, then casts in the seed; so God, by the convincing work of the law, breaks a sinner's heart, and

---

4 Ibid.

5 Beeke and Smalley, *Prepared by Grace*, 45.

makes it fit to receive the seeds of grace. Such as were never convinced are never called.... Conviction is the first step in conversion.[6]

Both the sinner and his pastor need to look for these humbling dispositions to determine the state of the pre-conversion process.[7]

Preaching the Law

The Reformed pastor's responsibility in preparing a sinner for salvation begins with the preaching of the law. John Calvin, for example, writing about "men whom the law leads by its tutelage to Christ," describes those who "are too full of their own virtue of assurance of their own righteousness, they are not fit to receive Christ's grace unless they first be emptied. Therefore, through the recognition of their own misery, the law brings them down to humility in order thus to prepare them to seek what previously they did not realize they lacked."[8]

Other Reformers, as well as the Reformation creeds and catechisms, taught that the preaching of the Old Testament law was an important step in bringing a sinner to Christ. Question 115 of the Heidelberg Catechism asks, "Why will God then have the ten commands so strictly preached, since no man in this life can keep them?" Zacharias Ursinus, in his commentary on this question, replies:

The law accuses, convinces, and condemns all those who are not regenerated, because they are unrighteous before God and subject to eternal condemnation. ... The use of the law, which consists in a knowledge of sin, and of the judgment of God against sin, produces in itself in the unregenerate hatred of God, and an increase of sin, and if they are reprobate it drives them into despair.... This knowledge of sin, however, is by an accident *a preparation to conversion* as it respects the elect, seeing that God by this means leads and constrains them to acknowledge

---

[6] Thomas Watson, *A Body of Divinity* (1692; repr., London: Banner of Truth, 1974), 224. Seventeenth-century Reformed theologians believed that Scriptures such as Mark 12:34, Acts 2:37, and Galatians 3:24 gave credence to the doctrine of preparation.

[7] For three seventeenth-century Puritan sermons on conversion, see *The Puritans on Conversion*, ed. Don Kistler (Morgan, PA: Soli Deo Gloria Publications, 1990). The three sermons included are "Sin—The Greatest Evil," by Samuel Bolton; "The Conversion of a Sinner," by Nathaniel Vincent; and "The One Thing Necessary," by Thomas Watson.

[8] John Calvin, *Institutes of the Christian Religion*, ed. John T. McNeill, trans. Ford Lewis Battles (Philadelphia: Westminster), II.VII.11:359.

their unrighteousness, to despair of any help in themselves, and to seek by faith righteousness and life in Christ the mediator.[9]

Preaching the law is therefore necessary before a person can be converted.

Reformed theologians were not the first to think about preparing the sinner for salvation, of course. There are many illustrations of this doctrine in the conversion experiences of famous people in church history. The conversion of Augustine as told in his *Confessions* is an example of the steps one may go through to come to salvation. Martin Luther's conversion is another illustration. In line with these examples, most Reformation and scholastic Reformed theologians taught that there is some preparation of the sinner for salvation through the impact of the Old Testament law.

The Puritans' Systematization of Preparation

The English and American Puritans explored the doctrine of preparation in more detail than had other Reformed theologians. They were heirs of Reformed Pietism, so they were concerned about the issues involved in a person's experience of salvation.[10] Moreover, the American Puritans had decided at the beginning of their arrival in New England that only those who could narrate an experience of salvation could be a member of a church. This in effect was a requirement not only for church membership but also for involvement in the civil affairs of the colony since participation in the governmental affairs was limited to church members. As Cor Harinck points out, "This requirement exerted tremendous pressure on the members of the church. The question was, 'What can we do to be born again, and what will enable us to believe in Jesus Christ?' This prompted the Puritans to formulate directives that could lead to regeneration and faith in Jesus Christ."[11]

[9] Zacharias Ursinus, *The Commentary of Zacharias Ursinus on the Heidelberg Catechism*," trans. G. W. Williard (n.p.: Forgotten Books, n.d., but originally published in 1564), 613, emphasis mine.

[10] See Edwin C. Deibler, "The Chief Characteristic of Early English Puritanism," *Bibliotheca Sacra*, 129:516 (Oct–Dec, 1972):326-335.

[11] Cor Harinck, "Preparationism As Taught By the Puritans," *Puritan Reformed Journal*, 02:2 (July 210):161.

William Perkins

Both William Perkins and William Ames, for significant examples, discuss the involvement of the sinner on his way to Christ. Perkins, whom we met in the previous chapter as a proponent of supralapsarianism, explains his doctrine of preparation, among other places, in his book, *The Cases of Conscience*. Perkins takes up the foundational question: "What must a man do, that he may come into God's favor and be saved?"[12] He says that in God's "first grace," there are "ten several actions" that a sinner, dead in his sins, would take in order to lay hold of salvation. Summarized, they are as follows:

1. "God gives man the outward means of salvation, especially the ministry of the Word: and with it, he sends some outward or inward cross, to break and subdue the stubbornness of our nature, that it may be made pliable to the will of God."

2. "This done, God brings the mind of man to a consideration of the Law and therein generally to see what is good, and what is evil, what is sin and what is not sin."

3. "Upon serious consideration of the Law, he makes a man particularly to see and know his own peculiar and proper sins, whereby he offends God."

4. "Upon the sight of sins he smites the heart with legal fear, whereby when man sees his sins, he makes him to fear punishment and hell, and to despair of salvation, in regard of anything in himself."[13]

5. "The fifth action of grace therefore is to stir up the mind to a serious consideration of the promise of salvation propounded and published in the Gospel."

6. 6. "After this, the sixth is to kindle in the heart some seeds or works of faith, that is, a will and desire to believe, and grace to strive against doubting and despair. Now at the same instant when God begins to kindle in the heart any sparks of faith then also he justifies the sinner, and withal begins the work of sanctification."

---

[12] William Perkins, *The Whole Treatise of the Cases of Conscience* (London: John Legatt, 1642; reprinted by Early English Books Online, n.d.), I.1, 30. This book was published posthumously. I've updated his old English in this section.

[13] Perkins notes that a reprobate may take these first four special actions, but never be saved from his sins (31).

7. "Then so soon as faith is put into the heart, there is presently a combat; for it fights with doubting and despair and distrust. And in this combat faith shows itself by fervent, constant, and earnest invocation for pardon; and after invocation follows a strength and prevailing of this degree."

8. "Furthermore God in mercy quiets and settles the conscience as touching the salvation of the soul and the promise of life whereupon it rests and stays itself."

9. "Next after this settled assurance and persuasion of mercy follows a stirring up of the heart to evangelical sorrow, according to God, that is a grief for sin because it is sin, and because God is offended; and then the Lord works repentance wherein the sanctified heart turns itself unto him."

10. "Lastly God gives a man grace to endeavor to obey his commandments by a new obedience. And by these degrees, does the Lord give the first grace."[14]

The second special grace is the continuance of the first special grace, specifically the grace to repent and believe throughout the believer's life.

For modern day evangelicals, the sequence in Perkins' explanation is intriguing. He puts the salvation of the sinner in number six and follows it with a season of doubt and distrust. Contemporary evangelicalism, a movement born in the optimism of the Enlightenment, often promotes the idea that once we make the decision for Christ, we should no longer have doubts. But this was neither the theology nor experience of the Puritans. Perkins' list reminds us of John Bunyan's *Pilgrim's Progress* (published about three-quarters of a century after Perkins' death) in which Pilgrim, even after his burdens fall off at the cross, must fight off the enemies of discouragement and doubt.

William Ames

William Ames believed that the inner call of God to the sinner was not always efficacious. In other words, the inner call could sometimes come to those who would reject it. "The inward offer," wrote Ames, "is a kind of spiritual

---

[14] Perkins, *Cases of Conscience*, 30-31. See also Martyn McGeown, "The Notion of Preparatory Grace in the Puritans," for his analysis of Perkins' list. This helpful essay, originally published in the *Protestant Reformed Journal* and available on-line in a slightly modified form, represents a strong Reformed position critical of what McGeown considers to be the excesses of the doctrine of preparation. (http://www.cprf.co.uk/articles/preparationism.htm#.WHzeZmYzWP8)

enlightenment whereby the promises are presented to the hearts of men, as it were, by an inner word." But then he adds that this inner enlightenment "is sometimes and in a certain way granted to those who are not elected."[15] Thus the gracious predispositions—fear, sorrow, regret, and shame—that softened the elect sinner and convicted him of his need of a Savior, also could be found in a non-elect sinner.

Understood in this way, the inner call sounds a little like the doctrine of prevenient grace that was taught by James Arminius. It was not the same, however, because the Puritans did not believe that this inner call brought the sinner to a neutral spiritual place whereby he could exercise his free will as the final act of the salvation experience. Still, the fact that the inner call could come to the non-elect moderates its impact. Even though the inner call was always successful with the elect, the inner call could be resisted by the non-elect.

Ames' view on the inner call leads to more focus on the response of the sinner. John Eusden, the editor and translator of Ames' *Marrow of Theology*, though exaggerating Ames' impact, writes:

> But Ames, almost alone in the orthodox party, found that the Remonstrant insistence on man's response in the drama of salvation was a needed corrective for Reformed theology.... There was much that man had to do; "spiritual preparation" was called for if grace was to be experienced. He differed from such straight-arrow orthodox theologians as Franciscus Gomarus (1563-1641) and Johannes Maccovius (1588-1644), his colleague at the University of Franeker, both of whom were seemingly unconcerned with the human side of the religious life.[16]

Thomas Hooker

Other Puritans emphasized the doctrine of preparation even more than Ames and Perkins. Beeke and Smalley point out that "perhaps no Puritan is as famous on the subject of preparation as Hooker."[17] Thomas Hooker (1586-1647), one of the founders of the Connecticut colony, wrote *The Soul's Preparation for*

---

[15] William Ames, *The Marrow of Theology*, John D. Eusden, trans. and ed. (Boston: Pilgrim Press, 1968, original publication in 1629), 158.

[16] John Eusden, "Introduction," *Marrow*, 7.

[17] Beeke and Smalley, *Prepared by Grace*, 71.

Christ, Being a Treatise of Contrition.[18] As typical of books in this era, the title continues—"Wherein is discovered How God breaks the Heart, and wounds the Soul, in the conversion of a Sinner to Himself."

Much of the book is a detailed systematization of sin and repentance, urging the sinner "to examine every commandment of God, and the breach thereof," because "you know not your sins." Therefore, "get you home to the Law and look into the glass thereof." [19] And then the sinner was to meditate on his sins until his soul came to "such a loathing of sin, that it may never love it more."[20] "Did the soul feel only the delight in sin, it would never part from it."[21] Hooker, along with Thomas Shepherd, believed that the sinner in preparation for conversion should come to the place in his humiliation where he so despised his sin that he would be "content to bear the estate of damnation."[22]

The Criticisms of Preparationism

Not all Reformed theologians, or even all Puritans, appreciated the emphasis on preparation for salvation.[23] Some were afraid of the emphasis on the work of the law in contrast to the work of grace in Christ, and others believed that the extremes of preparation were leading to Arminianism.

---

[18] Thomas Hooker, *The Soul's Preparation for Christ, Being a Treatise of Contrition* (1632; repr., Ames, IA: International Outreach, Inc., 1994).

[19] Ibid., 92.

[20] Ibid., 97.

[21] Ibid., 113.

[22] Thomas Hooker, *The Soules Humiliation*, 112, quoted in Beeke and Smalley, *Prepared by Grace*, 83. John Norton (1606-1663), another American Puritan and the successor to John Cotton as pastor of the First Church of Boston, wrote a classic study of preparation entitled *The Orthodox Evangelist*. Historians have debated whether John Cotton believed in preparation like the rest of the Puritans. He did, as Beeke and Smalley have shown. Even the fact that his hand-picked successor wrote a book on preparation seems to prove this. But Cotton was not interested in systematizing preparation into a doctrine like other Puritans. Cotton seems to have been an independent thinker, and, in my opinion, did not emphasize the Old Testament law as a standard for the Christian's life after salvation. This is why Cotton has often been accused inaccurately of being an Antinomian. Cotton believed that the Christian, by his union with Christ and through the power of the Holy Spirit, was to follow the law of Christ.

[23] See Norman Pettit, *The Heart Prepared* (Middletown, CT.: Wesleyan University Press, 1989), particularly his chapter, "Early Criticism and the Antinomian Controversy," 125-157.

Later Puritans

Beeke and Smalley reference two later English Puritans, Thomas Goodwin (1600-1679) and Philip Nye (1595-1672), who had two criticisms of the process of preparation:

> First, they thought Hooker's preaching held his congregation "too long" under preparation. They might have been referring to Hooker's lengthy expositions about conviction of sin with few references to Christ and His grace. For example, Hooker's ninth and tenth books in *The Application of Redemption* devote more than seven hundred pages to the evil of sin and how to meditate on it as preparation for conversion.[24]

The other criticism was that Hooker "sometimes confused preparation with true faith," and thus kept a seeking sinner from having assurance of his salvation. He in effect kept the listener "too long under John Baptist's water."[25]

Reformed theologians known as Antinomians rejected the doctrine of preparation in any form. Those involved in the antinomian debates (the word meaning "against the law") asked specific questions like, (1) Should the preacher preach the "moral law" to bring conviction? The majority of the Reformed theologians said "yes," but some antinomians said "no." (2) Does assurance of salvation come to a Christian by doing good works? The majority said "yes," specifically emphasizing the Mosaic Law as the standard of righteousness.[26] But the antinomians said "no." Peter Thuesen observes that antinomians "repudiated all legalistic means of assurance and instead looked to the immediate witness of the Spirit as the distinguishing mark of the elect. The Holy Spirit, in other words, communicated directly with the chosen, giving them an unparalleled, indeed supernatural, sense of assurance."[27]

---

[24] Beeke and Smalley, *Prepared by Grace*, 162. This is not to say that these later Puritans did not believe in preparation at all, including the preaching the law to sinners. They seem to be critical of the excessive emphasis on this doctrine.

[25] Ibid., 163.

[26] For an in-depth discussion of antinomianism, see Mark Jones, *Antinomianism, Reformed Theology's Unwelcome Guest* (Phillipsburg, NJ: Presbyterian and Reformed Publishing, 2013); and David D. Hall, *The Antinomian Controversy, 1636-1638* (Middletown, CT: Wesleyan University Press, 1968).

[27] Peter J. Thuesen, *Predestination, The American Career of a Contentious Doctrine* (New York: Oxford, 2009), 70-71. This second question was the issue in the New England antinomian controversy between the "orthodox" Puritans and John Cotton and his follower, Anne Hutchinson.

Modern Reformed Critics

Some more recent Reformed theologians have also been leery of Arminian-sounding theology that in their opinion sometimes could be found in the doctrine of preparation. Abraham Kuyper (1837-1920), a Dutch journalist, statesman, Calvinist theologian, and philosopher, thought that the doctrine of preparation taken to extremes tended to diminish the sovereignty of God. He wrote two chapters on preparation for salvation, one on "What It Is," and one on "What It Is Not."[28]

For Kuyper, "there is a *'gratia preparans,'* as our old theologians used to call it, i.e., a preparatory grace; not a preparation of grace, but a grace which prepares, which is in its preparatory workings real grace, undoubted and unadulterated."[29] "But," he wrote, "it should not be abused to reestablish the sinner's free will, as the Pelagians did, and the Arminians after them.... . There is no gradual transition; conversion is not merely the healing of disease, or an uprising of what had been suppressed...."[30] Kuyper held that the teaching "out of the many who received preparatory grace, some choose life and others perish" is the confession "not of Augustine, but of Pelagius."[31]

Kuyper even rejected the metaphor used by John Owen (1616-1683) of drying out wood in preparation for the fire.[32] Kuyper writes, "Even the representation still maintained by some of our best theologians, that preparatory grace is like the drying of wet wood, so that the spark can more easily ignite it, we can not adopt. Wet wood will not take the spark [they say]. It *must* be dried before it *can* be kindled."[33] For Kuyper, "this does not apply to the work of grace. The disposition of our souls is immaterial. Whatever it may be, omnipotent grace can kindle it."[34]

---

[28] Abraham Kuyper, *The Work of the Holy Spirit*, trans. Henri de Vries (Grand Rapids: Eerdmans; repr., 1956), 283-292.

[29] Ibid., 283.

[30] Ibid., 288.

[31] Ibid., 289.

[32] John Owen, *The Works of John Owen*, vol. 3, ed. William H. Goold (repr., Edinburgh: Banner of Truth, 1966), 229.

[33] Kuyper, *Work of the Holy Spirit*, 291.

[34] Ibid. Cf. strict Reformed theologian, Martyn McGeown's five objections against the doctrine of preparation: (1) The unregenerate do not hunger after righteousness; (2) The unregenerate will is not pliable to God's will; (3) Preparationism makes grace common and resistible; (4) Preparation complicates conversion; (5) Preparation destroys assurance and breeds despair. His conclusion is that preparatory grace is "a deadly compromise, not only of total depravity, but also of sovereign election and reprobation and of limited atonement" ("The Notion of Preparatory Grace in the Puritans").

Reformed theologian, J. I. Packer (b. 1926), also criticized the excesses of the Puritan doctrine of preparation in his book, *A Quest for Godliness*. He argues first that many of these Puritans, in spite of their disclaimers, implied that every sinner must experience every detail of the process of salvation. They inferred that those "who labor and are heavy laden" could not go directly to Christ without moving through the several steps of preparation.[35] Second, the extremists, such as Hooker and Thomas Shepard, went beyond the teaching of Scripture in suggesting that a sinner has to hate his sins so much that he be willing to suffer in hell for them.

Historian Edmund S. Morgan, in his analysis of the doctrine of preparation, argues that though the Puritans denounced Arminianism, there was a tinge of Arminianism to be found in some of the Puritans' analysis of how a depraved sinner comes to Christ. Morgan believes that "the history of New England theology for a century and a half after the founding is the history of this steady tendency toward Arminianism, punctuated by periodic reassertions of the Calvinist dogma of divine omnipotence and human helplessness."[36]

THE SOFTENING IMPACT
OF FEDERAL THEOLOGY

Historical theologians have often proposed that the covenant structure itself also tended to soften High Calvinism. Nineteenth century theologian, G. P. Fisher, asserts, "The scheme of the Covenants, whatever may be thought of it in other respects, softened this rigor of Calvinistic teaching by setting up jural relations in the room of bare sovereignty."[37] Sixteenth-century theologians like William Perkins and Caspar Olevianus, for examples, teach that "the covenant idea provides objective certitude by assuring the believer of the absolute reliability and trustworthiness of God."[38] Because God was willing to make a covenant with us, we don't need to fear a sovereign God. God is faithful to His covenant. Furthermore, as Herman Witsius in the seventeenth century, explains, "But man, upon accepting the covenant, and performing the condition, does acquire

---

[35] J. I. Packer, *A Quest for Godliness* (Wheaton, IL: Crossway Books, 1990), 172.

[36] Edmund S. Morgan, *The Puritan Dilemma* (Boston: Little, Brown and Co., 1958), 136.

[37] G. P. Fisher, *A History of Christian Doctrine* (New York: Charles Scribner's Son, 1896), 348.

[38] Lyle D. Bierma, *German Calvinism in the Confessional Age, The Covenant Theology of Caspar Olevianus* (Grand Rapids: Baker, 1996), 177.

some right to demand of God the promise; for God has, by his promise, made himself *a debtor to man*."[39]

The Westminster Confession states in this regard: "The distance between God and the creature is so great, that although reasonable creatures do owe obedience unto him as their Creator, yet they could never have any fruition of him as their blessedness and reward, but by some *voluntary condescension on God's part*, which he hath been pleased to express by way of a covenant."[40] The covenant thus put a sovereign God under some self-imposed boundaries.

Johannes Cocceius

Reformed theologians developed a third theological covenant in the seventeenth century, further softening the impact of High Calvinism. The development of this covenant called the "*pactum salutis*" and the "covenant of redemption" is most closely associated with Johannes Cocceius, "that most eminent of 'federal theologians.'"[41] The covenant of redemption played such a decisive role in Cocceius' theology that his system has often specifically been called "federal theology," and Cocceius has sometimes been honored as the "father of covenant theology." Such acclaim would be debatable for many reasons. Covenant theology was already an established system by the time of Cocceius' contributions. And many covenant theologians in the seventeenth century disagreed with some of the innovative features of Cocceius' "federal theology." Nevertheless, his system does represent a mature covenant theology similar to mainline covenant theology in the twenty-first century.

Johannes Cocceius (1603-1669) was born in Bremen, Germany, a community that had accepted Reformed theology. As a boy he was interested in languages and eventually learned to read Greek, Hebrew, Chaldean, Aramaic, Arabic, and of course, Latin. One of his areas of focus at the University in Bremen was on Rabbinic studies and the Jewish Talmud. He took private lessons in Hebrew from a rabbi and wrote a major treatise in Greek on Turkish religion, having read sections of the Koran in Arabic. He later studied at the University of Franeker where one of his major professors was William Ames.

---

[39] Witsius, *The Economy of the Covenants Between God and Man*, I. I. I:48, emphasis mine.

[40] The Westminster Confession, VII.I, emphasis mine.

[41] Richard A. Muller, "Toward the *Pactum Salutis*: Locating the Origins of a Concept," *Mid-America Journal of Theology* 18 (2007):11.

Cocceius began his teaching career at the University of Bremen in 1630 as Professor of Biblical Philology. In 1636 he moved to Franeker where he was Professor of Hebrew, and in 1643, Professor of Theology. In 1650, he moved to Holland and was Professor of Theology at the University of Leyden until his death in 1669. His published works, encompassing theology, philology, and commentaries, when collected after his death, came to twelve volumes. One of his most important language books, for example, was a Hebrew-Aramaic lexicon published in the year of his death. His most important theological work is his biblical theological study of covenant theology entitled in English, *The Doctrine of the Covenant and Testament of God*.[42]

Federal Theology

Cocceius introduced several theological ideas into covenant theology, including (1) a new emphasis on the personal aspects of a covenant; (2) a different method of doing theology; (3) a new way of understanding the covenant of works in doing theology; (4) a different understanding of the Sabbath for New Covenant Christians; (5) a clear statement of a third covenant—the covenant of redemption.

A significant challenge in covenant Reformed theology in general was integrating God's eternal decree with His interaction with mankind in time and space. Cocceius' federal theology tended to concentrate more on God's time-space involvement with men and women. But we should not make the mistake of believing that Cocceius was somehow not a Calvinist. He certainly thought and wrote out of the context of full-blown Reformed theology. He labors to show that the atonement of Christ, for example, was intended only for the elect. Commenting on God's love for the world in John 3:16, he argues that "since the world without exception of any men is not so loved, it is necessary that it is explained regarding part of the world."[43] So Cocceian federal theology is an innovative manifestation of the larger theological world of seventeenth-century Reformed theology.

---

[42] Johannes Cocceius, *The Doctrine of the Covenant and Testament of God*, volume 3 of Classic Reformed Theology, trans. Casey Carmichael (Grand Rapids: Reformation Heritage Books, 2016), originally published by Cocceius in 1648. This 2016 English translation was based on a third Latin edition that was published in 1660.

[43] Ibid., (par. 130), 111.

The Covenants and God's Love

One of the interesting features of Cocceius covenant theology was his empha-sis on the expression of God's love as He entered a friendship relation with man in the covenant of grace. In fact, Willem J. van Asselt proposes that the "relationship between the covenant concept and the friendship model for the divine-human relationship constitutes the genuinely original element in Cocceius' thought."[44] Covenants made by man with man, Cocceius observed, are almost always made to benefit both parties in one way or another. But when God makes a covenant with man, God makes His covenant for the benefit of the human being. "Indeed," Cocceius asserts, "the covenant of God is nothing other than the divine declaration of the way of receiving the love of God as well as the union and communion of becoming partaker in Him. If man makes use of this way, he is in the friendship of God, or, the Creator is his own."[45]

Because of the progressive revelation of the covenants of God with man, Cocceius understood that this friendship relationship did become better after the death, burial, and resurrection of Christ. Van Asselt explains,

> In the Old Testament dispensation of the covenant of grace, friendship with God was still, as it were, in a state of infancy and was mixed with ignorance. That fades away when Christ appears in the flesh and effects reconciliation. This reconciliation indicates the complete work of joining alienated humanity with God in friendship. For Cocceius, Good Friday was the turning point in the history of God's friendship with His fallen creatures.[46]

Such divine friendship is at the basis of such spiritual blessings as prayer to God as well as friendship and love with fellow believers. Even the sacraments of the covenant of grace are "testimonies of the friendship of God...."[47]

---

[44] Willem J. van Asselt, *The Federal Theology of Johannes Cocceius*, trans. Raymond A. Blacketer (Boston: Brill, 2001), 313.

[45] Cocceius, *Covenant and Testament of God*, (par. 5), 22.

[46] van Asselt, Introduction to the *Covenant and Testament of God*, xxxiii.

[47] Cocceius, *Covenant and Testament of God*, (par. 202), 140. We might wonder how and why Cocceius came to this friendship insight. One possibility is the lectures that he heard from his professor, William Ames (1576-1633), when Cocceius studied at the University of Leyden. Ames was a Pietistic Puritan who emphasized the Christian's personal relationship with God. It is intriguing to see that Ames described the covenant relationship in the Old Testament in terms of friendship with God. (William Ames, *The Marrow of Theology*, trans. John D. Eusden [Boston: Pilgrim Press], I, xxii.13), 150.

The Covenants in Progressive Revelation

Another important innovation developed by Cocceius was *not* to approach the study of the covenants by means of dogmatic theology. The word "dogma" "consistently stands for something that is established and not subject to doubt."[48] Cocceius would have agreed that the Bible does present dogma, but the best way to approach theology is to study the covenants as they unfold successively through progressive revelation in Scripture. As van Asselt explains, "Cocceius sought to formulate a covenant theory that described all of salvation history, by introducing the overall structure of consecutive covenants, or *foedera*."[49]

This means that instead of systematizing the Scriptures into doctrines with proof texts, the covenants would best be understood by examining the progressive revelation of what the covenantalists called the covenants of works and grace through the Old and New Testaments, passage by passage. More specifically, Cocceius attempted to understand the so-called theological covenants of works and grace in their Old Testament historic context rather than reading them only through the paradigm of the New Testament. Much of the rest of this chapter will demonstrate what Cocceius' methodology produced.

The Covenant of Works and Its Abrogations

Though Cocceius is known for his development of the covenant of redemption, the most remarkable feature of Cocceius' theology of the covenant may be his focus on the so-called covenant of works. Indeed, it can be startling for a non-covenant theologian to observe the central place that it plays in Cocceius' entire doctrine of salvation. Karl Barth correctly observes that for Cocceius the covenant of works "is the all-controlling principle that cuts across all of the events of salvation history; and it remains the perpetual criterion and norm for the covenant of grace."[50] Cocceius begins his study of the covenant of works, not in Genesis, but in Paul's letter to the Galatians:

---

[48] Herman Bavinck, *Reformed Dogmatics*, vol. I, trans. John Vriend (Grand Rapids: Baker Academic, 2003), 29.

[49] Willem J. van Asselt, Introduction to *Covenant and Testament of God*, xix. Van Asselt is a helpful guide through Cocceian federal theology.

[50] Karl Barth, "The Doctrine of Reconciliation," *Church Dogmatics*, ed. G. W. Bromiley and T. F. Torrance (Peabody, MA.: Hendrickson, 2010), IV.1:63.

The covenant of works (*foedus operum*), or friendship with God (*amicitia cum Deo*), and the righteousness (*justitia*) that is from works (*ex operibus*) is summarized in these two statements: 'The one who will do these things, he will live by them,' and 'cursed is everyone who does not remain in all things written in the book of the law, that he may do them' (Gal 3:12, 10). Indeed, law, promise, and threat are all included in these pronouncements.[51]

The Perpetuity of the Covenant of Works

For Coccceius, the covenant of works was given to mankind in two ways. First, it was given naturally in the Garden of Eden as man and woman were created in the image and likeness of God with a conscience. Second, it was written in the book of the law. The commandments in the Mosaic Law, therefore, "are not of another kind than what the *law of nature* (*naturae lex*) [the covenant of works] commanded to the original man...."[52] Thus the covenant of works does not end in the Garden, but is expressed in more detail and specificity in the Mosaic Law.

The perpetuity of the covenant of works was not a new idea with Coccceius. As we saw in a previous chapter, Zacharias Ursinus, the first theologian to publish a definition and explanation of the covenant of works, taught the perpetuity of the covenant of works some eighty years before Coccceius published his major work on the topic. Robert Rollock (d. 1598), fifty years at least before Coccceius, taught "that the fall does not abrogate the covenant of works."[53] Rollock writes, "Adam, in the state of his innocency, was under the covenant of works. Man, after the fall, abideth under the covenant of works; and to this day, life is promised him under condition of works done by strength of nature."[54] Even Christ, as far as His human nature was concerned, was under the covenant of works, according to Rollock.[55]

Thus, the covenant of works with its one commandment: "Don't eat of the tree of the knowledge of good and evil!" did not end when man sinned, but

---

[51] Coccceius, *Covenant and Testament of God*, (par. 12), 28.

[52] Ibid., (par. 13), 28, emphasis his.

[53] J. V. Fesko, *Death in Adam, Life in Christ* (Geanies, Fearn, Ross-shire, UK: Christian Focus, 2016), 82.

[54] Robert Rollock, *Select Works of Robert Rollock* (Edinburgh: Woodrow Society, 1844-1849; repr., Grand Rapids: Reformation Heritage Books, ed. William M. Gunn, 2008), 52.

[55] Ibid. Whether Christ was required to keep the covenant of works and law in His human nature is debated later by covenant theologians. Some would argue that if Christ were not required to keep the covenant of works and law, He would be free to keep it for the rest of the elect.

instead, morphed into the Old Testament Law. In fact, as we will see, Cocceius believed that the covenant of works continues until the resurrection for both the believer and unbeliever. For the unbeliever, one of the consequences of the perpetuity of the covenant of works is his eternal punishment. He suffers in hell forever at least in part because of his violation of the covenant of works throughout his lifetime.

The Gradual Elimination of the Covenant of Works

Cocceius' surprising addition to the doctrine of the perpetuity of the covenant of works is a system of abrogations whereby the original covenant of works is canceled step by step. In his words, the covenant of works "approaches abolition, with gradual abrogation. ... Indeed, the abolition of the law or of the covenant of works proceeds according to the following steps," [56] which are (1) the Fall; (2) the giving of the covenant of grace; (3) the inauguration of the New Covenant; (4) the death of the body; (5) the resurrection of the body. Thus, all of biblical history encompasses the progressive cancellations of the covenant of works, from the Garden of Eden to the resurrection.

The Fall

The first abrogation of the covenant of works occurred when Adam and Eve sinned in the Garden. Cocceius argues that in the Fall, the main "promise of life to man ... became useless. Hence it is the case that the law cannot give life: Gal 3:21."[57] So the pre-Fall covenant of works was the first expression of law, and law in this case promised eternal life if obeyed. But because Adam and Eve did not obey this law, the covenant of works was abrogated (at least weakened) in the sense that it lost its eternal life-giving power. It was not canceled, however. It continued via the law of nature until it was given detailed expression in the Mosaic Law. Cocceius says that Adam "nevertheless remains obligated to do all things which not only the law of nature, but also God, demands from man by right of His lordship."[58] So, the covenant of works was not voided entirely by the Fall, but transformed.

---

[56] Ibid., (par. 58), 58.

[57] Ibid., (par. 59), 59.

[58] Ibid., (par. 71), 68.

The Covenant of Grace

The second abrogation is the covenant of grace.[59] The covenant of grace provides for the same goal and means that the covenant of works did in the Garden. The goal is eternal life, and the means is perfect righteousness before God. The way that God confers this righteousness is by a gift. Since the sinner is not able to provide his own righteousness, that righteousness is provided for him by God through the righteousness of a "third person" who has kept the covenant of works perfectly. The "third person" cannot be a sinner, but he must be from the human race. God then justifies the sinner based on the righteousness of this perfect human being, Jesus Christ, who is also a divine person. Sinners receive forgiveness of sins and righteousness by faith in Christ's shed blood on the cross, on the basis of Christ's law-keeping. Consequently, the condemnation found in the penalty of the covenant of works is abrogated through the covenant of grace.[60]

The New Covenant

And yet, the covenant of works continues on—or does it? The third abrogation of the covenant of works "happens through the promulgation of the New Covenant, expiation of sin having been made to abolish terror and servitude."[61] We might think that through the arrival of the New Covenant, the covenant of works was finally annihilated. But Cocceius didn't think that. Positively, the covenant of works is abrogated in the sense that the promises of the New Covenant are better than the covenant of works under the Old Covenant. As van Asselt says, "When Christ actually does appear in the flesh, then there is freedom and joy, because what was promised has now occurred—it has become *history*.[62]

Negatively, the New Covenant Christian still has to battle with the flesh. Thus, he still needs the covenant of works as expressed through the paradigm of the old Mosaic Covenant, particularly the Ten Commandments, to guide him in the process of sanctification.

---

[59] Cocceius defines the covenant of grace as "an agreement between God and man the sinner, in which God declares His free, gracious purpose concerning the righteousness and certain inheritance of the seed, to be given in the Mediator by faith, for the glory of His grace, and by the mandate of repentance and faith." Ibid., (par. 76), 71.

[60] Ibid., (par. 76-87), 71-84.

[61] Ibid., (par. 275), 170.

[62] van Asselt, *Federal Theology of Johannes Cocceius*, 279.

Positively again, the covenant of works/Mosaic Law does have a different impact on him than it did before he became a believer. Cocceius asserts,

> Therefore, those who are sanctified by the Spirit of Christ are not under the law, as once they were miserable sinners under the law. But under the law of the Spirit of life in Christ they are set free from the law of sin and death (Rom 8:2).... Therefore, in this manner they are not under the covenant of works ..., but under the law of the Holy Spirit who writes the law on the heart and renews them in the image of God."[63]

Negatively again, the teachings of Christ, as in the Sermon on the Mount, are derived from the Mosaic Law where we are commanded to love God and our neighbor. Christ's commandments are not new commandments but are old commandments "restored by Christ."

The Death of the Body

The fourth abrogation of the covenant of works occurs when a Christian dies. Yet he still is under the covenant of works because "the death of the body continues to dust."[64]

The Resurrection of the Body

Finally, the last abrogation of the covenant of works is the resurrection of the Christian's body. "Every effect of the covenant of works ceases in the righteous through the resurrection from the dead.... Every effect of the covenant of works and every fruit of sin is removed through the final effect of the covenant of grace."[65] Through these five abrogations, therefore, the covenant of works is progressively modified, and man's standing before God changes from condemnation to full salvation from sin. Thus, the covenant of works continues from the Garden of Eden until the Second Coming of Christ.

---

[63] Cocceius, *Covenant and Testament of God*, (par. 544), 325.

[64] Ibid., (par 610), 358.

[65] Ibid., (par. 609), 358.

The Covenant of Redemption

These abrogations of the covenant of works leading to full salvation in Christ occur in earth time. There is yet another covenant that is cut in eternity past that undergirds the process of abrogations. This eternal covenant, according to federal theologians, is made among the members of the Trinity, specifically between the Father and the Son. In this covenant, the Father gives the Son to be the Redeemer of elect sinful human beings, the Son voluntarily accepts this office of the Redeemer, and the Father guarantees a kingdom for His Son as a reward for His redemptive work. In Cocceius' words, "the Father requires the obedience of the Son unto death and for that promises Him a Kingdom and a spiritual seed; and the Son presents Himself to do the will of God and requires from the Father the salvation of a people given to Him out of the world, or, to speak more clearly, each side makes requirements."[66] This covenant or pact therefore "concerns a *negotiated state of affairs*."[67]

The "covenant of redemption," as it was eventually named, was usually called the *pactum salutis* by the seventeenth-century federal theologians. This name comes from the Latin translation of a phrase in Zechariah 6:12-13 that occurs in the context of the rebuilding of the post-exilic temple and the crowning of Joshua:

> And say to him, "Thus says the LORD of hosts, 'Behold, the man whose name is the Branch: for he shall branch out from his place, and he shall build the temple of the LORD. It is he who shall build the temple of the LORD and shall bear royal honor, and shall sit and rule on his throne. And there shall be a priest on his throne, and the *counsel of peace* shall be between them both'" (Zech 6:12-13, emphasis added).

The "counsel of peace" in Latin is the "*pactum salutis*."

In Cocceius understanding, the Holy Spirit was not directly involved in the covenant agreement itself though He was willing to administer the whole plan of salvation. "The Holy Spirit exercises the power of the Godhead by regenerating us," explains Cocceius, "and its charity by uniting us to God and by sealing our inheritance."[68] But the Spirit is not a legal partner in the pact.

---

[66] Ibid., (par. 88), 85.

[67] van Asselt, *Federal Theology of Johannes Cocceius,* 229 (emphasis his).

[68] Cocceius, *Covenant and Testament of God,* (par. 90), 89.

The Origin of the Concept

Since the covenant of redemption does not show up in theology until the seventeenth-century, federal theologians have suggested that it has roots much earlier in church history. J. V. Fesko, for example, says that some of the church fathers, Jerome in particular, "hinted at the doctrine in their exegesis."[69] The concept was not born in the seventeenth century, he argues, just refined or refocused as theologians worked through the mediatorial role of the Son.[70] But it is clear, he admits, that "the doctrine does not explicitly appear until the middle of the seventeenth century."[71]

It is difficult to know for sure who originated the covenant of redemption.[72] Herman Witsius (1636-1708), a younger contemporary of Cocceius, makes some suggestions. He writes,

> As the doctrine of the covenant between the Father and the Son is so expressly delivered in scripture, it is unjustly traduced as a new and late invention. Though I find few among the more ancient who have professedly handled the subject, yet some of the greatest divines has sometimes made mention of this covenant. I say nothing now of Arminius, who does not carelessly discourse on the covenant, in his oration for the degree of doctor.[73]

Intriguingly, Arminius is a candidate to be named the founder of the covenant of redemption. In addition to Arminius' oration in 1603, Witsius suggests William Ames and Franciscus Gomarus, both of whom were stern adversaries of Arminius in other areas of soteriology. Ames, as we have already mentioned, was one of the teachers of Cocceius.

Regardless of who first came up with the concept, it is fairly certain that the first public use of the English term, "covenant of redemption," occurred in an address by David Dickson to the General Assembly of the Church of Scotland in 1638. Dickson speaks of "the Covenant of Salvation betwixt God

---

[69] J. V. Fesko, *The Trinity and the Covenant of Redemption* (Geanies, Fern, Ross-shire, UK: Christian Focus, 2016), 6.

[70] Ibid., 7.

[71] Ibid., 4.

[72] For a full discussion of the origin of the covenant of redemption, see Richard A. Muller, "Toward the *Pactum Salutis*": 11-65.

[73] Herman Witsius, *The Economy of the Covenants Between God and Man*, I. II.III: 176.

and man" and "the Covenant of Redemption betwixt God and Christ."[74] Without choosing an exact date or one specific person, we can ascertain that the third covenant of covenant theology, the *pactum salutis* or the covenant of redemption, was being developed nearly one hundred years after the beginning of the Reformation.

The Theological Need of the Covenant of Redemption

So the question is, why was the covenant of redemption necessary? What did it do that was lacking in covenant theology? The primary benefit for covenant theology is that it demonstrates that salvation originates in the Godhead. As mentioned before, covenant theology has two somewhat opposite concepts running through it. One is the eternal decree of God which seems to stand opposite to the second concept, God's working in time and space in the covenants of works and grace. Or to say it in a question, how does God's immutability and unchangeable decree interact with the covenant of works and the covenant of grace as God's plan unfolds in salvation history?

The covenant of redemption is not the decree, but it is the Trinitarian agreement resulting from the decree. Thus, for Cocceius and his followers, "the stability of the covenant of grace derives from the fact that the covenant rests, not on the human fulfillment of an obligation, but on a testament or inheritance—and the solidity of the testament, in turn, rests on an eternal *pactum*, not between God and the fallen humanity but between God and the mediator."[75] In other words, the covenant of grace is "stable" because it is based, not on God's progressive interaction with the sons of Adam, but on the divine covenant of redemption. The covenant of redemption, in turn, is stable because it rests on the sovereign decree of God. The covenant of redemption, therefore, serves a mediating role structuring the decree into the plan of salvation.

The Scriptural Support for the Covenant of Redemption

The seventeenth-century federal theologians did not find the covenant of redemption spelled out in one or more passage of Scripture like we can the biblical covenants. Cocceius used Zechariah 6:13; Psalm 16:2-7; 40:7ff.; 119:122; Isaiah 38:10-14; 43:4; 49:5-12; 53:10-11; Luke 22:29; Romans 5:15; Galatians

---

[74] Referenced in Muller, "Toward the *Pactum Salutis*," 17.

[75] Ibid., 23.

3:17; and Hebrews 7:22ff., as biblical sources. And there were other texts that found their way into the defenses of this covenant from other federal theologians. For a non-covenant theologian, however, it is nearly impossible to find the covenant of redemption taught or implied in any of these passages. It is clear that the method of theological study employed by the seventeenth-century Federal theologians was not to focus on a single passage, but to collect many texts that deal with the Son's work of redemption. Muller explains,

> The point, of course, is not to expect to find the term *pactum salutis* or *foedus redemptionis* embedded in the exegesis: that does not even occur consistently in the commentaries on key texts written by later proponents of the fully developed doctrine. The point is to identify the establishment of an exegetical ground for the eventual inference of the doctrine by way of comparison and collation of texts, given that this was the theological method of the time.[76]

Muller doesn't mean by this that the texts used were not related at all to a covenant of redemption. These texts reflect, he says, "not an arbitrary effort to proof-text a doctrine but an understanding of theological issues already raised in the exegetical tradition."[77]

Indeed, covenantalists often attempt to turn this lack of specific reference to the covenant of redemption in Scripture into a positive. David Garner, for example, discussing Ephesians 1:3-14, argues that "historic Reformed hermeneutics has avoided the word-concept fallacy, and discerned that the redemptive decree of the triune God was accomplished in an intra-Trinitarian covenant—the *pactum salutis* ('covenant of redemption' or 'covenant of peace')."[78] He asserts that covenantalists have deduced this covenant from Ephesians 1:3-14. To non-covenant theologians, however, it may appear that covenant theologians have deduced the covenant of redemption from Scripture because they needed it to complete their system which they had previously deduced from Scripture.

---

[76] Ibid., 29.

[77] Ibid., 47.

[78] David B. Garner, *Sons in the Son* (Phillipsburg, NJ: P&R, 2016), 62.

The Theological Accompaniments of the Covenant of Redemption

Several other soteriological doctrines interact with the covenant of redemption. For one, the covenant of redemption is based on a law-keeping motif. Cocceius says that the Father maintains the role of "legislator, requiring demonstration of righteousness and punishing sin in the Son...."[79] Cocceius was even willing to teach, with some qualifications, that Christ obeyed the Father under punishment, the same as we do. "The fear of the Lord would not truly be in Him (Isa 11:2)," Cocceius argues, if the threat of punishment had not hung over His head.[80] Nevertheless, the Son obeyed freely.

Covenantalists have also connected the *pactum salutis* with unconditional election and limited atonement (though Arminius seems to have avoided this connection). It is highly unlikely that the Son would have agreed to enter into a covenant in which He would suffer the ignominy of the kenosis and the cross, they reason, if it were possible that none would be saved through His suffering. William Ames, Cocceius' teacher, contends, "If the redemption of Christ were of uncertain outcome, the Father would have appointed the Son to death and the Son would have undergone it without any certainty whether any would be saved by it or not, and all the fruit of this mystery would depend upon the free will of men." Thus, "redemption applies to all those and only to those for whom it was obtained by the intention of Christ and the Father." [81] Likewise, the covenant of redemption, in connection with the covenant of works, assumes the doctrines of the active and passive obedience of the Son, both of which we will assess in the next chapter.

Reformed Orthodoxy Versus Federal Theology

Not every seventeenth-century covenant theologian appreciated the innovations they perceived in the Cocceian approach to the Reformed faith. Many agreed with a well-known opponent of Cocceius, Gisbertus Voetius (1589-1676). Voetius is "widely acknowledged as both the greatest Dutch Reformed scholastic theologian and one of the greatest representatives of the practical,

---

[79] Cocceius, *Covenant and Testament of God*, (par. 89), 88.

[80] Ibid., (par. 97), 95. Cocceius presents seventeen reasons as to why Christ had to be fully under the law, including the threat of punishment.

[81] Ames, *Marrow of Theology*, I.xxiv, 7-8:150. Cocceius emphasizes the connection between unlimited atonement and the covenant of redemption in paragraphs 111-112, and 118-149 of *Covenants and Testament of God*. The covenant of redemption also interacts with significant Trinitarian matters with which we will analyze in the following chapter.

experiential movement of the Dutch Second Reformation."[82] For our purposes in this chapter, we need to know that Voetian's kind of covenant theology is sometimes called "orthodox" Reformed theology because it defended with scholastic tools the Reformed covenant theology that had been constructed by such theologians as Bullinger and Ursinus.

An Anthropological Theological Methodology

There were some practical ethical differences between the Voetians and Cocceians to be mentioned, but the "main issue was a different interpretation of the continuity and discontinuity of redemptive history in the Old and New Testaments."[83] We have already observed Cocceius somewhat different method of doing theology. In simple terminology, the orthodox Voetians took a snapshot of salvation revelation from God's viewpoint, and the Cocceian federalists took a video from the viewpoint of man. Herman Bavinck's critique is that "Cocceius exchanged the theological for the anthropological viewpoint." He explains,

> Cocceius' novelty lay rather in the fact that he was the first to divide all the material of dogmatics in terms of the covenant idea and planned in this way to offer a more biblical-theological and antischolastic dogmatics. Furthermore, in the arrangement of the material, he followed the dispensations so sharply that their unity was lost and could be preserved only by arbitrary typological exegesis. In addition, finally, he viewed the entire history of the covenant of grace from beginning to end as an abolition of the covenant of works.[84]

Bavinck's criticisms echo the criticisms of the orthodox Voetians in the seventeenth century.

---

[82] Joel R. Beeke, *Gisbertus Voetius, Toward a Reformed Marriage of Knowledge and Piety* (Grand Rapids: Reformation Heritage Books, 1999), 18. The Dutch Second Reformation, sometimes translated as the "Further Reformation," emphasized piety and godliness to accompany the theological reformation.

[83] van Asselt, Introduction to *Covenant and Testament of God*, xx.

[84] Bavinck, *Reformed Dogmatics*, 104. Bavinck specified five problems with the federalist methodology: (1) Its starting point was not in the doctrine of God, but in the covenants between God and man; (2) It could treat the doctrines of God and man only by way of presuppositions; (3) It undermined dogmatics; (4) It was highly repetitious; (5) It exaggerated the distinctions between the various dispensations.

An Inadequate Model of Abrogations

The orthodox Reformed theologians also rejected Cocceius' system of a series of abrogations of the covenant of works. Herman Witsius, sometimes considered a mediating theologian between the Cocceians and the Voetians, argued that instead of saying that the covenant of grace abrogates the covenant of works, the covenant of grace "supposes the abrogation of the covenant of works."[85] So, contra Cocceius, the covenant of works was already abrogated when God instituted the covenant of grace.

A Conditional Righteousness for Old Testament Believers

More substantively, Cocceius differed from the orthodox Voetians by deducing out of his system a different assessment of the spiritual condition of the Old Testament believer. Cocceius taught that God only passed over the sins of the Old Testament believers rather than forgiving their sins. They were therefore still liable for their sins until Christ's payment on the cross. If, as the orthodox Voetians were saying, that Christ had paid for their sins already, possibly from eternity past, then why would Christ even need to die? So Christ was only a conditional surety in Cocceius' system. As Fesko observes, "The debt of sin, therefore, was not actually canceled until the crucifixion and not a moment sooner."[86] The Voetians, however, argued that Christ was an absolute surety and his surety was from eternity past. The Cocceian view, they thought, minimized the eternal decree of election.

The Sabbath as a Ceremonial Law

Perhaps the most obvious difference between federal and orthodox Reformed theologians was the role of the Sabbath for New Testament Christians. The Cocceians maintained that the Sabbath commandment was not a universally morally binding precept. It was a ceremonial law that was part of the covenant of works, and it is now abrogated. The Sabbath, he affirmed, did not begin in Genesis 2. It began during the days of the sojourn of Israel in the wilderness. Even the Old Testament prohibition of work on the Sabbath was a ceremonial law that was no longer binding for New Testament Christians.

---

[85] Witsius, *Economy of the Covenants Between God and Man,* I. I, IX:160.

[86] J. V. Fesko, *The Trinity and the Covenant of Redemption,* 33. For a full discussion of this debate, see further, Willem J. van Asselt, "Expromissio Or Fideiussio?" *Mid-America Journal of Theology* 14 (2003):37-57.

The Voetians, however, argued that the Christian life is one of obedience to the biblical precepts as set forth in the Decalogue—particularly obedience to the Fourth Commandment. The Sabbath in their view was a perpetually binding moral principle. The Lord's Day was to be spent entirely in religious devotion and resting from all unnecessary work. The Voetians therefore regarded the teaching of Cocceius as a serious deviation from the moral law of God. The practical outflow of these distinctive theologies produced two camps within the Dutch Reformed Church that observed the Lord's Day in two noticeably different ways, even to the point of the two groups dressing differently on the Sabbath.

The debates between the followers of Voetius and Cocceius continued in Dutch Reformed circles for several decades. Despite opposition, Cocceian federal theology gradually became "the ruling orthodoxy of the Reformed Church" in the second half of the seventeenth century.[87]

CONCLUSION

We have come to the end of our historical survey of supersessionism and covenant theology. Supersessionism (or continuity theology, or fulfillment theology) originated with the early church fathers to solve the problem of Israel. The church began in Acts 2 with a core of Jewish believers and proselytes that were present in Jerusalem on the Day of Pentecost. Then other ethnic groups were supernaturally brought into the church: the Samaritans in Acts 8, and the Gentiles in Acts 10-11.

These remarkable developments raised many questions. At first, the perplexity was how Gentiles fit into this new organism (Acts 15). But as the church entered the post-apostolic era, the perplexity became how Jews fit into a church that was mostly populated with Gentiles. The usual solution of the early church fathers was that the church had permanently superseded Israel. That meant, for example, that the church was now the recipients of the Old Testament prophecies about the glorious future for Israel. Augustine, who had been a premillennialist in his early ministry like the early fathers, became an amillennialist in his later life. In part because of the lasting impact of Augustine, supersessionism

---

[87] Barth, *Church Dogmatics*, IV.1:55. Barth gives a short summary of how Cocceian theology impacted various religious groups. As we might suspect, Barth liked the way Cocceius "tried to understand the work and Word of God attested in Holy Scripture dynamically and not statically, as an event and not as a system of objective and self-contained truths."

and amillennialism were standard doctrines in the theology of the Roman Catholic Church throughout the Middle Ages.

With the coming of the Reformation, the Roman Catholic sacramental system of salvation was replaced by the wonderful *solae*: *Sola scriptura* ("by Scripture alone"), *Sola fide* ("by faith alone"), *Sola gratia* ("by grace alone"), *Solo Christo* "through Christ alone"), *Soli Deo gloria*, ("glory to God alone"). The Reformers retained supersessionism, and some of the Reformed theologians began to remodel supersessionism, step by step, into what has become known as covenant theology.

The first steps in developing this system occurred in the German-Swiss canton of Zurich where Ulrich Zwingli was battling the Anabaptists. For Zwingli, there was one theological covenant that unified the two Testaments. Zwingli's successor, Heinrich Bullinger, agreed and wrote a treatise on this one theological covenant, making it the center piece of his theological system. This covenant would eventually become known as the covenant of grace. The second theological covenant, the covenant of works, was added into the system in the fourth quarter of the sixteenth century. Apparently, Zacharias Ursinus was the first Reformed theologian to assert the second covenant in a publication. Ursinus called this second covenant the "covenant of nature" and the "covenant of creation," though it eventually came to be known as the "covenant of works." Covenantalists added a third covenant into their system, the covenant of redemption, in the seventeenth century. It solved the problem for them as to how the covenants of works and grace were related to God's eternal and unchangeable decree.

When covenant theology reached this fully systematized form, it had effectively dogmatized its rejection of the Bible's promises about the future of a redeemed national Israel in God's plan. The following chapters present biblical and theological assessments of supersessionism and covenant theology.

FORSAKING ISRAEL

Part Two: *Why It Matters*

6

AN ASSESSMENT OF COVENANT THEOLOGY

Larry D. Pettegrew

The Reformation theologians who inaugurated and refined covenant theology were brilliant students of Scripture with excellent abilities in ancient and modern languages, able to produce a logically consistent system of theology. More importantly, the covenant system has historically upheld key doctrines of the Christian faith such as the inspiration and inerrancy of Scripture, the Trinity, the deity and bodily resurrection of Christ, justification by faith alone, salvation by grace through faith, the Second Coming of Christ, and heaven and hell. Present-day evangelical covenant theologians are scholarly and godly. The authors of this book have great respect for the Reformed tradition and have friends who are devotees to covenantalism.

Nevertheless, non-covenantalists disagree with several distinctive doctrines in covenantalism. Some of our disagreements are predictable, and we begin with these. Then, as we get deeper into our assessment, we will analyze some of the less obvious defects that may be defended or ignored by covenantalists and overlooked by some dispensationalists.

UNJUSTIFIABLE SUPERSESSIONISM

First of all, supersessionism, a major foundation of covenant theology, is not supported by Scripture. To review, supersessionism, "is the view that the NT Church is *the new and/or true Israel that has forever superseded the nation of Israel as the people of God.*"[1] It is true, of course, that the church since the Day of Pentecost has partially and temporarily replaced Israel as the center of God's program. This is what Paul teaches in Romans 11:25-27.[2] But it is a temporary replacement.

It is also typical for contemporary non-dispensationalists to argue that it is not that the church has replaced Israel, but rather that Christ, the ultimate Israelite, has replaced Israel permanently. Since members of the church are "in Christ," when Christ permanently superseded Israel, the church in effect superseded Israel. We will analyze this specific argument in a later chapter. But whether it is the church that has replaced Israel, or that the church by being in Christ has replaced Israel, there is no future for the nation of Israel other than as individual Jews are saved and become a part of the mostly Gentile church.

In summary form, supersessionism has been improperly inferred from Scripture for the following reasons:

1. The Bible teaches that God's covenants (i.e., grace contracts) with Israel are "irrevocable" (Romans 11:29). When God made the covenant with Abram (later "Abraham"), God and Abram went through a somewhat mystical ceremony in which God asked Abram to kill a dove and a pigeon, and then to cut in two a three years old heifer, a three years old female goat, and a three years old ram. Abram "brought him all these, cut them in half, and laid each half over against the other. But he did not cut the birds in half" (Gen 15:9-10).

The story continues, "As the sun was going down, a deep sleep fell on Abram. And behold, dreadful and great darkness fell upon him…. When the sun had gone down and it was dark, behold, a smoking fire pot and a flaming torch passed between these pieces. On that day the LORD made a covenant with Abram" (Gen 15:12,17-18). It is also important to notice that the specific content of the covenant in Genesis 15 dealt with the land of Israel (vv. 18-21). It is clear that this covenant is one-sided. God, in a fiery form, walked through the bloody sacrifices by Himself and made specific promises to Abram. The book of Hebrews adds, "For when God made a promise to Abraham, since he had no one greater by whom to swear, he swore by himself" (Heb 6:13).

---

[1] Michael Vlach, *Has the Church Replaced Israel?* (Nashville: B&H Academic, 2010), 12, emphasis his. This excellent book presents a clear and convincing case for why supersessionism does not measure up to the Scriptures' teachings about the future of Israel. See also, Barry E. Horner, *Eternal Israel* (Nashville: Wordsearch Academic, 2018).

[2] See chapters eight and eleven for expositions on the Apostle Paul's explanation that one of the church's responsibilities in our age is to make Israel jealous so that she will turn to her Messiah.

The covenant that God made with King David (2 Sam 7) was also an irrevocable covenant, as was the New Covenant. When God introduces the New Covenant, He says, "Behold, the days are coming, declares the LORD, when I will make a new covenant with the house of Israel and the house of Judah" (Jer 31:31). Walter Kaiser correctly asserts, "The 'New Covenant' was made with the house of Israel and Judah. God never made a formal covenant with the church."[3] Since these covenants with Israel are irrevocable, supersessionism cannot be correct.[4]

2. Supersessionism relies on a faulty hermeneutical concept that asserts that the New Testament should reinterpret the Old Testament. Much better is the hermeneutical principle that *"the primary meaning of a specific passage, whether from the OT or NT, is found in that passage and not in other passages."*[5] The New Testament adds further revelation to the Old Testament, but it does not reinterpret the Old Testament.

3. The Bible clearly teaches in both the Old and New Testaments that there is coming a restoration of the nation Israel (see, for one among many examples, Ezekiel 36-37). The failure of the Jews was calculated in the plan of God (Rom 11:8). But the New Testament teaches that God has not cast off disobedient Israel (Rom 11:1, 25-26). Supersessionism is an unstable foundation for a theological system.

IMPROPER THEOLOGICAL METHOD

A proper theological method, all evangelicals would agree, begins with the Christian Scriptures in which the one triune God has self-attestingly revealed Himself.[6] The most important issue in a theological method, therefore, is its connection between Scripture and the system. The student of God's Word must first study the Scriptures with the exegetical tools that are available to him or

---

[3] Walter C. Kaiser, "An Assessment of 'Replacement Theology,'" (*Mishkan* 71 (2013), 42.

[4] For another good study of these irrevocable covenants, see Robert L. Saucy, *The Case for Progressive Dispensationalism* (Grand Rapids: Zondervan), especially 39-139.

[5] Michael Vlach, *He Will Reign Forever* (Silverton, OR: Lampion Press, 2017), 42, emphasis his.

[6] God has also revealed Himself in general revelation that comes to us through nature and the moral law within us (Romans 1 and 2). Through general revelation everyone learns that God exists, He is powerful, and He is just when He condemns the unbeliever. But general revelation is limited. We can't learn from general revelation, for examples, that God is a God of love, or that He is a Trinity, or who Christ is. These truths are only available for us through special revelation. Whatever information that we find in general revelation, moreover, is best interpreted through the lens of special revelation that we find in Scripture.

her, using the grammatical historical method of hermeneutics. The interpreter next incorporates the truths found in his careful study of Scripture into a biblical theology, thus disclosing the doctrines that come out of the passage under consideration. Biblical theology in turn becomes the source for one's systematic theology that harmonizes the truths found in Scripture. This procedure is not one and done, so the interpreter should always be willing to go back to the exegesis of a passage as needed to improve his or her theology, especially since one's pre-understandings can corrupt the procedure at several places.

The primary founders of covenant theology, however, employed a different theological methodology. Instead of beginning with an exegesis of Scripture, they seem to be asking and answering questions such as, how can we justify infant baptism? How can we systematize the continuity of the Old and New Testaments? How can we tie in the legal requirements of the Old Covenant program with the New Testament? How can we correlate the eternal decree of God and the covenants of works and grace in time and space? Consequently, they deduced their system of theological covenants from the Bible to answer these kinds of questions.

Zwingli, for example, was motivated not primarily by the exegesis of Scripture, but by his desire to accomplish his reformation in Zurich through the state-church. To maintain the state-church, every citizen had to be baptized into citizenship when he or she was born, and thus infant baptism was absolutely required. To justify the state-church and infant baptism in his struggles with the Anabaptists, Zwingli devised a single theological covenant that transcended both the Old and New Testaments. By this over-arching covenant, he could support his argument that infant baptism replaced circumcision in the Old Testament. The baptismal issue then led, as we have seen, to the beginning of a process that over a period of a hundred years developed into covenant theology. Our point is that exegesis of Scripture was not the first step in Zwingli's theological method. Consequently, covenant theology was a system "more autonomous in relation to Scripture than it would admit to itself and gave impression to others."[7]

---

[7] Karl Barth, *Church Dogmatics*, IV.1, "The Doctrine of Reconciliation," ed. G. W. Bromiley and T. F. Torrance (Peabody, MA: Hendrickson Publishers, 2010), 56. Barth's analysis of federal theology in this section of his book is detailed, interesting, and important since Barth is neither a covenant nor dispensational theologian. Barth is here critical of covenant theology. Admittedly, what Barth might have said about dispensationalism, if he knew anything about it, would also not be favorable, to say the least. Neither evangelical covenant theologians nor dispensationalists accept Barth's theological method.

PHANTOM COVENANTS

Another defect in covenant theology is that its three covenants—grace, redemption, and works—are not found explicitly in any passage of Scripture. The biblical covenants, such as the Abrahamic, Mosaic, Davidic, and New are clearly identified in several passages. But we cannot turn to a passage and find stated the theological covenants of covenant theology.

The Covenant of Grace

The covenant of grace, as we saw earlier, "may be defined as that gracious agreement between the offended God and the offending but elect sinner, in which God promises salvation through faith in Christ, and the sinner accepts this believingly, promising a life of faith and obedience."[8] Covenantalists attempt to support the existence of this covenant by collecting many texts that deal with the Bible's teaching about salvation and grace. Of course, the grace of God is wonderfully displayed throughout Scripture. Immediately following the Fall of Adam and Eve, God laid out the foundational features of His plan of salvation (Gen 3). Adam and Eve were told that a descendant of the woman would, unlike Adam, bruise the head of the Wicked One. And the substitutionary blood principle was introduced as God killed animals to provide clothing for the couple. From this starting point in the Garden, salvation is progressively clarified and enriched in biblical revelation. But we never find a passage describing God cutting a covenant of grace with mankind.

We cannot minimize this fact. Steve Lehrer is correct when he says, "The danger of calling something a covenant that Scripture does not refer to as a covenant increases the likelihood of making something a cornerstone of our theology that in fact is not an emphasis in Scripture. This of course would lead to an unbalanced and unbiblical theological system."[9]

The Covenant of Redemption

There is also no Scripture passage that specifically teaches the existence of a covenant of redemption, the proposed "agreement between the Father, giving the Son as Head and Redeemer of the elect, and the Son, voluntarily taking the

---

[8] Louis Berkhof, *Systematic Theology* (Grand Rapids: Eerdmans, 1959), 277.

[9] Steve Lehrer, *New Covenant Theology: Questions Answered* (n.p., self-published, 2006), 37. Lehrer is a new covenant theologian.

place of those whom the Father had given Him."[10] Covenantalists freely admit that they do not find the covenant of redemption spelled out in any passage of Scripture. J. V. Fesko writes, "In a sense, no one text serves as the fulcrum for the doctrine." Putting the best spin on this problem, he continues, "In historic explanations, the pactum does not precariously rest upon one passage but lies upon multiple pillars scattered throughout Scripture."[11]

Lack of Scriptural Basis

Fesko takes readers of his book through some passages from both the Old and New Testaments that he considers key for the covenant of redemption. His interpretations of Psalms 1-2 and Psalm 110, for examples, are helpful. These Psalms are based on the covenant that God made with David as explained in 2 Samuel 7, and Fesko teaches this appropriately. But even though he claims that "Psalm 110 is one of the clearer pieces of evidence for the *pactum salutis*,"[12] it is difficult to find a legitimate connection between a biblical covenant like the Davidic Covenant and the proposed covenant of redemption that does not explicitly appear there or anywhere in the Bible.

Michael Horton goes even further than Fesko and claims that "the covenant of redemption, therefore, is as clearly revealed in Scripture as the Trinity and the eternal decree to elect, redeem, call, justify, sanctify, and glorify a people for the Son."[13] This is an astonishing claim that is historically and biblically unfounded. Historically, the church understood and explicitly taught the Trinity for over sixteen hundred years before anyone spoke of a covenant of redemption. Biblically, the Trinity, as a doctrine, is taught beautifully in such Scriptures as the Upper Room Discourse (John 13-17). Indeed, the Gospel of John has been accurately described as a "trinitarian tract." And we clearly see the three persons of the Godhead being presented at the baptism of Jesus.

Moreover, Horton's claim that the covenant of redemption is as clear in Scripture as "the eternal decree to elect, redeem, call, justify, sanctify, and glorify a people for the Son" is unsupportable. We can turn to Scriptures where the eternal decree to elect, redeem, call, justify, sanctify, and glorify a people for the

---

[10] Berkhof, *Systematic Theology* (Grand Rapids: Eerdmans, 1959), 271 (emphasis his).

[11] J. V. Fesko, *The Trinity and the Covenant of Redemption* (Geanies, Fern, Ross-shire, UK: Christian Focus, 2016), 15.

[12] Ibid., 106. Modern day commentaries, even the study notes written by covenant theologians in study Bibles, do not reference the covenant of redemption in these and similar passages.

[13] Michael Horton, *God of Promise* (Grand Rapids: Baker, 2006), 82.

Son is clearly taught—Romans 8:29-30, for example. But we cannot turn to a Scripture where the covenant of redemption is presented. The Bible does not teach the covenant of redemption. It was constructed by its proponents to solve a glitch inherent in the system.

Puzzling Portrayal of the Trinity

The portrayal of the Trinity in the "covenant of redemption" is also not helpful. The relationship of the three persons of the Trinity is complex, to say the least, and no one has or ever will understand fully the triune God.[14] Nevertheless, certain truths about the Trinity are clear in Scripture and are accepted by both covenantalists and non-covenantalists.[15]

The covenantalists' addition that the Father and Son made a covenant in eternity past, however, is a perplexing concept. Since this covenant supposedly is made in eternity past, it sounds as though there was a point in eternity past when the covenant was made. But there is no time (at least as we know it) in eternity past. So, it would seem that the covenant theologians' best explanation of the reality of the covenant of redemption is that this agreement has always existed. This essentially means that the Father and the Son exist together in an eternal covenant relationship for the salvation of mankind.[16]

This is still strange, however, because, according to covenantalists, the third person of the Trinity, the Holy Spirit, does not directly participate in

---

[14] See further Robert Reymond, *A New Systematic Theology of the Christian Faith* (Nashville: Thomas Nelson Publishers, 1998), 320-38, for a helpful discussion of the relation of the three persons within the Godhead.

[15] Some of these generally accepted truths are specifically essential for the proposed covenant of redemption to be a possibility. One is the eternal Sonship of Christ. The second person of the Trinity has eternally been the Son. Another is the functional subordination of the second and third persons of the Trinity. Though the Son and the Spirit are equally God, they willingly accept lesser functions that subordinate their activities to the Father. Evangelicals normally hold these doctrines, and non-covenantalists do so without believing in a "covenant of redemption."

[16] A related issue concerns the timing for when the functional subordination of the Son and Spirit occurred. Some evangelicals teach that this functional subordination occurred at the incarnation of Jesus Christ. In other words, the Son was not functionally subordinate in eternity past. Others teach that the Son is eternally functionally subordinate to the Father, even before His incarnation. This latter view seems to be the position of at least some of the covenant theologians who formulated the covenant of redemption in the seventeenth century. Caspar Olevianus, one of the sixteenth-century Reformed theologians who laid the foundation for the covenant of redemption, saw the pact between the Father and the Son as "an agreement between master and servant: The Father decrees and commands; the Son obeys" (Lyle D. Bierma, *German Calvinism in the Confessional Age, The Covenant Theology of Caspar Olevianus* [Grand Rapids: Baker, 1996], 112). The English Reformed theologian, William Perkins, seems to agree with Olevianus, saying, "This subordination, which is of the Son to the Father, is not in the divine essence severally and distinctly considered, but in the relation or manner of having the essence." William Perkins, *A Golden Chain*, ed. Greg Fox (Cambridge: John Legate, 1597; Puritan Reprints, 2010), xviii, 41. Muller interprets Perkins as saying that the Son's functional subordination is "not merely of the human nature to be assumed, but of the pre-incarnate Son." Richard A. Muller, "Toward the *Pactum Salutis*: Locating the Origins of a Concept," *Mid-America Journal of Theology* 18 (2007):55-56.

this covenant. He is not a covenant partner. Two-thirds, so to speak, of the Godhead are the legal partners, but the Spirit, though He agrees to administer this plan, is not a legal partner. These are odd concepts that force weird pictures into our minds. Barth asks, "Can we really think of the first and second persons of the triune Godhead as two divine subjects and therefore as two legal subjects who can have dealings and enter into obligations one with another? This is mythology, for which there is no place in a right understanding of the doctrine of the Trinity."[17]

To be sure, the Bible teaches a God-centered soteriology from beginning to end that is based on His eternal decree. Each detail of salvation was ordained by God and procured through the death of the God-man on the cross and His resurrection. Every person comes to God when God calls him or her to Himself through the drawing of the Holy Spirit. But the Bible does not proclaim a covenant of redemption.

DOMINANT COVENANT OF WORKS

Perhaps the most bewildering and problematic feature of covenant theology for non-covenantalists is the impact of the covenant works in this system. According to covenantalists, the covenant of works is an agreement in the Garden of Eden between God and Adam wherein God promises life for perfect obedience and death for disobedience. "The Westminster Shorter Catechism, 1647," asserts, "When God had created man, he entered into a covenant of life with him, upon condition of perfect obedience: forbidding him to eat of the tree of knowledge of good and evil, upon pain of death."[18] But as we have seen, according to covenantalists, the covenant of works did not end when Adam and Eve sinned, but continues on into the future until the final resurrection. Even now, according to the covenant system, mankind is under the covenant of works. The covenant of works is thus a central piece of the doctrine of salvation for covenant theologians. Michael Allen, a contemporary covenant theologian, writes:

> Second, the covenant of works witnesses to God's universal designs for communion with his human creatures.... We may say, then, that the covenant of works

---

[17] Barth, *Church Dogmatics*, IV.1:65. On the other hand, evangelical theologians have questioned Barth's "one God in three modes of being" interpretation of the Trinity.

[18] "The Westminster Shorter Catechism, 1647," in *Creeds of Christendom*, vol. 3, ed. Philip Schaff (repr., Grand Rapids: Baker, 1977), 678.

bound all humans at its time of inception to approach fellowship with God in this particular way, and we should confess still further that the covenant of works *continues to bind all men and women to relate to God in this specific manner.*[19]

It is highly unlikely, however, that God made a covenant with Adam in the Garden of Eden. Some covenantalists argue that Hosea 6:7 infers a covenant of works. Through Hosea, the Lord says, "But like Adam they transgressed the covenant; there they dealt faithlessly with me." The verse is somewhat difficult to translate and interpret in that "Adam" is the word for "man" in Hebrew, so it could as well be understood to be saying just as mankind rebelled against God, so Israel transgressed against the Mosaic covenant. The Isaac Lesser (Jewish Bible) translates, "But they, like an ordinary man, have transgressed the covenant: there have they dealt treacherously against me" (Hos 6:7 LEE).

Furthermore, "Adam" is also a city in the Old Testament (Josh 3:16). The Elberfelder translation of the German Bible translates the verse as "the inhabitants of Adam." Some English Bibles do as well. The New Jerusalem Bible translates the verse, "But they have broken the covenant at Adam, there they have betrayed me" (Hos 6:7 NJB). This translation makes sense in the context because three geographic areas are then mentioned in succession: Gilead, Adam, and Shechem. At any rate, one verse, difficult to translate, located late in Old Testament revelation, is an unsure foundation for this major covenant of covenant theology. Many covenantalists, in fact, look elsewhere in the Bible for the covenant of works.

Even granting for the sake of discussion that there is a covenant in the Garden of Eden, is it a covenant of works, or is it a covenant of faith? There are hardly any instructions about works in the first three chapters of Genesis. God only tells Adam to "be fruitful and multiply and fill the earth and subdue it, and have dominion over the fish of the sea and over the birds of the heavens and over every living thing that moves on the earth" (Gen 1:28). Even this is stated in the context of a blessing: "God blessed them and said...."[20]

The test in the Garden was not about works, therefore. It was about the central question of human life: Will Adam and Eve trust Satan or God? Who will be Lord? As the representative of the human race, Adam answered this

---

[19] Michael Allen, *Sanctification* (Grand Rapids: Zondervan, 2017), 111 (emphasis added).

[20] See Vlach's analysis of the situation in the Garden of Eden as a starting place for the kingdom of God here on earth with Adam as the appointed king. Vlach, *He Will Reign Forever*, 59-70.

question by replacing his allegiance and obedience to God with allegiance to Satan. Adam liked the idea of having the authority of an autonomous being, having the right to decide what is good and what is evil. To repeat, if there is a covenant made between God and Adam in the Garden of Eden (and this is unlikely), it would be a covenant of faith in God's person and authority, a covenant of Lordship. There is no such thing as a covenant of works.

Even some covenant theologians do not like the terminology "covenant of works." John Murray, for example, long-time professor of theology at Westminster Theological Seminary, argues that a better term for the situation in the Garden of Eden would be "The Adamic Administration." Murray explains:

> This administration has often been denoted "The Covenant of Works." There are two observations. (1) The term is not felicitous, for the reason that the elements of grace entering into the administration are not properly provided for by the term "works." (2) It is not designated a covenant in Scripture.... Covenant in Scripture denotes the oath-bound confirmation of promise and involves a security which the Adamic economy did not bestow.... The first or old covenant is the Sinaitic. And not only must this confusion in denotation be avoided but also any attempt to interpret the Mosaic covenant in terms of the Adamic institution. The latter could apply only to the state of innocence and to Adam alone as representative head. The view that in the Mosaic covenant there was a repetition of the so-called covenant of works, current among covenant theologians, is a grave misconception and involves an erroneous construction of the Mosaic covenant, as well as fails to assess the uniqueness of the Adamic administration.[21]

Dispensationalists agree with Murray's assessment. There is no such thing as a covenant of works.[22] Since, as we have seen, the covenant of works is a centerpiece of covenant theology, it unfortunately serves as a major division point between covenantalists and non-covenantalists.

---

[21] John Murray, *Collected Writings of John Murray*, vol.2 (Carlisle, PA: Banner of Truth, 1977), 49-50. Murray clearly disagrees with Cocceius' series of abrogations of the "covenant of works" that we analyzed in a previous chapter.

[22] With apologies to covenantalists and Ogden Nash: "As I was going up the stair, I met a covenant that wasn't there. It wasn't there again today. I wish I wish it'd stay away."

The Impact of Original Sin on the Doctrine of Salvation

Covenantalists and non-covenantalists do agree that Adam's sin in the Garden of Eden had a devastating impact not only on him, but on the entire human race. "Therefore, just as sin came into the world through one man, and death through sin, and so death spread to all men because all sinned" (Rom 5:12). Theologians have suggested two main ways to explain how Adam's sin—a broken relationship with God, guilt, and depravity—is passed down to the rest of humanity.[23]

The first is called realism or seminalism. This view states that human nature in its individualized unity existed in its entirety in Adam. Thus, when Adam sinned in the Garden of Eden, not only did he sin, but the common humanity which existed in its unity in him also sinned. Since each person who comes into the world is an individualization of this common human nature, he or she is both guilty and punishable for the sin committed by the unity. Augustus Hopkins Strong explains, "Adam's sin is imputed to us immediately, therefore, not as something foreign to us, but because it is ours—we and all other men having existed as one moral person or one moral whole, in him, and, as the result of that transgression, possessing a nature destitute of love to God and prone to evil."[24] Thus, all of us are born with a depraved nature, guilty, and deserving of condemnation and judgment, ultimately because we sinned in Adam. There is truth in this view. All of Adam's descendants were in Adam in seed form. But seminalism does not adequately explain why we are guilty.

The second way to explain our connection with Adam's sin is called representative imputation or federalism and is primarily based on the parallelism between Adam and Christ (Rom 5:14; 1 Cor 15:20-22, 45). According to this view, both Adam and Christ were representative heads of humanity: Adam of the human race and Christ of the redeemed race. So, Adam's sin not only constituted him guilty and corrupt, but also constituted all those whom he represented guilty and corrupt. This view has been taught by Reformed theologians such as Charles Hodge and John Murray. Murray explains, "We are compelled

---

[23] There are other ways to analyze this. Pelagians deny that Adam's sin had any impact on anyone other than himself, although he was a bad example. Mediate imputation, sometimes called Hopkinsianism, asserts that the human race receives a depraved or corrupt nature from Adam, and this corrupt nature, not Adam's sin, is the ground for man's condemnation. Consequently, there is no direct imputation of Adam's sin in Hopkinsianism.

[24] Augustus Hopkins Strong, *Systematic Theology* (Valley Forge, PA: The Judson Press, 1907), 620. Other notable theologians to hold this view include nineteenth century Reformed theologian, W. G. T. Shedd, and Puritan theologian, Thomas Watson.

to recognize an identity of modus operandi because Adam is the type of Christ. Why, we may ask, should we seek for any other principle in terms of which the reign of sin, condemnation, and death operates than the principle which is exemplified in the reign of righteousness, justification, and life? We cannot posit less."[25] That which is true of Christ's representation of the redeemed is also essentially true of Adam's representation of the human race.

So, which view is better? The correct answer, in one sense, if we understand the views properly, is "both." From Adam's original sin, there is (1) representative imputation of guilt as well as (2) seminal or realistic transmission of depravity. As Anthony Hoekema has taught us, "It is my conviction, however, that they [representative imputation and seminal transmission] ought to be combined. In other words, the decision we should make about these two understandings of the transmission of sin is not an either-or but rather a both-and."[26] Hoekema continues,

> When he [Adam] sinned, he did so as our representative, and therefore we are all involved in the guilt of that sin, and in the condemnation that results from it. We may call this involvement in guilt and condemnation *imputation*. God imputes to us the guilt of Adam's first sin. This imputation is not mediated by our innate corruption but is direct and unmediated. As an implication, and therefore as result, of our involvement in Adam's guilt, all human persons are born in a state of corruption. This corruption (also called pollution or depravity) is transmitted to us through our parents. Our involvement in and identification with Adam's sin carries with it the perversity apart from which sin does not exist. We are born in a state of corruption because we are in solidarity with Adam and his sin.[27]

In other words, because all of us are born into the human race with a broken relationship with a holy and sovereign God, we are born both (1) guilty because

---

[25] John Murray, *The Imputation of Adam's Sin* (Grand Rapids: Eerdmans, 1959), 40. An illustration of representation that I use in teaching is the battle between David and Goliath. Goliath concocts a plan: "Choose a man for yourselves, and let him come down to me. If he is able to fight with me and kill me, then we will be your servants. But if I prevail against him and kill him, then you shall be our servants and serve us" (1 Sam 17:8-9). Of course, when David won, the Philistines ran away. But the principle of representation is apparent here. And in the case with Adam, our representative, we cannot run away from his failure.

[26] Anthony Hoekema, *Created in God's Image* (Grand Rapids: Eerdmans, 1986), 160. Hoekema says that "such Reformed theologians as Herman Bavinck, J. Gresham Machen, A. D. R. Polman, John Murray, and Louis Berkhof have held this view" (161).

[27] Ibid., 161.

the guilt of Adam's sin is imputed to our account, and (2) depraved because Adam's corruption is transmitted to us through our parents.

This two-fold impact of Adam's original sin on the human race has powerful implications for the doctrine of salvation. Above all else, salvation must bring us a restored relationship with God. Because we are born guilty, we need a pronouncement by God in salvation that declares us not guilty. The Bible calls this declaration justification. And because we are born in corruption, totally depraved, we need God's act of regeneration whereby we receive a new nature (2 Cor 5:17). "Regeneration, or new birth, is an inner re-creating of fallen human nature by the gracious sovereign action of the Holy Spirit."[28] As we will see, both justification and regeneration occur simultaneously and instantly at the moment of our salvation through our union with Christ.

The Active Obedience of Christ and Law-Keeping

How does the covenant of works help solve the problems of guilt and corruption for covenantalism? As we discovered in our previous historical study, one of the centerpieces of historic covenant theology is the continual existence of the covenant of works beginning in the Garden of Eden and lasting until the resurrection. Covenant theologian, Robert Reymond, asserts:

> It is true that the covenant of works *per se* contained no provision for redemption from sin in the event that Adam should fall, but this fact should not be construed to mean that the covenant of works is no longer in force or was rendered null and void by the entrance of the covenant of grace. Rather, the covenant of grace should be seen as providing the requisite redemptive provisions and a second-level "covenant overlay" upon the covenant of works.[29]

Thus, in covenantalism, the covenant of grace overlays the covenant of works, and we are all responsible to keep the covenant of works.

---

[28] J. I. Packer, "Regeneration," *Evangelical Dictionary of Theology*, 3rd edition, ed. Daniel J. Treier and Walter A. Elwell (Grand Rapids: Baker, 2017), 734.

[29] Robert Reymond, *A New Systematic Theology of the Christian Faith*, 439-40. Reymond lists four ways that the covenant of works is still normative. Interestingly, Herman Witsius, fellow covenant theologian with Cocceius in the seventeenth century, doesn't seem to think that the covenant of works is ongoing. He argues that "the covenant of grace does not abrogate, but supposes the abrogation of the covenant of works. . ." (Herman Witsius, *The Economy of the Covenants Between God and Man* [Kingsburg, CA: van Dulk Christian Foundation, 1990], I.I.IX:160. This is a reprint of the English translation of the Latin, *De Oeconomia Foederum Dei cum hominibus*, published in 1677).

The Covenant of Works and the Ten Commandments

In covenant theology, this means that the only way for a human being to gain eternal life is to keep perfectly the covenant of works as formulated into law. As Charles Hodge declares, "The law demands, and from the nature of God, must demand perfect obedience.... No man since the fall is able to fulfill these demands, yet he must fulfil them or perish."[30]

Usually "law" means the Mosaic Law, specifically what covenant theologians call the "moral law." The *Westminster Confession* asserts:

> The moral law doth forever bind all, as well justified persons as others, to the obedience thereof; and that not only in regard of the matter contained in it, but also in respect of the authority of God the Creator who gave it. Neither doth Christ in the gospel any way dissolve, but much strengthen, this obligation (Chapter XIX, V).

Question 41 of *The Westminster Shorter Catechism*, 1647, further explains: "Wherein is the law summarily comprehended? Ans. The moral law is summarily comprehended in the ten commandments." So, keeping the covenant of works, as formulated primarily in the ten commandments of the Mosaic Law, is an absolute necessity for salvation. The Mosaic Law also serves as the ethical standard for Christians.

Dispensationalists have a different understanding of what constitutes the moral law. But whatever we believe the moral law is, there is a huge problem: sinners cannot keep it (Gal 3:11). Covenantalists thus teach that God covenanted with His Son to earn righteousness for us through His life of law-keeping and then suffer eternal death on the cross for us so that God could forgive our sins. These two provisions provided for us by Christ—law-keeping and substitutionary death—are often described as the active and passive obedience of Christ. "By the righteousness of Christ," explains Charles Hodge, "is meant all he became, did, and suffered to satisfy the demands of divine justice, and merit for his people the forgiveness of sin and the gift of eternal life. The righteousness of Christ is commonly represented as including his active and passive obedience."[31] In covenantalism, therefore, it is through the active and

---

[30] Charles Hodge, *Systematic Theology*, vol. II (Grand Rapids: Eerdmans, 1871-73), 517.

[31] Ibid., vol. III, 142. Some Reformed covenantalists do not like these phrases, "active obedience" and "passive obedience." Robert Reymond argues that they "are not satisfactory terms" and suggests "preceptive" and "penal" as better." "'Preceptive'

passive obedience of the substitute, Jesus Christ, that God justifies the sinner and considers him to have kept the covenant of works.[32]

The Imputation of Double Righteousness through Justification

In covenant theology, consequently, justification by faith, based on the active and passive obedience of Christ, provides a double righteousness for the sinner. Heber Carlos de Campos Jr., a leading scholar of this doctrine, explains that the active obedience of Christ is:

> the understanding that in order for a Christian to be justified, the second Adam, Christ, needed not only to pay for the penalty resulting from the transgressions of the laws (both original and actual sins) but also to fulfill the law perfectly in order to acquire the right to eternal life. In other words, justification was understood as going beyond simply having sins remitted. It also includes having positive righteousness (doing what the law commands) through the imputation of Christ's active obedience.[33]

Forgiveness of sins only takes us to neutral, according to the covenant view. We still need positive righteousness from justification to give us eternal life. Justification is thus a two-step event. Both forgiveness of sins and imputed law-keeping "are required within a covenantal structure (covenant of works) where eternal life comes as a result of obeying the law."[34]

---

righteousness refers to 'Christ's full obedience to all the prescriptions of the divine law.' "'Penal'" refers to Christ's willing obedience in bearing all the sanctions imposed by the law against his people because of their transgressions" (Reymond, *A New Systematic Theology of the Christian Faith*, 631).

[32] Julie Canlis observes that the doctrines of the active and passive obedience of Christ underemphasizes the resurrection of Christ. She writes, "Although this obedience has been divided into 'active' and 'passive,' I am not sure that is the best way to go about it (apologies here to the Reformed tradition). It is a whole self-offering in life and death and resurrection. The temptation is to think of our justification only in terms of what Christ went through 'passively' on the cross, with our sanctification residing in his 'active' life. The resurrection is usually left out of the picture" (Julie Canlis, "The Fatherhood of God and Union with Christ in Calvin," in *"In Christ" in Paul*, ed. Michael J. Thate, Kevin J. Vanhoozer, and Constantine R. Campbell [Grand Rapids: Eerdmans, 2014], 410, n.79).

[33] Heber Carlos de Campos, Jr. *Doctrine in Development, Johannes Piscator and Debates Over Christ's Active Obedience* (Grand Rapids: Reformation Heritage Books, 2017), 9. Campos' book is a well-written, helpful study and informs this section of our study. He has a good grasp of the primary sources which are valuable for anyone interested in studying this doctrine in more depth. I have no reason to think that Campos does not believe in the imputation of Christ's active obedience, but he does a careful historical and unbiased theological evaluation. His book is based on his doctoral dissertation at Calvin Theological Seminary. See Heber Carlos de Campos Junior, "Johannes Piscator (1546-1625) and the Consequent Development of the Doctrine of the Imputation of Christ's Active Obedience," Ph. D. diss., Calvin Theological Seminary, 2011).

[34] Ibid., 9.

The Availability of Extra Righteousness from Christ

There is some vagueness in the details of how active obedience works. We can understand how God the judge can declare us not guilty and forgive our sins because of the substitutionary death of Christ. But how can the righteousness of one person be legally credited to someone else?

This raises another question: Did Christ need to keep the law for His own sake, being both God and man? On the one hand, He was God, so we might think that He didn't. In fact, we can be sure that God Himself is not under His law because the moral law is an expression of the nature of God. On the other hand, Christ was man, so we might think that He had to keep the law for Himself. Covenantalists usually teach that the God-man was not required to keep the law for Himself, so He could keep it for others. A. A. Hodge writes "that being, *as to person*, above all law, and as to dignity of nature, infinite, he might render to the law in behalf of his people a free obedience, which *he did not otherwise owe for himself*, and that his obedience and suffering might possess an infinite value."[35] Hodge's point is that Christ did not need the righteousness for Himself that He earned from His keeping of the covenant of works/law since He was the God-man.

Thus, for covenantalism, there is a sort of Protestant "treasury of merit," so to speak, containing the infinite righteousness that Christ earned by keeping the covenant of works, not for Himself, but for others. God withdraws from this infinite "treasury of righteousness," when He justifies the repentant sinner.

The Historical Development of the
Covenantalist Doctrine of Active Obedience

It is important for us to know when the systematized doctrine of the active obedience of Christ became a part of covenant theology. A few medieval Roman Catholic scholastic theologians "did mention the importance of Christ's life for redemption, though never with a proto-Protestant understanding of Christ's work being imputed."[36] The founders of the Reformation likewise did not teach the systematized doctrine of the active obedience of Christ that incorporated a

---

[35] A. A. Hodge, *Outlines of Theology* (Carlisle, PA: The Banner of Truth Trust, repr., 1999; rewritten and enlarged edition originally published in 1878), 391, emphasis mine.

[36] Campos, *Doctrine in Development*, 63.

covenant of works, though what they taught about justification was compatible with the doctrine as it was later established.

John Calvin and the Active Obedience

As we saw earlier, Calvin specialists have a difficult time agreeing about the role of John Calvin in the development of covenant theology. Likewise, they also have suggested various interpretations of how Calvin tied together the imputation of the righteousness of Christ, the active obedience of Christ, regeneration (sanctification) and the union with Christ.[37] After surveying the various interpretations, William B. Evans concludes, "This brief and selected survey of Calvin scholarship regarding the relationship of justification, sanctification, and union with Christ underscores an extraordinary lack of consensus on a matter that most agree is central to Calvin's soteriology."[38]

A few concepts are clear in Calvin's theology. First, Calvin teaches that justification by faith provides a double righteousness for the sinner at the time of his salvation. He writes, "Therefore, we explain justification simply as the acceptance with which God receives us into his favor as righteous men. And we say that it consists in the remission of sins and the imputation of Christ's righteousness."[39] Calvin didn't include a covenant of works in his theology, but this is not surprising because the concept of the covenant of works had not yet been fully developed by the time that Calvin died. It is evident, therefore, that one could believe in double righteousness in justification by faith without the covenant of works.

Second, unlike some of the later covenant theologians, the "in Christ" relationship is at the heart of how Calvin conceives that believers receive the righteousness of God. Calvin declares that because God alone is the source of righteousness, "we *are righteous only by participation in him*...."[40] As Mark Garcia asserts, Calvin's doctrine of the union with Christ "does appear to stand

---

[37] See the survey of the various viewpoints of contemporary scholars in William B. Evans, *Imputation and Impartation, Union with Christ in American Reformed Theology* (Milton Keynes, Great Britain: Paternoster; repr., Eugene, OR: Wipf and Stock edition, 2008), 8-14. This is a helpful book.

[38] Ibid., 14.

[39] John Calvin, *Institutes of the Christian Religion*, ed. John T. McNeill, trans. Ford Lewis Battles (Philadelphia: Westminster Press), III.xi.2:727.

[40] Ibid., III.xi.8:735, emphasis mine.

as a singularly determinative idea in Calvin."[41] Evans contends that "Calvin accords a *causal* priority of union with Christ." Union with Christ in Calvin, he continues, is "the instrumental basis of both justification and sanctification."[42] In other words, a Christian is justified and sanctified because he or she is in union with Christ. It is not that a person is joined to Christ because he or she has been justified.

In distinction from Calvin, the doctrine of union with Christ as a foundation for justification and law-keeping righteousness is not highlighted by many of the later covenantalists.[43] The scholastic Reformed theologians instead built their soteriology on the "ordo salutis," in which "justification and sanctification were treated in a logical sequence which assured the priority of justification."[44] In these later covenantalists' system, therefore, salvation is conceived through the paradigm of justification rather than through union with Christ. In other words, the foundational doctrine of salvation is justification by faith, not union with Christ.

Though Calvin held to double imputation of justification, he taught that union with Christ was the foundation of the righteousness that we receive at salvation. Calvin thus does not have a developed doctrine of the active obedience of Christ. Calvin's commentaries, moreover, "on the crucial passages lack clarity."[45] Since Calvin and most of the other early Reformed theologians were mainly focusing on the justification by faith alone in opposition to the Roman Catholic sacramental system of salvation, the responsibility for systematizing the finer points of justification fell on the next generations of theologians.[46] It

---

[41] Mark A. Garcia, *Life in Christ* ((Milton Keynes, Great Britain: Paternoster; Eugene, OR: Wipf and Stock edition, 2007), 18. This book is subtitled, *Union with Christ and Twofold Grace in Calvin's Theology*.

[42] Evans, *Imputation and Impartation*, 38. "Sanctification" in Evans' analysis includes how we actually become righteous beginning with regeneration and continuing on in what we usually call progressive sanctification.

[43] The role of the doctrine of union with Christ in Calvin's theology is currently under debate. Julie Canlis notes, "Anyone who has read the recent explosion of material in Calvin studies concerning union with Christ realizes that this consoling doctrine is now being consumed by controversy" (Canlis, "The Fatherhood of God and Union with Christ in Calvin," 422).

[44] Evans, *Imputation and Impartation*, 40.

[45] Campos, *Doctrine in Development*, 77. One of Campos' thesis ideas is that the doctrine of the active obedience of Christ did not become important in Reformed circles until after the debate between Piscator and Beza.

[46] It may be that an important early step in the building of the doctrine of the imputation of Christ's law-keeping obedience was taken before the death of Calvin. J. V. Fesko suggests, that Wolfgang Musculus (1497-1563) was the "the first Reformed theologian to give the doctrine of the covenant its own specific locus in his theological system. Musculus notably connects law and covenant when he states that the law is part of God's covenant. By joining law and covenant, Musculus opened a new window to view imputation and Christ's law-keeping accredited to believers." J. V. Fesko, *Death in Adam, Life in Christ* (Geanies, Fearn, Ross-shire, UK: Christian Focus, 2016), 72. Fesko has a helpful survey of the doctrine of imputation in the Reformation and post-Reformation eras.

was thus "the era of orthodoxy that provided the context for a resolution of the issue of the imputation of Christ's active obedience to believers."[47]

The Debate Between Beza and Piscator

The imputation of Christ's law-keeping first became an important issue among Reformed theologians through a somewhat friendly series of letters between Theodore Beza (1519-1605), the successor to John Calvin at Geneva, and Johannes Piscator (1546-1625). Beza could be considered the innovator of the doctrine of the active obedience of Christ even though he "may not have been totally consistent."[48] But he seems to teach (1) the double imputation of justification, and (2) the capability of Christ to keep the law for others and impute this righteousness to believers. Beza even taught that Christ's virgin birth took "care of our problem of original sin."[49] Christ's life was thus substitutionary for the sins of the elect from the moment of His conception, according to Beza.

Johannes Piscator, is not as well known as Beza. He spent his adult life as a professor at several Reformed divinity schools in the Germanys, the longest stint at the Herborn Academy from 1584-1625. His writings include a translation of the German Bible, a summary of Calvin's *Institutes*, and commentaries on every book of the Bible. He was essentially orthodox. Campos explains,

> Before analyzing Piscator's opinions on Christ's obedience to the law, the ortho-
> doxy of Piscator needs to be asserted with respect to the doctrine of justification,
> which encompassed his views on Christ's active obedience. He upheld a forensic
> view of justification with an extrinsic notion of righteousness imputed rather than
> the medieval and Catholic notion of infusion. He vehemently excluded our works
> from justification, clearly distinguishing justification from sanctification. And he
> believed in the mere instrumentality of faith to grasp the righteousness of Christ
> rather than being the root from which works of righteousness for our justification
> come.... The issue of active obedience is probably the only one in the book which
> would stir some controversy among the Protestant orthodox.[50]

---

[47] Campos, *Doctrine in Development*, 227.

[48] Ibid., 79.

[49] Ibid., 80.

[50] Ibid., 108.

Piscator agrees with many components of the active obedience of Christ. He believes that Christ did perfectly keep the law. He believes that the Old Covenant moral law was still in existence in the church age. And he believes that a sinner does need both the forgiveness of sins and the righteousness that provides for eternal life.

Piscator was also committed to defending the Protestant teaching that justification is a forensic (legal) act.[51] Protestants in the Reformation emphasized that in justification, God *declares or pronounces* the sinner righteous. This differs from the Roman Catholics who believed that in justification, God *makes* the sinner righteous over a period of time through the sacramental system. It may be that Piscator's ultimate concern about the Reformed teaching that justification not only legally declares the sinner forgiven, but also legally imputes righteousness to the sinner, was too close to the Roman Catholic doctrine that in justification, God *makes* the repentant sinner righteous.

At any rate, Piscator rejected the doctrine of the imputation of Christ's law-keeping in justification. As a theologian who had written a commentary on every book of the Bible, he "confidently attested that the Scriptures were silent in respect to the imputation of Christ's active obedience."[52] Also, though he believed that the law of God was unchanging and continued until the resurrection, he taught that the way to eternal life through law-keeping had been closed. Campos explains that for Piscator, "the gospel appears to supplant the legal framework with a new form of attaining righteousness (not only of receiving it); the legal form of attaining life through perfect obedience is now defunct."[53] So, the purpose of the law was "pedagogical," to convict us of our sin and lead us to Christ (Rom 10:4).[54] Indeed, for Piscator, to see the law-keeping of Christ as part of justification would be to minimize the cross. In Campos' analysis of Piscator's view, "One cannot hold to the imputation of Christ's active obedience providing us with righteousness and still regard the cross as necessary for our righteousness."[55]

---

[51] Johannes Piscator, *A Learned and Profitable Treatise of Man's Justification* (London: Thomas Creede, 1599; reproduction by Early Books Online.

[52] Campos, *Doctrine in Development*, 10.

[53] Ibid., 158.

[54] Another key purpose of the law was to be "the dividing wall of hostility" (Eph 2:14) which kept the Jews and Gentiles separated until the death of Christ.

[55] Campos, *Doctrine in Development*, 163.

Piscator thus concludes that the doctrine of justification only provides for the forgiveness of sins and not the imputation of Christ's righteousness. Fesko explains, "According to Piscator Christ had to be perfectly obedient in order to qualify Himself to serve as mediator; if he was not personally holy, He would have been incapable of pleasing God. But Piscator does not take the next step and claim that God then imputes Christ's obedience to believers by faith alone."[56]

Piscator does not mean, however, that a believing sinner does not receive a new righteous nature when he is saved. He argues that those who teach the imputation of the active obedience of Christ through justification combine doctrines that are joined but distinguished at salvation. "Forgiveness of the punishment," he maintains, is different from the "cleansing of the faults." Forgiveness of the punishment occurs in justification. Cleansing of the fault "is by regeneration."[57] Discussing Romans 4-5, Piscator asserts,

> Although it is true that Christ by his obedience, hath obtained also that justice is infused into the elect by the regeneration of the Holy Ghost: as Adam by his disobedience caused that injustice is infused into his posteritie by carnal generation; nevertheless the Apostle speaketh not here of that thing, because here he handleth not regeneration (which he handleth in the 6, 7, and 8 chapters) but justification."[58]

In other words, for Piscator, Christ's righteousness is infused into the believer's moral nature by regeneration, not by justification.

Along with the doctrine of regeneration, Piscator also comments on the believer's adoption into God's family as the means of attaining the righteousness needed to have eternal life. So, yes, according to Piscator, we need positive righteousness in addition to the forgiveness of sins. But this righteousness comes through the new nature that believers receive through regeneration when we are adopted into the family of God. It does not come through the imputation of Christ's law-keeping.

---

[56] Fesko, *Death in Adam, Life in Christ*, 88. Cf., 89-102.

[57] Johannes Piscator, *A Learned and Profitable Treatise of Man's Justification*, 20.

[58] Ibid., 49-50, old English translation.

The Turning Point in the Debate

In Campos' analysis, "Piscator's objections to the imputation of Christ's positive righteousness functioned as a turning point in the Reformed understanding of active obedience, since it generated responses that brought together several other doctrines to support the imputation of Christ's active obedience in a
way that Reformed theologians had not previously done."[59] Other well-known
opponents of the imputation of the active obedience of Christ's law-keeping
include John Cameron, Moises Amyraut, Johann Heinrich Alsted, and Richard
Baxter.[60] Most Reformed theologians, however, accepted the imputation of
Christ's active law-keeping obedience to the believer's account in justification,
and Piscator's views were censored by some Reformed councils.

Seventeenth Century Developments

The first generation of Reformed theologians did not use the terminology
"active and passive" obedience. It was in the seventeenth-century that this terminology came to the forefront, especially among British Puritans.[61] Though
composers of the Westminster Confession (1646), debated the doctrine, they
"do not devote much space to the active obedience, but list it before going on
to the issues involved in his atoning death."[62] The Confession does not use the
terminology "active and passive obedience," but states "by imputing the obedience and satisfaction of Christ unto them" (ch. 11).

In 1658, the Savoy Declaration of the Congregationalists states that in justification, God imputed "Christ's active obedience to the whole law, and passive obedience in his death for their whole and sole righteousness" (11:1). The
Second London Confession of the Baptists (1689) which copied word for word
most of the Westminster Confession (other than the sections on the Baptist
distinctives) adds a statement about God "imputing Christ's active obedience
unto the whole law, and passive obedience in his death for their whole and
sole righteousness by faith" (ch. 11, par. 1). Cocceius, as we have seen teaches
this doctrine in 1648 and employs the terminology, "the active and passive

---

[59] Campos, *Doctrine in Development*, 7.

[60] Fesko, *Death in Adam, Life in Christ*, 102.

[61] Douglas F. Kelly, *Systematic Theology*, vol. 2 (Geanies, Fearn, Ross-shire, UK: Christian Focus, 2014), 318. Kelly
emphasizes that it was the terminology that was new, not the main features of the doctrine.

[62] Ibid., 329.

righteousness" of Christ in his book, *The Doctrine of the Covenant and Testament of God*.[63] It is obvious from Cocceius' extensive development of the covenant of works that the doctrine of the active obedience of Christ in keeping the law had become a central concept for federal theology by the middle of the seventeenth century. Campos writes,

> Secondary literature has shown that the notion of a prelapsarian covenant, not only the terminology 'covenant of works,' consistently became a locus in Reformed theology from the late sixteenth century onward. As this locus solidifies in Reformed theology it is brought as a framework in which the imputation of Christ's active obedience seems to fit. By the end of the seventeenth century, the covenant of works and Christ's active obedience are so intertwined that a Brakel writes of the former, "Acquaintance with this covenant is of the greatest importance, for whoever errs here or denies the existence of the covenant of works, will not understand the covenant of grace, and will readily err concerning the mediatorship of the Lord Jesus. Such a person will very readily deny that Christ by His active obedience has merited a right to eternal life for the elect."[64]

An Assessment of the Imputation of Christ's Law-keeping

The doctrine of the imputation of the active obedience of Christ through justification is highly regarded in much of Protestantism. Probably most evangelicals, including many non-covenantalists, teach this concept, though non-covenantalists leave out the covenant of works in their explanation. For the covenant theologians who stand in the line of Beza, Cocceius, and the Princeton theologians, the imputation of the active obedience of Christ is a sine qua non of their fully developed system. If the doctrine of the imputation of the active obedience of Christ as a part of justification were to be removed from covenant theology, covenant theology would unravel.

Non-covenantalists who have concluded that this doctrine should be modified, do agree that (1) Christ was required to keep the law; (2) Christ provided

---

[63] Johannes Cocceius, *The Doctrine of the Covenant and Testament of God*, volume 3 of Classic Reformed Theology, trans. Casey Carmichael (Grand Rapids: Reformation Heritage Books, 2016, originally published by Cocceius in 1648), (par. 93), 92. Cocceius writes, "Therefore by no means is it necessary that the active and passive righteousness of Christ be so divided that He claims one for Himself and gives the other to us." See also Willem J. van Asselt, *The Federal Theology of Johannes Cocceius*, trans. Raymond A. Blacketer (Boston: Brill, 2001), 46.

[64] Campos, *Doctrine in Development*, 234-35. Campos is quoting Wilhelmus a Brakel, *The Christian's Reasonable Service*, 1:355.

for justification by His passive obedience on the cross; and (3) there is a need for positive righteousness beyond God's forgiveness of our sins.

The Truth of Christ's Law-Keeping

The Bible teaches that Christ was required to keep the law while He was on earth. Christ's perfect life of obedience:

1. Qualified Him to be the sin-bearer—"For our sake he made him to be sin *who knew no sin*, so that in him we might become the righteousness of God" (2 Cor 5:21);

2. Enabled Him to fulfill the Old Covenant—"Do not think that I have come to abolish the Law or the Prophets; I have not come to abolish them but to fulfill them" (Matt 5:17; cf. 27:50-51);

3. Enabled Him to open the New Covenant—"Being therefore exalted at the right hand of God, and having received from the Father the promise of the Holy Spirit, he has poured out this that you yourselves are seeing and hearing" (Acts 2:33);

4. Qualified Him to be declared the Son of God—"and was declared to be the Son of God in power according to the Spirit of holiness by his resurrection from the dead, Jesus Christ our Lord" (Rom 1:4). David Garner correctly writes, "God chose *Jesus* as his adopted Son because he had obeyed exhaustively."[65]

5. Qualified Him to be our High Priest—"Therefore he had to be made like his brothers in every respect, so that he might become a merciful and faithful high priest in the service of God, to make propitiation for the sins of the people. For because he himself has suffered when tempted, he is able to help those who are being tempted" (Heb 2:17-18). As Garner observes, "The primary soteriological point is that Christ obeyed as the suffering Son, and that by his obedience in life and death, he became qualified in his resurrection as the ever-interceding Savior of Sinners."[66]

---

[65] David B. Garner, *Sons in the Son* (Phillipsburg, NJ: P&R, 2016), 214.

[66] Ibid., 218. Garner's covenant theology permeates his book and is a distraction. The word, "typological," or "type," shows up more than twenty times in pages 145-69 when he is discussing the role of Israel in God's plan. Otherwise, the book is an excellent study of the sonship of Jesus and our sonship "in Christ." For me, significant sections of the book were a breath of fresh air in contrast to other covenantalists' literature on this important theme of the New Testament.

A Refinement of the Covenantalist Construct

There are thus many biblical reasons for teaching that Christ was required to keep the law of God while He was here on earth. Nevertheless, for those of us that do not believe in a covenant of works, there are good reasons to think that the doctrine of the active obedience of Christ, especially as taught by covenant theologians, needs to be refined.

Salvation Is Not Based on Law-keeping

First, the covenantalist stress on law-keeping as the solution for sin needs refinement. According to covenantalism, Christ was freed from keeping the law for Himself; therefore, His law-keeping righteousness was available for God to impute to others. But are we sure that Christ did not need to keep the law for Himself? As we just noted, there are at least five reasons why Christ did need to keep the law for Himself. By so doing, (1) He was qualified to be our sin-bearer; (2) He was enabled to fulfill the Old Covenant; (3) He was enabled to open the New Covenant; (4) He was qualified to be declared the Son of God; (5) He was qualified to be our High Priest. How can a theologian make a broad general statement that Christ did not need to keep the law for Himself?

Furthermore, the concept that Christ was not required to keep the law for Himself raises the question as to whether this compromises the Bible's teaching that Christ was our sympathetic High Priest: "Therefore he had to be made like his brothers in every respect, so that he might become a merciful and faithful high priest in the service of God, to make propitiation for the sins of the people. For because he himself has suffered when tempted, he is able to help those who are being tempted" (Heb 2:17-18; cf. Heb 4:15). How does what Cocceius claimed, that Christ had to keep the law under threat of punishment, agree with the teaching that Christ did not have to keep the law for Himself. If He were under the threat of punishment, He had a very personal stake in keeping the law for Himself.[67] Perhaps covenantalists could argue that Christ had to keep the law for Himself, but in the end, He didn't need the earned righteousness for Himself. But the concept that Christ did not need to keep the law for Himself is at best confusing.

---

[67] Cocceius, *Covenant and Testament of God* (par. 97), 95. As we noted in the previous chapter, Cocceius presents seventeen reasons as to why Christ had to be fully under the law, including the threat of punishment.

More importantly, perhaps, are the legalistic overtones that pervade the covenantal theory that humans can only be saved from their sins by works (law-keeping). In covenantalism, Christ ends up fulfilling the covenant of works for us. Nevertheless, the bottom foundation stone of covenantalist soteriology is the big idea that works (law-keeping) is at the basis of salvation. Indeed, I have heard covenantalists say, "We are saved by works—Christ's works."

Dispensationalists do not doubt that the sons of Adam are required to keep the moral law of God. The moral law of God is the expression of God's nature in the form of moral requirements for human beings. It is articulated and applied in different ways throughout Scripture. In the Garden of Eden, God tested Adam's and Eve's loyalty to Himself by requiring them not to eat of the tree of the knowledge of good and evil. After they disobeyed, there was moral law between the Fall and the Mosaic covenant (Gen 18:19). Then, after the Mosaic Law, the Law of Christ became and remains the expression of the moral law of God (1 Cor 9:21; Gal 6:2). Everyone throughout history has been required to keep the moral law of God as it has been stated and applied in his or her time. Indeed, sin "is the lack of conformity to the moral law of God, either in act, disposition, or state."[68] But the obligation to keep the law of God is not the foundational stone in salvation.

The reason that Christ was obedient to the Law throughout His life is that He had perfect faith in God. Unlike Adam, Christ trusted God when Satan tempted Him, gaining victory through His reliance on the Old Testament Scriptures (Matt 4). In the Garden of Gethsemane, He prayed, "My Father, if this cannot pass unless I drink it, your will be done" (Matt 26:42). The Apostle Peter summarizes, "When he was reviled, he did not revile in return; when he suffered, he did not threaten, but continued entrusting himself to him who judges justly (1 Pet 2:23). Christ's law-keeping was a subset of the main requirement to trust God.

Furthermore, not only did Christ trust God perfectly, He also loved God perfectly. He kept the command of Deuteronomy 6:5 as no one else: "You shall love the LORD your God with all your heart and with all your soul and with all your might." Indeed, He taught us that this was the greatest commandment (Matt 22:37-38). Thus, Christ's obedience was based on a loving, trusting, personal relationship with God. The Servant of the Lord, the Messiah, happily says, "I delight to do your will, O my God; your law is within my heart" (Ps

---

[68] Strong, *Systematic Theology*, 549.

40:8). Jesus was not a legalist, and law-keeping must be kept in its proper context of the greatest commandment.[69]

Our point is that bare law-keeping was never intended to provide salvation. Even in the Garden of Eden, as we have seen, confirmation of Adam's and Eve's state of righteousness was available by faith and trust in God. Concerning the command not to eat of the tree of the knowledge of good and evil, Vlach correctly states,

> This command did not function as a call for Adam and Eve to merit or work for their salvation. Adam was created as a son and king in fellowship with God. Instead, this was an opportunity for these volitional beings to willingly express obedience to their Creator with their hearts. Avoiding the "tree of knowledge of good and evil" was to be an expression of worship.[70]

When the test came, however, Adam and Eve liked the idea that they could determine for themselves what is good and what is evil. So, they chose to believe Satan's lie and distrust the Lord God.

No one in the history of the human race, including Adam and Eve, could earn salvation by doing good works or keeping the law. A relationship with God has always been based on a loving trust in Him. Ultimately, the specter of the law that hangs over the head of every human being is solved in one way: the cross of Christ. In the words of the Apostle Paul, "Christ redeemed us from the curse of the law by becoming a curse for us—for it is written, 'Cursed is everyone who is hanged on a tree'" (Gal 3:13). It is the cross of Christ that removes the curse of the law from us.

Salvation Is Based on One Act of Obedience

Moreover, like other features of covenant theology, the imputation of Christ's law-keeping righteousness is never mentioned in Scripture. Many admit this, but then go on to teach it anyway. George Eldon Ladd, for example, asserts,

---

[69] Some covenantalists are alert to the need to emphasize that Christ's law-keeping came from the heart and was not just a legalistic obedience. Robert Reymond expresses this truth well: "Christ's obedience always came from his heart as a willing, joyous yielding up of himself to his Father's will and law; never was it merely artificial and outward, executed mechanically and perfunctory. His entire life was one of delight in doing his Father's will" (Reymond, *A New Systematic Theology of the Christian Faith*), 630.

[70] Vlach, *He Will Reign Forever*, 65. From a dispensationalist perspective, the misunderstanding and misuse of what covenantalists call the covenant of works is a fatal flaw in covenant theology.

"In classical Reformed theology, a corollary of justification is the doctrine of the imputation of Christ's righteousness to the believer. However, Paul never expressly states that the righteousness of Christ is imputed to believers."[71] Two paragraphs later, however, he concludes, "It is an unavoidable logical conclusion that people of faith are justified because Christ's righteousness is imputed to them."[72]

Similarly, Brandon Crowe states that though Scripture does not explicitly teach this doctrine, nevertheless what is taught in Scripture is "tantamount to imputation."[73] Michael Bird writes that in his study of justification he "became convinced of two things. First, there simply is no text in the New Testament which categorically states that Christ's righteousness is imputed to believers." But second, because of Christ's and Adam's representative roles, "imputed righteousness remains a legitimate way of expressing the forensic nature of justification...."[74] As these three scholars reluctantly admit, there is no specific statement in Scripture concerning the forensic imputation of Christ's law-keeping righteousness.

Instead, the Apostle Paul proclaims that a sinner is declared righteous on the basis of one act of Christ: "Therefore, as one trespass led to condemnation for all men, so one act of righteousness leads to justification and life for all men. For as by the one man's disobedience the many were made sinners, so by the one man's obedience the many will be made righteous" (Rom 5:18-19)."

"Obedience" in this passage does not refer to Christ keeping the law. In the previous eleven verses of chapter five, Paul focuses on the death of Christ, not His life of law-keeping. Then in verses 18-19, he specifically contrasts two individual acts: Adam's and Christ's. Adam's one act of disobedience was his repudiation of the Lordship of God when he ate of the fruit of the forbidden tree. Christ's one act of obedience was His willingness to go to the cross and die for our sins. It is "one act of righteousness"—the passive obedience of Christ on the

---

[71] George Eldon Ladd, *A Theology of the New Testament* (Grand Rapids: Eerdmans; revised edition, 1993), 491.

[72] Ibid.

[73] Brandon D. Crowe, *The Last Adam* (Grand Rapids: Baker Academic, 2017), 204.

[74] Michael Bird, *The Saving Righteousness of God* (Milton Keynes, Great Britain: Paternoster; Eugene, OR: Wipf and Stock edition, 2007), 2-3. There is no question that Scripture teaches that the forgiveness of sins in justification is a forensic event. God the judge declares the repentant sinner "not guilty." But Dr. Bird is arguing that the righteousness that we receive at salvation is also a forensic act—which is the issue that we are considering. Our point here is that this concept is never found in Scripture. Nevertheless, Bird's book is an excellent contribution to the discussion, and his point about the representative roles of Adam and Christ in this discussion is well-taken. In my view, however, key Scriptures about the representative roles of Adam and Christ assert that it is the "in Christ" relationship of the believer, not justification as such, that is the means of receiving our righteousness (i.e., 1 Cor 15:20). The righteousness that we receive from God in salvation, I will argue, is participative ("in Christ") rather than forensic.

cross followed by His resurrection—that "leads to justification and life." John Murray writes that on the basis of Rom 5:19, Phil 2:8, Heb 5:8,9 and 10:9,10, "our thought of the atonement is not biblically oriented unless it is governed by this concept of obedience."[75] In Scripture's words, "And being found in human form, he humbled himself by becoming obedient to the point of death, even death on a cross" (Phil 2:8).

Thus, Christ did not save us from the condemnation of the law by keeping the law (though He did perfectly keep it). Rather, as quoted above, "Christ redeemed us from the curse of the law by becoming a curse for us—for it is written, 'Cursed is everyone who is hanged on a tree'" (Gal 3:13). God justifies a repentant sinner on the basis of the death, burial, and resurrection of Jesus Christ. "The death on the cross was the supreme act of obedience."[76]

"Justification" Is Found in the Context of the Death of Christ

The verb, "justify," furthermore, is always found in the context of the substitutionary death of Christ in the New Testament when the context is salvation. Andrew Snider writes,

> The verb for justification ... appears in the NT thirty-nine times. Twenty-two of these occurrences speak of justification in a soteriological sense, and all are found in Paul's writings. In none of these occurrences is the active obedience of Christ associated with justification, nor is it present in the context. A check of the uses of other words in the same word group reveals a similar conclusion. Justification is always by faith in Christ because of his death on behalf of sinners.[77]

Snider points out that the covenant theologians' traditional solution to this challenge is to assert that these passages are synecdoches, that the New Testament writers include only a part for the whole. Admittedly, they argue, even if we don't find the active obedience of Christ in the Scriptural passages teaching justification, both the cross and law keeping are represented though only the cross is mentioned. Although this might be a legitimate solution if this happened

---

[75] John Murray, "The Obedience of Christ," *Collected Writings of John Murray*, vol.2 (Carlisle, PA: Banner of Truth, 1977), 152.

[76] Ibid., 134.

[77] Andrew Snider, "Justification and the Active Obedience of Christ: Toward a Biblical Understanding of Imputed Righteousness" (Th. M. Thesis, The Master's Seminary, 2002), 87.

only once, it is highly unlikely that such a figure of speech (a part for the whole) is employed in all twenty-two occurrences.

It is better to understand that justification provides the forgiveness of sins, but does not include the imputation of Christ's law-keeping righteousness. The righteousness of God that we need to enter heaven comes from a different doctrine in the multi-faceted doctrine of salvation.

Salvation Is Based on the "Righteousness of God"

The "righteousness of Christ" is mentioned twice in the New Testament. First John 2:29 teaches that Christ is righteous, and 2 Peter 1:1 asserts that the readers of this letter "have obtained a faith of equal standing with ours by the righteousness of our God and Savior Jesus Christ" (2 Pet 1:1), a reference to the fairness and justice of Christ.[78]

But the New Testament authors, especially Paul, consistently discuss the "righteousness of God" (Rom 1:17; 3:5; 3:21; 3:22; 3:25; 3:26; 10:3 twice; 1 Cor 1:30; 2 Cor 5:21; Eph 4:24; Phil 3:9; Jas 1:20). The righteousness that is provided for us in salvation is described twice as "the righteousness from God." Paul tells the Philippians that he counted all of his previous law-keeping good works as rubbish so that "he would be found *in him*, not having a righteousness of my own that comes from the law, but that which comes through faith in Christ, *the righteousness from God* (ἐκ θεοῦ) that depends on faith" (Phil 3:9, emphasis added). Similarly, Paul tells the Christians at Corinth that because of God "you are in Christ Jesus, who became to us wisdom from God, righteousness and sanctification and redemption, so that, as it is written, 'Let the one who boasts, boast in the Lord'" (1 Cor 1:30-31). By being in Christ, Christians receive the wisdom, righteousness, sanctification, and redemption "from God."

In other passages, when Paul discusses the righteousness of God, he seems to be referring to the whole composite of salvation blessings. He writes, "For in it [i.e., the Gospel] the righteousness of God is revealed from faith for faith, as it is written, 'The righteous shall live by faith.'" (Rom 1:17). Michael Bird comments,

> Thus the righteousness of God, at least in Rom 1:17, introduces the entire package of salvation including justification, redemption, propitiatory sacrifice, forgiveness

---

[78] R. H. Strachan, "The Second Epistle General of Peter," *The Expositor's Greek Testament*, vol. V, W. Robertson Nicoll, ed. (Grand Rapids: Eerdmans, 1970), 123; also Michael Green, *The Second Epistle of Peter and the Epistle of Jude*, Tyndale New Testament Commentaries, ed. R. V. G. Tasker (Grand Rapids: Eerdmans, 1980), 60.

of sins, membership in the new covenant community, reconciliation, the gift of the Holy Spirit, power for new obedience, union with Christ, freedom from sin, and eschatological vindication. God's righteousness is an all-encompassing action that includes both redemption and renewal.... God's righteousness is all that God does in salvation in our behalf.[79]

No aspect of the doctrine of salvation is outside of the "righteousness of God."

In another important Scripture, Paul writes, "For our sake he [God] made him [Christ] to be sin who knew no sin, so that *in him* we might *become the righteousness of God*" (2 Cor 5:21, emphasis mine in these verses). Here Christians actually *become* the righteousness of God by being "in Christ" (δικαιοσύνη Θεοῦ ἐν αὐτῷ). To "become" in this context expresses coming into a certain state, to experience a change in nature, to enter into a new creation.[80] In salvation, our corrupt moral nature is changed into a divinely righteous nature. A Christian, therefore, is to put off his old self which belonged to his "former manner of life," "and to put on the new self, created after the likeness of God in true righteousness and holiness" (Eph 4:22-24).

So, yes, there is a need for a righteousness beyond God's forgiveness of our sins. At salvation we are justified by faith alone, God declaring our sins past, present forgiven, and future sins not imputed to our account (Rom 4:7-8). And we receive the righteousness of God. The righteousness of and from God is obviously *extra nos*, the ultimate "alien righteousness."

Union with Christ

The final question is, how do we "become the righteousness of God"? If the righteousness of Christ's law-keeping is not forensically imputed to us in justification, how do we receive it? As important as the doctrine of justification by faith alone is to our eternal salvation, it does not comprise all of the doctrine of salvation. Some theologians have nearly taught that it is. It was common for

---

[79] Bird, *The Saving Righteousness of God*, 16. The Old Testament believer received righteousness from God, as the well-known case of Abraham illustrates (Gen 15:6; Rom 4:22) and is well-defined as "all that God does in salvation." But there are added benefits that come with the New Covenant. Old Covenant believers did receive "both redemption and renewal." This means that they were both justified and regenerated by their faith in God on the basis of the future substitutionary death, burial, and resurrection of Jesus Christ. From Bird's list, Old Covenant righteousness from God included justification, redemption, propitiatory sacrifice, forgiveness of sins, reconciliation, and eschatological vindication.

[80] See Walter Bauer, W. F. Arndt, F. W. Gingrich, and F. W. Danker, *Greek-English Lexicon of the New Testament and Other Early Christian Literature*, 3rd ed. (Chicago: University of Chicago, 2000), 198-99.

both Lutherans and some Reformed theologians to emphasize justification by faith to the neglect of other important soteriological truths during the post-Reformation era.[81] Justification by faith alone for some Lutherans, notes Garner, "was not merely a facet of theology, but the essence of it. The forensic served paradigmatically for their interpretive method and continues to do so today for much of Lutheran scholarship." Garner speaks of this almost exclusive emphasis on law-keeping and justification as "soteriological disproportion" that "generates numerous negative consequences."[82]

The negative consequences of which Garner speaks include antinomianism, legalism, and a failure to recognize the equal importance of the personal intimate relationship with God that the New Covenant Christian has through his or her union with Jesus Christ. Indeed, this forensic exclusivity in the Reformation brought about the rise of the Pietist movement which impacted both Lutheran and Reformed theology. Pietists insisted that being a Christian was not limited to a correct legal standing before God. They believed that the essence of Christianity is to be found in the personally meaningful relationship of the individual with God. The evangelical Anabaptists also rejected forensic exclusivity.

There is on-going debate even now among American covenantalists over whether justification (forensic) or union with Christ (participationist) is at the foundation of salvation. The side arguing that union with Christ is foundational think that certain post-Reformation covenantalists corrupted Calvin's doctrine of justification by emphasizing it to the place where union with Christ is ignored.[83]

---

[81] Simo Peura, a contemporary Lutheran scholar, points out that second generation Lutherans in the Formula of Concord (1577) included the forensic, but, in contrast with Luther, left out "the renewal of a Christian and the removal of sin from the doctrine (locus) of justification" (Simo Peura, "Christ as Favor and Gift (donum): The Challenge of Luther's Understanding of Justification," in *Union with Christ*, ed. Carl E. Braaten and Robert W. Jensen [Grand Rapids: Eerdmans, 1998], 45. For Luther, "Christ himself is the grace that covers a sinner and hides him from God's wrath, and Christ is the gift that renews the sinner internally and makes him righteous. This occurs, then when Christ unites himself with a sinner" (53). So, for Luther, justification in all its facets is based on union with Christ. But for Luther, "union with Christ is effected in baptism" (53). Peura warns the Lutherans that in their dialogues with Roman Catholics and the Orthodox, "we Lutherans will encounter great difficulties if we try to represent only the forensic aspect of justification" (43).

[82] Garner, *Sons in the Sons*, 224.

[83] For a helpful analysis of this debate among covenantalists, see Timothy Miller, "The Debate Over the *Ordo Salutis* in American Reformed Theology," *Detroit Baptist Seminary Journal* 18 (2013): 41-66. Westminster Seminary of Philadelphia apparently emphasizes the view, which they say was Calvin's view, that union with Christ is the foundation of salvation. Westminster Seminary in California seems to argue that it is justification. Of course, faculties from both seminaries believe that Calvin taught both union with Christ and justification by faith alone. Michael Horton, for example, who argues that the relational is grounded in the forensic, still believes that "even though Jesus Christ has been exalted to the throne of God, absent from us in the flesh, we may nevertheless only now be united to him in a manner far more intimate than the fellowship enjoyed by the disciples with Jesus during his earthly ministry" (Horton, *The Christian Faith*, 587; cf. 588).

So, to come to the point, if we do not receive the righteousness of God by the imputation of Christ's active obedience, how do we receive it? Simply answered, the Bible teaches that we receive it by being "in Christ." And we get into Christ through Spirit baptism at the time of salvation. As the Scripture says, "For as many of you as were baptized into Christ have put on Christ" (Gal 3:27). James Dunn says, "To be baptized into Christ is complementary to or equivalent to assuming the persona of Christ. In both cases [Spirit baptism and putting on Christ] some sort of identification or sense of bound-up-with-ness is implicit."[84] The only way that we can experience the many blessings of New Covenant salvation, therefore, is to be baptized by the Spirit into union with Christ.[85]

When we are placed into union with Christ at the instant of our salvation, we receive multiple New Covenant salvation benefits. Even the forgiveness of sins through justification is made possible by our union with Christ (Rom 8:1). D. A. Carson writes, "I cannot too strongly emphasize how often Paul's justification language is tied to 'in Christ' or 'in him' languages." He continues, "In other words, the language of incorporation or of identification is precisely what grounds 'the great exchange': when Christ died, he died my death, so I can truly say I died in him; now that Christ lives, his life is mine, so I can truly say I live in him."[86]

The "in Christ" intimacy saturates the New Testament epistles and shows up specifically in Paul's writings more than one hundred times. In Garner's words, "Union with Jesus Christ renders a comprehensive complex of redemptive benefits—legal, moral, somatic (the resurrection of the body), and relational-*filial*."[87] The New Testament clearly reveals this "comprehensive complex of redemptive benefits" that come through union with Christ as follows:

---

[84] James D. G. Dunn, *The Theology of Paul the Apostle* (Grand Rapids: Eerdmans, 1998), 405.

[85] Though salvation is essentially the same in both the Old and New Covenants, a more personal and intimate relationship with God was made available when Christ opened the New Covenant on the Day of Pentecost. The Apostle Peter, on his Pentecost day sermon, teaches, "Being therefore exalted at the right hand of God, and having received from the Father the promise of the Holy Spirit, he has poured out this that you yourselves are seeing and hearing" (Acts 2:33). The outpouring of the Holy Spirit was a signal that the New Covenant soteriological benefits were available. So, by means of the New Covenant, we receive some wonderful new soteriological benefits through the mediatorial ministry of Jesus Christ.

[86] D. A. Carson, "The Vindication of Imputation: On Fields of Discourse and Semantic Fields," in *Justification, What's at State in the Current Debates*, ed. Mark Husbands and Daniel J. Treier (Downers Grove, IL: IVP Academic, 2004), 72, 74 (see further, Romans 6:3-5; Galatians 2:20-21). Dr. Carson is not here repudiating the doctrine of the imputation of Christ' active obedience in the act of justification.

[87] Garner, *Sons in the Son*, 230.

1. God chose us in Christ: "even as he chose us *in him* before the foundation of the world, that we should be holy and blameless before him" (Eph 1:4);

2. We are adopted as God's sons in Christ: "In love he predestined us for adoption to himself as sons *through Jesus Christ*, according to the purpose of his will, to the praise of his glorious grace, with which he has blessed us *in the Beloved*" (Eph 1:4-6).

3. We are justified in Christ: "There is therefore now no condemnation for those who are *in Christ Jesus*" (Rom 8:1).

4. We are regenerated in Christ: "Therefore, if anyone is *in Christ*, he is a new creation. The old has passed away; behold, the new has come" (2 Cor 5:17).

5. We are sanctified in Christ:
    Positional sanctification: "to those sanctified *in Christ Jesus*" (1 Cor 1:2).
    Progressive sanctification: "that in every way you were enriched *in him* in all speech and all knowledge" (1 Cor 1:5).

6. We are preserved in our salvation in Christ: "For I am sure that neither death nor life, nor angels nor rulers, nor things present nor things to come, nor powers, nor height nor depth, nor anything else in all creation, will be able to separate us from the love of God *in Christ Jesus* our Lord" (Rom 8:38-39).

7. We receive the righteousness of God in Christ.
    "For our sake he [God] made him [Christ] to be sin who knew no sin, so that *in him* we might become the righteousness of God" (2 Cor 5:21).

    "And be found *in him*, not having a righteousness of my own that comes from the law, but that which comes through faith in Christ, the righteousness from God that depends on faith" (Phil 3:9). All of the benefits of our salvation come to us through our union with Christ and thereby we receive a new relationship with God. God sees us as righteous because of our identification by faith with His Son. Indeed, we are "sons of God."

Implications of Union with Christ

The doctrine of union with Christ actually helps to maintain the correct teaching of justification. It provides a biblical response to the Roman Catholic accusation that the Protestant doctrine of justification by faith was legal fiction since it supposedly declared a person righteous but didn't make a person righteous. The best answer to such an accusation is that "in Christ Jesus," we also receive the righteousness of God.

The emphasis on union with Christ also focuses our lives on the centrality of Jesus Christ. Timothy Miller points out, "In other words, all of the benefits of salvation—past, present, and future—are obtained through our union with Christ. Only a robust theology of the priority of union in the ordo does justice to the central place of Jesus and His work in salvation."[88]

Furthermore, the doctrine of union with Christ tends to minimize the dangers of either antinomianism or legalism: Antinomianism: Since we have been justified by faith, we can live how we want; Legalism: Salvation is about fulfilling the law rather than our relationship with God. Even such doctrines as election and predestination are better understood and made more intimate through the biblical emphasis on union. The Apostle Paul delighted in his union with Christ:

> Blessed be the God and Father of our Lord Jesus Christ, who has blessed us *in Christ* with every spiritual blessing in the heavenly places, even as he chose us *in him* before the foundation of the world, that we should be holy and blameless before him. In love he predestined us for adoption to himself as sons *through Jesus Christ*, according to the purpose of his will, to the praise of his glorious grace, with which he has blessed us *in the Beloved* (Eph 1:3-6, added emphasis).

Christians are blessed, adopted, and chosen *in Christ*.

Justification by faith alone is a major doctrine in the plan of salvation in which God the righteous Judge declares us not guilty. It is what Martin Luther longed for; it was what the Apostle Paul longed for; and it is what all of us long for: "Therefore, since we have been justified by faith, we have peace with God through our Lord Jesus Christ" (Rom 5:1). The forensic must be "studied, proclaimed and celebrated, but never in a way that obscures the full bounty of redemptive grace in Christ Jesus."[89] In other words, as Canlis emphasizes, "participationist categories do not destroy, undermine, or call the forensic into question. They simply

---

[88] Miller, "The Debate Over the *Ordo Salutis* in American Reformed Theology," 65.

[89] Garner, *Sons in the Son*, 230.

renegotiate the forensic, by insisting that it always be drawn into the larger arena of the person of Christ and incorporation into him."[90]

Thus, "the forensic and transforming benefits of salvation are insepara-ble because both are communicated to the believer in the same way through union with the mediatorial person of Christ by the power of the Holy Spirit."[91] Amazingly, through union with Christ, we become new creations in Christ (2 Cor 5:17). We are justified, we are regenerated, we are adopted into the fam-ily of God, and we "become partakers of the divine nature, having escaped from the corruption that is in the world because of sinful desire" (2 Peter 1:4).

CONCLUSION

Covenantalism has many admirable features. It is based on the fundamentals of the faith, and promotes our great God's holiness, love, and sovereignty. But dispensationalists are convinced that covenantalism lacks Scriptural support for its distinctives. The system is based on supersessionism that insists that the church has permanently replaced the nation of Israel as God's channel of grace to the people of earth. But the Bible clearly teaches in both the Old and New Testaments that there is coming a conversion and restoration of the nation. In our view, covenant theology, as it was developed in the Reformation era, is based on an inadequate theological system that was formed for polemical and apologetical reasons rather than from an inductive study of Scripture.

The three theological covenants of covenantalism are not found in the Bible. The founders of covenant theology in the Reformation era formulated a covenant of grace that was designed to tie the Old and New Testaments together. Their apparent purpose for so doing was to justify their state-church system and infant baptism. But there is no such thing as a covenant of grace in Scripture. The covenant of redemption, supposedly a covenant between God the Father and God the Son, was constructed in the seventeenth century in order to harmonize the decree of God (which is in Scripture) with the covenants of grace and works, which are not in Scripture. Besides not being in Scripture, the covenant of redemption presents a rather peculiar perception of the Trinity. Finally, the covenant of works, which supposedly continues from the Garden of

---

[90] Canlis, "The Fatherhood of God and Union with Christ in Calvin, 423. Canlis is specifically summarizing the doctrine of the union in Christ in Calvin's theology.

[91] Evans, *Imputation and Impartation*, 34.

Eden until the resurrection, became the center of soteriology for covenantalism, bringing with it unhelpful sub-doctrines.

Is it possible that dispensationalism, built on the major biblical covenants, is a step-up from covenantalism and supersessionism? That question is the topic of our next chapter.

7

DISPENSATIONALISM: A STEP UP FOR THE "ISRAEL OF GOD"

Larry D. Pettegrew

Dispensational premillennialism may not be as popular today as it was during the twentieth century. Indeed, one of the authors of this book has observed, tongue in cheek, that it sometimes seems as though we can no longer speak the word, "dispensationalism," in polite company. Consequently, some young men and women, originally discipled in circles that are friendly to dispensational premillennialism, may have too quickly abandoned it in their ministry preparation.[1] They may have been taught or read that dispensationalism, with its pretribulational premillennial eschatology, is only a populist movement, sustained primarily in popular prophecy novels, and thus not worthy of significant theological consideration. Or they may have been persuaded that biblical hermeneutics is complex, and the dispensational approach to hermeneutics is just too simplistic. Or perhaps they have become convinced that some form of supersessionism is a necessary accompaniment to embracing the doctrines of grace.

I think these are myths. So, I will argue in this chapter that dispensational premillennialism, when compared with other systems, consistently provides the best understanding of both the Old and New Testaments, and best honors

---

[1] I don't want to overstate this problem. I know that the reverse is also sometimes true, that those reared in non-dispensational circles sometimes later come to accept dispensational premillennialism.

the faithfulness of God to His promises to Israel. All of God's promises to the nation of Israel have been or will be fulfilled. God has not forsaken Israel.

DISPENSATION AND DISPENSATIONALISM

The differences between dispensationalism and other systems are not found in the explanation of a dispensation. A "dispensation" is a translation of the Greek word, οἰκονομία, meaning a stewardship, or an administration (Luke 12:42; Eph 3:9). When we speak of the Reagan or Obama administrations, for example, we are identifying a stewardship that these men had when they were in the oval office. They were required to take responsibility for their office and were thus stewards, responsible to the American people.

Similarly, each Christian is a personal steward of God's revelation. The apostle Paul considered himself a steward of the revelation that he had received from God about the church. He writes, "This is how one should regard us, as servants of Christ and *stewards* of the mysteries of God. Moreover, it is required of *stewards* that they be found faithful" (1 Cor 4:1-2, emphasis added; cf. Eph 3:2-3). In other Scriptures, an era is called a stewardship. Paul describes the church age as "the administration [οἰκονομία] of the mystery which for ages has been hidden in God who created all things" (Eph 3:9 NAU).

The name of the theological system, "dispensationalism," apparently derives from the idea that adherents to this system understand that God's plan for the human race is unfolded through a succession of administrations or stewardships. But no serious Bible student, dispensationalist or otherwise, doubts that there are successive dispensations in Scripture. One of the early proponents of covenant theology, Herman Witsius (d. 1708), for example, has a chapter in his two-volume set entitled "Of the different Economies or dispensations of the Covenant of Grace."[2] Witsius explains, "We shall exhibit, in this chapter, a short representation of these dispensations." Witsius discusses two dispensations in this chapter, the Old Testament dispensation that begins after the fall, and the New Testament dispensation. In another place, Witsius speaks of a third "economy" in the Garden of Eden under which the covenant of works administered God's affairs.[3] In another section of his book, Witsius introduces his chapter on the covenant of grace with similar words: "Let us now more

[2] Herman Witsius, *The Economy of the Covenants Between God and Man* . (London: R. Baynes, 1822; original Latin version, 1677 repr., Kingsburg, CA: den Dulk, Christian Foundation, 1990), I.III.III:317-24.

[3] Ibid., I.I.II:54.

particularly take a view of the two Economies, or the different dispensations under which that covenant was administered."[4] In succeeding chapters he discusses the covenant of grace "under Noah," "from Abraham to Moses," "Of the Decalogue," and "Of the Prophets."

Covenantalists, dispensationalists, and premillennial supersessionists thus use the term "dispensation" with similar understandings. Sam Storm, a covenantalists arguing for amillennialism, states, "It must be noted, however, that the recognition of distinct epochs or periods in biblical history is *not* the primary characteristic of dispensationalism. *All* Christians recognize the presence in Scripture of developments within God's redemptive purpose."[5]

Dispensationalists such as John Feinberg have emphasized this point again and again. Feinberg writes,

> The initial error is thinking that the word "dispensation" and talk of differing administrative orders only appears in dispensational thinking. Which covenant theologian thinks οἰχονομία is not a biblical word? Moreover, covenantalists
> often speak, for example, of differing dispensations of the covenant of grace. Since both dispensationalists and non-dispensationalists use the term and concept of a dispensation, that alone is not distinctive to Dispensationalism. It is no more distinctive to Dispensationalism than talk of covenants is distinctive to Covenant Theology. Dispensationalists talk about covenants all the time."[6]

Dispensationalists have always been aware of dispensations in Scripture, but so have other theological systems.

It may even be true that the name, "dispensationalist" was originated by opponents of what became known as "dispensationalism." Todd Mangum believes that 1936 is the first time that dispensationalists "accepted the label 'dispensationalist' for themselves. It appears that 'dispensationalists' accepted the label only reluctantly, and largely in response to articles written against them by Northern

---

[4] Ibid., II.IV.I:108.

[5] Sam Storm, *Kingdom Come, The Amillennial Alternative* (Geanies, Fearn, Ross-shire, UK: Christian Focus, 2013), 50.

[6] John S. Feinberg, "Systems of Discontinuity," in *Continuity and Discontinuity*, ed. by John S. Feinberg (Westchester, IL.: Crossway Books, 1988), 169. See also Peter J. Gentry and Stephen J. Wellum, *Kingdom Through Covenant* (Wheaton, IL: Crossway, 2012), 41; and Michael Vlach, "What Dispensationalism Is Not? in *Christ's Prophetic Plan*, edited by John MacArthur and Richard Mayhue (Chicago: Moody, 2012), 52.

Presbyterians."[7] "Dispensationalism," therefore, is not the best name for this system that honors God's promises to Israel. Dispensationalists didn't choose it, it has only been an identification name for their views for less than one hundred years, and it implies to some people weird doctrines such as multiple ways of salvation. Some dispensationalists have proposed that we call this system "futuristic premillennialism," and others have suggested "restorationism," i.e., the system that believes in the restoration of a redeemed Israel to the center of God's plan. Another possible good name is "biblical covenantalism" because this system is not built on the foundation of dispensations, but on the major biblical covenants, specifically the Abrahamic, Mosaic, Davidic, and New.[8] These biblical covenants form the backbone of what is usually called dispensationalism.

Dispensationalists have also tried to make other clarifying points about a dispensation, First, a dispensation is not essentially a period of time. A period of time is involved, but the point of a dispensation is that there is a distinguishable stewardship or administration. Second, the different dispensations in Scripture are not different ways of salvation. God's provision of salvation has always been by grace through faith based on the finished work of Christ. A dispensation, rather, deals with different ways that God administers His rule in the world. Third, each dispensation does have unique features to it that are clearly revealed by God, but some principles carry over to later dispensations (capital punishment, for example). Fourth, there are different opinions among dispensationalists as to how many dispensations there are. It's common to teach seven dispensations, but some dispensationalists have as few as four. One does not have to commit to a certain number of dispensations to be a dispensationalist.

EVANGELICAL

If we cannot identify dispensationalists by their distinctive use of the biblical word, "dispensation," then who are dispensationalists? Dispensationalists generally are Bible-believing Christians who hold to the fundamentals of the faith,

---

[7] Mangum, *The Dispensational-Covenant Rift*, 6. Mangum is specifically discussing dispensationalists in the southern Presbyterian Church. See also Lewis Sperry Chafer, "Dispensationalism," *Bibliotheca Sacra* 93 (October-December, 1936):390-449.

[8] Dr. Reluctant, Paul Martin Henebury, may have coined the term, "biblical covenantalism." See his blog, "Dr. Reluctant."

and often are described as evangelicals. Church historians in recent years have identified the essence of evangelicalism in four points:[9]

1. The authority of Scripture.

2. The uniqueness of redemption through the death of Christ upon the cross.

3. The need for personal conversion.

4. The necessity, propriety, and urgency of evangelism.

These characteristics apply to dispensationalists and other evangelicals. Many of those Christians who have been a part of historic fundamentalism and prefer to call themselves "fundamentalists" are also dispensationalists. It has never been true, however, that all evangelicals were dispensationalists. As noted above, dispensationalism with its eschatological teachings of pretribulational premillennialism may have lost ground in recent years.

One of the more significant articles about evangelicalism pertinent to our study was published in *Christian Life* magazine in March of 1956, and was entitled "Is Evangelical Theology Changing?"[10] The article identified eight ways in which evangelical theology was changing in the middle of the twentieth century: (1) A friendly attitude toward science; (2) A willingness to reexamine beliefs concerning the work of the Holy Spirit; (3) A more tolerant attitude toward varying views on eschatology; (4) A shift away from so-called extreme dispensationalism; (5) An increased emphasis on scholarship; (6) A more definite recognition of social responsibility; (7) A re-opening of the subject of biblical inspiration; (8) A growing willingness of evangelical theologians to converse with liberal theologians.

Concerning point three, the article states that "it used to be that most fundamentalists were premillennial and pre-tribulation.... But for the last ten years debate has been raging on these subjects."[11] Paul Woolley of Westminster

---

[9] See, for example, David W. Bebbington, *The Dominance of Evangelicalism*, vol. 3, A History of Evangelicalism (Downers Grove, IL: InterVarsity, 2005), 23-40.

[10] "Is Evangelical Theology Changing?" *Christian Life*, March 1956, 16-19. The article was written by the *Christian Life* staff and featured the views of faculty members from Fuller Theological Seminary, Wheaton College, Asbury College, Denver Conservative Baptist Theological Seminary, and Baylor University. The key interviews were from well-known evangelicals at that time including Vernon Grounds, E. J. Carnell, Lloyd Kalland, Stanley Horton, Carl F. H. Henry, Bernard Ramm, Wilbur Smith, and Paul Woolley.

[11] Ibid., 18.

Theological Seminary contributed, "The average evangelical Christian realizes
that the exegesis (explanation) of the Scriptures on this point is not so simple
that he can be cocksure about every detail. The result is that there is a more
healthy open-mindedness about the details of the eschatological scheme."[12] In
explaining point four, the author of the article declares, "Theologians are probably closer to agreeing on the fact that dispensationalism is facing a real test
today than on any other statement. Warren Young's comment, 'The trend today
is away from dispensationalism—away from the Scofield Notes—to a more
historical approach,' is echoed by many evangelical theologians."[13]

These predictions about the possible demise of dispensationalism have
not come true to the extent that these authors implied.[14] Still, "evangelical
theology is not monolithic,"[15] and has become even more amorphous over-all
since that article was written. Not all evangelicals are dispensationalists. Not
all fundamentalists are dispensationalists. But many are. Significantly, *there
has never been nor ever will be a theologically liberal dispensationalist—nor, for
that matter, a liberal pretribulational premillennialist.* It is impossible because
of dispensationalists' intense devotion to the grammatical-historical interpretation of Scripture.

CONSISTENT GRAMMATICAL-HISTORICAL INTERPRETATION

The aim of the grammatical-historical method of interpretation is to discover
the meaning of a passage of Scripture as the original author would have intended
and as the original hearers would have understood the message. Finding this
meaning may not always be the end of interpretation, but it should always be
the most important first step.[16]

Scripture is not mysterious, so it is usually not difficult to understand a
passage of Scripture. "Historical" in "grammatical-historical interpretation"
means that the student of God's Word will understand Scripture better if he

---

[12] Ibid.

[13] Ibid.

[14] Some of the other points made in this article anticipated weaknesses entering the evangelical movement rather than
strengths.

[15] Feinberg, "Systems of Discontinuity," 310.

[16] Since many books have been written to discuss and debate the issues in hermeneutics, the following discussion is only
an overview of the way many dispensationalists think about interpreting Scripture.

understands the historical, social, and cultural contexts of the biblical writers. "Grammatical" interpretation means studying the sentences word by word, knowing what the main clause in the sentence is, and observing how the verbs, nouns, and adjectives fit into the sentence structure. It also includes an investigation of the immediately preceding and immediately following contexts. Of course, the interpreter should also keep in mind the genre of the literature where a text is found: poetry (Psalms), prophecy (Isaiah, Revelation), a letter (Romans), history (Genesis), or a narrative (Acts). Acknowledging the genre of a passage of Scripture, however, does not blur the effort of trying to understand what the original author meant. Given the quality of our English translations in our era, plus some wonderful commentaries written by Bible-believing scholars, all Christians can potentially understand by serious study what a passage of Scripture means.

Trustworthiness of the Old Testament Prophets

The Old Testament Prophets are at the center of disagreements over consistent grammatical-historical interpretation. All evangelicals believe in the grammatical-historical method of interpretation of Scripture to some extent. Otherwise, they would not be evangelicals. But dispensationalists are more consistent in this matter, especially regarding Old Testament prophecy. *Dispensationalists believe and teach that an Old Testament prophecy must not be stripped of its original meaning.* If an Old Testament prophet prophesied the grandeur of a future kingdom here on earth, led by King Jesus, and centered in Jerusalem, dispensationalists believe that this is what is going to happen. For example, what did Isaiah mean when he prophesied the following?

> The word that Isaiah the son of Amoz saw concerning Judah and Jerusalem. It shall come to pass in the latter days that the mountain of the house of the LORD shall be established as the highest of the mountains, and shall be lifted up above the hills; and all the nations shall flow to it, and many peoples shall come, and say: "Come, let us go up to the mountain of the LORD, to the house of the God of Jacob, that he may teach us his ways and that we may walk in his paths." For out of Zion shall go the law, and the word of the LORD from Jerusalem. He shall judge between the nations, and shall decide disputes for many peoples; and they shall beat their swords into plowshares, and their spears into pruning hooks; nation shall not lift up sword against nation, neither shall they learn war anymore (Isa 2:1-4).

Dispensational premillennialists believe that this is exactly what is going to happen. The interpreter of the Bible, say dispensationalists, must treat with integrity an Old Testament passage in its own context. And since the Old Testament includes sixteen prophetic books, this is no minor issue. Similar prophecies about a future earthly kingdom before the eternal kingdom are also revealed in the historical and poetic sections of the Old Testament.

Interpretative Errors of the Medieval Church

The Roman Catholic Church throughout the Middle Ages prohibited the consistent grammatical-historical method of interpreting Scriptures. Thomas Aquinas (d. 1274), one of the major Roman Catholic theologians, argued that the meaning of a passage of Scripture can only be constituted by later interpretation. All historical material is subject to further interpretation because "things passing through their course signify something else."[17] This means that the New Testament reinterprets the Old Testament. But what about the New Testament? What clarifies it? Since there is no "third testament," "the obvious answer is ... his [Christ's] mystical body, the Church, endowed with the Spirit."[18]

Later Roman Church theologians such as Jean Gerson (d. 1429) went as far as to argue that the authority to judge and declare the meaning of Scriptures rests in the Church alone. Instead of the correct meaning being the plain sense of a passage of Scripture as it expressed the meaning of the author, the correct meaning "became the private property of the Spirit endowed Church."[19] Instead of a grammatical-historical interpretation of Scripture, Gerson and other medieval theologians argued for an ecclesial-literal understanding. So, "in the last analysis, the Bible itself has no theologically authoritative literal meaning."[20]

The Roman Catholic Church officially defended this view at the Council of Trent during the counter-reformation:

---

[17] Thomas Aquinas, *Quaestiones Quodlibetales*, VII q. 6 a 3 corp, in *Opera Omnia* IX, 546 ff., translated and quoted in James Preus, *From Shadow to Promise* (Cambridge, MA.: Harvard University Press, 1969), 56.

[18] Preus, *From Shadow to Promise*, 57. Preus' book is based on his Harvard dissertation. His translations from Latin and analyses of the medieval theologians inform this brief section of the chapter.

[19] Ibid., 79.

[20] Ibid., 81.

In order to restrain petulant spirits [the Council] decrees, that no one, relying on his own skill, shall,—in matters of faith, and of morals pertaining to the edification of Christian doctrine,—wrestle the sacred Scripture to his own senses, presume to interpret the said sacred Scripture contrary to that sense which holy mother Church,—whose it is to judge of the true sense and interpretation of the holy Scriptures,—hath held and doth hold.[21]

Thus, the medieval Roman Catholic Church effectively prohibited consistent grammatical-historical interpretation.

The Reformers and the Clarity of Scripture

Christian hermeneutics and theology started to change beginning in the Reformation era. One of the major principles of the Protestant Reformation was the priesthood of the believer. Thus, the believer is his own priest before God and has the right to interpret Scripture for himself. The corollary principle was that Scripture was clear and every Christian could understand it. As James Callahan explains, the clarity of Scripture means, "Scripture can be and is read with profit, with appreciation and with transformative results. It is open and transparent to earnest readers; it is intelligible and comprehensible to attentive readers. Scripture itself is coherent and obvious. It is direct and unambiguous as written; what is written is sufficient."[22] Callahan continues,

> Yet, while Protestants did not invent the notion [of clarity of Scripture], Protestantism certainly linked its own identity with a reinvented version of Scripture's clarity, making the claim to Scripture's "plain meaning," a logically necessary article of the Protestant faith.... This has its origins in Zwingli and Luther, and is particularly evident in the Protestant scholastic tradition.[23]

The Reformers thus committed themselves to the clarity of Scripture and an awareness of the dangers of allegorical interpretation that had plagued the medieval church.

---

[21] "Canons and Decrees of the Council of Trent" (fourth session, April 8, 1546), in *The Creeds of Christendom*, vol. II, ed. Philip Schaff (New York: Harper and Brothers; repr., Grand Rapids: Baker, 1977), 83.

[22] James Patrick Callahan, *The Clarity of Scripture* (Downers Grove, IL: InterVarsity, 2001), 8.

[23] Ibid., 128.

The True Meaning of Progressive Revelation

One issue of interpretation, however, remained unchanged in the Reformation era. What about the Old Testament? Is it clear, coherent, and unambiguous? Is there a plain meaning in the Old Testament text? The Reformers reawakened to the value of the history and theology of the Old Testament, to be sure. They studied it more and developed their idea of the theological covenant out of Old Testament theology. But one hermeneutical principle from medieval attitudes toward the clarity of Scripture remained: the subordination of the Old Testament to the New Testament.

Explaining the Functions of the Two Testaments

The subordination of the Old Testament to the New Testament so that the New Testament corrects the Old Testament continues to this day to be the covenant theologians' method of doing theology. Covenant theologian, Hans K. LaRondelle, for example, argues that the Christian interpreter of the Old Testament is obliged to read the Hebrew Scriptures in the light of the New Testament. The Old, he claims, is interpreted authoritatively, under divine inspiration, in the New Testament as God's continuous history of salvation. According to LaRondelle, historic Christianity has always confessed that the New Testament is the goal and fulfillment of the Old.[24] For covenantalists and other non-dispensationalists, therefore, doing theology proceeds as follows:

1.   The formulation of a biblical theology from the New Testament;

2.   The formulation of a biblical theology from the Old Testament;

3.   The production of a systematic theology by harmonizing points 1 and 2.[25]

At first glance, this formula may sound good. Dispensationalist agree that the New Testament helps us understand the meaning of the Old Testament.

---

[24] Hans K. LaRondelle, *The Israel of God in Prophecy* (Berrien Springs, MI.: Andrews University Press, 1983), 19. Unfortunately, the "historic Christianity" that he was referring to in this case is the medieval method of interpretation. LaRondelle was a Seventh-day Adventist, but his book has been recommended by other covenant theologians. See further, Larry D. Pettegrew, "The Perspicuity of Scripture," *The Master's Seminary Journal* 15:2 (Fall, 2004): 216-25; and "The New Covenant and New Covenant Theology," *The Master's Seminary Journal* 18:2 (Fall, 2007): 181-89.

[25] See the helpful study by Mike Stallard, "Literal Hermeneutics, Theological Method, and the Essence of Dispensationalism," (Unpublished paper, Pre-Trib Research Center, 1995), 13-16. The following discussion is adapted from this paper.

But the problem arises when non-dispensationalists use the New Testament to undermine what the Old Testament prophets proclaimed. Covenantalists admit that the Old Testament says one thing about the future of the nation of Israel, but it must mean something different. In effect they "undo, or replace the results that would have been obtained in performing a true biblical theology of the OT."[26] In doing theology, the Old Testament is almost an afterthought in this procedure. The New Testament is used like the "presidential power of veto"[27] over legitimate exegetical results in Old Testament passages. Consequently, there is no true Old Testament biblical theology that serves to form the production of systematic theology. Their systematic theology is "one-legged."[28]

Employing Grammatical-Historical Interpretation in Both Testaments

The proper approach for doing theology, dispensationalists insist, based on a grammatical-historical interpretation of Scripture, proceeds as follows:

1. The formulation of a biblical theology from the Old Testament;

2. The formulation of a biblical theology from the New Testament;

3. The production of a systematic theology by harmonizing all biblical inputs to theology.

And why is this better? For at least three reasons. First, because this is the nature of progressive revelation. In progressive revelation, revelation builds upon previous revelation. Second, because this process enables the interpreter to read the Old Testament with a consistent grammatical-historical hermeneutic. And third, because in this procedure, there is really no priority of one testament over another except in a chronological order of progressive revelation. In the end, it is superior to be able to insist that an Old Testament text must not be stripped of its original meaning in its context, found through grammatical-historical interpretation and biblical theology.

---

[26] Ibid., 15.

[27] Ibid.

[28] Ibid.

Dispensationalists believe in progressive revelation in the legitimate under-standing of this method of Bible study. God, the ultimate author, directs later prophets or apostles to add further details to a previously given prophecy. All doctrines of Scripture are progressively developed from earlier revelation to later revelation like an acorn grows into a large oak tree over time.[29] The doctrine of salvation, for example, was in place as soon as Adam and Eve were created. After their fall into original sin, God provided further revelation: salvation involves sacrificial death and the coming of a Savior (Gen 3). Further truths are imbed-ded in the Levitical system as well as prophecies like Isaiah 53. Then the Gospel writers explain the life and death of the Redeemer in great detail, and other Apostles plumb the depth of this wonderful doctrine of salvation in the epistles.

Eschatology works the same way. The Old Testament prophets, for exam-ple, often prophesy about the future kingdom of God. In the New Testament, the Apostle John explains that there are two stages of the kingdom. The first stage will last one thousand years before the eternal kingdom begins. The Bible thus reveals an added dimension to the doctrine of the kingdom. But even if there is a "development of the divine meaning of an individual text of Scripture as the canonical context grows, in that development or further dimension of meaning the original meaning is not lost."[30]

The difference between covenant theology and dispensational theol-ogy should be apparent. The hermeneutical system of covenantalism often undermines or jettisons the Old Testament's meaning. Instead, both the New Testament and the Old Testament should be treated as perspicuous, subject to grammatical-historical interpretation. Following this procedure will result in later revelation elaborating on earlier revelation, but not obscuring or demolish-ing earlier revelation.

Maintaining Confidence in the Old Testament Writers

Depending on the New Testament authors to reinterpret the Old Testament can also lead to a lack of confidence in the Old Testament. Some covenant

---

[29] See Geerhardus Vos, *Biblical Theology, Old and New Testaments* (Grand Rapids: Eerdmans, 1948), 15-16. The study of progressive revelation is the essence of biblical theology. Vos defines biblical theology as "the branch of Exegetical Theology which deals with the process of the self-revelation of God deposited in the Bible. ... Biblical Theology deals with the revelation as a divine activity, not as the finished product of that activity" (13).

[30] W. Edward Glenny, "The Divine Meaning of Scripture: Explanations and Limitations," *Journal of the Evangelical Society* 38:4 (Dec. 1995):481.

theologians imply that the Old Testament authors, writing under the super-intendence of the Holy Spirit, were not quite up to the task and could not express what they really meant—either because the prophet was not able to do so, and/or because the people could not have understood the prophecy if he had explained it as it really will be. For example, how should we interpret this prophecy of Isaiah?

> No more shall there be in it an infant who lives but a few days, or an old man who does not fill out his days, for the young man shall die a hundred years old, and the sinner a hundred years old shall be accursed. They shall build houses and inhabit them; they shall plant vineyards and eat their fruit. They shall not build and another inhabit; they shall not plant and another eat; for like the days of a tree shall the days of my people be, and my chosen shall long enjoy the work of their hands. They shall not labor in vain or bear children for calamity, for they shall be the offspring of the blessed of the LORD, and their descendants with them (Isa 65:20-23).

Clearly Isaiah tells us that in this glorious future time, children will be born, there will be long life, but there will be death.

One covenant theologian, however, gives this explanation: "The best and most intelligible way that the original author of this prophecy could commu-nicate the *realistic future* glory of the new heaven and the new earth, to people who were necessarily limited by the progress of revelation to that point in time, was to portray it in the hyperbolic or exaggerated terms of an *ideal present*."[31] For the amillennialist this means that when Isaiah wrote these verses, he was doing the best that he could, but he didn't really prophesy what actually will happen. "His point isn't to assert that people will actually die or that women will continue to give birth."[32]

To be frank, the "ideal future" explanation was invented to obscure the meaning of the passages that talk about a future millennial kingdom on earth. It gives evidence of being a hermeneutical escape from the prophecies that do not fit in with a predetermined eschatology. These interpreters have already concluded that a future one-thousand-year literal kingdom on earth with a temple located in Jerusalem where all the world will worship, and where

---

[31] Storm, *Kingdom Come, The Amillennial Alternative*, 35.

[32] Ibid., 36.

Christ will be king over the whole earth "is an egregious expression of the worst imaginable redemptive regress."[33]

Dispensationalists believe that the proper way to interpret a prophecy like Isaiah 65:20-23 is to believe that what the prophets tell us about the future in plain words is true. To repeat, Old Testament prophets like Isaiah were revealing a future that includes both (1) an earthly Messianic Kingdom here on the present earth, centered in Jerusalem (Ezek 37; 39:25-29; Zech 12:10-14; 14:1-21; cf. Rom 11; et. al.), followed by (2) the eternal state in the new heavens and the new earth. Even as the Old Testament prophets did not always separate out the first coming of Christ from the second coming of Christ, they sometimes did not separate out the Millennium from the Eternal State. In the Messianic Kingdom, described as lasting one thousand years by the Apostle John, people give birth and die. But people do not die in the eternal state. Both stages of the future kingdom are taught in Scripture and will come to pass.

To return to the point, believing in the integrity of the Old Testament prophets is one of the main foundations for dispensational premillennialism. We are happily compelled to this principle if we practice consistent grammatical-historical interpretation of both the Old and New Testaments. If the Old Testament prophets are telling us the truth, therefore, Christ will establish His kingdom on the earth, centered in Jerusalem, and, according to the New Testament apostle, reign from there for one thousand years. In this kingdom, God will demonstrate His glory in keeping His promises to Israel.

Figures of Speech Versus Figurative Interpretation

Critics of dispensationalism often imply that dispensationalists do not take into consideration figures of speech (such as metaphors, similes, allegories) in the interpretation of Scripture, especially in the interpretation of prophecy. Sam Storm writes,

> We simply cannot escape the fact that metaphor is dominant in Scripture, especially in prophetic texts. This recognition does not undermine the authority or infallibility of the word. Evangelicals must stop their knee-jerk reaction to the word as if it is nothing more than the liberal scholar's way of dismissing the historicity

DISPENSATIONALISM: A STEP UP FOR THE "ISRAEL OF GOD"

of the Bible. The concepts and principles communicated via figurative language are true and real as those communicated via more "literal" language. To say that a text or phrase is metaphorical does not mean it isn't true or that it is emptied of concrete reality. It simply means that ordinary, flat-footed literalism would fail to fully and properly communicate what God intended.[34]

All biblical dispensationalists would agree with this, but the statement seems to imply that dispensationalists would not.

The Scriptures indeed are full of figures of speech. The Old Testament authors use metaphors, for example, to describe the Lord: "The Lord is my rock and my fortress and my deliverer" (2 Sam 22:2). Yahweh is not literally a "rock" or "fortress." The Apostle Paul explains spirituality as "walking in the Spirit," exhibiting the "fruit of the Spirit," and that the Spirit is the "seal" of our salvation. When Christ said, "I am the door" (John 10:7, 9), or when He described Herod as an "old fox" (Luke 13:32), he was employing figures of speech.

Likewise, there are figures of speech in the prophetic sections of Scripture. The Apostle John, describing the future millennial kingdom in Revelation 20, writes,

> Then I saw an angel coming down from heaven, holding in his hand the key to the bottomless pit and a great chain. And he seized the dragon, that ancient serpent, who is the devil and Satan, and bound him for a thousand years, and threw him into the pit, and shut it and sealed it over him, so that he might not deceive the nations any longer, until the thousand years were ended (Rev 20:1-3).

Are the key and the chain symbolic? Yes, in the same way as the sword coming out of Christ's mouth is symbolic (Rev 19:15). The key and the chain are visionary metaphors for describing the binding of Satan. Probably every interpreter of Scripture recognizes symbolism here. But this does not mean that Bible students are supposed to *interpret the passage* figuratively. Nevertheless, this is exactly what some non-dispensationalists seem to be saying. Storm writes,

---

[34] Storm, *Kingdom Come, The Amillennial Alternative*, 34. See also Kenneth Gentry's confusion about the differences between methods of interpretation and literary phenomena, *He Shall Have Dominion*, 3rd edition (Draper, VA: Apologetics Group, 2009), 144 ff.

But if the premillennialist insists on saying that Satan's being cast into the abyss in Revelation 20 must be interpreted in a literal, spatial way, what does he do with the rest of the imagery in that passage? Must we believe that the angel who down from heaven was physically holding a literal key that literally could lock and unlock a pit? What kind of door was on this pit? What kind of lock held it fast?[35]

Such a statement confuses literary phenomena with methods of interpreting language. The symbolism or figures of speech do not change the meaning of the passage. John is explaining that during this future one-thousand-year period of time, the Devil will be bound and inoperative on earth while at the same time his arch- enemy, Jesus Christ, rules over His Messianic Kingdom (Rev 19). This meaning of the passage is nearly unavoidable if we employ grammatical-historical interpretation. And to make that point, John employs conceptual metaphors.

The following chart demonstrates the differences between figures of speech and figurative interpretation.[36]

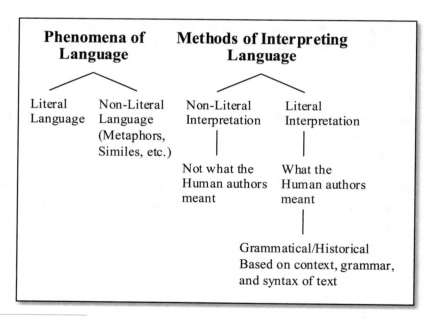

Phenomena of Language		Methods of Interpreting Language	
Literal Language	Non-Literal Language (Metaphors, Similes, etc.)	Non-Literal Interpretation	Literal Interpretation
		Not what the Human authors meant	What the Human authors meant
			Grammatical/Historical Based on context, grammar, and syntax of text

---

[35] Storm, 442-43. Storm does admit that "most, if not all, premillennialists would readily acknowledge that all of this is symbolic imagery designed to teach a very real and, yes, even literal spiritual and theological truth." But he argues that this passage is not describing a future Millennium but was fulfilled in the first century.

[36] John S. Feinberg, "Salvation in the Old Testament," *Traditions and Testament* (Chicago: Moody, 1981), 47-48. The following chart comes from Dr. Feinberg's guest lectures at The Master's Seminary in 1999 entitled, "Continuity between the Testaments."

Dispensationalists believe that the biblical authors employed both literal language and non-literal language as features of the phenomena of language. They take metaphors, similes, and the like into consideration when they interpret any passage of Scripture. At the same time, they believe that they should follow the literal method of interpretation.

THE CHURCH A DISTINCT ORGANISM

In addition to their devotion to consistent grammatical-historical interpretation, dispensationalists believe that the church is not just an updated Israel, as covenant theologians teach, nor does the church replace Israel permanently. In some ways, both Old Covenant and New Covenant believers are similar. For example, both are saved by grace through faith based on the substitutionary death of Christ. Nevertheless, we learn in Scripture: (1) the church was a mystery in the Old Testament and is thus a distinctive organism that began at Pentecost (Acts 2); and (2) the term "Israel" always refers to the covenant nation in biblical history, during the church age, and in predictive prophecy.

The Church a Mystery in the Old Testament

It is theologically incorrect to speak of the "Old Testament church" or "the church in the Old Testament," as non-dispensationalists often do. The New Testament states explicitly in Ephesians 2-3 that the church was something new, unknown in the past. Beginning in verse eleven of chapter two, the Apostle Paul details the horrifying predicament confronting the Gentiles under the Old Covenant by summarizing five privileges that the people of Israel had which the Gentiles did not:

> Therefore remember that at one time you Gentiles in the flesh, called "the uncircumcision" by what is called the circumcision, which is made in the flesh by hands—remember that you were at that time separated from Christ, alienated from the commonwealth of Israel and strangers to the covenants of promise, having no hope and without God in the world (Eph 2:11-12).

According to Paul, (1) the Gentiles were without the messianic hope ("separated from Christ"); (2) they were alienated from the commonwealth of Israel; (3) they were excluded from the covenants of promise; [37] (4) they had no hope for salvation; (5) they were alienated from the God of Israel ("without God in the world").

Then Paul reveals the solution to this horrifying predicament for the Gentiles: "But now in Christ Jesus you who once were far off have been brought near by the blood of Christ" (2:13). The door to salvation was opened to them through Spirit baptism into union with Christ (cf. Gal 3:27) on the basis of the shed blood of Christ. The result is that Jews and Gentiles are together on equal footing in the church as one: one new man, one body, one Spirit (2:14-18).

Oneness and newness are the chief characteristics of this new organism. Though formerly strangers to the plan of God, saved Gentiles are now fellow-citizens with the saved Jews in the household of God and fellow members of the body of Christ, and fellow partakers of the promised Messianic salvation with its attendant blessings of the New Covenant ministries of the Holy Spirit (2:19-22).

Furthermore, the union of believing Jews and Gentiles in a new body was a mystery in the Old Testament (3:3).[38] The word, "mystery," does not mean mysterious, or mystical, or confusing. "Mystery" simply means "secret." The church was a secret in the Old Testament. The content of this secret is actually a definition of the church. As Paul explains, "This mystery is that the Gentiles are fellow heirs, members of the same body, and partakers of the promise in Christ Jesus through the gospel" (3:6). Thus, the church, as defined by Paul, is *Jew and Gentile together in one body on equal footing.*[39] It was a secret, Paul adds, because it was not previously revealed (3:5).[40] But the secret is no longer secret because it has now been revealed by the Spirit. And the Spirit revealed the secret to the world through the apostles and New Testament prophets (cf. Col 1:25-27).

---

[37] Note the plural. This is the perfect place to use the singular if the covenant of grace were the issue. But the covenants of promise are the biblical covenants such as the Abrahamic, Davidic, and New.

[38] See further Carl Hoch, "The Significance of the SYN-Compounds," *Journal of the Evangelical Theological Society* (June, 1982), 175-83. To be clear, Paul's point is not that the church is an afterthought of secondary importance to God. We who are believers in the church age were chosen in Christ "before the foundation of the world, that we would be holy and blameless before him" (Eph 1:4).

[39] The word "church" is a translation of a common Greek word that essentially means "assembly." A few times in the New Testament the word "church" does not refer to the New Testament church made up Jew and Gentile together on equal footing. In a non-technical sense, the word just means "assembly." See Acts 7:38; 19:32-41. In the latter passage, the Greek word refers to an unruly mob, and then to a lawful assembly.

[40] Some non-dispensationalists argue that the church was revealed in the Old Testament, just not as clearly revealed as it was in the New Testament, basing their argument on the "as." The parallel passage in Colossians 1:26, however, proves this view incorrect. Here the word "as" is not found. So the Ephesian passage should not be interpreted, "not so clearly as." The church, as Jew and Gentile together in one body on equal footing, was not revealed at all in the Old Testament.

If the church was not revealed in the Old Testament, then there is no such thing as an Old Testament church. Whatever happened on the Day of Pentecost when the New Testament church was formed is not just an absorption or update of an "Old Testament church." Yes, both are saved by grace through faith. Soteriologically, there is one people of God. But the church is a distinct organism different from the nation of Israel that was formed on the Day of Pentecost. Both the church and Israel continue to be important in God's plan for the future.

The Church Is Not "New Israel"

Not only is it theologically incorrect to speak of the "Old Testament church," it is also incorrect to say that the church is the "new Israel." There is no biblical evidence for this terminology. Paul Benware explains,

> The term "Israel" is used a total of seventy-three times in the New Testament, and in each case it refers to ethnic Israel. Out of these seventy-three occurrences only three are used by covenant theology to prove that Israel equals the church, which could hardly be seen as overwhelming evidence for an Israel-equals-church idea. Interestingly covenant theologians are not in agreement in two out of these three references. Some see two of them (Rom 9:6 and 11:26) as referring to ethnic Israel.[41]

The main verse in which non-dispensationalists think they find the church specifically identified as the "new Israel" is Galatians 6:16. The phrase "the new Israel" is not in Galatians 6:16 and never appears in Scripture. But in this passage, Paul uses the phrase "Israel of God" (Gal 6:16). Non-dispensationalists claim that Paul is saying that "the Israel of God" is a name for the church and that the church updates and replaces Israel and thus becomes the "new Israel." This verse, according to some covenant theologians, is "the chief witness in the New Testament in declaring that the universal church of Christ is the Israel of God, the seed of Abraham, the heir to Israel's covenant promise (see Gal 3:29; 6:16)."[42] The better interpretation, however, is that the "Israel of God" is not a name for the church but refers to godly Jews in the churches of Galatia.

---

[41] Paul N. Benware, *Understanding End Times Prophecy* (Chicago: Moody, 1995), 87.

[42] LaRondelle, *Israel of God in Prophecy*, 110-11.

The verse appears near the end of Galatians where Paul is sending his final admonitions to the churches of Galatia. Much of this letter is a warning about the Judaizers, and Paul reasserts his warning as he is about to finish:

> [12] It is those [Judaizers] who want to make a good showing in the flesh who would force you [Gentile Christians] to be circumcised, and only in order that they may not be persecuted for the cross of Christ.
>
> [13] For even those who are circumcised [Judaizers] do not themselves keep the law, but they [Judaizers] desire to have you [Gentile Christians] circumcised that they [Judaizers] may boast in your [Godly Gentiles'] flesh.
>
> [14] But far be it from me to boast except in the cross of our Lord Jesus Christ, by which the world has been crucified to me, and I to the world.
>
> [15] For neither circumcision counts for anything, nor uncircumcision, but a new creation.
>
> [16] And as for all who walk by this rule [Godly Gentiles], peace and mercy be upon them, and upon the Israel of God [Godly Jews] (Gal 6:12-16).[43]

Non-dispensational theologians support their view that the church is "the new Israel" by focusing on the conjunction translated here "and." They claim that the Greek word (καὶ) sometimes means "even," and should be translated this way in verse 16. Paul would therefore be equating believing Gentiles with the "Israel of God." Thus "Israel of God" is another name for the church, they say. But reliance on a secondary use of a conjunction for such an important theological point is not compelling.[44]

More important for understanding correctly the "Israel of God" is the immediately preceding context. All agree that Paul is specifically addressing the Gentile believers who have not been circumcised (12-13). He speaks to them in the second person plural ("you"). Both covenant theologians and dispensationalists also agree that the "them" in verse 16 is also referring to the Gentile Christians who commit to the truth that circumcision is not a part of salvation. Then Paul blesses ("peace and mercy") the two groups within the Galatian

---

[43] Pronoun identification is mine.

[44] Some editions of the *New International Version*, unfortunately in my opinion, give the same impression by replacing the "and" with a dash.

churches who will not be overwhelmed by the arguments of the Judaizers: (1) Gentile Christians ("them") and (2) *godly Jews* ("the Israel of God").[45] Paul is not stating that the church should now be known as "the Israel of God" or as "new Israel."[46] He is referencing believing Jews in the Galatian churches who reject the Judaizers. These godly Jews are the "Israel of God."

We should also remember the seventy-two other uses of the word, "Israel," that always refer to ethnic Israel. And it would certainly be unusual if, in the concluding admonitions to his letter, he dropped this new "bombshell" on the Galatians churches that they were now the "new Israel," the "Israel of God." The truth of the matter is that the terms, "Israel" and "the Israel of God" are never used in the New Testament as synonyms for the church. Thus, there is no such thing as the "Old Testament church," and the church is not "new Israel"[47]

REALISTIC BIBLICAL ESCHATOLOGY

Dispensationalists teach premillennialism and pretribulationism. Christ's Second Coming will occur before (pre) the millennial kingdom, and the rapture of the church will occur before (pre) the seven-year Tribulation. In the Tribulation, God's plan is to bring Israel to a place where she will accept Jesus as her Messiah when He returns.[48] After Christ returns, He will establish a righteous world-wide kingdom on earth over which He will rule for one thousand years. At the end of Christ's millennial reign and after the Great White Throne judgment, God will make a new heavens and a new earth and inaugurate the eternal state. Premillennialism and pretribulationism are both biblical and realistic.

---

[45] Also the joint themes of Israel and "mercy" throughout Paul's argument in Romans 9-11 adds evidence to the proper interpretation of mercy and Israel here in Galatians 6:16. See further Cilliers Breytenbach, "'Charis' and 'eleos' in Paul's Letter to the Romans," *The Letter to the Romans* (ed. U. Schnelle: BETL, 226; Louvain: Walpole, MA: Peeters, 2009), 266.

[46] See chapter two for an analysis for when the phrase "New Israel" first shows up in the church fathers.

[47] For further discussion on Galatian 6:16, see S. Lewis Johnson, Jr., "Paul and the 'Israel of God': An Exegetical and Eschatological Case-Study," in *Essays in Honor of J. Dwight Pentecost* (Chicago: Moody Press, 1986), 181-96). Johnson lists several commentaries that hold to one of these two views, 183-87.

[48] Many books have been written detailing pretribulational premillennialism, so we will concentrate here on the big picture.

Biblical Accuracy

Most importantly, the key features of dispensational eschatology are taught in the Bible:

1. There is a rapture of the church.

   Paul asserts, "For the Lord himself will descend from heaven with a cry of command, with the voice of an archangel, and with the sound of the trumpet of God. And the dead in Christ will rise first. Then we who are alive, who are left, will be caught up together with them in the clouds to meet the Lord in the air, and so we will always be with the Lord (1 Thes 4:16-17).[49]

2. The nation of Israel is the center of prophetic events.
   This is not because there is anything special about Israel, but because of God's special grace to this people (Deut 7:7-9).[50] On the basis of His irrevocable covenants with Israel, the Lord made irrevocable promises like the following:

   "For a brief moment I deserted you, but with great compassion I will gather you. In overflowing anger for a moment I hid my face from you, but with everlasting love I will have compassion on you," says the LORD, your Redeemer. "This is like the days of Noah to me: as I swore that the waters of Noah should no more go over the earth, so I have sworn that I will not be angry with you, and will not rebuke you. For the mountains may depart and the hills be removed, but my steadfast love shall not depart from you, and my covenant of peace shall not be removed," says the LORD, who has compassion on you (Isa 54:7-10).

3. A wicked dictator, known by various names in Scripture, will come to power over the Middle East.[51]

---

[49] "Caught up" is an English translation of the Greek word, ἁρπάζω. The Latin translation of the Greek word is *rapio* that means "to catch up" or "take away." Our English word thus comes from *rapio*.

[50] "It was not because you were more in number than any other people that the Lord set his love on you and chose you, for you were the fewest of all peoples, but it is because the Lord loves you and is keeping the oath that he swore to your fathers..." (Deut 7:7-8). The eventual redemption of Israel is focused more on God's honor and glory than it is on Israel's: "Therefore say to the house of Israel, Thus says the Lord God: It is not for your sake, O house of Israel, that I am about to act, but for the sake of my holy name, which you have profaned among the nations to which you came" (Ezek 36:22).

[51] For examples: "little horn" (Dan 7:2-28, "prince who is to come" (Dan 9:26), "Gog" (Ezek 38-39), "man of lawlessness" (2 Thes 2:3-4), "antichrist" (1 John 2:18), "beast" (Rev 13:1-8).

He will make a seven-year covenant with Israel, break it after three and one-half years, gather a coalition of ten nations together to attack and temporarily defeat Israel. "For I will gather all the nations against Jerusalem to battle, and the city shall be taken and the houses plundered and the women raped. Half of the city shall go out into exile, but the rest of the people shall not be cut off from the city" (Zech 14:2).

4. During the seven years of Tribulation, awful judgment will be poured out on the entire world (Rev 5-18), some of which specifically impacts Israel (Zech 13:8).

5. Jesus Christ will return, destroy the Antichrist and the nations gathered against Israel.

    "Then the Lord will go out and fight against those nations as when he fights on a day of battle" (Zech 14:3; cf. Dan 7:26; Rev 19:11-21).

6. One-third of the nation of Israel will survive the Tribulation and convert to Christ, person by person (Zech 12:10-13:1).

7. Christ's kingdom will be established centered in Jerusalem, and Christ will rule over the world for one thousand years (Dan 7:27; Zech 14:9; Rev 20:1-6).

8. At the end of the one-thousand-year reign of Christ, there will be a brief, but unsuccessful rebellion against Christ (Rev 20:7-10).

9. A final judgment known as "the great white throne" judgment will follow (Rev 20:11-15).

10. God will remake the heavens and the earth (Rev 21:1; 2 Pet 3:10-13).

11. The eternal state will be inaugurated, and the resurrected believers will live in the New Jerusalem located on the remade earth.

Realistic Expectations

Dispensational eschatology not only describes the big picture of God's revelation of the future accurately, but the system is also in harmony with current events in the Middle East. If dispensational premillennialism is correct, what would we expect to see take place, sooner or later, as God providentially prepares the world for the Second Coming of Christ?

Restoration of the Nation of Israel

First, we would expect to see Jews from the far parts of the world regathering in the land of Israel.[52] As we know, the Jews were dispersed from their homeland (the diaspora) after Jerusalem and the temple were destroyed in A. D. 70. For nearly 2000 years, the Jews had no homeland to occupy. Then, in the 1890's, the Zionist movement was founded with its goal to reestablish the nation of Israel in her historic land. At least one early American dispensationalist, William E. Blackstone, was instrumental in promoting this movement. Jonathan Moorhead writes,

> At a time when Jews were seeking relief from oppression, Blackstone petitioned the U.S. President Benjamin Harrison to campaign for their return to Israel. The "Blackstone Memorial" was the first petition of its kind, which predated the work of Theodor Herzl's Der Judenstaat (The Jewish State). The efforts of Blackstone on behalf of the Jews have resulted in some Jewish groups and even a U.S. Supreme Court Justice to name Blackstone the "Father of Zionism."[53]

In the aftermath of defeat of Turkey in World War I, four hundred years of Muslim rule over the Middle East was ended. The League of nations divided "Palestine" between the Arabs and the Jews, though the Jews only had about 20% of the land. Jerusalem, moreover, was given to the Arabs. But within three decades (1948), the nation of Israel was established. Further, in 1967, as a result of the Six Day War, Israel defeated a coalition of Arab[54] nations and gained control of Jerusalem. We cannot overestimate how amazing—even stunning— these events are.[55] So, if dispensational premillennialism is correct, we would

---

[52] See chapter ten for a few more details of the Bible's teachings on this from the Old Testament perspective.

[53] Jonathan Moorhead, "The Father of Zionism: William E. Blackstone?" *Journal of the Evangelical Theological Society* 53/4 (Dec. 2000):787.

[54] We shouldn't forget that there are many wonderful Arab Christians living in the Middle East and throughout the world.

[55] There was no nation of Israel when I was born. So I have had the privilege of watching God's sovereign providential power at work in Israel. It would be interesting to know what supersessionists think the reason is for God's preserving the Jews as a distinct people for thousands of years and enabling them now to form their own nation in their historic, God-given land.

expect to see the reestablishment of the nation of Israel. And that is exactly what has happened by God's providential control of history.

Coalition of Surrounding Enemy Nations

Second, if dispensational eschatology provides a correct understanding of the Bible's teaching about the future, we would expect to see Israel living under a threat from neighboring nations. Both the Old and New Testaments tell about a future ten-nation alliance that eventually attacks Israel and brings her to her knees. The prophet Daniel, for example, has a night-vision in which he sees "a fourth beast, terrifying and dreadful and exceedingly strong. It had great iron teeth; it devoured and broke in pieces and stamped what was left with its feet. It was different from all the beasts that were before it, and it had ten horns" (Dan 7:7). Daniel asks one of the persons in his vision to explain further, and the person says,

> As for the fourth beast, there shall be a fourth kingdom on earth, which shall be different from all the kingdoms, and it shall devour the whole earth, and trample it down, and break it to pieces. As for the ten horns, out of this kingdom ten kings shall arise, and another shall arise after them; he shall be different from the former ones and shall put down three kings (Dan 7:23-24).

This new coalition of ten enemy nations of Israel, led by the Antichrist ("little horn"), is temporarily victorious over Israel: "As I looked, this horn made war with the saints and prevailed over them" (Dan 7:21; see further Rev. 13:1-7).

Several times in Daniel's prophecies, Daniel or an angel declares that a particular prophecy will be fulfilled in the "latter days" (Dan 2:28; 10:14), or "days yet to come" (Dan 10:14), or the "times of the end" (Dan. 8:17 and 19). Thus, if dispensationalists are interpreting biblical prophecy correctly, we would expect to see at some point in earth history—now or later—a developing coalition of enemy nations surrounding the nation of Israel, waiting for the right moment and the right leader to unleash a devastating attack. It would seem that the Middle East is already being prepared for these events.[56]

But this victory will be temporary. The prophets always finish their descriptions of struggles between latter-day Israel and its enemies with a clear

---

[56] This coalition of nations that will attack Israel will most likely be a revived Islamic caliphate. For a discussion of the war on Israel, see Joel Richardson *Mideast Beast* (Washington, D.C.: WND Books, 2012), especially 159-221.

announcement that these events will be followed by the Second Coming of
Christ and the inauguration of His kingdom. Daniel records:

> I saw in the night visions, and behold, with the clouds of heaven there came one
> like a son of man, and he came to the Ancient of Days and was presented before
> him. And to him was given dominion and glory and a kingdom, that all peoples,
> nations, and languages should serve him; his dominion is an everlasting domin-
> ion, which shall not pass away, and his kingdom one that shall not be destroyed
> (Dan 7:13-14; cf. Rev 19:11-16).

We have to be humble when we interpret prophecy, so no one knows whether
the current tensions in the Middle East between Islamic nations and Israel are
the beginning of the "latter days" or only a foreshadowing. Nevertheless, the
eschatology of dispensational premillennialism is not like Star Wars or Never-
Never Land. Dispensational premillennialism is both biblical and realistic.

HISTORICAL CREDIBILITY

A common question about dispensationalism is, why was it late in redevelop-
ing? If it is the correct way to understand Scripture—especially eschatology—
why didn't Christians understand the principles of dispensational theology until
the early nineteenth century?

There are many answers to this question, and we have analyzed some of
them in our earlier chapters. Like covenant theology, dispensational theology has roots in early church history. Dispensational schemes, for example,
were common in the church fathers' literature.[57] And the early church fathers
were premillennialists and believed in imminency. But this does not mean
that the church fathers were dispensationalists in the way that we understand
the term today. Dispensationalists believe that the main features of dispensationalism were taught by the New Testament apostles; but the distinctives
of dispensationalism were gradually lost by the church fathers, forgotten by
the Roman Catholic Church of the Middle Ages, and not revived by the
Protestant Reformers.

In the broad scheme of historical theology, moreover, different doctrines
have been understood better and developed more accurately and precisely at

[57] See Larry V. Crutchfield, "Ages and Dispensations in the Ante-Nicene Fathers," part two of "Rudiments of
Dispensationalism in the Ante-Nicene Period," *Bibliotheca Sacra* 144 (Oct-Dec, 1987):377-401.

different times in church history. The early church fathers systematized the biblical teaching on the Trinity, then the person of Christ, and then the nature of man. The Reformers took up the important matter of salvation and taught and wrote about it more clearly and precisely than it had been taught for hundreds of years. In more recent centuries, many Bible students have concentrated on ecclesiology—the place of the church in God's plan, the doctrine of pneumatology, and the doctrine of eschatology—and their study has led many to accept the principles of dispensationalism.

We should also remember that dispensationalism, pretribulationism, and premillennialism are not the only truths that were forgotten or neglected for hundreds of years. Many of us believe that baptism of believers by immersion, for example, is a Scriptural teaching which was lost early in church history and not revived until the seventeenth century. Even an important doctrine like justification by faith alone was hardly recognized until the Reformation. And covenant theology itself was not fully systematized until the seventeenth century. Furthermore, for dispensationalism to revive, other doctrines and hermeneutical principles had to be in place first—especially grammatical-historical interpretation. Dispensational premillennialism was also dependent on a futuristic approach to the Book of Revelation (rather than historicism or preterism), and futurism was a post-Reformation redevelopment.

Premillennialism is also foundational to dispensational theology, but it was only rediscovered in the Reformation era. Indeed, the fact that there were pastors and professors teaching premillennialism as early as the late Reformation is an important part of the story. William C. Watson has demonstrated that important English and American theologians in the seventeenth and eighteen centuries were premillennialists.[58] He lists eleven members of the Westminster Assembly (1643-1653) who were either premillennialists or who had written about a future conversion of the Jews.[59] Watson also surveys other significant sixteenth and seventeenth century theologians who expected a future revival in the nation of Israel and concludes,

---

[58] William C. Watson, *Dispensationalism before Darby: Seventeenth-Century and Eighteenth-Century English Apocalypticism* (Silverton, OR: Lampion Press, 2015). See, for examples, chapter 8, "American Colonial Premillennialism," 179-204; and chapter 9, "Historic and Futurist Premillennialism in Late Seventeenth- and Early Eighteenth-Century England," 205-24.

[59] Ibid., 24. Also worthy of more research are premillennialist Baptist pastors such as Henry Jessey, Benjamin Keach, and John Gill who lived in the seventeenth and eighteenth centuries.

Love of the Jewish people and an expectation of their return to reestablish the nation of Israel constitutes a primary element in dispensational theology. Anti-dispensationalists deny any future eschatological role for the Jews as a distinct redeemed people, and the most vocal anti-dispensationalists of late are theologians of the Reformed tradition. How surprised they should be to discover that many seventeenth-century Puritan theologians whom they admire had a similar expectation of the return of the Jews to the Land promised to Abraham and his descendants four thousand years ago.[60]

The regathering of Jews to the land of Israel was not something thought up by dispensationalists in the nineteenth century.

Gerald R. McDermott makes a similar observation and demonstrates that the following theologians believed in the return of the Jews to their land: John Bale (d. 1563); *Foxe's Book of Martyrs* (1563); Thomas Drake (d. 1618), a disciple of William Perkins; Thomas Brightman (d. 1607); Joseph Mede (d. 1638); John Cotton (d. 1652); Henry Fench (d. 1662); William a Brakel (d. 1711); Increase Mather (d. 1723); Jonathan Edwards (d. 1758), and others. None of these should be understood to be dispensational pretribulationists. Some were premillennialists, and many were postmillennialists. But they all taught that the Jews were prophesied to return to their land.[61]

Some of these post-Reformation theologians and pastors were also writing about a rapture, the Tribulation, a futurist interpretation of the book of Revelation, and two resurrections—all foundational doctrines for dispensational premillennialism. Indeed there are also occasional references to a pretribulational rapture in church history. Francis X. Gumerlock has identified at least twelve examples from the Middle Ages, as well as in the seventeenth and eighteenth centuries. For examples, Gumerlock writes,

> From the 1700's, Morgan Edwards's 1788 *Two Academical Exercises* and Grantham Killingworth's 1761 *Immortality of the Soul* have Christ appearing in the air years prior to the Second Coming to take away the saints from the earth, which

---

[60] Ibid., 44.

[61] Gerald R. McDermott, "A History of Supersessionism: Is Christian Zionism Rooted Primarily in Premillennial Dispensationalism?" in *The New Christian Zionism*, ed. Gerald R. McDermott (Downers Grove, IL: IVP Academic, 2016), 58-71. A major thesis of this book is that Christian Zionism predated dispensationalism by hundreds of years. He is right, of course. But, as noted above, dispensationalists, such as William E. Blackstone (d. 1935), author of *Jesus Is Coming*, were early supporters of the Zionist movement.

afterward experiences the tribulations of the book of Revelation. From the1600's, John Brown's 1654 *Brief Survey of the Prophetical and Evangelical Events of the Last Times* and John Birschensha's 1600 *History of the Scripture*, have the saints being taken up to heaven before the tribulation and destruction of Babylon on earth.[62]

But to ask the same question that we asked about covenant theology in earlier chapters, "do we have dispensationalism yet?" The answer is "no, not yet."

John Nelson Darby is correctly considered as the one person who first put several of these foundational doctrines together and redeveloped biblical dispensationalism. According to his testimonies, his pilgrimage began in 1828 when he discovered in Isaiah 32 that there was a yet future age to come, and that Israel had a special place in that future age. In a letter dated 1848, Darby describes his conviction that the church age was "in the extraordinary suspension of prophetic testimony, or period, which comes between the sixty-ninth and seventieth week of Daniel."[63] In his study of Scripture, he also came to believe in a rapture of the church that would occur before the Tribulation. He brought up the doctrine of the pretribulational rapture at the 1833 Powerscourt Bible Conference. The historian Ernest Sandeen points out that "Darby never indicated any source for his ideas other than the Bible—indeed, he consistently affirmed that his only theological task was explicating the text of Scripture"[64]

MINISTRY IMPACT

Beginning in the latter part of the nineteenth century and continuing throughout the twentieth century, several different kinds of dispensationalist ministries networking with each other impacted American culture and Christianity for the glory of God. Many American evangelicals accepted dispensationalism as a result of the Bible conference movement and the literature that the leaders

---

[62] Francis X. Gumerlock, "The Rapture in an Eleventh-Century Text," *Bibliotheca Sacra* 176 (January-March 2019):82-83.

[63] John Nelson Darby, "Letters," May 1, 1848, vol. 1., no. 66, http://www.stempublishing.com/authors/darby/letters/51066E.html

[64] Ernest Sandeen, *The Roots of Fundamentalism* (Chicago: University of Chicago, 1970; repr. Baker, 1978), 64. Other early dispensationalists, such as James Hall Brookes, who deserves to be known as the "father of American dispensationalism," also insisted that he had changed from postmillennialism to pretribulational premillennialism only because of his study of the Bible. See James Brookes, "How I Became a Premillennialist," *The Truth*, XXII (1896):331. Brookes' son-in-law and biographer, David Riddle Williams, also tells this story. See David Riddle Williams, *James H. Brookes: A Memoir* (St. Louis: Presbyterian Board of Publication, 1897). For a refutation of the outrageous claim that Darby got his idea of the pretribulational rapture from a prophetess or the Irvingites, see Thomas Ice, "Did Edward Irving Invent the Pre-Trib Rapture View?" *Master's Seminary Journal* 27/1 (Spring 2016):57-73.

of these conferences published.[65] Dispensationalism was popularized in the Scofield Reference Bible (1909, 1917), and taught in the nineteenth- and twentieth-century Bible institutes and Bible colleges, as well as in some significant evangelical theological seminaries.

A good case can be made that a revival brought dispensationalism to the attention of American pastors, missionaries, and evangelists. George C. Needham (1840-1902), an Irish evangelist who ministered in Ireland and England, came to the United States in 1868 with a letter of recommendation to the American churches from Charles Spurgeon.[66] Needham, a Baptist, pastored Moody Church in Chicago for two years, then spent the rest of his life in full-time evangelistic work. According to Needham's testimony, he became a premillennialist in the Irish Believers' Meetings that he attended after the Irish revival of 1859-1861. Needham writes:

> It was then, in journeying through the Gospels, and subsequently in the Epistles, we discovered the prominence given to the second advent of Christ. With limited ideas of what the work outside, or the church around, believed regarding this doctrine, we investigated the word alone, being neither helped or hindered by traditional theology. The glorious coming of our Lord, as an advent hastening near, became to our souls an inspiring, energizing hope. It was not death; it was no mysterious spiritual coming; it was not even a literal coming thousands or millions of years hence which we were led to embrace.[67]

When Needham arrived in the United states, "with the thrill of these mighty [Irish] gatherings in his soul, "he looked for similar believers' meetings but didn't find any. He eventually met James Inglis (1813-1872), a pretribulational, premillennialist, who published an early dispensational paper entitled *Waymarks in the Wilderness*. Inglis and Needham subsequently organized a private Bible study in 1868 in the Irish tradition of the Believers' Meetings. These private Believers' Meetings for Bible Study were opened to the Christian public in 1876. In due course the public Believers' Meeting for Bible Study was

---

[65] See further, Larry D. Pettegrew, "The Historical and Theological Contributions of the Niagara Bible Conference to American Fundamentalism," Th. D. diss., Dallas Theological Seminary, 1976.

[66] George C. Needham, *The Spiritual Life* (Philadelphia: American Baptist Publication Society, 1895), 9. Needham also wrote a biography of Spurgeon: George C. Needham, *The Life and Labors of Charles H. Spurgeon* (Boston: D. L. Buernsey, 1881).

[67] George C. Needham, "Introduction," James H. Brookes, *Present Truth* (Springfield, IL: Edwin A. Wilson, 1887), 13.

named the Niagara Bible Conference which existed until 1900. Other Bible conferences were later organized throughout America. Thus, the Irish revivals of 1859-1861 led to private Bible studies, which led to Bible conferences.

One of the results of the Bible conferences was the faith missions movement. Throughout the history of the Niagara Bible Conference, pastors and missionaries such as A. T. Pierson and J. Hudson Taylor challenged the Conference hearers to respond to the spiritual needs of nations of the world. In some cases, the leaders of the Niagara conference acted as their own faith mission board, and the mission volunteers had their support "spontaneously pledged by the Conference or by individual members."[68] In at least one other case, a faith mission board, the American branch of the China Inland Mission, was organized and promoted in connection with the Niagara Conference.[69]

Dispensational missionaries were leaders of evangelical missions in the twentieth century. Joel Carpenter points out that "of all the activities the fundamentalists pursued outside of their own congregations, perhaps the most important to them and the most indicative of their contrasting fortunes with the major Protestant denominations was their foreign missionary work."[70] David Hesselgrave states that at the beginning of the twentieth-century, "mainline denominational churches in the U. S. supplied 80 percent of the North American missionary force. At the end of the twentieth century they supplied no more than 6 percent of it!"[71] Carpenter adds that for fundamental dispensationalists, "missions were not just a sideline to which local churches absent-mindedly tossed a portion of their discretionary funds. They were a major concern."[72] Clearly their pretribulational premillennialism was an impetus for missions and evangelism. As missiologist Michael Pocock observes,

[68] W. J. Erdman, "Believers' Meeting for Bible Study," *The Truth*, XV (1889):264. Our next chapter presents a lecture by a participant in the First American and Bible Conference in 1878.

[69] Stewart G. Cole, *The History of Fundamentalism* (Westport, CT: Greenwood Press, 1931), 34.

[70] Joel A. Carpenter, *Revive Us Again* (New York: Oxford University Press, 1997), 28. Most fundamentalists who led the faith missions movement were dispensational premillennialists.

[71] David J. Hesselgrave, "Saving the Future of Evangelical Missions: How to Survive a Tsunami" (unpublished paper, n.d.), 1. Hesselgrave (1924-2018) was a dispensationalist as was George W. Peters, two of the leading evangelical missiologists in the twentieth and early twenty-first centuries.

[72] Carpenter, *Revive Us Again*, 30.

"Premillennialists are, as the name suggests, more concerned about what they should be doing before the millennium than during that period."[73]

Revivals, private Bible studies, Bible conferences, and the faith missions movement also led to the formation of Bible institutes and Bible colleges, some of which eventually became Christian colleges or universities. Many of the leaders of the nineteenth-century Bible conferences lost confidence in the existing denominational theological colleges and seminaries. James Brookes, the president of the Niagara Bible Conference, wrote in 1888 that he had received many letters through his periodical *The Truth,* pointing out that the seminaries were too academic, too long, and failed to teach the Bible.[74] Many denominational seminaries were no longer teaching orthodox theology. Brookes once said, "As there is a growing disregard of the Bible in Theological Seminaries, so there is a growing disregard of Theological Seminaries among Christians who love the Bible above all other books in the world."[75] Brookes believed in seminary education if the seminaries could maintain a proper theological position and add English Bible content to their curriculum.

Many of the early American dispensationalists, however, began to promote the idea of instituting a new type of school, a Bible school, often called a Bible institute. The curriculum of these premillennial Bible institutes focused on the English Bible and a practical Christianity that included evangelism and missions. Indeed, most of the early Bible institutes had "missions" or "evangelism" in their names: Missionary Training Institute for Home and Foreign Missionaries and Evangelists (1882, later Nyack College); Chicago Evangelistic Society (1886, later Moody Bible Institute); Boston Missionary Training School (1889, later Gordon College and Divinity School); Northwestern Bible and Missionary School (1902, later Northwestern College and Seminary, now University of Northwestern).

Other schools which did not have "missionary" in their name, like the Bible Institute of Los Angeles, emphasized evangelism and missions just the same. According to Carpenter, "by 1938, the Bible Institute of Los Angeles (founded

---

[73] Michael Pocock, "The Influence of Premillennial Eschatology on Evangelical Missionary Theory and Praxis from the Late Nineteenth Century to the Present," *International Bulletin of Missionary Research,* 33:3 (July 2009):129.

[74] James Brookes, "Bible Schools," *The Truth,* XIV (1888):385-86.

[75] James Brookes, "Meeting for Bible Study," *The Truth,* VII (1881):483. Brookes, a Presbyterian, attended Princeton Theological Seminary, but did not graduate.

in 1908) had produced 426 [missionaries], and over 120 in the last decade."[76] Carpenter adds that "Bible schools considered the training of missionaries to be one of their major tasks and they proudly announced how many of their alumni were now in overseas service."[77]

CONCLUSION

The history of dispensationalism in America demonstrates a wonderful intertwining of biblical ministries dedicated to fulfilling the Great Commission. Many well-known dispensational evangelists, Bible scholars, pastors, professors, radio and television ministers, and well-taught lay people were devoted to the fundamentals of the faith, believed that the Bible means what it says, looked for the premillennial return of Christ, and busied themselves in various Christian ministries. Biblical dispensationalists, in other words, have not been spending their time drawing prophecy charts and setting dates for the Second Coming. As Carpenter observes, "Until Jesus came for them at the Rapture, Bible-believing Christians were to win the lost, heed the signs of the times, keep themselves pure from error, and expose and condemn false religion."[78] What better description could be written about a theological movement?

[76] Carpenter, *Revive Us Again*, 30.

[77] Ibid.

[78] Ibid., 111.

8

A WHALE AND AN ELEPHANT

Douglas D. Bookman

INTRODUCTION

The word picture at stake? I once heard a very influential special creationist (who was an Old Testament linguist and a first-rate theologian as well) explain why, though unusually qualified and equipped to do so, he refused to engage in formal debates with naturalistic evolutionists: "Those debates are very much like a struggle between a whale and an elephant. There is a great deal of sound and fury and thrashing about, but when the dust and the foam settle neither has laid a single blow on the other—simply because they are operating in two entirely different spheres."

The persuasion which animates this chapter is that the very real and important debate between the dispensational premillennialist and his evangelical brethren who reject that construct is crippled by that same reality. The important and fraternal discussion is frustratingly hamstrung by the fact that a genuine worldview dissonance is involved, but it is usually unrecognized. The conversation, whether academic or popular, is ineffectual in persuading or dissuading in either direction—neither contender lands a telling blow—at least in part because the combatants do not comprehend (let alone appreciate) the defining construct which gives shape to their opponent's arguments and position.

Note that the issue here is not surgical exegetical disagreements over specific biblical texts, or even distinctions of hermeneutical philosophy or method, whether broad or nuanced. To be sure, all these issues are real and important and worthy of discussion in the context of the debate at issue. But my contention is that the debate over these "constituent" issues will be

235

more fruitful and fraternal if each side accurately comprehends the "cosmic" construct from within which his opponent perceives the overarching and all-inclusive set of ideas which frame and shape the way he reads and interprets specific texts and theological issues.

Thus, this essay. The *plan* is to focus on one underappreciated but defining and animating distinction of dispensational premillennialism—a distinction which will likely be off-putting to many readers (thus its underappreciation) but which ramifies to virtually every aspect of the set of ideas which is dispensational premillennialism, and which, therefore, must be factored into any careful assessment of that construct. The *spirit* of the essay is deliberately fraternal and irenic. The *purpose*, honestly, is not so much to persuade as to inform.

THE COMMON GROUND: A THEOCENTRIC UNDERSTANDING OF HUMAN HISTORY

God's grand purpose in human history is His own glory. About this proposition there will be no debate whatever in the evangelical world. That God's basic purpose in all of His dealings with mankind is to display His own glory is a truth made necessary by the ontological reality of who God is and affirmed unmistakably throughout the Scriptures, both in specific affirmation and in the narratives that unfold. The most familiar theological articulation of this reality is, perhaps, the first Question / Answer of the 1647 Westminster Shorter Catechism:

Question 1. What is the chief end of man?

Answer. Man's chief end is to glorify God, and to enjoy him forever.[1]

One Scriptural passage which makes this point as forcefully as any other is Isaiah 48:9-11, where in three short verses Yahweh *six times* explicitly grounds His persevering goodness to Israel in His determination to display His own glory:

"For my name's sake I defer my anger, for the sake of my praise I restrain it for you, that I may not cut you off. Behold, I have refined you, but not as silver; I have tried

---

[1] http://creeds.net/Westminster/shorter_catechism.html.

you in the furnace of affliction. For my own sake, for my own sake, I do it, for how should my name be profaned? My glory I will not give to another."[2]

In his discussion of this biblical reality, Gaffin states simply, "God is 'the Father of glory' (Eph 1:17). Glory begins and ends with him and his plan is to share his glory."[3] All thinking believers will acknowledge with Paul, "For from him and through him and to him are all things. To him be glory forever. Amen" (Rom 11:36). Indeed, God glorifies Himself in many ways. Even the heavens "declare the glory of God" (Ps 19:1).

Now let it be stated unequivocally here that no claim is made that the dispensational-premillennial world is distinct by reason of its commitment to this foundational reality of the moral and physical universe. This is in fact common ground for all thinking Bible believers, whether dispensational premillennial or otherwise. Indeed, many who deliberately reject the dispensational-premillennial construct have been much used of God in celebrating and championing the centrality of God's glory. And virtually all who today do embrace the dispensational premillennial construct have been taught and challenged and helped by the doxological emphasis in the ministries and writings of such thinkers and preachers from beyond their camp.

THE MODEST SUGGESTION:
THE DISTINCTIVE PERSPECTIVE OF
DISPENSATIONAL PREMILLENNIALISM

The proposition to be developed here is that the dispensational-premillennial understanding and application of this basic reality (i.e., of the fundamentally and preeminently doxological focus of human history) is consciously distinguishable from that of the non-dispensational world in two particulars. And those two points of fine-tuning are basic to the construct and must be factored into any attempt to understand and assess the construct.

---

[2] See John Piper's very helpful treatment of this subject in "Biblical Texts to Show God's Zeal for His Own Glory," Nov 24, 2007, found at http://www.desiringgod.org/articles/biblical-texts-to-show-gods-zeal-for-his-own-glory.

[3] R. B. Gaffin Jr., "Glory, Glorification" in *Dictionary of Paul and His Letters* (Downers Grove, IL: InterVarsity Press, 1993), 348.

An Emphasis Upon Glory Displayed

First, dispensational premillennialism, by definition, maintains a more sustained and deliberate emphasis upon one element of the biblical concept of glory,[4] namely the reality that God's glory cannot be reduced to a simple abstraction, especially in reference to this issue of His ultimate purposes in human history. That is, the biblical concept of God's glory includes but is more than His intrinsic worth and majesty. The biblical concept of God's glory necessarily focuses on—indeed, emphasizes—the *display* of that majesty to rational creatures. This nuance is intrinsic to the Old Testament word for "glory," כָּבוֹד (*kābôd*), a term whose "basic meaning is 'to be heavy, weighty.'"[5] This physical dimension, basic to the term, plays into the biblical idea of glory in terms of its *objectivity*, its *manifest and palpable reality*. In short, God's glory is not just His majesty; it is *His majesty on display*. John Piper made this point well when asked to define the biblical idea of "glory":

> I believe the glory of God is the *going public* of his infinite worth. I define the holiness of God as the infinite value of God, the infinite intrinsic worth of God. And *when that goes public in creation,* the heavens are telling the glory of God, and human beings are manifesting his glory, because we're created in his image, and we're trusting his promises so that we make him look gloriously trustworthy. The *public display* of the infinite beauty and worth of God is what I mean by "glory," and I base that partly on Isaiah 6, where the seraphim say, "Holy, holy, holy is the Lord God Almighty. The whole earth is full of his—and you would expect them to say "holiness" and they say "glory." They're ascribing "Holy, holy, holy is the Lord God Almighty. The whole earth is full of his glory"—and *when that goes public in*

---

[4] C. C. Ryrie, in a work which was significantly definitional to the dispensationalist construct, (*Dispensationalism Today* [Chicago: Moody, 1965], 46) reduced that set of ideas to a 3-fold *sine qua non*, the third element of which was the conviction that "the underlying purpose of God in the world" was and is "the glory of God." Ryrie set this in contrast to what he represented as the position of "the covenant theologian [who] in practice makes this [underlying] purpose salvation." That specific claim was received quite negatively in many quarters. Thus I beg the reader's patience as I acknowledge that I am returning to that theme, but only because the fine points of the dispensationalist approach to this issue are pivotal to the construct and demand to be considered.

[5] John N. Oswalt, "943 כָּבֵד," *Theological Wordbook of the Old Testament* (Chicago: Moody, 1999), 426–27. He goes on to acknowledge that the literal physical sense of "heavy" is rarely used in the OT (cf. the High Priest Eli [1 Sam 4:18] and the hair of Absalom [2 Sam 14:26]), but "the figurative (e.g. "heavy with sin") [is] more common." He concludes, "From this figurative usage it is an easy step to the concept of a 'weighty' person in society, someone who is honorable, impressive, worthy of respect. This latter usage is prevalent in more than half the occurrences."

the earth and fills it, you call it "glory." So God's glory is the *radiance* of his holiness, the *radiance* of his manifold, infinitely worthy and valuable perfections.[6]

Again, Nixon avers that the term *kābôd* "is used of men to describe their wealth, splendor or reputation"[7]—that is, it is used of the visible display of their honor. Gaffin also emphasizes the idea of palpable manifestation of worth or value as intrinsic to *kābôd*: "In ancient cultures the wealthy and the powerful were *marked by* the finery of their dress and jewels. Hence, a person's glory meant the *ostentatious signs* of wealth and power.... In the OT the glory of God means *something obvious* about God."[8]

Further, that this element of the meaning of *kābôd* was basic to the way it was used and understood is reflected in the fact that the meaning of the Greek word used to translate *kābôd* in the LXX, and then adopted throughout the NT, was fundamentally altered by that usage.[9] That Greek word is δόξα/*doxa*. Oswalt emphasizes that this palpable dynamic was so basic to the meaning of *kābôd* that it changed the popular meaning of *doxa*. Having made the point that Scriptures often belittle man's claim to "glory," he states:

> Over against the transience of human and earthly glory stands the unchanging beauty of the manifest God (Ps 145:5). In this sense the noun *kābôd* takes on its most unusual and distinctive meaning. Forty-five times this form of the root relates to a *visible manifestation* of God and whenever "the glory of God" is mentioned this usage must be taken account of. Its force is so compelling that it remolds the meaning of doxa from an opinion of men in the Greek classics to something *absolutely objective* in the LXX and NT.[10]

---

[6] Found at http://www.desiringgod.org/interviews/what-is-gods-glory. Emphasis added.

[7] R. E. Nixon, "Glory," *New Bible Dictionary* (Leicester, England; Downers Grove, IL: IVP, 1996), 415.

[8] Gaffin, "Glory, Glorification," in *Dictionary of Paul and His Letters*, 348. Emphasis added.

[9] Nixon, "Glory," *New Bible Dictionary*, 348, states that in the NT, "... the LXX is followed in translating *kābôd* by *doxa*. In secular Greek [*doxa*] means 'opinion' or 'reputation'. The former idea disappears entirely in the LXX and NT."

[10] Oswalt, "943 כָּבֵד," *Theological Wordbook of the Old Testament*, 426-27, emphasis added. Cf. Gerhard Kittel, δόξα *TDNT* 2:237. After surveying the use of δόξα in Greek literature, he states, "Even a cursory survey of the position in the NT reveals a totally different picture. The old meaning ... 'opinion,' has disappeared completely. There is not a single example in either the NT or the post-apostolic fathers.... There has been added the meaning ..."radiance," "glory," which is not found in secular Greek."

In sum, a biblically framed and robust conception of God's glory must include the element of objectified worth, the truth of God "gone public" and thus perceived and acknowledged by rational creatures, divine majesty *on display*.

And it is this dynamic of God's glory which is *distinctively* honored, indeed celebrated, by the dispensational premillennialist construct. Central and basic to that construct is the insistence that human history on this fallen earth will conclude with a real kingdom in which Jesus of Nazareth will reign as King over all the earth in perfect righteousness, in which—in careful and exact fulfillment of covenant promises—a redeemed generation of the seed of Abraham will acknowledge as Savior and Lord that One whom once they pierced, and in which there will be the fulfillment of God's design that "every knee should bow, in heaven and on earth and under the earth, and every tongue confess that Jesus Christ is Lord, *to the glory of God the Father*" (Phil 2:10-11). That kingdom is the grand, physical, triumphalist culmination of human history. It is, in fact, the cosmic expression of God's majesty *on display*.

This is indeed distinctive to dispensational premillennialism. In contrast, amillennialism, the predominant eschatological system of covenantalism, denies that this future physical kingdom will exist.[11] That system affirms that the kingdom has already come, that what obtains on earth today is as good as God plans to do with human history, that the "kingdom" has to do simply and exclusively with spiritual victories and individual salvation. That construct anticipates an eternal state, a heavenly realm, in which God will be appropriately glorified, but *that kingdom glorification does not happen in any sustained and undeniably manifest fashion within human history.*

Historic premillennialism, different from dispensational premillennialism and based on supersessionism, acknowledges a literal kingdom (which persuasion the dispensational premillennialist is quick to commend) and (generally) teaches that a great company of Jewish people will be welcomed into that marvelous kingdom as they accept the Gospel and become part of the Universal Church. But to the degree that it insists that the Church has replaced Israel and thus denies ethnic Israel—the people with whom Yahweh formed a unique covenant relationship—a primary place in that kingdom, it compromises the

---

[11] This point hardly demands reinforcement; it is definitional to amillennialism. One example of that claim is Louis Berkhof, *Systematic Theology* (Grand Rapids: Eerdmans, 1938, 708): "All the great Confessions of the Church represent the general resurrection as simultaneous with the second coming of Christ, the final judgment *and the end of the world*" (emphasis added).

integrity of the fundamental truth regarding the character of Yahweh which is so deliberately on display in the Kingdom, viz., His covenant-keeping character.[12]

In sum, whereas all thinking Bible believers will affirm that human history is ultimately about the glory of God, dispensational premillennialism is distinctive in this particular: it is a set of ideas which by definition celebrates with full throat the very important dynamic so basic to the biblical concept of God's glory–the element of triumphalism, of divine majesty really and fully on parade for all the worlds (human and angelic, mortal and immortal) to marvel at and learn from. It is dispensational premillennialism which distinctively acknowledges and celebrates this dynamic of God's determination to demonstrate His glory *within* the course of human history: He has so framed the drama of mortal time that it culminates with a sustained, inescapable, breath-taking *physical display* of the triune God's majestic Person, and specifically of His attribute of truth—He is a God who keeps covenant. In short, the millennial kingdom is God's truth and truthfulness going public.

A Consistent and Prevailing Focus on the Glory of God

But there is a second particular at which dispensational premillennialism distinctively embraces the centrality of God's glory in human history. I would argue that all competing theological systems and constructs, though they honestly and deliberately acknowledge that God's glory is the grand purpose of all human history, give theological pride of place—functional priority—to the divine program of redemption from sin. The (seemingly airtight) syllogistic reasoning is this: (1) God's grand purpose is His own glory; (2) His most important strategy in demonstrating His glory is the plan of redemption from sin through Jesus Christ; (3) therefore human history is properly conceived of as ultimately all about God's unfolding plan of redemption. Thus, in terms of the way God's activity in history is conceived, and *in terms of how the biblical narrative is read and biblical theology is framed,* the divine plan of redemption is regarded as the single most defining factor.

That this is so—that most of the evangelical world holds that the divine plan of redemption is the center and core of all that God is doing in the course of time is obvious on the face of it. Indeed, it is spoken of as a first truth,

---

[12] These characterizations are made with neither polemical nor pejorative intent. The only design is to identify what seems on the face of it to be a point of distinction between these systems of thought on the one hand and dispensational premillennialism on the other.

a given, an axiomatic and *a priori* settled reality.[13] In fact, the debate here would almost certainly not be whether that proposition is widely embraced, but *whether there is any virtue or theological integrity in challenging that proposition.* And it is frankly acknowledged here that such a question as that is reasonable, and that the intuitive and impassioned response of many would be that there is *no* integrity or nobility in such a challenge. But it is precisely at this point that carefully-articulated dispensational premillennialism must take humble and gentle exception.[14]

To be specific, the exception is taken with the second element of the syllogism suggested above. Again, it seems fair to distill the argument in favor of regarding the work of redemption as the center of God's purpose and activity to this: (1) God's grand purpose in all of history is His own glory; (2) His most defining *strategy* in demonstrating His glory is the plan of redemption from sin through Jesus Christ; (3) therefore human history is properly conceived of as ultimately all about God's unfolding plan of redemption. Quite simply, dispensational premillennialism would argue—humbly and cautiously—that the second factor in that syllogism is incorrect. Rather, the *primary* strategy in God's plan to glorify Himself in human history is His dealings with a people called Israel, and specifically His design to *fulfill a covenant which He made with ethnic Israel to make them a "great nation" in whom "all the families of the earth shall be blessed"* (Gen 12:2, 3). Thus, dispensational premillennialism would recast the syllogism as follows: (1) God's grand purpose is His own glory; (2) His most defining *strategy* in demonstrating His glory is the fulfillment of a redemptive covenant He made with a people called Israel; (3) Therefore human history is properly conceived of as ultimately about God's patient and wise and persevering dealings with Israel so as ultimately to bring a generation (and subsequent

---

[13] Examples are legion, but it does not seem necessary to multiply them here. One prevailing iteration of the idea is formal Covenant Theology which, with many nuances and variations, regards history as the unfolding of the one Covenant of Grace, the covenant by which God "freely offers sinners life and salvation through Jesus Christ" (Westminster Confession, Chap VII, Art III). For instance, Daniel Hyde of Ligonier Ministries writes, "Reformed Christians speak of Scripture as the unfolding drama of God's covenant of grace" (Web article, Sep 26, 2014, at http://www.ligonier.org/blog/what-covenant-grace). Again, an article in the *Christian Research Journal* states, "The Bible is fundamentally a history book — the history of God's redemptive acts, past, present, and future.... The Bible, therefore, may best be understood as a history of the administration of a single divine plan for the redemption of the cosmos" (27:5, 2004).

[14] This was the basic point that Charles Ryrie was making in the third element of his *sine qua non* of dispensationalism (Ryrie, *Dispensationalism Today*), the point for which he was so often remonstrated. Though the point that I am developing in this chapter is fairly standard in dispensationalism, I am not asserting that every dispensational premillennialist would necessarily explain this concept as I am.

generations, Isa 61:9) of that people to Himself.[15] Thus, the plan of redemption wrought through the finished work of Messiah Jesus—as inexpressibly blessed, infinitely important, bottomlessly wondrous, and magisterially praiseworthy as it is—must be seen as a necessary means to the end of making possible the fulfillment of that covenant made with Israel, and thus of powerfully demonstrating the glory of Yahweh's covenant-keeping, truth-telling character.

I am compelled to beg the reader's patience and attention here—patience because I am in fact treading on sacred and sensitive ground, and attention because it is so important that I not be misunderstood. There is no denial that that plan of redemption is a central theme which runs throughout Scripture from the moment of man's fall (Gen 3:15) to the final transformation of the cosmos, or that it is incumbent upon believers to carefully trace that unfolding plan of redemption and to wallow in its goodness. Indeed, as Michael Vlach points out, "The reason why Jesus is worthy to take the book and establish God's kingdom on earth is because He has been slain and has purchased His people with His blood. Cross and kingdom work in perfect harmony"[16] (cf. Rev 5:9-10; Col 1:15-20; Heb 2:5-9). So, there is here no intent to belittle or disparage the blessed and noble plan of redemption as revealed in Scripture and accomplished by Jesus Christ. God is glorified through His plan of redemption.

The suggestion is simply that the biblical testimony demonstrates that this plan of redemption *in and of itself* is not God's primary doxological strategy, though it is in fact pivotal and necessary to the accomplishment of that which is His primary strategy. The reality that there will be an *entire generation* of Abraham's descendants who repent and are saved—is very much at the heart of the covenant promise made by God with Israel. Paul's affirmation of this reality in Romans 11:26, 27—"And in this way, all Israel will be saved,"—is clearly informed by promises recorded in the Hebrew Scriptures. This is evidenced by what follows in that sentence: "... as it is written, 'The Deliverer will come from Zion, he will banish ungodliness from Jacob; and this will be my covenant with them when I take away their sins.'" Paul's citation is from Isaiah 59:20-21a,

---

[15] This concept may seem novel, but as we will see in the last paragraph of chapter ten, Episcopal Bishop William B. Nicholson made this same point in 1878 in his message at the first International Prophecy Conference. Nicholson says, "Oh, this restoration of Israel is the very centre of God's gracious purposes concerning the world."

[16] Michael Vlach, *He Will Reign Forever* (Silverton, OR: Lampion Press, 2017), 479.

but he conflates that verse with Isaiah 27:9.[17] And in fact those Old Covenant Scriptures are replete with the specific promises that—not because of their righteousness, but *for the sake of God's glory*—the covenant people *as a nation* is going to turn to God in the day of His choosing.[18]

But at the same time, it is acknowledged that the very concept of an entire generation turning to Messiah Jesus in saving faith is distinctively non-intuitive—perhaps incoherent—certainly to the non-dispensationalist worldview and even to many who would embrace some iteration of a dispensational-premillennial construct. Thus, Paul's phrase πᾶς Ἰσραὴλ is given many interpretations and nuances,[19] and one's persuasion regarding both the broader purposes of God and the details of an end-time drama will turn, to a significant degree, on how that phrase is understood.[20] But the purpose here is not to adjudicate among those suggested interpretations. Rather, for purposes of a thought experiment, the reader is asked to accept the most tightly construed understanding of the phrase—that the phrase is intended to signify every Jewish person (physical descendant of Abraham) still alive when the White-Horsed Rider descends at the end of the seven-year Tribulation.[21]

Given the fact that this reading of πᾶς Ἰσραὴλ is intuitively difficult for many, here are two comments in clarification and modest defense of its legitimacy. First, a clarification. According to dispensation-premillennialism, an

---

[17] There is some discussion about the specific passage being cited in the final phrase of Paul's argument in Romans 11:27—"when I take away their sins." Indeed, Lange cites several commentators who trace the statement to Jeremiah 31:33, and then alludes to one who "… thinks it probable 'that here, as elsewhere, [Paul] does not intend to refer exclusively to any one prediction, but to give the general sense of many specific declarations of the ancient prophets.'" Lange appropriately rejects both of those proposals. But the latter surmise serves to make the point that the simple affirmation that Yahweh will "take away [Israel's] sins" is in fact an oft-repeated promise in the Hebrew Scriptures—so much so that it is hard to know what specific promise he has in mind in 11:27b.

[18] E.g.: Ps 130:7-8; Isa 33:24; 35:8-10; 44:3-5,21-23; 45:17; 46:13; 62:1,10-12; Jer 31:31-34; 33:7-9; 50:20; Ezek 11:18-19; 36:22-28; Joel 2:28-29,32; 3:21; Mic 7:18-20; Zech 12:10-12; 13:1-2. The same Heb 8:8-12; 10:16,17.

[19] Cranfield lists four interpretations and suggests as most likely that "the nation Israel as a whole, but not necessarily including every individual member" (C. E. B. Cranfield, ICC: *Romans*, Edinburgh: Clark, 1975-79, 2:576–77). Other commentators and/or scholars list dozens of suggested meanings.

[20] Or, perhaps, vice versa: one's theological construct will strongly influence the way πᾶς Ἰσραὴλ is interpreted. But it would be better if it were the other way around.

[21] Not every Israelite alive at the beginning of the Tribulation will be saved at the Coming of Christ because God uses the last half of the Tribulation to "purge out the rebels" (Ezek 20:38; cf. 33-38). Zechariah proclaims, "'In the whole land,' declares the Lord, 'two thirds shall be cut off and perish, and one third shall be left alive. And I will put this third into the fire, and refine them as one refines silver, and test them as gold is tested. They will call upon my name, and I will answer them. I will say, 'They are my people'; and they will say, 'The Lord is my God'" (Zech 13:8-9). The generation that unanimously accepts Messiah is thus one-third of the generation alive when the severe judgments of the Tribulation begin. Scripture also seems to teach that most of this generation's descendants will be believers in Jesus Christ (Isa 61:9), so that the accursed Jew (that is a non-believer) in the Millennial Kingdom is a rare exception (Isa 65:20).

entire generation of Jewish people will be saved at a divinely orchestrated climactic moment, but they will not be saved *en masse*—that is, the salvation
experience and commitment is not corporate. Individual salvation must be individual. And Zechariah is explicit that this is what will happen in the moment to
which Paul is alluding when he exults, "All Israel shall be saved":

> The land shall mourn, each family by itself: the family of the house of David by
> itself, and their wives by themselves; the family of the house of Nathan by itself,
> and their wives by themselves; the family of the house of Levi by itself, and their
> wives by themselves; the family of the Shimeites by itself, and their wives by them-
> selves; and all the families that are left, each by itself, and their wives by themselves
> (Zech 12:12-14).

So the claim is not that the entire nation will be pronounced "saved" as a group
"by some unilateral action of God."[22]

Rather, a sovereign God, for the purposes of His own glory, will orchestrate
and oversee a series of earth-shaking and -shaping circumstances and events
that will bring those Jews who are alive at the culminating coming of Messiah,
all of them, to a place of such existential and individual despair that, by reason
of God's grace, they will *individually* but *universally* look in faith to the One
Whom once they pierced (Zech 12:10). In short, all Israel will be saved, but
salvation will be embraced by each individual Jewish person because God sends
a spirit of "grace and pleas of mercy" (Zech 12:10)—*grace* the ground of and
supplication the means of redemption for every individual Jewish person at that
grand moment, just as has been true of every person ever brought from death
to life from Adam forward.

Second, the concept of God demonstrating His glory *through the nation
of Israel as a nation* is not new to sacred history. This was explicitly the divine
strategy in the Old Testament, most recognizably perhaps during the days of
the Theocracy in Israel. Quite simply, at Mt Sinai Yahweh made Himself King
over Israel in the most real, literal, physical and actual sense,[23] and Scriptures

---

[22] Robert H. Mounce, *Romans*, vol. 27, The New American Commentary (Nashville: Broadman & Holman Publishers, 1995), 224. Mounce's full comment on Romans 11:26: "Obviously this was not some unilateral action of God on behalf of his people. Israel's salvation would be on the same basis as anyone else's, that is, by responding in faith to the forgiveness made possible by the death and resurrection of Jesus Christ."

[23] For a characterization of the Theocracy and a survey of the role it plays in the OT narrative, see Appendix A: "The Nature of the Old Testament Theocracy."

are clear that He did so in order to put Himself on display to the nations of the world *through His dealings with Israel as a people.* That is, in blessing that nation's obedience and cursing her disobedience, the Lord Himself would cause the nations across the world to realize who Yahweh is (Exod 9:13-16; Ps 106: 7-8; 1 Sam 4:6-8; 5:6; 2 Sam 7:23; Jer 13:11).

The simple point here: after Gen 12, God's strategy was primarily a function of His relationship to the family of Abraham/nation of Israel, as opposed to His personal relationship to individual Israelites. Indeed, King Yahweh's capacity to accomplish His doxological purposes was not directly a function of the spiritual condition of individual Israelites. If the nation was led and dominated by wickedness, they suffered punishment; if righteousness prevailed in the homes and in the palace, they experienced blessings. But in either case, Yahweh put His character on display to the nations *through His rule of Israel as a nation.*

Because the reality of the theocracy in the Hebrew Scriptures is so underappreciated, and because the New Testament program is so thoroughly personal and individual (as opposed to national and corporate), Bible believers are often intuitively uneasy with the idea of God accomplishing His purposes through the nation of Israel as a whole. But that is the pattern God established in the Old Testament. To be sure, in God's eschatological dealings with the nation of Israel the issue of individual standing before God will be entirely central simply because the promise to which He has committed Himself is that an entire nation (generation) will be saved. At this point, the end-time program is different from the Old Testament program. But the similarity is important and the ramification instructive: God has worked His purposes through Israel *as a nation,* and He has promised to do so again.

A THOUGHT EXPERIMENT: WELCOME TO OUR WORLD(VIEW)

First, a brief review. The distinctive element under discussion in this essay is the claim of dispensational premillennialism that the central doxological strategy of God is not ultimately the work of redemption itself, but rather God's faithful fulfillment of covenant promises made to the people of Israel, and specifically the promise that He would "make a new covenant *with the house of Israel and the house of Judah,*" and that by reason of that regenerating covenant, Israel's relationship to Yahweh would be made eternally perfect: "I will be their God, and they shall be my *people*.... they shall all know me, from the least of them to the greatest, declares the LORD. For I will forgive their iniquity, and I will remember their sin no more" (Jer 31:31-34).[24]

Indeed, the issue I am attempting to address is perhaps crystallized in the following multiple-choice question:

Q: Which is *most central* to God's purpose to glorify Himself in mortal time?

A. The salvation of the *elect* (i.e., the blessed work of redemption by which an innumerable host from every tribe, tongue and nation are rescued from the curse of sin and reconciled to God)

B. The salvation of *Israel* (i.e., the application of that redemptive work to a generation of ethnic sons of Abraham who are finally brought to saving dependence on Messiah Jesus.

The non-dispensational evangelical world will certainly answer A. The thesis here is that a careful, if cautious, dispensational premillennialist answer would be B.[25] Clearly, that latter perception of God's doxological plan will dramatically and inexorably frame one's understanding of all that God is doing and will do in order to bring human history to its most God-glorifying denouement. But the thesis itself, as well as the theological universe into which it takes the dispensational premillennialist, are as unfamiliar and off-putting to the non-dispensationalist as watery ocean depths to an elephant or the verdant jungle to a whale (to rather overwork the metaphor!).

In the interest of getting beyond that whale/elephant impasse, the skeptical reader who has graciously persevered to this point is asked to engage in a modest thought experiment: Step into the worldview of the dispensational premillennialist and consider very briefly God's purposes for today and tomorrow *as understood from that worldview*—first, the present age (The Interregnum: a patient pedagogy), and then the drama by which a culminating kingdom will

---

[24] The passage is selectively cited and emphasized to make the point at stake, but in so doing I have taken care not to distort or compromise the meaning of this all-important text. The reader is implored to consider the passage carefully to determine whether I have been successful in that effort.

[25] Again, this proposition must not be read to suggest any disregard for or deemphasis of the glorious and all-important work of redemption in Christ. The attempt is not to taxonomize God's activities as to their intrinsic worth or majesty; it is to identify the primary strategy God has chosen as the means of His own glory according to the Scriptures.

be introduced (The Tribulation: a terrible kindness), and finally one distinct element of that kingdom itself (The Millennial Kingdom: a final doxological nail).
And please know that the intent here is not to persuade the non-dispensational
premillennialist of any of these elements as understood from within that construct. Rather, it is to help the unpersuaded to contemplate the cogency and
coherency of that construct itself given this animating and defining thesis—that
God's primary strategy by which He has determined to glorify Himself publicly
in the course of human history is His covenant faithfulness to Israel.

The Interregnum: A Patient Pedagogy

The present age—the period between the first and final comings of Messiah
Jesus—is variously comprehended by theological thinkers who inhabit it. To
the non-dispensationalist, it is the *culminating* age of earthly human history:
the work of redemption is "finished" (John 19:30), the Gospel goes freely to
all men in every place, God is gathering His own from every tribe, tongue and
nation, and all that awaits is for the full number of individuals to be drawn to
the truth so that the redeemed might be granted eternal rest and communion
with the God they have been taught to love and trust. A delightful set of ideas
in all of its parts.

But the exercise before us is to contemplate this element of God's design,
the interregnum, from a dispensational-premillennial worldview, and thus to
ask how this present age might speak to the purpose of bringing a generation of
Israel to faith.[26] In that regard, two preliminary points of refinement.

Regarding Gentile Salvation During the Interregnum

It is popularly perceived that the grand distinction of this age is that the
Gospel is open to Gentiles. But certainly, Gentiles could get saved in the Old
Testament. In fact, God's purpose in His relationship with Israel was that that
people might be a blessing to all nations (Gen 12:3), a "kingdom of priests"[27]
mediating the truth of Yahweh to the entire world (Exod 19:6), that through

---

[26] Dispensationalists have sometimes spoken of this present age as a "parenthesis," and have thus been accused of treating
it as an "afterthought," an exigency that God in some sense did not anticipate, or a "Plan B" made necessary because Plan A
had failed with the rejection of Jesus by the generation to which He came. I don't think that latter accusation is legitimate
(i.e., no thinking dispensationalist ever so conceived the present age as Plan B), though I acknowledge that dispensationalists
have sometimes made it easy to level the charge. But such a notion plays no part in the discussion at hand.

[27] That is, a "kingdom with a priestly function," a nation which God would use—as a nation—to mediate the truth of
Yahweh to the rest of mankind, *and* a people through whose divinely provided Levitical system the rest of mankind would
be enabled to approach Yahweh.

His dealings with Israel His name might be "proclaimed in all the earth" (Exod 9:6). The Mosaic Law demands that the "stranger who dwells with you"—that is, the Gentile proselyte who has abandoned his gods and given his allegiance to Yahweh—is to be accepted and treated as a full citizen of the kingdom of Yahweh (Lev 24:22; Num 9:14; 15:14, 15; et al.).

Indeed, Gentiles could be and were saved before Pentecost, but *only as they were willing—to one degree or another—to surrender their "Gentile-ness" and identify with the nation of Israel.* The various Gentile peoples were identified most importantly by the gods they served. But Yahweh, the God of Israel, insisted He was the one God, that all other purported gods were fictions at best and demons at worst. One could not "serve the living and true God" without turning "from idols" (1 Thess 1:9), and to turn from the patron god in whose name your Gentile monarch ruled was to surrender your rights as a citizen of that land. Thus, she who confessed, "Your God will be my God" had already decided that "Your people shall be my people" (Ruth 1:16).[28] It is in this sense that "salvation is of the Jews" as Jesus said to a Samaritan woman (John 4:22). Indeed, the book of Acts is in large part the record of God's efforts to bring the early Christian community—an entirely Jewish community—to acknowledge that now "Then to the Gentiles also God has granted repentance that leads to life" (Acts 11:18).

Thus, the refinement: the grand distinctive of this age is not that Gentiles can now be saved; rather, it is that Gentiles can now be saved *as Gentiles.* The divinely ordained protocol for two thousand years had been that Yahweh was uniquely and manifestly the God of Abraham, of the family that came from his loins and of the nation that issued from his twelve sons, and that to pledge allegiance to that God was to identify with His people. But now, a remarkable change in God's purposes: Gentiles can serve and honor the *God* of Israel apart from any identification with the *nation* of Israel. Clearly, something is afoot.

There is, of course, more to the blessed story. Jesus was "crucified and killed by the hands of lawless men" (Acts 2:23), the generation of Jewish people to whom He had come. Indeed, a partial hardening has come upon Israel, until the

---

[28] Not all converts/proselytes made a dramatic a commitment as did Ruth. Compare Naaman, the Syrian leper (2 Kgs 5:17).

fullness of the Gentiles has come in" (Rom 11:25).[29] God, furthermore, has raised up an organism in which, "the dividing wall of hostility" between Jew and Gentile has been broken down in order that "He might reconcile us both to God in one body through the cross, thereby killing the hostility" (Eph 2:14-16).

But the point to be stressed here is that the radical change in God's salvific purposes which prevails during the present inter-advent age is *not* that Gentiles can be saved, but that they can be saved *as Gentiles*. This blessed reality can only be appreciated against the backdrop of the concomitant reality that throughout the ages from Abraham onward salvation was "of the Jews" (John 4:22). In short, this age is not so much the grand and final *culmination* of all that went before as it is a *departure* from the method by which God invited men to know and approach Him for centuries before. And further, the dispensational premillennialist will argue, it is a departure with a purpose, a departure designed with infinite divine wisdom as a key step in God's strategy to manifest to the universe the majesty of His covenant-keeping nature. This conviction takes us, in the interest of the thought experiment before us, to the second of the preliminary propositions.

Regarding New Covenant Blessings During the Interregnum

Again and again, prophets ministering under the "old covenant"[30] revealed God's purpose to one day bless Israel with a "new covenant" (Jer 31:31), a "covenant of peace (שָׁלוֹם)" (Isa 54:10; Ezek 34:25; 37:26).[31] It is perhaps fair to

---

[29] The phrase "until the fulness of the Gentiles is come in" is widely—universally, as far as I can determine—taken to mean "until the full number of Gentiles has been redeemed"—a happy thought, especially to this Gentile writer. But the phrase will be read as an unhappy thought if informed by two antecedent and closely related passages: first, Daniel 2 and 7, in which two visions introduce a period of Gentile rule which Israel must endure before the promised Messianic Kingdom is established, a period when the name of God will be much maligned and the purposes of God will be despised and defied; and second, Luke 21:24, where Jesus affirms that Jerusalem will be trampled by Gentiles until "the times of the Gentiles" are fulfilled—best understood as a reference to that concept defined in Daniel 2 and 7. If this phrase in Rom 11:25 is understood to be a reference to the period of Jewish suffering and divine dishonor which is foretold in Dan 2 and 7 (a reading consistent with the thesis that God's primary doxological strategy is His gracious dealing with Israel), it is a most melancholy thought to anyone with a heart for God's glory. Might it be indicative of the tendency of the Gentile reader to put himself overmuch at the center of God's purposes that the phrase is so often taken, absent any attempt to ground it in closely relevant former Scriptures, to refer to an ingathering of Gentile converts? And might not such a reading constitute a violation of Paul's twice-made warning in this passage: the injunction not to be "arrogant" against the branches which were cut off (11:18), and later the warning not to be "wise in your own sight" (11:25).

[30] So identified in retrospect in 2 Cor 3:14 and Heb 8:13. The reference is to the Law, the Mosaic covenant, by which at Mt. Sinai the family of Abraham became the nation of Israel, and by which Yahweh became King over that people.

[31] For a survey of the "new covenant" promises found in the Hebrew Scriptures, see "Dispensationalism, The Church, and The New Covenant," R. Bruce Compton, *Detroit Baptist Seminary Journal,* 8 (Fall 2003):3–48, esp. the section entitled, "Old Testament Survey."

distill the promises of that new covenant to two almost unimaginable blessings. First, Jeremiah celebrates the promise of *sins once and for all forgiven* (Jer 31:34), a confidence which the Old Testament (or "covenant") saint could never know (Heb 10:1-4). And second, Ezekiel anticipates a covenant by which Yahweh would give His people "a new heart" and put a "new spirit" within them; indeed, He promised His covenant people, "And I will remove the heart of stone from your flesh and give you a heart of flesh" (Ezek 36:26). The apostle Paul exults over the unimaginable intimacy with the Father made possible under that "covenant of peace" when he speaks of receiving "the Spirit of adoption as sons, by whom we cry, 'Abba! Father!'" (Rom 8:15; Gal 4:6). And clearly, all of this because of "the blood of the covenant, which is poured out for many for the forgiveness of sins" (Matt 26:28; Mark 14:24; cf. Luke 22:20; 1 Cor 11:27; Heb 9:15; 13:20).

But here is a bit of a conundrum: that new covenant was promised explicitly and exclusively to the nation of Israel (Jer 31:31),[32] and yet all of those who during the present interregnum are "in Christ," believers both Jew and Gentile, are happy beneficiaries of those new covenant blessings (Matt 26:28; Luke 22:20; 1 Cor 11:25; 2 Cor 3:6; Heb 7:22; 8:6; 13:20).

Rivers of ink have been spilt in the effort to explain this conundrum.[33] But the thought experiment at hand is simply to ponder how our understanding of God's purposes (including here His determination to visit all believers in this age with new covenant blessings originally promised to Israel) might be framed given the defining dispensational-premillennial commitment that God's primary doxological strategy is faithfulness to His covenant with the

---

[32] Most explicitly in the most definitional text, "I will make a new covenant with the *house of Israel and the house of Judah,* (Jer 31:31), and again in 31:33, "For this is the covenant that I will make *with the house of Israel* after those days, declares the Lord" (Jer 31:33). Yahweh further specifies the recipients of the anticipated "new covenant" when he states that it will not be "like the covenant that I made with their fathers on the day when I took them by the hand to bring them out of the land of Egypt, my covenant that *they* broke (Jer 31:32, my emphasis throughout those scriptural quotes). This is a reference to the Mosaic covenant which God certainly made only with the nation of Israel. Finally, with reference to the recipients of that new covenant, Yahweh avers that only if the lights He has placed in the heavens should stop shining "shall the offspring of Israel cease from being a nation before me forever" (Jer 31:36).

[33] The biblical fact that believers of this age are vouchsafed new covenant blessings has often been appealed to as evidence for supersessionism. For example, Loraine Boettner, *The Meaning of the Millennium: Four Views,* ed. Robert G. Clouse (Downers Grove, IL: InterVarsity Press, 1977), states, "... the Old Covenant, which we have in the first part of our Bibles in the Old Testament, was made exclusively with the nation of Israel. ... it now has been replaced by the New Covenant, which we call the New Testament, which was made exclusively with the church." Indeed, the conundrum before us has generated sharply divergent explanations even within the dispensational premillennial camp; for a survey of those explanations, see, Compton, "Dispensationalism, The Church, and The New Covenant, *DBSJ,* under "Major Views."

nation of Israel. That is, how might the present-day Christian's unanticipated[34] possession of those new covenant blessings serve to bring a generation
of Israel to faith?

The Riddle Solved: A Suggestion

Paul speaks directly to this question. In Romans 9-11 the apostle is addressing
the issue of God's character: How can a covenant-keeping God set aside the
nation of Israel with whom He has made an everlasting covenant? Central to
his reply is the truth that the setting aside of Israel is temporary, that "if they do
not continue in their unbelief, will be grafted in, for God has the power to graft
them in again" (Rom 11:23). But in making that argument Paul speaks directly
to the two-fold question before us: first, why has the door of salvation been
thrown open to Gentiles as Gentiles so late in the history of God's working with
mankind, and second, why do believers of this age enjoy the New Covenant
blessings promised to a regenerated Israel? Having acknowledged that national
Israel has indeed been set aside, the apostle argues:

> So I ask, did they stumble in order that they might fall? By no means! Rather,
> through their trespass *salvation has come to the Gentiles, so as to make Israel jealous.*
> Now if their trespass means riches for the world, and if their failure means riches
> for the Gentiles, how much more will their full inclusion mean! Now I am speak-
> ing to you Gentiles. Inasmuch then as I am an apostle to the Gentiles, I magnify
> my ministry in order somehow *to make my fellow Jews jealous, and thus save some of*
> *them.* For if their rejection means the reconciliation of the world, what will their
> acceptance mean but life from the dead? (Rom 11:11-15, emphasis mine).

Paul is explicit: "*salvation has come to the Gentiles, so as to make Israel jealous.*"[35]
He goes on to celebrate his own unique ministry as "apostle to the Gentiles"
because his efforts among Gentiles will be used to make fellow Jews in his life
jealous, and thus to save some in his own day (11:13, 14). But the force of his

---

[34] That is, unanticipated *in the promises of the Hebrew Scriptures.* Certainly, this reality was in no sense unanticipated by
God; in fact, it is best appreciated as a deliberate and integral part of the infinitely wise and persevering plan of God to fulfill
His covenant promise to the seed of Abraham.

[35] εἰς τὸ παραζηλῶσαι, purpose expressed by εἰς with the articular infinitive; a strong statement of purpose, "in order to.
…" God uses the Gentiles to bring Jews to Christ, and, on the other hand, God uses the salvation of the nation of Israel to
bring the Gentile nations to Himself (see Ezek 36:23-36; Rom 11:30-31). There is no racial prejudice with God (Rom 2:11-
12). See further our Chapter Eleven—an exposition of Romans 11.

argument here has to do with the grander hope that "all Israel will be saved" (11:26) in a day when the "natural branches" will be "grafted back into their own olive tree" (11:24).

It is in the light of this reality that the unanticipated participation in new covenant blessings by saints of the present interregnum is biblically understood. God's ultimate doxological strategy in all of human history is the ineffably brilliant display of His own covenant-keeping character by means of His persevering and resourceful accomplishment of His promise to Israel—specifically, the promise to bring a generation of that people to Himself. The very idea of an entire living generation of Jewish people coming to faith in Messiah Jesus seems beyond possibility, a blessedness even God in heaven could scarcely accomplish. But the overwhelming "impossibility" of such an event is key to the pedagogical impact it will have throughout eternity as redeemed and glorified saints contemplate the ages-long history of God's faithfulness to His covenant promises to Israel.

And key to the means by which that grand and staggering promise will find fulfillment is this: for 2000 years (and counting) the Jewish people have been surrounded by a great company of those who have confessed their faith in Messiah Jesus and thus live out their lives as happy beneficiaries of the bottomlessly delightful blessings of the New Covenant promised to Israel in the Hebrew Scriptures. That testimony will excite sacred jealousy in that culminating generation just as it does today. The testimony of individual Jews who come to faith in Messiah Jesus so often includes this note of longing for what he or she saw in the life of someone who had embraced the Christian faith.[36] Indeed, the intimacy and confidence the Christian enjoys in his relationship with his Father God and through the finished work of Messiah Jesus is intended to be the "aroma of Christ … the fragrance from life to life" (2 Cor 2:15-16). This is clearly a basic and gracious dynamic of the divine strategy to draw the lost to Himself; God convicts and persuades and attracts the rebellious unbeliever in significant part by means of the redeemed and transformed lives of those around him who have come to know the blessedness of a right relationship with their Heavenly Father.

And in that same way the corporate remembrance of a generation of Israel who finds themselves the targets of unimaginable murderous rage in an end-time

---

[36] See https://www.oneforisrael.org/met-messiah-jewish-testimonies/ for example, the testimony of a Jewish woman who came to Christ because of the testimony and changed life of her sister.

drama,[37] the remembrance and observation of Christ-followers delighting in those New Covenant blessings, will be one part of the divine strategy by which God does indeed accomplish the unimaginable, by which He woos to faith in His now-appearing Messiah a generation of that people to whom so long ago He made the covenant-promise to do exactly that.[38]

In sum, given Paul's instruction, the interregnum is best understood not as a final or culminating age, but as a two-millennia teaching time, exciting in the Jewish people a "jealousy" for what the Gospel provides. It is an integral element of the infinitely wise and deliberately doxological scheme of God to prove His covenant-keeping character by bringing to Himself a generation of Jewish people. This age is, in truth, a Patient Pedagogy.

THE TRIBULATION: A TERRIBLE KINDNESS

A second step in the thought experiment before us: how does the seven-year Tribulation—by dispensational lights the centerpiece of the divinely revealed end-time drama by which the promised kingdom shall be brought in—relate to God's purposes to glorify His name by bringing to Himself a generation of Israel? I acknowledge that at this point the discussion charges into a hermeneutical worldview and an eschatological framework to some degree foreign and unfamiliar to the non-dispensationalist. Thus, in the attempt to make the thought experiment viable for brethren beyond our pale, I will offer a number of simple propositions which are intrinsic to the dispensational-premillennialist construct as it relates to the question at hand. Again, the intent is to inform rather than to persuade; thus, the propositions will be neither expanded nor defended. They are iterated here simply as a very basic characterization of the broad construct from which the dispensational premillennialist ponders the question, "How does the Tribulation fit into God's more cosmic doxological purposes for human history?"

---

[37] See the next section of this chapter.

[38] It is in this connection that Gentile believers throughout this age might acknowledge with a Syro-Phoenecian woman who so long ago impressed our Lord with her submissive and trusting spirit that we, too, are the "dogs under the table who eat the children's crumbs" (Mark 7:28). In Jesus' word picture, that woman was a "dog" rather than one of "the children" only because she was a Gentile—as are so many of us. It is appropriately humbling to accept the Lord's contrast between the Jewish "children" and the Gentile "dogs." But certainly, the point to be stressed is that it is infinitely and eternally blessed to be made partakers of the New Covenant blessings promised to Israel but provided for Gentiles in God's time and purposes. Indeed, to apply Jesus' word picture theologically, those New Covenant blessings are very tasty crumbs!

Proposition #1: When the predictive prophecies of the Scriptures are read literally,[39] a remarkably detailed and definable end-time drama does in fact emerge.

Proposition #2: Very important to that drama is a seven-year Tribulation period first foretold in Daniel 9:24-27 as the culminating "week" (i.e., period of 7 successive years) in a period of 70 such "weeks" which will finally bring in the much-promised and long-awaited Messianic Kingdom (Dan 9:24). That end-time 70th Week, the Tribulation, is expanded upon in stunning detail in Revelation 4-19.

Proposition #3: The chief player and arch-villain of that seven-year Tribulation will be a profoundly wicked and alarmingly clever deceiver who will ultimately be entirely and immediately controlled by Satan; that end-time destroyer is identified in Scripture by various titles and descriptors, including "the little horn" (Dan 7:8), "the prince who is to come" (Dan 9:26), "the Man of lawlessness" (2 Thess 2:3), "the lawless one" (2 Thess 2:8), "the Antichrist" (1 John 4:3; cf. 2 John 7), and "a beast rising out of the sea" (Rev 13:1).

Proposition #4: During the last half of that seven-year period, the end-time arch-villain will determine to annihilate the people of God—to be sure, the believers of every tribe and tongue, but more specifically the entire ethnic nation of Israel irrespective of whether they have accepted the messianic claims of Jesus of Nazareth—in order to frustrate God's program to glorify Himself by fulfilling His covenant promises to that nation. In the effort, the Antichrist will marshal all the forces and resources of the world to that one God-defying purpose.

Proposition #5: Only when every whisper of hope to resist or escape has been entirely and inarguably stripped from the people of God, Messiah Jesus will descend with a heavenly army to powerfully destroy His enemies and rescue those about to be annihilated.

Proposition #6: At that moment, God will pour out "a spirit of grace and pleas for mercy" (Zech 12:10) and a generation of living Israelites will cry out

---

[39] To be sure, the term "literal" with respect to hermeneutics is much discussed and variously defined. I would ask the reader to maintain the "thought experiment" and assign the term the connotation intended by the dispensational premillennialist: "literally" in the sense of "normally," as written words are intuitively understood in everyday situations of life; "… the words of the authors of Scripture must mean what they ordinarily meant when they were accorded their *usus loquendi*, that is, their spoken sense in similar contexts of that day" (Walter C. Kaiser, Jr, *The Messiah in the Old Testament* [Grand Rapids: Zondervan, 1995], 25). Is this the proper way to read Scripture? Might the term "literally" be justifiably used to describe non-dispensational approaches to Scripture? These are questions worthy of discussion, but they are not the issue before us. In fact, the dispensational hermeneutic is certainly distinguishable from a non-dispensational hermeneutic. This is the most basic reason the competing systems of biblical thought exist. The intent here is to invite the non-dispensationalist to step into the dispensational premillennial thought universe in order to appreciate why he reads the Scriptures as he does.

to God for salvation, individually as to faith and universally as to number. Thus "all Israel will be saved" (Rom 11:26).

Given this over-simplified summary of the dispensational-premillennial understanding of what the Scriptures reveal concerning the end-time drama, we return to the question, "What specific role does the seven-year Tribulation play in God's doxological purposes?" Simply stated, the Tribulation is God's gracious strategy to bring an entire generation of Israel so entirely to the end of themselves that they will look upon Him whom once they pierced and cast themselves entirely upon Him for deliverance and salvation, both physical and spiritual. It is, in fact, a Terrible Kindness.

In this regard, it is important to note that in the Hebrew Scriptures Yahweh promises quite explicitly to employ this precise strategy. For example, in the reaffirmation of His covenant with Israel spelled out in Deuteronomy, God vows repeatedly to curse Israel for her persistent disobedience, but even as He does so He makes this promise to that people who will prove themselves recalcitrantly rebellious: "*When you are in tribulation*, and all these things come upon you *in the latter days*, you will return to the LORD your God and obey his voice. For the LORD your God is a merciful God. He will not leave you or destroy you or forget the covenant with your fathers that he swore to them" (Deut 4:30-31, emphasis added). The Tribulation will cause that generation of Israel to "return to the LORD ... and obey His voice."

Again, in the seminal vision of the chronology of the end-time drama, the prophet Daniel is told of the unspeakable terror to befall his people in the course of that drama. Two angelic watchers are standing by, and the one inquires of the other, "How long shall it be till the end of these wonders?" (12:6). In response, that other angel "swore by him who lives forever that it would be for a time, times, and half a time" (12:7, i.e., for the final 3½ years of the 7-year Tribulation). And then that angelic spokesman announced, "when the shattering of the power of the holy people comes to an end all these things would be finished" (12:7). In God's sustaining providences, Israel has again and again proved herself a stunningly proud and plucky people. But God has revealed something of the set of world-wide catastrophic circumstances which He will use to "completely shatter" the "power of the holy people," with the design that they might finally look to Him for deliverance. The Tribulation is central to those catastrophic circumstances.

Once more, Hosea the prophet was commanded to marry a "wife of whoredom" (1:2), then to buy her from the slave-market to which her wickedness had doomed her, and then to restore her to himself through care and chastening (3:2-3)—all this as a deliberate and explicit picture of how Yahweh would work with Israel to redeem her to Himself (3:4-5). In application of all this God states, "I will return again to my place, until they acknowledge their guilt and seek my face, and *in their distress earnestly seek me*" (5:15, emphasis added). As Hosea's wife had to be driven to despair before she would learn to love and trust the husband to whom she had sworn a marriage covenant, so with the nation of Israel. God has promised to deal thus with that people, bringing them so entirely to the end of themselves that they learn to trust and love the God with whom they enjoy a marvelously blessed and eternally abiding relationship.

Finally, in his very important description of the moment when Israel will be saved, Zechariah foretells the day when God will make Jerusalem "a cup of staggering to all the surrounding peoples. The siege of Jerusalem will also be against Judah" (12:2), when "all the nations of the earth will gather against it [Israel]" (12:3). But the prophet goes on: "On that day the LORD will protect the inhabitants of Jerusalem" (12:8); indeed, God promises through the prophet that "on that day I will seek to destroy all the nations that come against Jerusalem" (12:9). And note that God pledges that at just that moment of world-wide assault and powerful divine rescue, "I will pour out on the house of David and the inhabitants of Jerusalem a spirit of grace and pleas for mercy, so that, when they look on me, on him whom they have pierced, they shall mourn for him, as one mourns for an only child, and weep bitterly over him, as one weeps over a firstborn. On that day the mourning in Jerusalem will be great..." (12:10-11a)—clearly a mourning of repentance.

In short, the consistent and unmistakable teaching of the Hebrew Scriptures is that Yahweh will bring upon a latter-day generation of His covenant nation a horror so awful that they will be driven to absolute despair for their very existence. But in the moment of impending and certain doom, God will deliver, and the nation will mourn and repent. Thus, the terror will be the *means* by which God will finally bring that people to look to Him in trust and allegiance.[40] To the mind of the dispensational premillennialist, the seven-year

---

[40] Further, if the book of Revelation is read from the dispensational futurist/literalist perspective, it develops just this theme in gut-wrenching and graphic detail. That is, in a crescendo of terror and despair, seven seals are broken, seven trumpets are sounded, and seven bowls are emptied (chapters 4-18). And then, when there seems to be no hope for God's besieged people, the White-Horsed Rider descends to rescue that people. Indeed, the OT anticipation that God will use an end-time horror to turn His people to Himself is oft repeated in the NT, but that theme will likely be under-appreciated if one's reading of the NT is uninformed by the OT.

Tribulation, that end-time season of terror so carefully foretold and detailed in various passages of Scripture, is not an aberrant explosion of Thor-like anger or an eruption of ignoble divine pique; it is precisely what God promised in all of those Scriptures to use to bring Israel to repentance.

To return to our thought experiment, we are pondering the question, "How does the seven-year Tribulation relate to God's purpose to glorify Himself through His covenant people, Israel?" The suggested answer: all that we have appealed to as Scripturally revealed regarding that end-time season of terror—the seductive deception and diabolical murderous hatred of the Antichrist, the indescribable terror of the world's military and technological might arrayed for the destruction of God's covenant-people, the consequent absolute existential despair of that hitherto rebellious nation, the knowledge of the Gospel message which God causes to saturate so thoroughly the world even during the seven years of crescendoing dread, the shared remembrance of 2000 years of Christ-followers wallowing in New Covenant blessings, and now the glorious descent of a White-Horsed Rider whose name is Faithful and True, who bears a "sharp sword" to destroy His enemies, and who is accompanied by an army which no man can number—all of that will be used by a covenant-keeping God to bring a generation of living Israelites to cry out for salvation, individually as to faith and universally as to number.

No fallen son of Adam has ever turned to God until he has been taught his utter hopelessness apart from God's provision; thus it will be with the people of Israel. And because it is God who in His gracious providences brings prideful men so thoroughly to the end of themselves that they cast themselves on His provision, it is God who is to be glorified even for a man's finally coming to repentance. In this important and biblically consistent sense, the seven-year Tribulation may in truth be regarded as a Terrible Kindness.

THE MILLENNIAL KINGDOM: THE FINAL NAIL

A third and final stage in the thought experiment before us: how does the millennial kingdom relate to God's doxological purposes in human history? As in the last section, I will begin with a series of briefly stated propositions, undefended and undeveloped, which provide for the basic contours of this element of the dispensational premillennial worldview.

Proposition #1: The concept of a literal kingdom of God on earth is solidly grounded in real Old Testament history. At Mt. Sinai the family of Abraham became the nation of Israel and Yahweh—in the person of the Glory-Cloud—took His throne as that nation's king (Exod 40:33-38). This theocracy (real rule by Yahweh as king) endured until the Glory-Cloud departed in 592 BC (Ezek 11:22-23). Thus, for hundreds of years Yahweh did rule as a literal, abiding, active King in Israel. [41] He unilaterally pronounced the Law system by which the society would be governed; He went before the nation in their travels; He directed their warrior-kings in battle and often intervened directly on the nation's behalf; He was to be consulted on matters of governmental urgency or judicial difficulty; He invited His subjects to approach Him with whatever concern or spiritual impulse might be on their hearts. This reality of an entirely literal, physical, functioning kingdom ruled personally and practically by Yahweh, one more kingdom (albeit entirely unique) among all the other kingdoms of the world, is definitional to the way God's kingdom is conceived of in the mind of the dispensational premillennialist. [42]

Proposition #2: When, in exact fulfillment of covenant promises of judgment for sin, the theocratic relationship was suspended (592 BC, Ezek 11:22-23) God revealed clearly that the suspension was *temporary* (Dan 2 and 7), that after a succession of four Gentile kingdoms the Kingdom of God on earth would be established once again. Further, Daniel emphasized, as had other prophetic voices before him, that the latter-day kingdom of God on earth would be established and administered by the already long-awaited Messiah.

Proposition #3: As revealed in the Hebrew Scriptures, the righteous of all ages will be resurrected to that coming messianic kingdom and will dwell *eternally* in blessed fellowship with God and His saints (Dan 2:44; 7:14, 27; Ezek 37:25; Mic 4:7). Important to our purposes here: in the Old Testament the coming messianic kingdom is *eternal*—"an everlasting dominion which shall not pass away" (Dan 7:14).

Proposition #4: That kingdom so basic and definitional to God's revelation of Himself and His purposes in the Old Testament is *one with* the kingdom so much spoken of in the New Testament. In short, Jesus did not come to

---

[41] According to 1 Kgs 6:1, the Exodus and then the ratification of the Mosaic Covenant (by which Yahweh became King over the nation of Israel) occurred in 1446 BC. Ezekiel dates his vision of the departing Glory Cloud (8:1-11:23) as occurring in 592 BC. Thus the theocratic arrangement endured from 1446 to 592 BC, or about 8½ centuries.

[42] That is, the idea of a future literal kingdom of God on earth is the more compelling if one is persuaded that such a literal kingdom obtained in the past.

re-define the kingdom of the Old Testament, but to offer that kingdom to His generation.[43]

Proposition #5: The generation of Israel to which Jesus offered Himself as Messiah and King rejected His claims. Therefore, Jesus announced that "the kingdom of God will be taken away from you and given to a people producing its fruits" (Matt 21:43). Thus was introduced an unanticipated element of God's program: the Messiah has come but He will not at this time establish His kingdom; rather, He will depart for a time and come again later to bring in that kingdom promise. Further, Jesus promised that in the interregnum He would raise up an organism called "the church" (Matt 16:18) whose stewardship would be to put on display the power of the Gospel concerning Himself (Eph 3:8-11) and to carry that message to the ends of the earth (Matt 28:18-20).

Proposition #6: Very late in the progressive unfolding of New Testament revelation a new dynamic of the kingdom program of God was made known. In Revelation 20:1-10, John revealed that the eternal messianic kingdom would include an *initial* stage[44] which will be distinct from the eternal stage on at least four counts: (1) it will be temporary (i.e., it will last 1000 years—Rev 20:1-10); (2) it will include both mortal and immortal human beings; (3) though at its commencement it will include only regenerate mortals, by the end of the 1000 years there will be unregenerate people in the kingdom[45]; and (4) it will be mediatorial (i.e., King Jesus will be ruling *in the name of* God the Father).

---

[43] Many dispensationalists embrace the idea that Jesus did introduce some "mystery" element or form of the kingdom. Cf. Arnold Fruchtenbaum in a blogpost titled "The Mystery Form of the Kingdom" posits that the Jesus' parables teach a hitherto unrevealed "Kingdom that covers the age between the First and Second Comings of the Messiah. More specifically, it began with the rejection of His Messiahship in Matthew 12 and will continue until Israel accepts His Messiahship just before the Second Coming" (https://raptureforums.com/forums/threads/the-mystery-of-the-kingdom-by-dr-arnold-fruchtenbaum.128731/). Some dispensationalists reject this idea (including this writer). But dispensationalists will unanimously insist that however such a newly-introduced "mystery form" of the kingdom might be understood, it does not replace or compromise the literal, physical, world-wide kingdom of God's Christ which is foretold in the Hebrew Scriptures (cf. Dan 2:44; 7:27; Isa 2:2-4; 9:6-7; 11:1-9; Amos 9:11-15; Zech 2:10-12; 9:9-10; et al.). For an excellent exposition of the parables describing the mysteries of the kingdom in Matthew 13, see Michael Vlach, *He Will Reign Forever* (Silverton, OR: Lampion Press, 2017), 325-34.

[44] That the 1000-year kingdom of Rev 20:1-10 is to be understood as the initial stage of the eternal kingdom is a function of the dispensationalist's conviction that the OT must inform the NT. The OT is explicit that the kingdom will be eternal. By dispensational hermeneutical and bibliological lights, later revelation cannot reject or contradict earlier revelation, though it does enlarge and enhance.

[45] These two elements (2) & (3) are a function of two exegetical/theological realities. First, the judgment of Matt 25:31-46 ("the sheep and the goats") demonstrates that there are humans who survive the Tribulation and are ushered into the Kingdom in mortal bodies. Second, the rebellion at the end of the millennium (Rev 20:3, 7-10) shows that in time unregenerate human beings are part of that millennial kingdom. These lost persons must be those who were born to those believers who entered the kingdom in mortal bodies; those children then refused to give their allegiance to King Jesus.

Proposition #7: Messiah Jesus will reign in absolute righteousness and peace for 1000 years. The blissfully perfect utopian world-culture which man has idealized and desired since Eden will be a reality in all of its parts. That which is ignoble and wicked will be despised and forbidden; that which is God-honoring and virtuous will be practiced and celebrated. Satan will be rendered entirely impotent as accuser and tempter for all of those years. In short, "the earth will be filled with the knowledge of the glory of the LORD as the waters cover the sea" (Hab 2:14).

Proposition #8: But at the end of that 1000-year season, Satan will be loosed for a "little while" (Rev 20:3) and will gather a vast army of human rebels to rise up against King Jesus (Rev 20:7-10). Then in his revelatory vision, John sees that final rebellion powerfully put down: "but fire came down from heaven and consumed them, and the devil who had deceived them was thrown into the lake of fire and sulfur where the beast and the false prophet were, and they will be tormented day and night forever and ever" (Rev 20:9-10). And fire came down from God out of heaven and devoured them.

Proposition #9: At this point comes "the end, when he [Messiah Jesus] delivers the kingdom to God the Father" (1 Cor 15:24).[46] The New Jerusalem will descend to a "new heaven and a new earth" (Rev 21:1-2), the physical cosmos itself will be "set free from its bondage to corruption" (Rom 8:21), the dwelling place of God will once again be "with man. He will dwell with them, and they will be his people, and God himself will be with them as their God" (Rev 21:3-4).

Such is the Kingdom program of Scripture as conceived by the dispensational premillennialist. The one element of that construct which is the most incongruous to the non-dispensationalist—perhaps even incoherent and troubling—is, curiously enough, the element which most directly addresses the question that faces us in the thought experiment at hand. That question: how does the millennial kingdom relate to God's doxological program for human history? The incongruous element: what rationale or purpose could there be for an initial *abortive* stage of the eternal kingdom? That is, why would God

---

[46] An important note: it is at this point that the kingdom of God ceases to be *mediatorial*. That is, in the past days of the theocracy and during the future millennial kingdom, King Yahweh ruled and will rule through some human intermediary (Moses, Joshua, local Judges, human kings, the Son of Man). As the eternal stage of the kingdom begins Yahweh establishes His throne-room among men and rules and fellowships directly with redeemed creation. In fact, all four distinctions of the initial millennial stage of the eternal kingdom will be eliminated.

inaugurate the long-awaited messianic kingdom, only to have it culminate in a brief sinful rebellion which is once again put down by God's strong hand?

Full disclosure: we acknowledge that the Scriptures do not answer that question explicitly. On the other hand, to the dispensational premillennialist a satisfying answer readily suggests itself. That answer can be synthesized as follows:

1. God's primary doxological strategy to glorify Himself in human history is the staggering display of His covenant faithfulness as seen in the redemption of a generation of Israel, just as He had promised. Necessary to that redemption is the ineffably gracious and glorious cross-work of the incarnate Son of God. By the time of the millennial kingdom, all of that and infinitely more has been accomplished by Israel's God and His Christ. The story is fully told and thus rational creatures, mortal and immortal, can ponder that history-long narrative in order to learn how wise and loving and faithful and worthy of worship is the God who has framed and accomplished that staggering drama.

2. Now God has one more cosmic teachable moment for the human race, a teachable moment designed to practically and undeniably and concretely confront mankind with the infinite splendor and ineffable majesty of the Creator. But the fact is that such realities cannot be conceived or comprehended by man and women (even *redeemed* men and women) as amorphous concepts or pure abstractions. To be sure, finite human beings will never fully comprehend the infinite splendors of God. But mankind's finite grasp will be made ever deeper and more soul-impacting as those divine splendors are *manifested in real history*. More specifically, finite rational creatures will be best enabled to celebrate the ineffable goodness of a redeeming God as they are made to recognize the staggering wickedness of the sons of Adam apart from that redemption.

3. To that end comes this teachable moment which is the initial stage of the eternal kingdom. Consider with what infinite care and design the lesson is prepared and presented. The Scriptures identify three "enemies of the soul," the world, the flesh, and the devil.[47] But during this initial stage of the eternal kingdom, Satan's influence is entirely absent.

---

[47] This is the very traditional summary of the sources of temptation faced by men. The passage which most clearly suggests this summary is Eph 2:1-3: "And you were dead in the trespasses and sins in which you once walked, following the course of this *world,* following *the prince of the power of the air,* the spirit that is now at work in the sons of disobedience—among whom we all once lived in the passions of our *flesh,* carrying out the desires of the body and the mind, and were by nature children of wrath...." Popularly, it has been said that the Christian is like a fortified city set upon by three enemies; the problem—one of those enemies is on the inside of the walls trying to let the others in.

Then I saw an angel coming down from heaven, holding in his hand the key to the bottomless pit and a great chain. And he seized the dragon, that ancient serpent, who is the devil and Satan, and bound him for a thousand years, and threw him into the pit, and shut it and sealed it over him, so *that he might not deceive the nations any longer, until the thousand years were ended* (Rev 20:1-3, emphasis added).

So no wickedness or rebellion of men during those 1000 years can be laid to the charge of a tempting Satan.

Again, during the millennial stage of the kingdom Jesus is ruling in absolute righteousness and peace. Isaiah rejoices that "the government shall be upon his [Messiah's] shoulder," that "of the increase of his government and peace there will be no end," and that He will sit "on the throne of David and over his kingdom, to establish it and to uphold it with justice and with righteousness from this time forth and forevermore" (Isa 9:6, 7). So the "world"—the κοσμος or world system engineered and dominated by Satan and bathed in wickedness and perversion for all the centuries since Adam's fall—will in that day be entirely redeemed and set right as "the kingdom of the world has become the kingdom of our Lord and of his Christ" (Rev 11:15).

So here is the moral laboratory contrived by God to provide for finite rational creatures this culminating and cosmic teachable moment. For as much as most of a thousand years, mortal human beings live under the beneficent and all-wise reign of Messiah/King Jesus. In all of their existence they know nothing of want or hunger or injustice or neglect. There is no spiritual enemy to assault them and no destructive world system to trouble them. And yet when, at the end of that millennial utopia, Satan is loosed for just a "little while,"[48] he is able "to deceive the nations that are at the four corners of the earth, Gog and Magog, to gather them for battle; their number is like the sand of the sea" (Rev 20:8).

How can this be? Those rebels were born into and lived out their years enjoying Eden restored. The gospel of the saving power of the finished cross-work of King Jesus was available to them throughout all the decades and centuries of their adult lives. Had they any doubt as to the truth of the biblical narratives or doctrines, they could consult with the resurrected players in those century-long

---

[48] Note that this is the point of the phrase μιχρὸν χρόνον, "little while," in the description of the final rebellion: after 1000 years of righteous rule by King Jesus, Satan will be able *very quickly* to gather an army of mortal rebels to make futile war against the Lord. Likewise, Satan and the rebels are immediately destroyed.

dramas; indeed, they could even enjoy an audience with His Majesty King Jesus Himself. And yet a multitude "whose number is as the sand of the sea" refused to bow the knee to that King throughout those centuries. Even as they lived under His gracious and loving rule, they harbored a spirit of defiant rebellion which arose out of a fallen and prideful unregenerate heart. And where is the moral blame to be laid for that wickedness? The devil is bound; the world is purified. There can be only one foul cesspit from which such a spirit of rebellion has arisen: the depraved immoral nature of the sons of Adam!

Thus does an all-wise divine teacher contrive to teach finite creatures—men and angels—the gut-wrenching truth concerning the wretched heart of fallen man. And to what end? In order that, against that sorry backdrop, those creatures might more thoroughly comprehend and celebrate the marvelous grace and goodness of a God who would provide a way to redeem such men and make them new creations worthy of acceptance by and fellowship with a perfectly holy and loving God.

What is the chief end of man? To glorify God and enjoy Him forever. But man cannot discover God because man is twice crippled: he is finite and thus cannot know God, and he is fallen and thus will not know God. So God must take—and has taken—the initiative. Throughout all of human history God has been carefully and patiently instructing rational creatures concerning who He is and why He is to be worshiped. And even as the culminating messianic kingdom is inaugurated, God continues to teach. Because the glories of God's goodness and power and wisdom will be best appreciated against the backdrop of man's wickedness and unworthiness, and because of man's reluctance to acknowledge his wretchedness, God contrives an initial stage of that eternal messianic kingdom which will in the most powerful and compelling way demonstrate the spiritual deadness of unregenerate man. How fully just is God's condemnation of men who refuse the truth shown to be, and thus how inexpressibly gracious and infinitely wise is God's rescue of just such men who come to a love of that truth. Thus, the millennial kingdom might well be understood as The Final Nail in the spiritual coffin of man apart from God's redeeming power.

REVIEW AND SUMMARY

We return a final time to the thought experiment at hand. The intent: to ponder the dispensational-premillennial construct from within the hermeneutical and theological worldview definitional to that community; to give the whale the opportunity to conceptually experience the world of the elephant (or vice versa—let the patient reader choose!).

Distilled, the story is this. Human history is not just about God's majesty; it is about the *display* of that majesty to rational creatures. Mortal history is in fact the divinely framed and administered narrative which will yield an innumerable multitude of immortal human beings who in an age to come will celebrate the splendors of the triune God. But that historical drama is also the *curriculum* which that rescued and resurrected company will relish and ponder throughout that never-ending age, the means by which minds and soul-spirits no longer crippled by sin will come to an ever-deeper but never exhaustive comprehension of the greatness of that God. And the centerpiece lesson to be learned from the eternal contemplation of that seven-millennia (and counting) drama is *who that God is*, His *truthfulness*, His *integrity*, His *faithfulness* to His word, indeed the *covenant-keeping loving-kindness* (חֶסֶד *hesed*). He manifested in all of His dealings with mankind. But most remarkable and instructive in the grand catalog of story-lines to be pondered, the plot-line to which everything relates, is God's dealings with a people called Israel.

CONCLUSION

Another elephant related analogy, and a bit of a stretch at that: It is said that in the ancient world Israel was renowned for three wonders: one day of the week when no one worked, a temple in which there was not one statue to be found, and a sea in which even elephants would float! But no elephant would enjoy testing that thesis in the briny waters of that Dead Sea; he would survive but he wouldn't be comfortable. We have asked the non-dispensationalist to explore the conceptual world of the dispensational premillennialist—to try to contemplate the construct so precious and defining to a significant company of his evangelical, Bible-believing brethren of today and yesterday—*from within that construct itself*. To the reader who has survived the experiment, genuine gratitude and commendations. No claim is made that the foregoing is any sort of authoritative or universally satisfying expression of that construct. But it is an honest attempt to focus on that which is distinctive to the dispensational-premillennialist construct, and to make the case that that construct is an internally coherent set of ideas. Is the construct exegetically and historically defensible? Is it reflective of a legitimate hermeneutic? Does it honor the appropriate catalog of theological principles and philosophical priorities? These are important issues for another place. This chapter was born of the persuasion that the conversation regarding competing hermeneutical/theological/eschatological systems of thought might just be advantaged by the effort. If that is the case in any place and to any degree, then—as in all things—to God be the glory.

9

THE MESSIAH'S LECTURE ON
THE FUTURE OF ISRAEL

Larry D. Pettegrew

Nothing could be more important in the doctrine of eschatology than to know what Jesus Christ Himself taught about the future. Thankfully, we have several opportunities in the New Testament to learn from Jesus' teaching on prophecy. One of these is the entire book of Revelation, often mistakenly entitled in some English Bibles, "The Revelation of St. John." But the first couple of verses of Revelation read: "The revelation of Jesus Christ, which God gave him to show to his servants the things that must soon take place. He made it known by sending his angel to his servant John, who bore witness to the word of God and to the testimony of Jesus Christ, even to all that he saw" (Rev 1:1-2).

Another special opportunity to learn from Jesus' teaching about the future is the Olivet Discourse that Jesus gave to His disciples shortly before His death.[1] This discourse is important, first, because it is the Messiah's ultimate exposition of future events while He was on earth. Second, the Olivet Discourse gives an outline of the future of Israel—the nation at the center of much of biblical eschatology. Third, the Olivet Discourse is particularly helpful in understanding the various eschatological systems. How the teachers of a system interpret the Olivet Discourse gives us a mini-picture of their theological system as a whole. We will find in this Discourse that Jesus was not a supersessionist.

---

[1] Mark records the Olivet Discourse in chapter 13, Luke in chapter 21, and Matthew in chapters 24-25. Other key passages of Scripture for the Lord's teachings about the future includes Matthew 13 and John 14-17.

A SURVEY OF THE DISCOURSE

The Olivet Discourse can be divided into four main divisions: (1) The immediately preceding context: Curses on the hypocritical religious leaders of Israel (Matt 23); (2) Questions from the confused disciples over the Lord's statement about the temple (Matt 24:1-3); (3) A lecture on the Tribulation and Second Coming (Matt 24:4-31; (4) The application of the Lord's teaching for living our lives in anticipation of the Second Coming (Matt 25).

The Scathing Rebuke—Matthew 23

Chapter 23 describes Christ's fierce denunciation of the unbelief and hypocrisy of the religious leaders of Israel. He concludes His condemnation with a curse on the Jerusalem temple, the center of first-century Judaism: "'See, your house is left to you desolate. For I tell you, you will not see me again, until you say, 'Blessed is he who comes in the name of the Lord'" (Matt 23:38-39).

The Stunned Disciples—24:1-3

The disciples were clearly alarmed by such a prophecy against the temple ("your house"). The temple was in many ways the patriotic symbol that evidenced the solidarity of Israel. The Lord's denunciation no doubt also reminded the disciples of the Lord's warning in the Old Testament immediately before the Babylonians destroyed Solomon's temple: "I swear by myself, declares the LORD, that this house shall become a desolation" (Jer 22:5).

In their alarm and confusion, the disciples point out the magnificence of the temple (Matt 24:1)—and Herod's temple was a glorious building indeed. It was constructed of huge white marble stones plated with gold. Some of the stones, in fact, weighed as much as 100 tons and shown so brightly in the sun that people could hardly look at them. The rabbis reportedly insisted, "He who has not seen Herod's Temple has not seen a beautiful building." So, the disciples could hardly believe their ears. "Did we hear you correctly, Lord? Is this marvelous temple to be made desolate?"

The Lord's answer was unequivocal. "You see all these, do you not? Truly, I say to you, there will not be left here one stone upon another that will not be thrown down" (24:2). This explicit prophecy was fulfilled some 40 years later when the Roman legions, comprised mostly of legions from the surrounding

Arab nations, destroyed the temple and the city.[2] The city was ruined to such an extent that one could hardly tell that the area had been previously inhabited. Thus, the setting for the Olivet Discourse is delivered in the context of coming judgment on Israel.

This shocking statement from Jesus was not at all what the disciples had expected when the Messiah came. So, when they arrived on the Mount of Olives, they asked Jesus two questions about the future of Israel—specifically about the destruction of Herod's temple, as it is often called, and a sign for the Second Coming and future Kingdom: (1) "Tell us, when will these things be?" and (2) "What will be the sign of your coming and of the end of the age?" (Matt 24:3). The rest of the teaching in the Olivet Discourse is given over to Jesus' answer to these questions.

The Tribulation and the Second Coming—24:4-31

The Lord explains first that, in contrast to what the disciples had thought, Christ's Kingdom on earth, ruled by the Messiah from Jerusalem, would not begin immediately. The great Messianic Kingdom promised by the Old Testament prophets was to be delayed, and instead there would be a period characterized by false Christs, wars, famines, earthquakes, persecutions, false religions, secularism, as well as the preaching of the gospel. Such events would typify the era from the time of the Lord's prophecy here in His discourse to the middle of the seven-year Tribulation (cf. Rev 6).

The Great Tribulation—24:15-22

The last half of the seven-year Tribulation, identified by Christ as a "great tribulation" (24:21), will be more horrendous than the first three and one-half years. Jesus says: "For then there will be great tribulation, such as has not been from the beginning of the world until now, no, and never will be" (Matt 24:21).[3]

---

[2] According to Tacitus and Josephus, the Romans commanders utilized mostly Middle Eastern legions from Syria, Turkey, and Egypt, and other Arab nations, to destroy the temple and the city. See Tacitus, *The Histories*, trans. Alfred John Church and William Jackson Brodribb, 5.1, http://classics.mit.edu/Tacitus/histories.5.v.html; Josephus, *The Works of Josephus*, trans. William Whitson, "The Wars of the Jews" (Peabody, MA: Hendrickson, 2007), 3.1.3 (639); 3.4.2 (642); 5.13.4 (725). For an interesting and eye-opening discussion of these armies, see further, Joel Richardson, *Mideast Beast* (Washington, D.C.: WND books, 2012), 89-102, and Chadwick Harvey, *God's Prophetic Timeline* (Washington D.C.: WND books, 2016), 44-48.

[3] Some 60 years later, the Apostle John, who was present to hear this lecture from His Lord, was given the details of this future horrible time on earth (Rev 4-18).

The Second Coming—24:23-31

At the conclusion of the Great Tribulation, the Lord will return to earth. Christ explains,

> Immediately after the tribulation of those days the sun will be darkened, and the moon will not give its light, and the stars will fall from heaven, and the powers of the heavens will be shaken. Then will appear in heaven the sign of the Son of Man, and then all the tribes of the earth will mourn, and they will see the Son of Man coming on the clouds of heaven with power and great glory (Matt 24:29-30).

These verses describe the glorious coming of Christ at the end of the Tribulation to establish His Kingdom.

The Application—24:32-25:46

This announcement of the Second Coming of Christ is then followed by a series of parables and illustrations emphasizing the need to be prepared, alert, and serving the Lord in anticipation of His arrival. David Turner points out, "Jesus spent only half as much time on the bare facts of the future as he did on the implications of those facts."[4] Chapter 25 explains that at the coming of Christ, there will be a judgment on believing Israel as well as on the Gentile nations. As a result of these judgments, believing Jews (the wise virgins) and believing Gentiles (the sheep) will "inherit the kingdom prepared for you from the foundation of the world" (Matt 25:34).[5] Unbelieving Jews (the foolish virgins) and unbelieving Gentiles (the goats) "will go away into eternal punishment" (Matt 25:46).

THE ESCHATOLOGICAL SYSTEMS

The four eschatological systems that we are analyzing are preterism, prewrath rapture, posttribulationism, and pretribulationism. Preterists teach that Christ's prophecies in Matthew 24 have already been fulfilled. The other three systems

---

[4] David L. Turner, "The Structure and Sequence of Matthew 24:1-41: Interaction with Evangelical Treatments," *Grace Theological Journal* 10.1 (1989):27.

[5] For an excellent study of the Sheep and Goats judgment, see Eugene W. Pond's three-part series: "The Background and Timing of the Judgment of the Sheep and Goats," *Bibliotheca Sacra* 159 (April-June, 2002):201-20; "Who Are the Sheep and Goats in Matthew 25:31-46?" *Bibliotheca Sacra* 159 (July-September, 2002):288-301; and "Who Are 'the Least of My Brethren'?" *Bibliotheca Sacra* 159 (October-December, 2002).

are based on premillennialism. According to the pre-wrath system, the rapture of the church occurs three-fourths of the way through the Tribulation, that is, twenty-one months before the Second Coming. In posttribulationism, the rapture occurs at the end of the Tribulation. And in pretribulationism, the rapture occurs before the Tribulation. Pretribulationism is the only system that consistently maintains that the main purpose of the Tribulation is to bring Israel to national conversion in preparation of her central role in the Messianic Kingdom that begins after the Second Coming.

Preterism and the Olivet Discourse

Preterists are not premillennialists. They teach that though the information in the Lord's discourse on the future was prophetic when He gave it, the prophecy has already been fulfilled. Among themselves, preterists differ over how much of prophecy, if anything, is still future. Thomas Ice explains,

> Mild preterism holds that the Tribulation was fulfilled within the first three hundred years of Christianity.... Moderate preterism ... sees the Tribulation and the bulk of prophecy as fulfilled in events surrounding the destruction of Jerusalem and the temple in A.D. 70; but they still hold to a future Second Coming, a physical resurrection of the dead, an end to temporary history, and the establishing of the consummate new heaven and new earth. Extreme or consistent (as they like to call themselves) preterism believes that the Second Coming, and thus the resurrection of believers, is all past. For all practical purposes all Bible prophecy has been fulfilled, and we are beyond the millennium and even now in the new heaven and the new earth.[6]

Extreme preterists, such as John Noe, claim to be evangelicals, believing in the inerrancy of Scripture.[7] But to maintain the view that essentially all of prophecy has been fulfilled requires fanciful interpretation of key Scriptures. What about 2 Peter 3:10, for example? "But the day of the Lord will come like a thief, and then the heavens will pass away with a roar, and the heavenly bodies

---

[6] Thomas Ice, Introduction to *The Great Tribulation, Past or Future?* (Grand Rapids: Kregel, 1999), 7. In this book, two evangelicals debate the rapture question, Thomas Ice representing the pretribulational view, and Kenneth L. Gentry Jr. representing a moderate preterism view.

[7] See John Noe, *Beyond the End Times* (Bradford, PA.: International Preterist Association, 1999); and John Noe, *Shattering the "Left Behind" Delusion* (Bradford, PA: International Preterist Association, 2000).

will be burned up and dissolved, and the earth and the works that are done on it will be exposed" (2 Pet 3:10). Has this already occurred? Noe says that this is describing the conversion experience of a person. "Individually, we become a 'new heaven' when God comes to dwell inside us, in our spirit.... The 'new heaven' is the new spirit God gives a person at salvation (1 Cor 3:16; Eph 2:6)."[8] Noe continues, "That means that our former earth consists of our unregenerated physical bodies, and our minds and emotions. This is what the Bible calls our 'flesh.'"[9] In this way extreme preterists argue that all the events that Jesus prophesied have already transpired.

Analysis of the Preterist Interpretation

The key verse for preterism is Matthew 24:34: "Truly, I say to you, this generation will not pass away until all these things take place." Preterists argue that "this generation" means the generation that was alive when Jesus was on earth, and so everything recorded in the Olivet Discourse took place by around A.D. 70.

Inadequate Hermeneutics

Once preterists have argued this point, however, they are in interpretive trouble because there are several events in Matthew 24 that have not occurred. Preterists are forced, consequently, to spiritualize these events. All forms of preterism, some more than others, rely on figurative interpretation. John Noe, for example, defends non-literal interpretation of prophecy as follows: "The popular stream of endsayers has assumed that the Bible's apocalyptic language must be interpreted literally and physically, and that since no one has witnessed a cataclysmic, earth-ending event of this nature, its time must lie in the future."[10] The result of such compromise of the integrity of hermeneutics is bizarre interpretations such as noted above of 2 Peter 3:10.

Indeed, much of the Olivet Discourse is taken figuratively in preterism. For example, Jesus says, "For as the lightning comes from the east and shines as far as the west, so will be the coming of the Son of Man" (Matthew 24:27). This passage is clearly teaching that Christ's coming will not be local only, but public

---

[8] Noe, *Beyond End Times*, 253-54.

[9] Ibid., 255.

[10] Ibid., 51.

and grandiose. But moderate preterist Gentry says that the lightning is a picture of "the Roman armies marching toward Jerusalem from an easterly direction."[11]

In verse 30 of Matthew 24, the Lord teaches that at the Second Coming, "all the tribes of the earth will mourn, and they will see the Son of Man coming on the clouds of heaven with power and great glory." But Gentry insists that "this is not a physical, visible coming, but a judgment coming upon Jerusalem in A. D. 70. They 'see' it in the sense that we 'see' how a math problem works: with the 'eye of understanding' rather than the organ of vision."[12] In this figurative interpretation, the prophetic events of the Olivet Discourse, including the Second Coming of Christ, were fulfilled in A.D. 70 when the Romans captured and destroyed Jerusalem.

Inadequate Interpretation

In addition to their hermeneutical method, the preterists' interpretation of "this generation" (24:34) is unlikely. Preterists argue that this means that the generation that was alive when Christ presented this discourse must not die until everything in the discourse is fulfilled.[13] For the extreme preterist, this means that the Second Coming occurred while that generation was alive. Noe insists, "Make no mistake about it, A.D. 70 was the Lord's promised and personal return!"[14]

The Old Testament prophets' predictions of the coming of the Messiah in power and glory (Zech 12-14), however, do not harmonize with the events of A.D. 70. The Old Testament prophets taught that when the enemy armies surrounded Jerusalem, Israel would be temporarily defeated. But then Messiah would come and fight for Israel and destroy Israel's enemies. But in A.D. 70, Jerusalem and the temple were demolished, and the times of the Gentiles was prolonged. The preterists' interpretation of "this generation" would seem to be flawed—or else the Old Testament prophets were wrong, an unthinkable idea.

---

[11] Kenneth L. Gentry, Jr., *The Great Tribulation, Past or Future?* 54.

[12] Ibid., 60.

[13] This interpretation is not unique to preterists. Even some pretribulationists agree with the preterist interpretation of "this generation." See Turner, "The Structure and Sequence of Matthew 24:1-41," 22-26.

[14] Noe, *Beyond End Times*, 196. Noe asks, "But where does Scripture say that Jesus' return must be 'visible'?" (198). Such a question makes sense only if one allegorizes away such Scriptures as Acts 1:9-11 and Matthew 24:23-31. Both of these passages teach that Christ's return will be visible.

The Chronological Generation

What does the Lord mean when He prophesies that "this generation" would not pass away until all these things take place (24:34)? Some premillennialists believe that "generation" is another way of saying "nation." Thus, Jesus is teaching that the nation of Israel would not pass away until all the events spoken about in the Olivet Discourse are fulfilled. This interpretation is possible and has been defended well.[15] And it states a truth that Scripture teaches elsewhere. But it still isn't the usual and most natural understanding of "generation."[16]

The better interpretation, in my view, is what has sometimes been called the "chronological generation" view. This simply means that "generation" describes a group of all of the people living at the same time. Matthew consistently uses "generation" in the chronological sense. In his genealogy in chapter one, for example, Matthew states: "So all the generations from Abraham to David were fourteen generations, and from David to the deportation to Babylon fourteen generations, and from the deportation to Babylon to the Christ fourteen generations" (Matt 1:17). Jesus could have used the term differently than Matthew. But elsewhere in the Gospels when Jesus spoke the word, "generation," it was in the chronological sense (see Matt 11:16; 12:39, 41, 42, 16:4; 17:17; 23:36). So "generation" in the Olivet Discourse means a group of all the people living at the same time.

The Tribulation Generation

Furthermore, the generation that Jesus describes in His discourse is a generation that will be in existence in the future Tribulation. This generation will not pass away until all of the events that Jesus had just previously enumerated about the Tribulation occur. Each of the three Gospel authors who narrates the Olivet Discourse place Jesus' statement about "this generation not passing away" after a list of Tribulational events. Mark, for example, begins his description of the Tribulation with the "Abomination of desolation" which takes place in the middle of the Tribulation. He records Jesus saying, "For in those days there will be

---

[15] See Kenneth E. Guenter's "'This Generation' in the Trilogy of Matthew 24:34-35," *Bibliotheca Sacra* 175 (April-June, 2018):174-194.

[16] The "until" could also be a problem for the "nation" view. It might imply that after these predicted events were completed, the nation of Israel would then "pass away." In Greek, the "until" could mean "until and subsequently" or "up to that point and no further." See A. Kretzer, "ἕως" *Exegetical Dictionary of the New Testament*, vol. 2, ed. Horst Balz and Gerhard Schneider (Grand Rapids: Eerdmans, 1961), 96.

such tribulation as has not been from the beginning of the creation that God created until now, and never will be. And if the Lord had not cut short the days, no human being would be saved" (Mark 13:19-20).

Following the description of these horrible judgments of the Tribulation, Mark records Jesus' explanation of His Second Coming (Mark 13:24-27) and the parable of the fig tree. Jesus then concludes, "So also, when you see these things taking place, you know that he is near, at the very gates. Truly, I say to you, this generation will not pass away until all these things take place" (Mark 13:29-30).

"This generation," therefore, is the generation *who will experience the terrible events of the Great Tribulation.* And because these terrible events are a sign, these people will know that the Second Coming is drawing near. Darrell Bock explains, "Once the beginning of the end arrives with the cosmic signs ..., the Son of Man will return before *that* generation passes away.... It is arguing that the end will occur within one generation; the same group that sees the start of the end will see its end."[17] The Tribulation generation is thus the primary reference for the generation that will not pass away before the Second Coming.

A Prophetic Foreshadowing

The phrase, "this generation," however, also applies to the disciples' first question about the destruction of Herod's temple. Jesus answers this question, although Matthew does not record His response.[18] But Luke does:

> But when you see Jerusalem surrounded by armies, then know that its desolation has come near. Then let those who are in Judea flee to the mountains, and let those who are inside the city depart, and let not those who are out in the country enter it, for these are days of vengeance, to fulfill all that is written. Alas for women who are pregnant and for those who are nursing infants in those days! For there will be great distress upon the earth and wrath against this people. They will fall by the edge of the sword and be led captive among all nations, and Jerusalem will

---

[17] Darrell L. Bock, *Luke*, The IVP New Testament Series, ed. Grant R. Osborne (Downers Grove, IL: InterVarsity Press, 1994), 343-44 (Bock's emphasis). Bock is not necessarily arguing for this view.

[18] The theme of the Gospel of Matthew is the kingdom, so Matthew focused on the questions about the events surrounding the Tribulation and the Second Coming of Christ to establish His kingdom.

be trampled underfoot by the Gentiles, until the times of the Gentiles are fulfilled (Luke 21:20-24). [19]

So the generation that saw the signs of the upcoming destruction of Jerusalem in A.D. 70 also would not pass away until that horrible event had occurred.

The Lord's method of prophesying was similar to the Old Testament prophets who sometimes spoke of two events in the same context without completely distinguishing between them. The prophets, for example, sometimes gave a revelation that included information about both the First Coming of Jesus and His Second Coming (Isa 61; cf. Luke 4:16-21). They also sometimes described characteristics of the first stage of the Kingdom of Christ, the Millennium, and the second stage, the eternal Kingdom, in the same passage without distinguishing the details of the first stage from the second (Isa 65:17-25). And some (but not all) of the information in these Old Testament prophecies seem to apply to both events.

Likewise, in the Olivet Discourse, Jesus answers both of the disciples' questions about the two attacks on Jerusalem that are at least nearly two thousand years apart. Some of the details in Christ's discourse reference both the attack in A.D. 70 and the attack at the end of the Great Tribulation. The flight from Jerusalem during the attack, for example, is common to both events. Luke tells us that a flight will take place during the attack on the temple in A. D. 70 (Luke 21:21). "In the strongest possible terms," writes Daniel Doriani, "Jesus tells his disciples how to survive the coming siege and sack of Jerusalem. When you see the Romans coming, he says, RUN! Get out fast and don't return."[20] Matthew and Mark indicate that the flight is also a sign of the Great Tribulation (Matt 24:15-21; Mark 13:18-19). There is an atmosphere of warning, urgency, and imminency that pervades Jesus' revelation about both attacks. So we need to see the unity of these two events without, at the same time, minimizing the different end results.

---

[19] It is noteworthy that Jesus consistently uses the phrase, "this generation," in a pejorative sense during His earthly ministry (Matt 11:16; 12:39, 41, 42, 45; 16:4; 17:17). That wicked generation was subsequently judged in the destruction of the city and temple. See Neil D. Nelson, Jr., "'This Generation' in Mat. 24:34: A Literary Critical Perspective," *Journal of the Evangelical Theological Society* 38/3 (September 1996): 369-85.

[20] Daniel M. Doriani, *Matthew*, vol. 2, *Reformed Expository Commentary*, ed. Richard D. Phillips and Philip Graham Ryken (Phillipsburg, NJ: P&R Publishing, 2008), 358. Doriani is an amillennialists, but his exposition of the Olivet Discourse (347-420) is somewhat different from the premillennial prewrath and posttribulational systems because he, like many pretribulationists, doesn't believe that the Lord teaches anything in the Discourse about the rapture of the church. Doriani's interpretation differs from pretribulationists because he believes that the church permanently replaced Israel.,

Indeed, the attack on Herod's temple in A.D. 70 seems to be a prophetic foreshadowing of the events leading up to the Second Coming of Christ. Jesus had in-depth knowledge of the Old Testament, and prophetic foreshadowing is common there. Some of the prophecies in the Book of Daniel, for example, foretell events that have an historic fulfillment and ultimate fulfillment in "the latter days," and in the "time of the end" (Dan 2:28-45). As Craig Blaising explains, "just as was the case in the Old Testament, it is possible for a type of the eschatological day of the Lord to appear in history in advance of the anti-type."[21] Thus, the events of A.D. 70 foreshadow the Tribulation events that become a sign of the Second Coming and the end of the age.

To return to our evaluation of preterism, preterists' claim that A.D. 70 fulfilled all of the prophecies in the Olivet Discourse cannot be true. "This generation" primarily refers to the future Tribulation generation. The specific events of the Great Tribulation (Matt 24:15-26) and the Second Coming of Jesus to earth (24:27-31) have not occurred. And there are different results from the two attacks on Jerusalem. In A. D. 70, the temple was destroyed, Israel was scattered, and the times of the Gentiles continued. But at the end of the future Great Tribulation when the attack on Jerusalem happens again and Israel is temporarily overwhelmed, the Lord will return and "will seek to destroy all the nations that come against Jerusalem. (Zech 12:9). As a result of His care of Jerusalem, a revival begins in Israel (Zech 12:10-14). The preterist interpretation of the Olivet Discourse thus fails specifically because of its figurative hermeneutics, its contradiction with the Old Testament prophets, and consequently, its failure to fit the facts of the Messiah's teaching.[22]

Prewrath Rapture and the Olivet Discourse

The prewrath rapture is a premillennial system developed by Marvin Rosenthal and Robert Van Kampen near the end of the twentieth century.[23] According

---

[21] Craig Blaising, "A Case for the Pretribulation Rapture," in *The Rapture, Pretribulation, Prewrath, or Posttribulation*, ed. Stanley N. Gundry and Alan Hultberg (Grand Rapids: Zondervan, 2010), 40.

[22] For an analysis of a moderate preterists explanation of Matthew 24:3, see Mike Stallard, "A Review of R. C. Sproul's *The Last Days According to Jesus*: An Analysis of Moderate Preterism, Part I, *The Conservative Journal* 6/17 (March 2002):45-71. Also, for a full critique of Preterism, see the helpful study by Brock David Hollett, *Debunking Preterism* (Kearney, NE: Morris Publishing, 2018).

[23] See Marvin Rosenthal, *The Pre-Wrath Rapture of the Church* (Nashville: Nelson, 1990); Robert D. Van Kampen, *The Sign* (Wheaton: Crossway, 1992); and Robert D. Van Kampen, *The Rapture Question Answered* (Grand Rapids: Fleming H. Revell, 1997).

to this view, the rapture takes place about three-fourths of the way through the seven-year Tribulation, though these authors insist that we shouldn't call the entire seven-years the "Tribulation." According to their interpretation of eschatological events, the Tribulation is only the first three and one-half years of the seven-year period. After the first three and one-half years, the Great Tribulation begins, but it is cut short and only lasts for twenty-one months—half of the second half of Daniel's Seventieth Week. God's wrath is actually not poured out on the earth until the last one-fourth (twenty-one months) of the seven-year period. The troubles on the earth in the first three-fourths of the seventieth week of Daniel are not God's wrath, according to the prewrath view, but are brought about by Satan and man himself.[24] The rapture of the church then takes place twenty-one months before the end of the seven-year period. Since God does not pour out His wrath until after the rapture, the rapture is prewrath, and thus the name of the system.

Teachers of the prewrath system look to Matthew 24:22 for support: "And if those days had not been cut short, no human being would be saved. But for the sake of the elect those days will be cut short." Rosenthal explains,

> To sum up, then, God will cut the Great Tribulation short; that is bring it to a conclusion before the seventieth week is concluded. The Great Tribulation will be followed by cosmic disturbance, which will indicate that the Day of the Lord is about to commence. At that time God's glory will be manifested.... First, the Rapture of the church will occur; that will then be followed by the Lord's judgment of the wicked as He begins His physical return to earth.[25]

Underlying the prewrath interpretation of the Olivet Discourse is the assertion that Jesus is giving a prophecy about the church—not Israel. Alan Hultberg, a teacher of the prewrath view claims,

> The disciples do not view themselves nor are they treated by Jesus in Matthew as anything other than faithful Jews who are beginning the community of the Messiah. It is not surprising then that the question and response recorded in the

---

[24] This means that the earthquakes described in Matthew 24:7 (which Rosenthal thinks will occur in the first half of the seven-year era) are the result of the power of Satan or man. Toussaint observes, "Interestingly, Rosenthal never explains how the earthquakes in Matthew 24:7 are triggered by humans!" (Toussaint, "Are the Church and the Rapture in Matthew 24?" *The Return*, Thomas Ice and Timothy J. Demy, eds. [Grand Rapids: Kregel, 1999], 133).

[25] Marvin Rosenthal, *The Pre-Wrath Rapture of the Church*, 112-13.

Olivet Discourse have such a Jewish character. But neither do they show that the church is not in view in the Olivet Discourse, unless one begins with the assumption of a radical discontinuity between the church and Israel. This assumption is very unlikely.[26]

Hultberg also argues that Jesus Himself in some way has replaced Israel. Jesus "fulfills the role of Israel itself," he writes. "Thus for Matthew, to belong to Israel one must belong to the Messiah, Jesus."[27] Also, since the word, "church," is related to "congregation" in the Old Testament, Hultberg asserts that "the messianic community that Jesus is founding is in some sense the 'true' or 'new Israel.'"[28] Jesus gives the kingdom to another nation (Matt 21:43), he continues, which means that Jesus has rejected "Israel as a whole."[29] Thus, "for Matthew the church is viewed as in some sense the inheritor of the Jewish Kingdom...."[30] This would mean, of course, that Jesus was a supersessionist, believing that the church has superseded Israel.[31]

Analysis of the Prewrath Rapture Interpretation

Besides the supersessionism of the prewrath view, there are some weaknesses that are distinctive to this understanding of the timing of the rapture. First, the Scriptures never divide the Tribulation period into thirds. Daniel's prophecy divides the seventieth week in two (Dan 9:27); half of the Tribulation is described as numbering 1260 days (Rev 11:3; 12:6). In fact, since Revelation 12:14 explains that God will protect fleeing Jews for "a time, and times, and half a time" (1260 days); and since the beginning of this period is the beginning of the last three and one-half years, the Great Tribulation (Matt 24:15-22) must last for 1260 days. The Bible never divides the 1260 days into two 630 days.

---

[26] Alan Hultberg "A Case for the Prewrath Rapture," in *The Rapture, Pretribulation, Prewrath, or Posttribulation*, ed. Stanley N, Gundry and Alan Hultberg, 112. I'm not sure what Dr. Hultberg means by "radical discontinuity." His eschatology is based on continuity between Israel and the church—i.e., supersessionism.

[27] Ibid., 113.

[28] Ibid.

[29] Ibid., 114.

[30] Ibid., 113.

[31] Apparently, some prewrath proponents do believe that Israel will be the center of God's coming millennial kingdom and are therefore not supersessionists.

Second, "cut short" does not teach what the prewrath view says. The question that should be asked is, "The Great Tribulation is shortened up from what?" A good answer is that the Great Tribulation is shortened from what Satan's forces—the Antichrist and his associates—want. Gerhard Delling writes, "That is, He has made it shorter than it would normally have been in terms of the purpose and power of the oppressors."[32] It is also shorter than what the wicked world deserves. If God were to pour out perfect judgment on the world for a longer time, no one would be alive. But God is merciful and thus limits the Great Tribulation to only 1260 days. It will not go on indefinitely. Paul Benware writes, "So Jesus is teaching that the decree of God, made in eternity past, had already determined that the Great Tribulation would be just three and a half years and not some longer period of time. This interpretation is verified by noting what the Scriptures say about the length of the Great Tribulation."[33]

A third flaw in the prewrath interpretation of Matthew 24:22 is its logical failure. The reason that the Great Tribulation is shortened, according to this verse, is that if it were not, no flesh would be saved. The point of the Scripture is that when the Great Tribulation is over, something better comes on the scene. In the prewrath scheme, however, something more horrible occurs after the Great Tribulation—the Day of the Lord. If no flesh would have survived if the Great Tribulation were allowed to continue on twenty-one months, surely no flesh would survive if the Great Tribulation were to be cut short and followed by twenty-one months of a more horrible Day of the Lord.

Moreover, Matthew 24:21 says that the Great Tribulation will be the worst time ever. So, how can it be replaced by the Day of the Lord which is more horrible? Wouldn't *that* be the worst time ever? In fact, the Great Tribulation (Matt 24:21) and the Day of the Lord (Dan 12:1; Jer 30:7) are both said to be the worst time ever, so they must be the same time period or at least overlap. Much better is the pretribulational interpretation of Matthew 24:22 which says that when the Great Tribulation mercifully concludes at the end of the 1260 days, Christ returns, God's wrath on the earth ceases, and the millennial Kingdom begins.[34]

---

[32] Gerhard Delling, "κολοβόω," *TDNT* 3:823-24.

[33] Paul N. Benware, *Understanding End Times Prophecy* (Chicago: Moody, 1995), 230.

[34] For critiques of the prewrath rapture system, see Paul S. Karleen, *The Pre-Wrath Rapture of the Church: Is It Biblical?* (Langhorne, PA: BF Press, 1991); Renald E. Showers, *The Pre-Wrath Rapture View* (Grand Rapids: Kregel, 2001), especially 93-151; Toussaint, "Are the Church and the Rapture in Matthew 24?" 133-35.

Posttribulationism and the Olivet Discourse

The most common contemporary form of posttribulationism interprets the Tribulation as a future seven-year time of judgment on the world after which the Lord will rapture the living believers and resurrect dead believers. Christ then immediately returns to the earth to conduct judgments and set up the millennial kingdom. Posttribulational premillennialism is taught today by some "New Covenant" theologians as well as those theologians who call their system "Progressive Covenantalism."[35]

In explaining the Olivet Discourse, posttribulationists teach that Jesus explains the Tribulation events through 24:29, and then describes a posttribulational rapture in verses 30-31. This is in contrast to pretribulationists who believe Christ explains His Second Coming here without any reference to a rapture. Jesus proclaims,

> Then will appear in heaven the sign of the Son of Man, and then all the tribes of the earth will mourn, and they will see the Son of Man coming on the clouds of heaven with power and great glory. And he will send out his angels with a loud trumpet call, and they will gather his elect from the four winds, from one end of heaven to the other (Matt 24:30-31).

According to posttribulationists, the rapture is described again in 24:40-42, where the Lord speaks of two men in the field, with the one taken and the other left; and two women at the mill, with one taken and the other left. Since the information here follows the Lord's discussion of the Tribulation in the chapter, posttribulationists insist that this passage must be describing a posttribulational rapture.

For the posttribulational interpretation of the Olivet Discourse to succeed, posttribulationists need to demonstrate that Jesus is explaining the future of the church, not the future of Israel. Otherwise, since the rapture applies to the

---

[35] For a defense of the most common form of contemporary posttribulationism, see George Eldon Ladd, *The Blessed Hope* (Grand Rapids: Eerdmans, 1956); and Craig L. Blomberg and Sung Wook, ed., *A Case for Historic Premillennialism* (Grand Rapids: Baker Academic, 2009). As we explained in the first chapter, most of the early church fathers taught a form of premillennial posttribulationism similar to contemporary posttribulationists. A few of the early fathers seem to be intra-tribulationists. They believed that they were in the tribulation already, that the tribulation was of indeterminate length (not 7 years), and that Christ would rapture the church at the end of the tribulation. Thus, for them, the rapture was imminent and still posttribulational because the church was already in the Tribulation. In the twentieth century, J. Barton Payne was the main, and almost only, evangelical writer, who held to intra-tribulationism. See J. Barton Payne, *The Imminent Appearance of Christ* (Grand Rapids: Eerdmans, 1962). For a helpful study of different kinds of posttribulationism, see John Walvoord, *The Blessed Hope and the Tribulation* (Grand Rapids: Zondervan, 1976).

church and not the nation of Israel, there could be no information given about the rapture. Thus, posttribulationists argue that the disciples in this passage represent the church rather than believing Israel. As Douglas Moo, a posttribulationist, says, "Thus, the crucial question becomes: Whom do the disciples represent in this passage—Israel or the church?"[36] Two evenings later, when the Lord's Supper is instituted, they represent the church. So, why not here, asks posttribulationist J. Barton Payne. "If they represented the church in Matthew 26 on Thursday, no arbitrary exegesis can make them represent anything else in Matthew 24 on Tuesday."[37] "For it is surely a legitimate assumption," writes Moo, "to think that the disciples in the Gospels are generally representatives of all disciples—or else why do we accept Jesus' teaching as relevant for the church in general? ... Are there clear indications in the Olivet Discourse that Jesus did not intend his words to apply to all the people of God, including the church?"[38] Thus, the posttribulational argument unfolds as follows:

1. The disciples were the original recipients of Jesus' teaching.

2. The nation of Israel had rejected Christ and had been permanently set aside.

3. Therefore, the disciples now represent the church, not Israel.

4. Therefore, in the Olivet Discourse, Jesus is explaining to the disciples the future of the church in the Tribulation.

5. Therefore, the Olivet Discourse teaches a posttribulational rapture of the church.

---

[36] Douglas J. Moo, "The Case for the Posttribulation Rapture Position," in *The Rapture, Pre,-Mid,-or Post-Tribulational?* (Grand Rapids: Zondervan, 1984), 192. The book is helpful for detailing the different views of the three rapture systems. Authors include Gleason L. Archer, Jr., Paul D. Feinberg, Douglas J. Moo, and Richard R. Reiter. For an interesting evaluation of the debate between pretribulationist, Paul Feinberg, and posttribulationist, Douglas Moo, in that book, see John S. Feinberg, "Arguing for the Rapture: Who Must Prove What and How?" in *When the Trumpet Sounds*, edited by Thomas Ice and Timothy Demy (Eugene, OR.: Harvest House, 1995) 187-210. A second edition of *The Rapture, Pre,-Mid, or Post-Tribulational?* with new contributors and including a representative of the prewrath view instead of mid-tribulationism, was published in 2010. Craig Blaising represents pretribulationism; Douglas Moo represents posttribulationism; and Alan Hultberg represents the prewrath position. See *The Rapture Pretribulation, Prewrath, or Posttribulation*, ed. Stanley N. Gundry and Alan Hultberg (Grand Rapids: Zondervan, 2010).

[37] Payne, *The Imminent Appearance of Christ*, 55.

[38] Moo, "A Case for the Posttribulation Rapture" in *The Rapture, Pretribulation, Prewrath, or Posttribulation*, 218-19.

Analysis of the Posttribulation Interpretation

Posttribulationists, however, as well as some prewrath proponents, have missed the point of the discourse.[39] The assertion that Jesus' teaching in the Olivet Discourse must be applicable and relevant to the church is a strawman argument because all Christians believe Jesus' teaching is applicable to the church. Matthew expected, no doubt, that his book would be used as a teaching manual for the church (Matt 28:19-20). So, all of us living in the present dispensation should find vital information in this passage for our own lives (2 Tim 3:16). We learn important information about Christ's Second Coming to earth, one of the most encouraging doctrines in Scripture. Chapter 25 applies to us by encouraging us to use our talents for God and to live our lives in preparation for the Lord's return. So, dispensational pretribulationists believe that the Olivet Discourse is *for* the church. Since no one is disagreeing about this, it ought not to be "the crucial question." The real question is, what is the Olivet Discourse *about?* And the answer is, it is *about* the future of Israel.

The Immediate Context: The Disciples' Question

As discussed above, the whole Olivet Discourse is based on two questions asked by the disciples:

1. When will the Temple be destroyed?

2. What will be the sign of the Second Coming and the end of the present age?

According to Old Testament theology, these three events—the attack on the temple, the coming of Messiah, and the beginning of the kingdom age— would follow one after another. The current age would end, and the Messianic Kingdom would be initiated (Zech 14:1-11). Since the disciples did not know that the temple in Jerusalem would be assaulted more than once in the future, they were confused, wondering if the attack on the temple would mean that the Second Coming was imminent.

---

[39] David Turner, however, apparently a pretribulationist, agrees with the posttribulationists at this point. See "The Structure and Sequence of Matthew 24:1-41," 5-7.

Questions About the Future of Israel

The point is that the disciples were not asking anything about the church or the rapture. They did not know much about either one (cf. Acts 10). But they did know a lot about Israel, the temple, Jerusalem, the coming of the Messiah to earth, and the Kingdom. Thus, the debate over who the disciples represent is not the focus of the disagreement between posttribulationists and pretribulationists.[40] The issue here is the immediate context. What do the disciples ask? And the answer is, they asked about the main events prophesied in the Old Testament and taught by Christ in His earthly ministry about the kingdom of God and the future of Israel. And Christ answers these questions in His discourse. Since the discourse is *for* the church but *not about* the church, there is nothing in it about the rapture of the church.

A Reference to an Old Testament Second Coming Passage

Indeed, when Jesus describes His Coming in the Olivet Discourse, He essentially quotes an Old Testament passage about the Second Coming as the following chart demonstrates:

Daniel 7:13-14 – Second Coming	Matthew 24:30 – Second Coming
"I saw in the night visions, and behold, with *the clouds of heaven* there came one like a *son of man*, and he came to the Ancient of Days and was presented before him. And to him was given dominion, glory, and a kingdom."	"Then the sign of the *Son of Man* will appear in heaven, and then all the tribes of the earth will mourn, and they will see the *Son of Man* coming on *the clouds of heaven* with power and great glory."

---

[40] Actually, the disciples could represent the church on some occasions and Israel on other occasions. For example, they represent Israel in the commission given by Christ in Matthew 10; and they represent the church in the commission given by Christ in Matthew 28:19-20. But this is not the issue here.

If the Coming of Christ in the clouds described in Daniel 7 is the Second Coming of Christ, then the Coming of Christ in the clouds described in the Olivet Discourse also must be the Second Coming, not the rapture.

The Nations Mourn

Furthermore, "all the tribes of the earth will mourn … when they see Christ coming "with power and great glory" (v. 30). The "mourning" of the nations describes the Second Coming, not the rapture. According to John's description of the Lord's return in the Book of Revelation, Christ returns as a warrior:

> Then I saw heaven opened, and behold, a white horse! The one sitting on it is called Faithful and True, and in righteousness he judges and makes war. His eyes are like a flame of fire, and on his head are many diadems, and he has a name written that no one knows but himself. He is clothed in a robe dipped in blood, and the name by which he is called is The Word of God. And the armies of heaven, arrayed in fine linen, white and pure, were following him on white horses. From his mouth comes a sharp sword with which to strike down the nations, and he will rule them with a rod of iron. He will tread the winepress of the fury of the wrath of God the Almighty (Rev 19:11-15; cf. Isa 62:2-3).

The Olivet Discourse correlates with this event, the Second Coming of Christ to earth to destroy Israel's enemies and establish His kingdom, not the rapture of the church.

Israel and the Ultimate Israelite

Posttribulationists and many prewrath defenders cannot accept the evidence that the Olivet Discourse is about Israel's future because they believe that Israel has been permanently replaced (or superseded) by the church. National Israel has no future, they believe, other than as individual Jews are saved and become a part of the body church. One of their arguments is that Jesus the Messiah, as the ultimate Israelite, has Himself replaced Israel, so Jesus is "true Israel."

As noted above, it is Hultberg's view, as a proponent of the prewrath rapture, that Jesus Himself "fulfills the role of Israel itself."[41] Christ replaces Israel, church-age believers are united to Christ at salvation, so the church united to

---

[41] Hultberg "A Case for the Prewrath Rapture," 113.

Christ permanently replaces Israel. As posttribulationist, Brent Parker, summarizes, "The case to be demonstrated is that Jesus really is the 'true Israel' in that he not only represents Israel but also fulfills Israel's identity, calling, and promises in inaugurating the new age, ratifying the new covenant, and bringing forth the dawning of the eschatologically restored Israel—the church."[42] The bottom line, then, is that for non-dispensationalists, the church replaces Israel through Christ who is the "new Israel." Thus, the church, as a result, becomes the "new Israel" and becomes the recipient through Christ of both the Old Testament covenants made with Israel and the Old Testament promises to Israel about the future kingdom. This also means that the nation of Israel no longer has a biblical claim to the land of Israel.

Almost all non-dispensational eschatological systems are based on the permanent replacement of Israel by the church through Christ. Amillennialists, postmillennialists, posttribulationists, some prewrath rapture adherents, Roman Catholics, theological liberals, and representatives of the New Perspective on Paul teach supersessionism. Kim Riddlebarger, an amillennialist asserts, "The New Testament writers claimed that Jesus was the true Israel of God and the fulfillment of Old Testament prophecies. So what remains of the dispensationalists' case that these prophecies will yet be fulfilled in a future millennium? They vanish in Jesus Christ, who has fulfilled them."[43] This view sounds logical and biblical at first look, but dispensational premillennialists are convinced that it is neither. Jesus is the *representative* of true Israel, but He is not the replacement of true Israel. There is a huge difference between representation and replacement. The claim that Christ replaces Israel is a defining issue in the differences in eschatology among evangelicals.

Christ the "True Israel"?

Is Christ the ultimate Israelite and "true Israel"? The answer depends on what one means by this. Everyone agrees that Christ is not called "Israel" in the New Testament nor is the phrase, "true Israel" found in Scripture. So "true Israel" is a summary term that some use for an analysis of Christ's earthly ministry. If "true

---

[42] Brent E. Parker, "The Israel-Christ-Church Relationship," *Progressive Covenantalism*, ed. Stephen J. Wellum and Brent E. Parker (Nashville: B&H Academic, 2016), 63. Dr. Parker later uses typological language to explain that "the church does not replace or absorb OT Israel; rather Israel was a type of Jesus and derivatively, of a new and regenerate covenant community" (68). We will discuss this concept later in this chapter.

[43] Kim Riddlebarger, *A Case for Amillennialism* (Grand Rapids: Baker, 2003), 70.

Israel" means that Christ identified with Israel and lived a life that exemplified everything that Israel was supposed to do including keeping the Mosaic Law perfectly, then there is no objection to the term. Christ was born a Jew who could trace His lineage back to Abraham, and indeed to Adam. The Gospel writers understand that part of Christ's ministry on earth was to "do-over" the mistakes that Israel had made in its history (Matt 2-4 for examples). Jesus specifically identified with believing Israel at John's baptism, and then obeyed God during the Satanic temptations in the wilderness, in contrast to Israel who had disobeyed God in her wilderness experience. Brandon Crowe observes, "Just as Israel passed through the waters of baptism into the testing of the wilderness, so Jesus comes through the waters of baptism into the testing of the wilderness, though Jesus remains fully faithful as God's Son, in contrast to Israel."[44]

Scripture expressly declares, moreover, that God's historical soteriological purposes are all fulfilled in Christ. God: "For in him all the fullness of God was pleased to dwell, and through him to reconcile to himself all things, whether on earth or in heaven, making peace by the blood of his cross" (Col 1:19-20). Thus, if "true Israel" means that Christ identified with Israel and lived an exemplary life of loving obedience to God, then there is no objection to the term, "true Israel."

If calling Jesus "true Israel," however, means that the nation of Israel is not truly Israel any longer, that she has no theological future, and that all the promises to Israel have been transferred to the church through Christ, then that is an unbiblical concept. As Michael Vlach writes, "There simply is no scriptural evidence for the non-dispensational view that Christ's identity as 'Israel' means the non-significance of the nation Israel in the future. The Scripture teaches the opposite—Christ's role as true Israel means the restoration of the nation Israel."[45]

Typological Fulfillment?

The case for the church superseding the nation of Israel through Christ is based, for the most part, on typology.

---

[44] Brandon D. Crowe, *The Last Adam* (Grand Rapids: Baker Academic, 2017), 76. Crowe is a non-dispensationalist.

[45] Michael J. Vlach, "What Does Christ as 'True Israel' Mean for the Nation Israel? Critique of the Non-Dispensational Understanding," *The Master's Seminary Journal* 23/1 (Spring, 2012):53.

A Non-Dispensational Case

According to non-dispensationalists, Israel is the type and the church in Christ is the antitype. The antitype cancels out the significance of the original type. To be specific, for non-dispensationalists, the type is not "Israel as an ethnic people group" since Jewish people can be saved and added to the church in the present and future ages. The claim "is that national Israel in terms of its role, vocation, calling, and identity is typological of Christ and thus rules out the notion of a future national role of Israel in the plans of God."[46] The type (Israel) has been surpassed and made obsolete by the antitype (the church in Christ).

This is certainly not a new argument for supersessionists. We came across Melito of Sardis (d. ca 190) in the second chapter of this book arguing for typological interpretation. In his meditation, *On Pasca*, Melito argues that typology begins with a "first draft," or a "preliminary sketch" (meaning Israel). But when the finished copy or the thing that was sketched comes into existence, "then the type is destroyed." Melito explains,

> But when the church arose and the Gospel came to be, the type, depleted, gave up meaning to the truth: and the law, fulfilled, gave up meaning to the Gospel. In the same way that the type is depleted, conceding the image to what is intrinsically real, and the analogy is brought to completion through the elucidation of interpretation, so the law is fulfilled by the elucidation of the Gospel, and the people is depleted by the arising of the church, and the model is dissolved by the appearance of the Lord. And today those things of value are worthless, since the things of true worth have been revealed."[47]

For Melito, Israel was just a type of the real—the church. And the type has been eliminated once and for all. Modern day non-dispensationalists have refined this explanation to say specifically that Christ (rather than the church) is the antitype; but the method and the result are essentially the same. Israel is permanently replaced by the church.

---

[46] Parker, "The Israel-Christ-Church Relationship," 52.

[47] Melito of Sardis, *On Pascha* (Crestwood, NY: St. Vladimir's Seminary Press, 2000), 43-44. See 56-65 for Melito's poetic attack on unbelieving Israel. Cf. Eusebius, XXIV.

An Analysis of the Non-dispensational Case

Types are certainly found in Scripture. Melchizedek, for an example, is a type of Jesus Christ (Gen 14:18; Ps 110:4; Heb 5-7). And Adam is a type of Christ (Rom 5:14). But there are problems in the way that non-dispensationalists employ typology. In the first place, antitypes do not change or obliterate the teaching of the type. If what the type taught were not true, it could not serve as a basis of a relationship with the antitype. John Feinberg makes this point:

> Non-dispensational systems stress that the type is shadow and the antitype is reality; therefore, the meaning of the antitype supersedes and cancels the meaning of the type in its own context. Dispensationalists do not think types necessarily are shadows, and they demand that both type and antitype be given their due meanings in their own contexts while maintaining a typological relation to one another.[48]

An antitype does not eliminate the historical reality and significance of the type itself.

Some dispensational premillennialists teach that there can be some unexpected inaugural fulfillments of a type in the New Testament antitype. The inaugural antitype, in turn, foreshadows the greater antitype yet to come.[49] In Acts 2, for example, Peter teaches that the outpouring of the Holy Spirit is that which was prophesied by Joel. But not all that was prophesied by Joel was fulfilled on the Day of Pentecost. The ultimate fulfillment of Joel 2 will take place near the end of the Tribulation period relating to the Second Coming of Christ. The prophet Zechariah is clear and precise about this (Zech 12). Isaiah even tells us what the Jewish prayers of repentance will be like when the "spirit of grace" is poured out on them (Isaiah 53). The Pentecost outpouring of the Holy Spirit that formed the church is an unexpected inaugural antitype foreshadowing the greater antitype.

Another example of this same kind of unexpected inaugural antitype already discussed is the attack on Israel's temple in A. D. 70 as a foreshadowing of the greater fulfillment that will take place in connection with the Second

---

[48] John S. Feinberg, "Israel and the Church: A Case for Discontinuity," *Continuity and Discontinuity*, ed. John S. Feinberg (Westchester, IL: Crossway Books, 1988), 78.

[49] See further, W. Edward Glenny, "The Israelite Imagery of 1 Peter 2," *Dispensationalism, Israel and the Church*, ed. Craig A. Blaising and Darrel L. Bock (Grand Rapids: Zondervan, 1992), 183-84.

Coming of Jesus Christ. Thus, a type may have an inaugural antitype and an ultimate antitype.

Non-dispensationalists might agree up to a point that a type might have more than one antitype. But if there is more than one fulfillment of a type, they say, "the text must dictate whether the type is completely annulled or fulfilled in Christ's first advent, or if there may be additional fulfillment or appropriation in the church and in the eschaton (the new creation.)"[50] Since they do not see an additional fulfillment indicated in Scripture, the church through Christ is the one and only antitype of Israel.

Dispensationalists believe, however, that Scripture does teach that even if there is an inaugural fulfillment of the type with the church through Christ, there will be further fulfillment of the type. The Apostle Paul states this in his letter to the Romans. The status of Israel is his topic:

> So I ask, did they stumble in order that they might fall? By no means! Rather through their trespass salvation has come to the Gentiles, so as to make Israel jealous. Now if their trespass means riches for the world, and if their failure means riches for the Gentiles, how much more will their full inclusion mean! (Rom 11:11-12).

According to this Scripture, the salvation of the Gentiles at the present time has as a purpose "to make Israel jealous" and bring about her conversion to her Messiah. As Russell Shedd points out, "God has the power to engraft again the natural broken branches of Israel; that is less remarkable or objectionable than the engrafting of wild slips (Rom 11:23-24)."[51]

This does not mean that Gentiles will be ignored in the future kingdom, as non-dispensationalists seem to think that dispensationalists teach. Parker writes, "How Jewish Christians can be recipients of OT nationalistic promises apart from Gentile Christians in a future millennial state is confounded by the fact that *all* believers have their identity in Christ."[52] Dispensationalists, however, do not believe that Gentile Christians somehow remain on a lower spiritual level than the Jews in the kingdom. The new covenant is here to stay, not

---

[50] Parker, "The Israel-Christ-Church Relationship," 49.

[51] Russell Phillip Shedd, *Man in Community* (Grand Rapids: Eerdmans, 1964), 202. See further Matt 19:28, Acts 1:6, Rom 9:4, and Rev 7:4-8.

[52] Parker, "The Israel-Christ-Church Relationship," 63-64.

only in the church age but in the future millennial age. Both Jews and Gentiles will be united in Christ in the kingdom.[53]

This does not negate the Biblical prophets' teaching that the nation of Israel will be in a place of prominence, living in her land, with her Messiah ruling from earthly Jerusalem. These prophecies are in perfect alliance with Paul's discussion in Romans 9-11. The purpose of God's election of Israel, as expressed in the Abrahamic covenant, is that Israel would be God's servant nation "representing God and His character before the surrounding nations of the world."[54] The Old Testament prophets affirm that after Israel's judgment, God would restore Israel to a place of blessing and bless all the Gentile nations through Israel (Isaiah 40-55, for example). As Michael Grisanti explains,

> Israel functions as Yahweh's vehicle to bless the nations at the same time as she holds a place of priority over them. After judging recalcitrant Gentiles, the Lord will sovereignly cause the nations to expedite the return of scattered Israelites to their homeland (43:5-7; 49:22-23a). These surviving Gentiles will bring tribute to Israel and be subject to her (45:14; 49:22b), recognizing Israel's role as God's servant nation. They will care for Israel as parents care for their child (49:22b). Nations that do not know Israel will hasten to her because of her relationship with Yahweh (55:5).[55]

If the church *temporarily* replaces and supersedes Israel through Christ, therefore, there is another replacement and supersession in the future. At the Second Coming, believing Israel, along with the Gentile nations, will supersede the church as God's focus during the Kingdom of Christ here on earth. A type is not fulfilled until what was communicated by the type is finally fulfilled in the antitype.

Corporate Personality

It may be debatable as to whether the type-antitype concept is an accurate way to talk about the relationship of Christ to Israel since the New Testament does

---

[53] Being "in Christ" soteriologically is different from being in the ecclesiological body of Christ which is true of all new covenant believers during the church age.

[54] Michael A. Grisanti, "Israel's Mission to the Nations in Isaiah 40-55: An Update," *The Master's Seminary Journal* 9/1 (Spring, 1998):40.

[55] Ibid., 60.

not say that as such. There is a specific biblical concept of the bond between Israel and Christ, however, that is based on the relationship of the one and the many, and that is found throughout Scripture.

Definition of Corporate Personality

This relationship has often been described as "corporate personality." Russell Shedd explains that "the application of the term to a group means that a nation or family including its past, present, and future members, might function as a single individual through any one of those members conceived as a representative of it. The community was therefore conceived as an interminable continuity. At the same time the group-consciousness was analogous to the idea of a personality."[56]

Examples of Corporate Personality

There are many examples of corporate personality in Scripture. The sin of the first man, Adam, contaminates the entire human race because Adam personally was mankind. When Achan sinned, God told Joshua that "Israel has sinned; they have transgressed my covenant that I commanded them; they have taken some of the devoted things; they have stolen and lied and put them among their own belongings" (Josh 7:11). A guilty party, in the Old Testament, could be punished in the son (see 2 Sam 21:1-14; 2 Kgs 9:26) because of the corporate personality of the family. David's "son" (2 Sam 7) incorporates Solomon, other kings, and ultimately Messiah. Daniel, as a righteous intercessor, identified himself with the nation in his prayer of repentance so that the individual functioned as the representative of the nation (Dan 9:4-19).

Russell Shedd observes, "There was a very strong sense of solidarity which produced a consciousness of continuous extension crossing the barriers of succeeding generations and uniting the whole group."[57] Not just the family, but the entire nation of Israel "as a whole forms a corporate personality or collective individual, making the history of the race the biography of the national super

---

[56] Shedd, *Man in Community*, 4. Shedd says that the term, "corporate personality," was apparently "coined and popularized" in 1936 by H. W. Robinson. But it is a common Scriptural concept.

[57] Ibid., 5.

individual."[58] A group, in the worldview of Old Testament people, was "a mass individual living through its constituent members."[59]

This "super individual" in the Old Testament was an extended physical family that was incorporated, so to speak, through a covenant. The covenant "served as an external frame within which the generic unity of the nation subsisted."[60] The Abrahamic covenant functioned as a family covenant binding the descendants of Abraham into this "super individual." The Mosaic covenant functioned as a national covenant binding the descendants of Abraham into a *national* corporate personality. The Davidic covenant functioned as a royal covenant binding David's "sons" into a *royal* corporate personality (2 Sam 7). Since the eternal and immutable God is one of the parties of each of these covenants, the continuity of the nation and the line of David is assured.

Oscillation between Individual and Group

One of the interesting features of the biblical concept of corporate personality is the oscillation between the individual and the group in many passages of Scripture. "Oscillation" is a term that some scholars have given to the "characteristic of the Hebrew thought process which enabled one to conceive of the individual as the embodiment of the group, and the group as an individual." Shedd continues, "It is found in a fluidity of transition from the individual to the society and vice versa. It must be accepted as a genuine characteristic of the Hebrew mind, manifesting itself in speech and writing, and requiring the conception of the corporate personality of the group for an adequate explanation."[61] In other words, the biblical author might write about a group—Israel for example—but also include in his mind the individual—Messiah. Or he could speak of Messiah but also include Israel in his thought process. There are some interesting examples of this in the Old Testament (Num 20:14-20; 21:22; Daniel 7; Isaiah 40-50).

---

[58] Ibid., 6.

[59] Ibid., 5.

[60] Ibid., 20.

[61] Ibid., 38-39. Disappointingly, after Shedd's helpful explanation of corporate personality, in his later chapters he asserts that the person replaces the corporate so that Israel has no future as a nation (126-99).

Representative Rather Than Replacement

It is also important to note that in corporate personality, the individual does not replace the group. The individual is the head of the group, the father of the family, the king of the nation, the Messiah of the nation. And the individual represents his corporate group, but he does not replace the group. In Daniel 7, for example, Daniel's vision outlining the future of the world culminates in the Ancient of Days presenting the everlasting kingdom to the "son of man." Daniel writes,

> I saw in the night visions, and behold, with the clouds of heaven there came one like a son of man, and he came to the Ancient of Days and was presented before him. And to him was given dominion and glory and a kingdom, that all peoples, nations, and languages should serve him; his dominion is an everlasting dominion, which shall not pass away, and his kingdom one that shall not be destroyed (Dan 7:13-14).

The dominion, glory, and kingdom were presented to the Son of Man, Israel's Messiah.

Daniel asks the heavenly person who is also in the vision for help in understanding what he had seen, and the heavenly being explains that the kingdom will be given to the "saints of the Most High" (7:18 and 22). The explanation concludes: "And the kingdom and the dominion and the greatness of the kingdoms under the whole heaven shall be given to the people of the saints of the Most High; his kingdom shall be an everlasting kingdom, and all dominions shall serve and obey him" (Dan 7:27).

So, to whom is the kingdom given? Is it given to the Son of Man? Jesus applies it to Himself (Matt 26:64). Or is the kingdom given to the saints? Brandon Crowe answers correctly,

> A plausible explanation for this interplay between the individual and the corporate is that the son of man is an individual figure who represents God's people corporately. This is consistent with the biblical paradigm in which the king represents his people. If this is correct, then the son of man in Daniel 7 is described both as an individual and as those whom this individual represents.[62]

---

[62] Crowe, *The Last Adam*, 39.

Thus, the Messiah is a representative of believing Israel, not the replacement of Israel.

Agreement with the Servant Songs

Another example of this interplay in the corporate personality occurs in the "Servant Songs" in Isaiah 40-53. The question is, who is the "Servant" that is described in these prophecies? In some of these prophecies, the Servant is obviously Israel. The Lord says, "But you, Israel, my servant, Jacob, whom I have chosen, the offspring of Abraham, my friend; you whom I took from the ends of the earth, and called from its farthest corners, saying to you, 'You are my servant, I have chosen you and not cast you off'" (Isa 41:8-9).

Other prophecies, however, are clearly about the Servant Messiah:

> Behold my servant, whom I uphold, my chosen, in whom my soul delights; I have put my Spirit upon him; he will bring forth justice to the nations. He will not cry aloud or lift up his voice, or make it heard in the street; a bruised reed he will not break, and a faintly burning wick he will not quench; he will faithfully bring forth justice. He will not grow faint or be discouraged till he has established justice in the earth; and the coastlands wait for his law. Thus says God, the LORD, who created the heavens and stretched them out, who spread out the earth and what comes from it, who gives breath to the people on it and spirit to those who walk in it: "I am the LORD; I have called you in righteousness; I will take you by the hand and keep you; I will give you as a covenant for the people, a light for the nations, to open the eyes that are blind, to bring out the prisoners from the dungeon, from the prison those who sit in darkness" (Isa 42:1-7).

The Servant, therefore, is Israel/Messiah. There are several other examples of this corporate personality in this section of Isaiah (43:10; 44:1-2, 21-22; 45:4; 48:20; 49:5; 53:4-9, et. al.).

Especially significant is one passage in which the Servant is instrumental in bringing Israel back to Yahweh. Isaiah writes,

> And now the LORD says, he who formed me from the womb to be his servant, to bring Jacob back to him; and that Israel might be gathered to him—for I am honored in the eyes of the LORD, and my God has become my strength—he says: "It is too light a thing that you should be my servant to raise up the tribes of Jacob and

to bring back the preserved of Israel; I will make you as a light for the nations, that my salvation may reach to the end of the earth" (Isa 49:5-6).

The Servant does not replace Israel. The Servant leads Israel back to God. H. H. Rowley comments that there is here an "oscillation between Israel, that was called to be the Servant of the Lord, and a future individual who should perfectly represent Israel and carry its mission to a unique degree in himself." Rowley continues,

> Nevertheless, it was probably not a linear development from community to individual, but a real oscillation. The mission the Servant would exercise would still be the mission of Israel, and in so far as he should be the representative of Israel he would call all Israel to enter into the mission, so that he might be truly its representative. Just as the High Priest could not truly represent the people in his confession on the Day of Atonement unless his confession was echoed in their hearts, so the Servant could not represent Israel unless she entered into his mission and realized that it was hers.[63]

The point is that "in all of these instances the one involves the inclusion of the many, not their substitution."[64] So, if Christ is the true Israelite, He does not replace Israel. In Vlach's words, "The presence of the true Israelite, Jesus, does not mean that the people of Israel lose their significance. On the contrary, the people of Israel are restored and made what they were supposed to be because of Jesus Christ."[65] Blaising adds, "Rather than indicating Israel's replacement, I would argue that such description serves to underscore both his Messiahship (as Messiah of Israel) and the surety of the hope of Israel.... [T]he Servant was expected to bring Israel back to God as well as extend salvation to the Gentiles."[66]

---

[63] H. H. Rowley, *The Unity of the Bible* (New York: Meridian Books, 1957), 61.

[64] Robert Saucy, "Is Christ the Fulfillment of National Israel's Prophecy? Yes and No!," *The Master's Seminary Journal*, 28/1 (Spring, 2017):24. This paper was originally presented at the national meeting of the Evangelical Theological Society, 2010.

[65] Vlach, "What Does Christ as 'True Israel' Mean for the Nation Israel?" 50.

[66] Blaising, "A Case for the Pretribulation Rapture," 157.

Jesus and Church Age Believers

The "in Christ" relationship that church-age believers enjoy with Jesus is a parallel with Christ and Israel. We who are "in Christ" in the church age are not obliterated into insignificance. We are not replaced by Jesus. Neither will Israel in Christ during the future kingdom be of no significance. The Apostle Paul, having deeply imbibed Old Testament theology, writes that God has "raised us up with him and seated us with him in the heavenly places in Christ Jesus" (Eph 2:6). Church believers, therefore, are unified with Christ as a corporate personality by being in Christ. Saucy writes, "Now we might ask, if the salvation promises related to the church are all fulfilled in Christ, does this negate any function for the church in the fulfillment of those promises, as is asserted [by non-dispensationalists] in relation to the promises of national Israel? Clearly this is denied in the New Testament."[67] Jesus is not fulfilling the roles of either Israel or the church in the sense that He replaces Israel and/or the church.

Thus, in the Olivet Discourse, when the disciples ask two questions about the future of Israel, the interpreter cannot legitimately override their questions and Jesus' answer to claim that they were actually asking about the church because Israel has been replaced by Christ and the church. This would violate the biblical concept of corporate personality, as well as the plain words of the disciples. Christ does not replace Israel. He represents Israel in a corporate personality. The non-dispensational interpretation of the Olivet Discourse therefore misses the point of Christ's answer to the disciples' questions. Both questions are about the future of Israel, not the church, and Jesus answers these questions.

Pretribulationism and the Olivet Discourse

Pretribulationism is the eschatological system within dispensational premillennialism that teaches that Jesus Christ will rapture away His church before the future seven-year Tribulation begins. This doctrine is one of the most delightful and encouraging doctrines in all of Scripture for church-age believers. Its blessing resides primarily in the fact that we might see our Lord and Savior in the next moment. Following the rapture of the church, God will bring Israel back to Himself through seven years of Tribulation.

There is no doubt that there are some within pretribulationism who tend to be reckless and superficial with Scripture. Who of us can forget sermons,

---

[67] Saucy, "Is Christ the Fulfillment of National Israel's Prophecy? Yes and No!," 26.

pamphlets, and booklets such as "88 Reasons Why the Rapture Will Occur in 1988"? But pretribulationism, in our opinion, when taught correctly, is still the most accurate harmonization of prophetic events, including the Bible's declarations about the future of Israel.

"One Taken, One Left"?

Some pretribulationists, however, are not consistent with their method of interpretation of Scripture, and this inconsistency is evident in their explanations of sections of the Olivet Discourse. It is not uncommon, for example, to hear pretribulationists preach about the rapture from Matthew 24:40-42: "Then two men will be in the field; one will be taken and one left. Two women will be grinding at the mill; one will be taken and one left. Therefore, stay awake, for you do not know on what day your Lord is coming." Though there is no one interpretation of these verses to which all pretribulationists advocate, most understand that though this may sound like a rapture passage to some, it is not.

The Lord's reason for using these examples in verses 40-42 is not to teach the imminency of the rapture. Christ does not have the rapture in view in these verses. Instead He is teaching that there will be a division of humanity at the Second Coming of Christ to earth. The Greek word for "taken" (παραλαμβάνω), is essentially a neutral word, used for both taken into good as well as taken into judgment. In Matthew 4, Matthew uses this word, for example, when the devil "takes" Jesus up to the pinnacle of the temple and to the exceedingly high mountain to be tempted (Matt 4:5, 8). "Taken" in that passage has a bad implication (cf. John 19:16). Thus, it is not necessarily good to be "taken."

If "taken" has any connotation in this passage, the immediately preceding context about the judgement of Noah's flood would lead us to understand that the one taken is taken into judgment, and the one left is left to enter the millennial kingdom. The wicked of Noah's day, though they might have expected some type of flood judgment watching Noah build an ark, missed the signs, and "did not know until the flood came and *took* them all away…."[68] And then the Lord adds, "so will be the coming of the Son of Man" (Matt 24:39). Just as the Noahic flood came and took away the unsuspecting and unprepared wicked, the judgments at the time of the Second Coming will come and take away the unsuspecting and unprepared wicked.

---

[68] The word for "take" (αἴρω) in verse 39 is a different word than in verses 40-41. It often has implications of violent action such as destroy, kill, or remove.

It is also significant that when Christ gives this illustration in Luke 17:34-37, the disciples ask, "Where will they be taken?" And the Lord answers, "Wherever the body is, there the eagles [i.e. vultures] will be gathered together" (Luke 17:37). This is not a description of the rapture, but an image of judgment. It is also noteworthy that preceding this illustration in Luke 17 is another illustration of judgment—this time God's judgment on Sodom. In other words, the taking from the field and the mill is consistently found amid a judgment context.

The "taken into judgment" interpretation also has some support by the word for "left" (ἀφίημι), that can have a positive idea of "permitted," or "to let someone have something." The best understanding of Matthew 24:40-41, therefore, is that the person who is "taken" is an unbeliever at the end of the Tribulation, and thus "taken" into judgment. The one who is "left" is left (i.e., permitted) to enter the Millennial Kingdom.

The Fig Tree

Several Bible students, including some pretribulationists, believe they have discovered hints about the time of the rapture in the parable of the fig tree:

> From the fig tree learn its lesson: as soon as its branch becomes tender and puts out its leaves, you know that summer is near. So also, when you see all these things, you know that he is near, at the very gates. Truly, I say to you, this generation will not pass away until all these things take place" (Matt 24:32-34).

Who or what is the fig tree? Some believe that it is Israel. In their view, when Israel became a nation in 1948, the timetable for a generation began, and the Tribulation and Second Coming events must take place before that generation dies out. Counting back seven years from the end of the Tribulation and the Second Coming, it would mean that the rapture would have to occur at least seven years before that generation passed away. If one could know for sure how long a generation was, therefore, he could know about when the rapture would take place.

The fig tree, however, does not illustrate Israel becoming a nation in 1948.[69] The fig tree is simply an illustration from nature. R. T. France writes, "This is simply a proverb-type saying which draws a simile from observation of the

---

[69] However, I am not saying that the inauguration of the nation of Israel in 1948 was insignificant for prophecy. I believe that it is extremely important—a vital part of latter days prophecies.

natural world: the fig tree is used because it is the most prominent deciduous tree in Palestine and one whose summer fruiting was eagerly awaited."[70] The disciples ask, what will be the sign of your coming and the end of the age? And the answer is the events of the Great Tribulation. The cycle of a tree illustrates this. When we see leaves on a tree, we know that summer is near. Similarly, when the events of the Great Tribulation unfold, believers in the Tribulation will know the Second Coming is near.

There are two evidences for this interpretation. First, when Jesus makes His point from the fig tree illustration, He says, "When you see *all these things*, know that it is near—at the doors!" (33). The Lord is not talking about a single event such as Israel becoming a nation in 1948, as astounding as that event is. Instead, He is speaking about all the events of the Tribulation being signs of the Second Coming. Second, in the parallel passage in Luke, Luke records Jesus adding the phrase, "and all the trees" (Luke 21:29). If the fig tree blossoming were a reference to the founding of Israel, what would the blossoming of the other trees be illustrating? The parable understood in this way doesn't seem to make sense. Again, the best understanding of the parable is that the Lord is simply giving an illustration from nature. MacArthur writes, "The point of the parable is utterly uncomplicated; even a child can tell by looking at a fig tree that summer is near. Likewise, the generation that sees all these signs come to pass will know with certainty that Christ's return is near."[71]

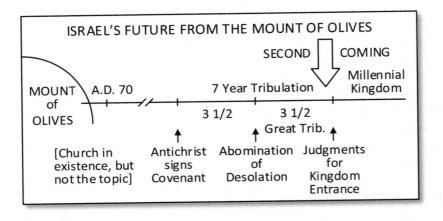

[70] R. T. France, "The Gospel of Mathew," *The New International Commentary on the New Testament*, ed. Gordon Fee (Grand Rapids: Eerdmans, 20007), 929.

[71] MacArthur, *Second Coming*, 134.

CONCLUSION

The Olivet Discourse is a majestic lecture presented by the Messiah in which He outlines Israel's future in the age between Israel's recent rejection of Him and the Second Coming when Israel finally embraces her Messiah. Supersessionists, including posttribulationists, argue that the lecture is about the church and the rapture, not Israel and the Second Coming. The disciples, they say, represent the church, and so the lecture must be about the future of the church. But the correct interpretation of this passage is not settled by whom the disciples represent. The questions that the disciples ask at the beginning of the Discourse settle it. Do they ask about the future of the church or the future of Israel? Clearly, they ask about the future of Israel in relationship to her temple, Messiah, and Kingdom. And thus Christ answers these questions.

This does not mean that the discourse has no application to the church. All Scripture is profitable to all believers for doctrine, reproof, correction, and instruction in righteousness. But Jesus Christ is not teaching some form of replacement theology in this lecture. Israel's Messiah knows that Israel's story has not ended.

10

THE GATHERING OF ISRAEL: A NINETEENTH CENTURY PERSPECTIVE

Bishop William R. Nicholson

The Bible conference movement was a feature of the late nineteenth- and early twentieth- centuries American Christianity. Summer after summer, Bible-believing Christians came together, often at resort locations, to study the Scriptures. Leading pastors and Bible teachers such as James Hall Brookes, A. J. Gordon, and Arno C. Gaebelein expounded on the fundamentals of the faith, often highlighting the doctrine of the premillennial return of Christ. Between 1875 and 1900, the most significant of these summer conferences, the Niagara Bible Conference, met for seven or eight days usually in July. This conference, originally called "the Believers Meeting for Bible Study," changed its name to the Niagara Bible Conference because it began to meet in the beautiful town of Niagara-on-the-Lake, Ontario, Canada.

Most summer Bible conferences, like Niagara, were nondenominational and fostered the spirit of interdenominational cooperation among conservatives in the emerging American fundamentalist/evangelical movement. Many of the participants at these conferences were struggling with the impact of theological liberalism in their denominations. But each summer they could come together to fellowship with other evangelicals and hear the Word of God taught accurately. The participants of the Niagara Bible Conference composed a fairly thorough fourteen-point doctrinal statement that became the basis of participation at the meetings. It taught the doctrine of inerrancy, an interdenominational ecclesiology, and premillennialism, as well as other fundamental doctrines.[1]

The leaders of the Niagara Conference decided that a conference more public and academic than the summer Bible conferences was needed.[2] James Brookes, the president of the Niagara Conference, wrote that an idea arose during the winter and spring of 1878 "without consultation with each other."[3] So they sent out a call for a national conference that would emphasize the premillennial Second Coming of Christ. The statement of the call began as follows:

DEAR BRETHREN IN CHRIST: When from any cause some vital doctrine of God's Word has fallen into neglect or suffered contradiction and reproach, it becomes the serious duty of those who hold it, not only strongly and constantly to re-affirm it, but to seek by all means in their power to bring back the Lord's people to its apprehension and acceptance. The precious doctrine of Christ's second personal appearing has, we are constrained to believe, long lain under such neglect and misapprehension.

In the Word of God we find it holding a most conspicuous place. It is there strongly and constantly emphasized as a personal and imminent event, the great object of the Church's hope, the powerful motive to holy living and watchful service, the inspiring ground of confidence amid the sorrows and sins of the present evil world, and the event that is to end the reign of Death, cast down Satan from his throne, and establish the kingdom of God on earth. So vital, indeed, is this truth presented to be that the denial of it is pointed out as one of the conspicuous signs of the apostasy of the last days.[4]

Eight well-known pastors and professors, including James Brookes, a Presbyterian, and A. J. Gordon, a Baptist, composed the committee that sent out the call for the meeting. Also included in the committee was Bishop W. R. Nicholson, a Reformed Episcopalian, the author of the essay that is included in this chapter. The call also lists 112 "bishops, professors, ministers, and brethren,"

[1] This Niagara Creed can be read, among other places, in David O. Beale, *In Pursuit of Purity* (Greenville, SC: Unusual Publications, 1986), 375-79.

[2] Larry D. Pettegrew, "The Historical and Theological Contributions of the Niagara Bible Conference to American Fundamentalism," Th. D. diss., Dallas Theological Seminary, 1976, 53-54.

[3] James Hall Brookes, "Believers' Meeting at Clifton Springs," *The Truth* (1878): 405.

[4] "Call for the Conference," *Premillennial Essays of the Prophetic Conference*, ed. Nathaniel West (Chicago: F. H. Revell, 1879; repr. by Bryant Baptist Publications of Minneapolis (Klock and Klock, 1981), 5.

who had sanctioned the call to the conference. The first International Prophecy Conference[5] (sometimes designated as the First American Bible and Prophecy Conference) met October 30 to November 1, 1878, at the Episcopal Church of the Holy Trinity in New York City. Dr. Stephen H. Tyng, Sr., gave the opening address entitled, "Christ's Coming: Personal and Visible." His son, Stephen H. Tyng, Jr., was the rector of the church and a member of the committee that sent out the call. The pastors and professors attending the conference included several denominations including forty-seven Presbyterians, twenty-six Baptists, sixteen Episcopalians, seven Congregationalists, six Methodists, five Adventists, four Dutch Reformed, and one Lutheran. They were not all dispensationalists, but many were, and they were all premillennialists.[6]

The conference unanimously passed a series of resolutions outlining their beliefs and concerns including a resolution "by the vast audience voluntarily rising *en masse* to its feet—a magnificent spectacle not soon to be forgotten: '*Revolved*, That the doctrine of our Lord's pre-millennial advent, instead of paralyzing evangelistic and missionary effort, is one of the mightiest incentives to earnestness in preaching the Gospel to every creature, until He comes.'"[7]

The leaders of the conference apparently were surprised and encouraged by the interest in the prophetic messages. A. J. Gordon reported:

Those who projected the Conference were fairly astonished at the interest which it awakened. From the first day until the last, the attention and the attendance were unabated, the large church of Rev. Dr. Tyng, Jr., being completely filled with the congregation of eager listeners. The papers read had more of the character of theological lectures than of popular addresses. Elaborate, critical and almost wholly expository, ranging in length from one hour to nearly two, they commanded the closest attention; and though two, and in one case three, of the papers followed in a single session, the audience was not perceptibly thinned.[8]

---

[5] The second International Prophecy Conference was held in Chicago in 1886.

[6] B. M. Pietsch writes: "Most historical accounts of early American premillennialism portray this movement as a peevish offshoot of the teachings of John Nelson Darby. ... The conference proceedings [of the 1878 conference], however, tell a different story. Neither Darby nor his separatist impulses were in attendance. Darby's works were not cited alongside those of the German scholars so evident in the speeches." B. M. Pietsch, *Dispensationalism Modernism* (New York: Oxford University Press, 2015), 50. See further Ernest Sandeen, *The Roots of Fundamentalism* (Chicago: University of Chicago, 1970; repr., Baker, 1978), 156.

[7] "Introduction," *Premillennial Essays*, 9.

[8] A. J. Gordon, "The Prophetic Conference," *The Watchword*, I (December, 1878): 40.

The meeting came to national attention partly through the *New York Tribune* that published an extra edition of 50,000 copies containing many of the addresses of the conference. In the following years the religious journals and magazines discussed and amplified the messages of the conference. Historian Ernest Sandeen, comments:

> The conveners of the [1878] conference, thus, succeeded beyond their expectations in alerting American Protestants to the nature of their movement. Whether they had anticipated the volume of criticism that would accompany the publicity ... is not known. But once initiated into the struggle, these leaders of millenarianism did not flinch or turn back.... They were utterly convinced that they were right.[9]

The following address concerning the regathering of the nation of Israel to its land was presented at the first International Prophecy Conference by Bishop William R. Nicholson (1822-1901). Nicholson was trained in the Methodist Church and preached his first sermon at the age of fourteen. He graduated from La Grange College in Alabama and was ordained a minister in the Protestant Episcopal Church. He pastored Episcopal churches in Louisiana, Ohio, and Massachusetts. In 1857 he received the Doctor of Divinity degree from La Grange College. In 1874, he resigned from the Protestant Episcopal Church, joined the Reformed Episcopal Church, and became rector of the Second (later called St Paul's) Church, in Philadelphia.[10] Two years later, in 1876, he was consecrated Bishop of the Synod of New York and Philadelphia. At the foundation of the Reformed Episcopal Seminary, he was appointed Dean of the faculty, and was elected to the chair of Exegesis and Pastoral Theology. He pastored until 1898 and served at the seminary until his death.

In his message at the first International Prophecy Conference, Nicholson summarized the Scriptures' teaching about the future return of the Jews to their land in the Middle East. It is a significant essay because it was written about seventy years before Israel had a country to which to return. Before 1948, there were individuals and some Jewish groups that returned to the land. But it was

---

[9] Sandeen, *The Roots of Fundamentalism*, 157.

[10] He left the Protestant Episcopal Church, according to a pamphlet that he wrote entitled, "Why I Left the Protestant Episcopal Church," because of his disagreement with the impact of the Roman Catholic Church on the Protestant Episcopal Church through the Oxford Movement. He was concerned about the increasing sacerdotalism, especially the new emphasis on baptismal regeneration of a baby, in the Protestant Episcopalian Church.

never a gathering like that which began in connection with the founding of the nation of Israel in 1948.

In his interpretation of the Old Testament prophets, Nicholson believed that there would be two phases to the return: a return in unbelief and a return with national belief in process. Such a view is similar to many dispensationalists today. Craig Blaising, for example, describes Israel's gathering to her historic land in the twentieth and twenty-first centuries "a preconsummate working of God in continuity with the divine plan for Israel and the nations."[11]

Nicholson's essay is noteworthy because much of what he said would happen has already happened. It is not that Nicholson was a prophet. He simply describes what the Scriptures say will transpire in Israel's future. His essay begins with quoting and commenting on significant Old and New Testament passages about the return of Israel to their land. The rest of the essay explains how Israel will gather to their land in two installments. Especially notable is the last three or four pages in which he surveys God's providential preservation of Israel in spite of severe chastening. Many dispensationalists living today can agree with almost everything that Nicholson proclaimed. As dispensational premillennialists often say, outside of Scripture, the greatest evidence for premillennialism is the existence of the nation of Israel. So here is Nicholson's address as it was given in 1878.[12]

"THE GATHERING OF ISRAEL"

Bishop William R. Nicholson,

Professor at the Reformed Episcopal Seminary of Philadelphia

By Israel is here meant, as the Scriptures speak, "Both the houses of Israel" (Isa 8:14); or "The house of Israel and the house of Judah" (Jer 31:31); or Judah and Ephraim (see Hosea); or the two tribes of Judah and Benjamin, and the ten remaining tribes. "Both the houses of Israel" is interchangeable with "the house of Israel," one house (Jer 31:31, 33) in which usage "the house of Israel" is conterminous with "the house of Jacob" (Psalm 114:1.) By the gathering of Israel

---

[11] Craig Blaising, "Biblical Hermeneutics: How Are We to Interpret the Relation Between the Tanak and the New Testament on This Question," in *The New Christian Zionism*, ed. Gerald R. McDermott (Downers Grove, IL: IVP Academic, 2016), 98.

[12] William R. Nicholson, "The Gathering of Israel," *Premillennial Essays*, 222-40, presented here by permission of Bryant Baptist Publications (Mpls.) and Klock and Klock publishers who reprinted the book in 1981. Nicholson quotes from an older edition of the King James Version.

is meant the gathering back of all the twelve tribes of Jacob from their dispersion, continued through so many ages, to their own covenanted land, Palestine,
and the resettlement of them there as one nation. Is this restoration of Israel a
foreshown fact in prophecy? And if so, what circumstances of the regathering,
if any, are at the same time predicted? This is our subject.

I. As regards the prophetical fact of the restoration.

In giving answer to this question I find myself in the midst of an embarrass-
ment of riches. It is impossible to exhibit within the limits of this paper the full
strength of the prophetical proof, since in that case I should have to quote an
immense proportion of the Bible. We can consider but a very few references, a
mere sample of the whole; these, however, shall be in themselves exhaustive and
all sufficient. We turn to Ezekiel 36:22-28:

> "Say unto the house of Israel, Thus saith the Lord God ... I will take you from
> among the heathen, and gather you out of all countries, and will bring you into
> your own land. Then will I sprinkle clean water upon you, and ye shall be clean;
> from all your filthiness, and from all your idols, will I cleanse you. A new heart,
> also, will I give you, and a new spirit will I put within you, and I will take away
> the stony heart out of your flesh, and I will give you a heart of flesh. And I will put
> My spirit within you, and cause you to walk in My statutes, and ye shall keep My
> judgments, and do them. And ye shall dwell in the in the land that I gave to your
> fathers; and ye shall be My people, and I will be your God."

Here, how positively stated is the purposed fact of their restoration. But
this restoration can not be the return from the captivity in Babylon; for,
besides that it takes place "out of all countries," instead of only one, it is
attended with the converting power of the Holy Spirit, giving new hearts to
the restored ones, and causing them to walk in all obedience to God; blessings of the Spirit, which were *not* fulfilled in the return from Babylon. Nor
is it the setting forth, whether typically, symbolically, or other wise, of the
conversion of the Gentiles and their restoration from Satan to God, or the
establishment of the Christian church among the Gentiles and its spiritual
prosperity; for it is expressly "the *house* of Israel" whom God here addresses,
and the land to which restoration is effected is identically that which "God
gave to the fathers" of that house, a land which, as God goes on to say in
the subsequent verses, has been "waste and desolate," and filled with "ruined

cities," but which is now to be tilled," and to abound in "corn, and the fruit of the tree, and the increase of the field;" *literally* the land of Israel, then, and not typically or symbolically something else. Thus the regathering of Israel spoken of in this passage can possibly refer only to the literal Israel, and to their restoration to Palestine. And since, as we have seen, it did not take place at the return of Babylon, by the same token, there never having been any other restoration of that people, it has, as yet, never taken place at all. It is yet in the future. Ezekiel 37:15-22:

> The Word of the Lord came again unto me, saying: Moreover, thou son of man take thee one stick, and write upon it, for Judah and for the children of Israel his companions; then take another stick and write upon it, For Joseph, the stick of Ephraim, and for all the house of Israel his companions; and join them one to another, into one stick, and they shall become one in thine hand. And when the children of thy people shall speak unto thee, saying, Wilt thou not show us what thou meanest by these? Say unto them: Thus saith the Lord God, Behold, I will take the stick of Joseph, which is in the hand of Ephraim, and the tribes of Israel his fellows, and will put them with him, even with the stick of Judah, and make them one stick, and they shall be one in mine hand. And the sticks whereon thou writest shall be in thine hand before their eyes. And say unto them, Thus saith the Lord God, Behold, I will take the children of Israel from among the heathen, whither they be gone, and will gather them on every side, and bring them into their own land; and I will make them one nation in the land, upon the mountains of Israel; and one king shall be king to them all; and there shall be no more two nations, neither shall they be divided into two kingdoms any more at all.

Anything more conclusive than this it is not possible to put into language, or even to conceive of: Both divisions of Israel are expressly mentioned, Judah and his companions, and Ephraim and his companions; they shall be taken "from among the heathen (the nations)" and be gathered "on every side" (out of all nations); they shall be "brought into their own land, the land upon the mountains of Israel," and in that land the two divisions shall be made "one nation," and never more shall they become "two nations," or be "divided into two kingdoms;" the reference being the rebellion of the ten tribes under Rehoboam, Solomon's successor, and their secession from his authority under Jeroboam. Reference to literal Israel could not be more demonstrated, nor the fact of their restoration to Palestine more positively stated; meanwhile the impressive effect of both the literalness and positiveness is made superlative, by means of a symbolism of the two sticks, bearing each the name of one of the two houses of Israel respectively, and joined together in the hand of the prophet.

And that this restoration is not the return from Babylon is beyond question, from what follows in the chapter; for God immediately proceeds to say, that, upon the occurring of this restoration of Israel to their own land, He will make a covenant of peace with them, an everlasting covenant with them, and "will set His sanctuary in the midst of them forevermore," and "they shall walk in His judgments, and observe His statutes," and "they shall dwell in the land that He has given unto Jacob, wherein their fathers have dwelt, they and their children, and their children's children forever;" none of which things were true of their going back from Babylon. Both houses of Israel are *yet to be* gathered out of all nations to their own land.

In the ninth chapter of the prophecy of Amos, at the ninth verse, the Lord says: "For lo, I will command and I will sift the house of Israel among all nations, like as corn is sifted in a sieve"—a vigorous description of their divinely inflicted dispersion, which, beginning so many ages ago, has continued to the present moment; "yet shall not the least grain fall upon the earth"—an equally vigorous description of their divinely wrought marvelous preservation as a people, although scattered through all nations during all those terrible ages of suffering. Now, for what purpose have they been so preserved? The Lord Himself answers, in the fourteenth verse, "And I will bring again the captivity of My people of Israel, and they shall build the waste cities, and inhabit them; and they shall plant vineyards, and drink the wine thereof; they shall also make gardens, and eat the fruit of them;" that is, He would preserve them in their national identity on purpose to return them to their national territory; to a land, their entrance into which would be His "bringing them again;" a land whose soil they should cultivate into vineyards and gardens, and whose grapes and vegetables they should enjoy; *literally* a land, then, and their own land; *Literally* the tribes of Jacob gathered back to where they had nationally dwelt long centuries before. Has this restoration of that people ever been effected? Nay, for the Lord continues: "And I will plant them upon their land, and they shall no more be pulled up out of their land which I have given them, saith the Lord thy God."

But their dispersion among the nations is a living experience before our eyes to-day; therefore, never did occur their restoration as spoken of in this passage from Amos; they have yet to be so planted in their land, as that they shall no more be pulled up out of it. The land is still waiting for them, and they are being kept of God for the land. So far we have but tasted of Old Testament teaching, on the point before us. Isaiah and Jeremiah are full of testimonies every whit as strong as the ones we have examined; and so are many others of the prophets.

But we now pass to the New Testament Scriptures, wherein is clearly recognized that there is yet to be a regathering of Israel to their own land; although consistently with the purpose and character of what we call the Christian dispensation, it is not so pervasively there as in the Old Testament. In Romans 9:4, 5, St. Paul, having mentioned the "Israelites," says that to them appertain "the adoption, and the covenants, and the promises, and the fathers." He expressly identifies the Israelites of whom he is speaking as "his kinsmen according to the flesh;" therefore, literal, national Israel.

Theirs is "the adoption," he says. But if their adoption or sonship as a people be only a past fact, having no influence for the yet future, how can it still be to them, as a people, a matter of privilege and blessing? Theirs are "the covenants," he says. But one of those covenants—is it not God's arrangement with Abraham to give to him and his seed "all the land of Canaan for an *everlasting* possession." (Gen 17.) Must they not, therefore, be reinstated in that land? Theirs are "the promises," he says. But what promises can belong to them as a distinct people, save such as those of which we have had a sample from the Old Testament? Theirs are "the fathers," he says. But what are Abraham, and Isaac, and Jacob to them as a people, if they, the descendants of those fathers are forever nationally defunct? So inevitably implied in St. Paul's enumeration of the privileges of his kinsmen according to the flesh is the prophetical fact of the gathering of them back to their own land.

In Romans 11:1, the Apostle exclaims, "I say, then, Hath God cast away His people? God forbid. For I, also, am an Israelite, of the seed of Abraham, of the tribe of Benjamin." That is, the literal, national Israel are God's ancient people; and *as such*, He has not cast them away. In Luke 21:24, Jesus said: "They shall be led away captive into all nations; and Jerusalem shall be trodden down of the Gentiles until the times of the Gentiles be fulfilled." When this fulfillment of the times shall have taken place, then shall Jerusalem be no longer trodden down; it shall be in the possession of its ancient owners, even of those who have been led away captive into all nations. And did not the Lord Jesus advert to the same prophetical fact, when He said to His apostles (Matt 19:28), "In the regeneration, when the Son of Man shall sit in the throne of His glory, ye shall also sit upon twelve thrones, judging the twelve tribes of Israel!" For how shall the apostles rule over the twelve tribes if as twelve tribes, they shall then have no existence, or if they be not gathered together as a nationality?

Let these instances suffice, as regards the New Testament, for the prophetical fact of Israel's yet future restoration. Other citations might be given, especially almost the whole of one entire book, the great prophetical Apocalypse, in which this fact is the underlying element, the very centre around which revolve its terrors and its grandeurs. As, however, I shall have occasion to refer to that book in another part of our subject, I here conclude the direct argument for the general fact. Limited though our selections of proof have been, they yet are ample. Undeniably, both houses of Israel, as one nationality, shall yet be re-established in Palestine, the land of their ancient inheritance. Moreover, the argument for the fact will be continually expanding and strengthening, while we shall be considering the predicted circumstances of the fact.

II. The gathering of Israel will be accomplished in two installments.

1. One movement in the process of their restoration will have taken place previously to the Lord's Second Coming.

"Behold," saith God, in Zechariah (14), "the day of the Lord cometh. For I will gather all nations against Jerusalem to battle; and the city shall be taken, and half of the city shall go forth into captivity, and the residue of the people shall not be cut off from the city." Now, if Israel be not there, why are the nations there to fight against them for that it is Israel against whom this battle is waged is sufficiently suggested by the word "nations" designating the attacking party; in fact, however, the whole chapter is express as to the presence of Israel. But it is in connection with this battle that "the day of the Lord cometh." And the prophecy proceeds: "Then shall the Lord go forth, and fight against those nations. And His feet shall stand in that day upon the Mount of Olives, which is before Jerusalem on the east."

This is the Second Coming, and lo, Israel are already in their own land. Again (Zechariah 12): "Behold, I will make Jerusalem a cup of trembling unto all the people round about, when they shall be in the siege both against Judah and against Jerusalem." Here the presence of Judah is expressly noted; meanwhile, in the last verses of the chapter, others of Israel besides those of the tribes of Judah and Benjamin are mentioned as being present, as "the family of the house of Levi," and "the family of Shimei" (or, according to the reading of the Septuagint, "the family of Simeon."). Representatives of the ten tribes, also, are there. But when is it that God will make Jerusalem this cup of trembling to the nations? When (8) "the Lord shall defend the inhabitants of Jerusalem, and the house of David shall be as God, as the angel of the Lord before them;" when the house of David shall have as its chief representative, visibly present, the incarnate God, Christ in His second coming, who is David, the Eternal King.

Nor, as it would seem, will it be more than a very few years before the Lord's coming, that this restoration of Israel will have been effected. It is in the last of Daniel's Seventy Weeks that they are presented to our view as nationally established in their own land; and that seventieth week is the seven years immediately preceding the Advent. It must be borne in mind, however, that some several years may be required before the beginning of that last week, in order to their regular settlement as a State.[13]

2. But all Israel will not have been gathered back to their land before the Advent; a second and finally complete movement in their restoration will occur subsequently to that great event. (Isa 11:11, 12, 15, 16):

> And it shall come to pass in that day, that the Lord shall set his hand again the second time to recover the remnant of his people, which shall be left, from Assyria, and from Egypt, and from Pathros, and from Cush, and from Elam, and from Shinar, and from Hamath, and from the islands of the sea. And He shall set up an ensign for the nations, and shall assemble the outcasts of Israel, and gather together the dispersed of Judah from the four corners of the earth. ... And the Lord shall utterly destroy the tongue of the Egyptian sea; and with his mighty wind shall He shake His hand over the river, and shall smite it in the seven streams, and make men go over dry-shod. And there shall be a highway for the remnant of his people, which shall be left, from Assyria; like as it was to Israel in the day that he came up out of the land of Egypt.

At what time is it appointed for this magnificent description of Israel's restoration to be realized? As we learn from the fourth verse, After the Lord with the breath of His lip shall have slain the Wicked One. Now from 2 Thess 2:8,

---

[13] The Futurist theory of the Apocalypse regards this Book [Daniel] as a "Book of the Time of the End"—the last world-week—i.e., the 70th of the 70 weeks of Daniel, the whole period between the First and Second Advents being a parenthesis between the 69th and 70th of these prophetic weeks. In this last week Israel's history is resumed for the final tribulation and glory. The Jew is the key to the Apocalypse. The first three and one half years of this world-week are occupied with the rise of Antichrist; the second three and one half with the fall of Antichrist. The albeit critical exposition of this theory is by *Kiefoth, Offenbarung*, Leipzig, 1874. See also Keil on Daniel, Clarks For. And Ev. Library, p. 337. The 1,000 years *follow* the Destruction of Antichrist. N.W. [N.W. is Nathaniel West, the editor of the book.]

we learn that "the Lord shall destroy that Wicked with the brightness of His coming." After the coming, then shall this restoration of Israel have place.

Again (Isa 66:20): "They shall bring all your brethren for an offering unto the Lord, out of all nations, upon horses, and in chariots, and in litters, and upon mules, and upon swift beasts, to my holy mountain, Jerusalem, saith the Lord."

When? After the Lord shall have "come with fire" (15), and after He shall have "pleaded by fire and by sword with all flesh, and the slain of the Lord shall be many" (16). Nay, the very persons who shall thus bring all Israel out of all nations, are those who escape the great destruction which the Lord at His coming shall inflict on the besieging armies around Jerusalem, and whom He will send on that errand back from Jerusalem to the nations (19). This recovery of Israel, then, is subsequent to the Advent. Thus there will be two distinct stages in the process of their gathering; the first, before the great Epiphany of the Lord Jesus; the second, after it; the first, partial; the second, complete. How utterly vain to attempt to make the passages which describe this second gathering apply to the return from the Babylonish captivity!

III. Particulars of the first gathering:

1. The number of them will be considerable.

This is indicated by the immense armies which Antichrist will bring together for the siege of Jerusalem (Joel 3:1, 2, 9, 14). But also Ezekiel describes the land as being, by reason of this first gathering back of the people, as a land of villages, and the people as having silver and gold, and cattle and goods (Ezek 38:11-13). See also Isa 2:7.

2. They will be gathered back in their unconverted state.

According to Zechariah 12:10, it will be only at the Lord's coming only in connection with "their looking upon Him whom they pierced," that "the spirit of grace and of supplications" shall be poured out upon them. Previous to the coming of the Lord, therefore, it will be still as rejecters of Christ and rebellious to God, that they will occupy their land. And it is as speaking of them at that very time, that Isaiah ascribes to them pride and haughtiness, the loftiness of the cedar of Lebanon, and the stiff sturdiness of the oak of Bashan (Isa 2:13).

3. They will have rebuilt their [Tribulation] temple and re-established their temple services: before the coming of the Lord.

For, according to the words of Jesus in the twenty-fourth of Matthew, they will "see the Son of Man coming in the clouds of Heaven with power and great glory," only after "the abomination of desolation," spoken of by Daniel the prophet, shall have stood "in the holy places."

4. The object of their gathering is ultimately their conversion, but primarily, their chastisement and suffering. In connection with the setting up of the abomination of desolation in the temple, Jesus said (Matthew 24):

> "Then shall be great tribulation, such as was not since the beginning of the world to this time, no, nor ever shall be." "Alas!" says God, in Jeremiah (30:7) "for that day is great, so that none is like it; it is even the time of Jacob's trouble." "Therefore thus saith the Lord God (Ezek 22:19-22), because ye are all become dross, behold, therefore, I will gather you into the midst of Jerusalem. As they gather silver, and brass, and iron, and lead, and tin, into the midst of the furnace, to blow the fire upon it, to melt it; so will I gather you in mine anger and in my fury, and I will leave you there and melt you. Yea, I will gather you, and blow upon you in the fire of my wrath, and ye shall be melted in the midst thereof. As silver is melted in the midst of the furnace, so shall ye be melted in the midst thereof; and ye shall know that I the Lord have poured out my fury upon you."

5. Their terrible sufferings, when ended, will have reduced them to a remnant.

"Except those days should be shortened," said Jesus (Matt 24), "there should no flesh (no Israelites) be saved; but for the elect's sake those days shall be shortened." Those elect ones will be but a remnant. Only "the third part shall be brought through the fire, and be refined as silver is refined." (Zech 13:9.) This elect remnant, spoken of so frequently by the prophets, is not to be confounded with "the remnant according to the election of grace," spoken of in Romans 11:5. That elect remnant consists of all those individuals of Israel who have, or will have, believed in Christ, during our Christian dispensation, and who, in company with all believers from among the nations, will constitute, together with the true people of God in Old Testament times, the church of the glorified at the time of the Lord's coming.

But the elect remnant with whom we now have to do is the comparatively few of Israel who will have survived, in their own land, the terrors of the great day. They are identical with the "hundred and forty and four thousand sealed" ones of the seventh of the Revelation. For those sealed ones are all Israelites, it being expressly said that they are taken from among "the tribes of the children of Israel and, besides, the twelve tribes being all enumerated by their names, as "the tribe of Judah," "the tribe of Reuben," "the tribe of Gad," etc. If that is not a description of the literal Israel, then is there no way of certainly identifying them at all?

I stop not to discuss whether the number of the sealed is to be interpreted literally or symbolically, but, however interpreted, that there are only twelve thousand out of each tribe presents the idea of a *remnant*. And, as it is said they are sealed, in whatever way the sealing may be done, on purpose that they shall be discriminated from others, and so be preserved through the judgments of the awful day; be brought to the end of and beyond those fiery sufferings of their people and themselves on the occasion of the Lord's Advent. Thus they are precisely the elect remnant of whom the Old Testament so often speaks. And preserved they will have been, when the dread grandeurs of that Epiphany from heaven shall have passed. There they stand in their Divine deliverance, God's chosen Israel, a wondrous company.

6. And now comes to pass their conversion to God.

They will have witnessed the terrors of the reign of Antichrist, will have seen the plagues of the Revelation poured out upon the nations under his control, will have beheld the heavens darkened, the Lord descend in glory, the graves open, the saints taken, the Day of the Lord come upon Jerusalem, the heavens and the earth shaken. They will see, and yet find themselves protected through all these things." [B. W. Newton] "They will look on Him whom they have pierced." God will pour upon them "the spirit of grace and supplications;" they shall mourn for their sins; and "there shall be a fountain opened to them for sin and for uncleanness." They will believe on the Lord Jesus Christ, and they shall be forgiven; and not forgiven only, but accepted in all the preciousness of that Name which they and their nation had rejected and abhorred.

IV. Particulars of the gathering subsequent to the Advent:

1. It will be effected by both human and divine agency.

Partly by human. (Isa 49:22, 23; 66:19, 20.) Partly by Divine. (Isa 11:15, 16.) In this latter circumstance it will contrast with the first gathering, for it is the unvarying implication of Scripture that Israel's recovery before the Advent will come about in a natural and ordinary way. As has been said by a late writer (Molyneux), "Israel[14] will be parceled out of the world's map, by common consent, for the occupation of its ancient possessors. The conviction of its expediency, and the stroke of a pen, on the part of one or two of the leading Continental powers, and the deed would be done." Even now we may almost speak of England's protectorate of the Holy Land. God's providence is moving apace, and evidently is rapidly nearing the crisis of Israel's first recovery. But their second restoration will be effected as well by miracle as by human agency.

2. In this second gathering, as in the first, returning Israel will as yet be unconverted (Ezek 36:24-38.)

3. Immediately upon their restoration, however, they will be converted.
    See Ezekiel as above. Also the Better Covenant (Jer 31:31-34.) "And so," exclaims Paul, "all Israel shall be saved." Then it is that that glorious anthem, the twelfth of Isaiah, will peal from the lips of an entirely converted nation.

4. And Israel's land in that day shall answer back to the gospel holiness of its inhabitants.
    In extent it will be according to the covenant with Abraham (Gen 15:18), wherein the Lord said, "Unto thy seed have I given this land, from the river of Egypt unto the great river, the river Euphrates." As to fertility and beauty, "The wilderness and solitary place shall be glad for them, and the desert shall rejoice and blossom as the rose. It shall blossom abundantly, and rejoice even with joy and singing. In the wilderness shall waters break out, and streams in the desert." (Isa 35.) "Instead of the thorn shall come up the fir tree, and instead of the brier shall come up the myrtle tree." (Isa 55.) "The mountains shall drop down new wine, and the hills shall flow with milk, and all the rivers of Judah shall flow with waters, and a fountain shall come forth of the house of the Lord, and shall water the Valley of Shittim." (Joel 3:18.) "The plowman shall overtake the reaper, and the treader of grapes him that soweth seed." (Amos 9:13.)
    As to universal harmony: "The wolf, also, shall dwell with the lamb, and the leopard shall lie down with the kid, and the calf, and the young lion, and the fatling together; and a little child shall lead them. And the cow and the bear shall feed, their young ones shall lie down together; and the lion shall eat straw like the ox. And the sucking child shall play on the hole of the asp, and

---

[14] The original text reads "India," but this is almost certainly a misspelling.

the weaned child shall put his hand on the cockatrice's den. They shall not hurt nor destroy in all my holy mountain; for the earth (land?) shall be full of the knowledge of the Lord, as the waters cover the sea." (Isa 11:6-9.) And as to duration, God said to Abraham, "I will give to thee and to thy seed after thee all the land of Canaan, for an everlasting possession." (Gen 17:8.) "Thou shalt no more be termed Forsaken," says God to the holy inhabitants, "neither shall thy land any more be termed Desolate; but thou shalt be called Hephzibah, and thy land Beulah; for the Lord delighteth in thee, and thy land shall be married." (Isa 62:4.)

5. The spiritual blessings of millennial Israel will be the same as are ours now.

They will be sons of God (Hosea 1:10); so are all Christians now. They will be under the mediatorship—sacrifice and priesthood—of the New Covenant (Jer 31:31; Heb 8:6); so are we. They will please God, and therefore must have been brought into living union with Christ, through the Spirit, even as we, for "they that are in the flesh (unregenerate) can not please God." (Rom 8:8.) They will say to Him, "The Lord our righteousness" (Jer 23:6); so do we. They will be raised in His likeness, at the last resurrection, in virtue of being in Him; we shall similarly be raised at the first resurrection, in virtue of being in Him. (1 Cor 15.) At the same time, however, the imprisonment of Satan and his angels, the presence of the visible glory of Christ and His saints, His investiture with the sovereignty of earth, the release of creation from its groan, the outpouring of the Holy Spirit upon all flesh, these and other like things will give to the millennial age a glorious difference and superiority, as contrasted with our present age.

6. Great and exalted will be millennial Israel's position and influence in the earth.

"And thou, O tower of the flock, the strong hold of the daughter of Zion, unto thee shall it come, even the first dominion; the Kingdom shall come to the daughter of Jerusalem." (Micah 4:8.) "Thou shalt also be a crown of glory in the hand of the Lord, and a royal diadem in the hand of thy God." (Isa 62:3.) "At that time they shall call Jerusalem the Throne of the Lord, and all the nations shall be gathered unto it, to the name of the Lord, to Jerusalem." (Jer 3:17) "Out of Zion shall go forth the law, and the word of the Lord from Jerusalem." (Isa 2:3) "He shall cause them that come of Jacob to take root: Israel shall blossom and bud, and fill the face of the world with fruit." (Isa 27:6). The children of Jerusalem shall be made princes in all the earth (Ps 45:16), and the nations shall at last be regulated according to God.

I have said nothing of the relations of millennial Israel to the Church of the glorified. But I must close. What a vast subject we have been surveying, yet only as by lightning glances! How strong the proof, from God's Holy Word, of these gatherings of Israel! And have we not confirmation superabounding, in the miraculous preservation of that people through well-nigh a score of centuries of transcendent sufferings?

Can the world show anything like it? Twice 1,800 years old, they saw the proud Egyptian perish in the waters of the Red Sea; they heard the fall of great Babylon's power; they witnessed the ruins of the Syro-Macedonian conquests. And now they have outlived the Caesars, and outlived the dark ages. They have been through all civilizations, shared in all convulsions, and have kept pace with the entire progress of discovery and art. And here they stand to-day as distinct as ever, occupying no country of their own, scattered through all countries, identical in their immemorial physiognomy, earth's men of destiny, before the venerableness of whose pedigree the proudest scutcheons of mankind are but as trifles of yesterday.

But have they suffered severely? One convulsive groan of agony breathing through eighteen centuries, and heard in every land but our own. At the siege of Jerusalem by Titus, besides the tens of thousands led into captivity, it was as if in a single action of a great war the slain on one side should amount to 1,300,000; and when, the remaining Jews having been expelled from their country, they attempted, sixty years afterward, to return, a half million more were slaughtered. For centuries they were forbidden, on pain of death, even to set foot in Jerusalem. Under King John of England, 1,500 were massacred at York in one day. Under Ferdinand and Isabella 800,000, by a single decree, were forced out to sea in boats, and the most of them perished in the waves. They have been fined and fleeced by almost every government known to history. They have been banished from place to place; banished and recalled, and banished again.

By the Code of Justinian, they were incapable of executing wills, of testifying in courts of justice, of having social and public worship. The Koran of Mahomet stigmatized them as wild dogs; the Romish Church excommunicated any one who held intercourse with them; the Greek Church uttered anathemas still more severe. They have been forced to dissemble to save their lives, and in Spain and Portugal have even become bishops, and have governed in convents. In the prophetic words of the Old Testament, they have been "a reproach and a proverb, a taunt and a curse;" they have been "taken up in the lips of talkers," and have been "an infamy of the people;" and the general estimate of them has ripened into the intense contempt of that dramatic conception—Shylock, the Jew of Venice. And now in this nineteenth century they are a suffering people still, but still as indissoluble as ever.

But now all this is not according to the established course of nations. The northern tribes came into Southern Europe, and are now not at all distinguishable. No Englishman can say that he derives from the Britons and not from the Romans, or from the Saxons and not from the Normans. On the contrary, the Jew is a Jew still. Even our own all-appropriating country, which denationalizes Germans, Irish, French, Spaniards, Finns, Swedes, has left untouched this wondrous people. Here they are, holding fast to that one tell-tale face, keeping up the sacred learning of their traditions, self-conscious in their isolation, irrepressible in their love of Jerusalem, sublime in their singular patriotism, evermore looking and longing for their Messiah, the same intense individuality as when, lord of the soil, He plucked His olives from the trees of Judea.

And, what is more, these world wanderers of the centuries, these tribes of the weary foot, have not only survived, but have now risen again as an element of power among mankind. The Jew is the broker of the world; he is among the foremost, whether in science, or literature, or government. In witchery of song unsurpassed, he enchants the world with some of the sweetest music it ever heard. Surely he is the standing miracle of the world's current history; the bush of Moses, ever burning, yet never consumed; an ocular demonstration of how God may energize the secret springs of a people's life, yet without disturbing individual freedom or social characteristics; an unanswerable refutation of that godless philosophy which would turn the Almighty out of His own universe. As for what have they thus been borne in the hands of God, all along the ages? Beyond a peradventure, if so literally have been fulfilled the prophecies which foretold their sufferings and their preservation, equally sure are the predicted grandeurs of their future.

But let us not take leave of our subject without making application of these two thoughts. First, it will be, as we have seen, their own true faith in the cleansing blood of Christ that shall open to them the golden gates of their millennial nationality. On what a flood of illustration is thus brought to our own hearts the exact truth of that Scripture, "He that believeth shall be saved, he that believeth not shall be damned." Have we now that faith?

Secondly, pray for the peace of Jerusalem. "For if the casting away of them be the reconciling of the world, what shall the receiving of them be but life from the dead?" (Rom 11:15); life from the dead in the resurrection bodies of the saints, since then shall occur the first resurrection (Isa 25:8, and 1 Cor 15:54), and life from the dead in the spiritual quickening of the nations. Oh, this restoration of Israel is the very centre of God's gracious purposes concerning the world. "For Zion's sake will He not hold His peace, and for Jerusalem's sake He will not rest, until the righteousness thereof go forth as brightness, and the salvation thereof as a lamp that burneth." Therefore, "Ye that make mention of the Lord, keep not silence, and give Him no rest till He establisheth, and till He make Jerusalem a praise in the earth" (Isa 62:1, 6, 7).

11

"IN THIS WAY, ALL
ISRAEL WILL BE SAVED"

Stephen Davey

Israel's survival through the millennia is impressive. Israel, as a people, has lasted thirty-five hundred years. We know when the nation began, why, and through whom. We have detailed written records of her ancient and modern history. Her language remains essentially the same, as do her religion, her traditions, her homeland, and her bloodline. The people still follow, though imperfectly, the original documents that outlined their faith—the Torah—the Old Testament law.

In light of the nation's history, that survival can be described only as miraculous. Israel has survived and even thrived. Yet throughout history no nation has been so robbed, so deported, so murdered, so hated. In 722 BC Israel's northern kingdom was decimated by the Assyrians, and the people were carried into captivity. In 586 BC, Jerusalem, the capital of the southern kingdom, was destroyed by the Babylonians, and the people were deported. Yet in 538–432 BC, groups of Jewish exiles returned like homing birds to rebuild Jerusalem. In AD 70 the nation again was destroyed, Jerusalem was razed, and much of the population fled.

For the next 1800 years they were scattered throughout Europe and Asia, where they faced periodic persecution. Meanwhile their homeland became the scene of hundreds of years of conflict, as Turks, Muslims, and Western powers ruled the land. Then, in the 1940s the Holocaust resulted in the deaths of millions of European Jews. Yet, amazingly, in 1948 the Zionist movement reestablished Israel as a nation in the original homeland, and in 1967 the Israelis regained control of Jerusalem, except for the Temple Mount. Today Israel is a thriving nation, though it is persistently threatened, attacked, and pressured.

Why has Israel survived despite four thousand years of war and destruction and deportation and genocide and persecution? The answer is simple. God said they would! Through His prophet Jeremiah, the Lord declares, "If the heavens above can be measured, and the foundations of the earth below can be explored, then I will cast off all the offspring of Israel for all that they have done" (Jer 31:37). In other words, until the universe is mapped and the center of the earth is explored, Israel will not cease to be a nation.

But we are dismayed at what ancient Israel did. They did not just kill the prophets; they called for the death of *The Prophet!* They did not just reject God's messengers; they rejected the Messiah! Surely, it would seem, God must be through with Israel. Indeed, in Romans 10:21, Paul notes that God says, "All day long I have held out my hands to a disobedient and contrary people." Clearly, the question remains: Since Israel rejected the Messiah, is God finished with Israel? This is the very question that opens chapter 11 of Romans.

THE PROMISE OF GOD TO ISRAEL
Romans 11:1-6

I ask, then, has God rejected his people? By no means! For I myself am an Israelite, a descendant of Abraham, a member of the tribe of Benjamin.[2] God has not rejected his people whom he foreknew. Do you not know what the Scripture says of Elijah, how he appeals to God against Israel? [3] "Lord, they have killed your prophets, they have demolished your altars, and I alone am left, and they seek my life." [4] But what is God's reply to him? "I have kept for myself seven thousand men who have not bowed the knee to Baal." [5] So too at the present time there is a remnant, chosen by grace. [6] But if it is by grace, it is no longer on the basis of works; otherwise grace would no longer be grace (Rom 11:1-6)

Paul anticipates this question and clearly spells it out: "I ask, then, has God rejected his people?" And he answers his own question: "By no means!" (Rom 11:1). Is God through with the nation Israel? Does the nation and her blessing and covenants experience a spiritualized makeover that is applied to the church? Is there to be no literal throne in Jerusalem? Is there no literal restoration of national Israel in their homeland? Here is the short answer: All these covenant promises to Israel will be fulfilled literally. Why? Because God said they will. John MacArthur writes,

> Contrary to what some sincere Christians maintain, God cannot be finished with the nation of Israel—for the obvious reason that all of His promises to her have not yet been fulfilled. If God were through with His chosen nation, His Word would be false, and His integrity discredited. Among those who most strongly insist that God is through with the nation of Israel are those whose theology is commonly referred to as covenant theology, which is ironic because they cannot escape the implication that God is not faithful to fully honoring His covenants.[1]

In other words, non-dispensational theologians view God as choosing *not* to literally honor His *covenants*. Israel is morphed into the church, and in covenant theology, circumcision is spiritualized into infant baptism, and the Old Covenant feasts are spiritualized into the Lord's Supper. Romans 11 should forever "turn us away from the presumptuous assertions of those who would teach that God is 'through with national Israel,'—that it has no future as an elect nation."[2]

Again, Paul asks in Romans 11:1: "I ask, then, has God rejected his people?" The antecedent of "His people" is found in the previous paragraph—it is the people of Israel. Paul builds his case to his climactic statement, "all Israel will be saved" (v. 26). The word translated "rejected" is *apotheo* (ἀπωθέω), which means to cast aside, or discard. Paul is asking: "God has not discarded the nation, has He?" His answer: "By no means!" God forbid! That is impossible!

This truth certainly has significance for Israel and our understanding of the future. But it also has very practical significance to every believer in Christ. If God does not literally keep His word to His chosen nation, how can we know He will keep His word to us? If God ever takes back even one tiny part of His covenant with Israel, we are all in deep trouble, in more ways than we can count. God *cannot* keep only some of His promises. God *cannot* be partially reliable. If God changes His mind about Israel's homeland, maybe He will change His mind about our heaven! Paul's answer is powerful: "By no means!" There is no way! The future of Israel is rooted in the honesty of God.

---

[1] John MacArthur Jr., *Romans*, vol. 2 (Chicago: Moody, 1994), 92.

[2] William R. Newell, *Romans* (Chicago: Moody, 1938), 410.

Paul's Personal Testimony

Paul next provides two evidences that Israel is not a castaway nation. The first piece of evidence is found in Paul's own testimony. The apostle essentially says, "God hasn't cast Israel aside—look, He chose me!" "For I myself am an Israelite, a descendant of Abraham, a member of the tribe of Benjamin. God has not rejected his people whom he foreknew" (Rom 11:1*b*–2*a*). In other words, "If God decided to get rid of the Israelites after they rejected the Messiah, why would He choose an Israelite like me to be his apostle?"

As exhibit A, Paul points to three things about himself. First, he declares, "For I myself am an Israelite." Interestingly, he does not say, "I am a Jew" or "I am a Hebrew," using either of the other two names for God's chosen people. "Hebrew" is probably derived from "Eber" in Genesis 10:21. "Jew" is a name derived from "Judah," the most prominent of Israel's twelve tribes. "Israelite" comes from Father Jacob, who was renamed Israel by God. This is the covenant name of the people, signifying their unique relationship with God. Michael Vlach asserts,

> It is not coincidental that all of Paul's uses of "Israel" or "Israelite" occur in Romans 9-11, when outside of these chapters in Romans he uses "Jew(s)." While the designation "Jew" comes from the single tribe of Judah, without excluding the other tribes, the title "Israel" often carries national implications and emphasizes the broader twelve tribes of Israel stemming from Jacob (i.e., "Israel").[3]

"Israelite" is the term Paul uses here, as if to say, "Listen, God hasn't rejected His covenant with Israel—look at me! God did not reject me, and I am an Israelite." Moreover, Paul was "a descendant of Abraham." Abraham, of course, was the father of all Israelites and the one to whom God delivered His covenant. Furthermore, Paul explains that he is "a member of the tribe of Benjamin." Paul was a direct descendant of Jacob's son Benjamin, the only son born in the Land of Promise. It is as if Paul were reminding his readers that there was nobody more connected to the covenant than he was. This is Paul's personal testimony: "You can't get any more Jewish than I am … any more Hebrew than I am … any more Israelite than I am! But God did not reject me … He saved me! And I was saved by grace."

---

[3] Michael Vlach, "A Non-Typological Future-Mass-Conversion View," in *Three Views on Israel and the Church*, ed Jared Compton and Andrew David Naselli (Grand Rapids: Kregel Academic, 2018), 26.

Israel's Continual Rebellion

In verse 2 Paul urges his readers to remember "what the Scripture says of Elijah, how he appeals to God against Israel?" Yes, Elijah was praying *against* Israel. He was tired of the nation's disobedience and idolatry. He was weary of Ahab, the faithless king of Israel, and Jezebel, his wicked wife. And so he poured out his heart to God: "Lord, they have killed your prophets, they have demolished your altars, and I alone am left, and they seek my life" (v. 3). We can hear the pain in his voice. He was alone in the wilderness—depressed, defeated, afraid. Yes, he had just come from Mount Carmel, where the fire of God fell from heaven and consumed his sacrifice. Yes, the false prophets of Baal had been humiliated and later executed. Yes, the people had shouted until they were hoarse, "The Lord He is God, the Lord He is God." Yes, rain had fallen after three years, in answer to Elijah's prayer. But instead of a national revival, there was continued rebellion. Jezebel even tried to kill Elijah, God's prophet. It was a horrible time in Israel. God gave Elijah some encouragement by telling him that there were seven thousand men in Israel who had not bowed the knee to Baal. But seven thousand was still a small percentage of the nation's population. God certainly would have been justified in abandoning Israel, but He did not.

So, Paul ties up all the evidence with this summary statement: "So too at the present time there is a remnant, chosen by grace. But if it is by grace, it is no longer on the basis of works; otherwise grace would no longer be grace" (vv.5–6). Israel had a long history of disobedience, but God's promise was on the basis of His grace, not Israel's works. And His promise cannot be annulled.

THE FAILURE OF ISRAEL AND ITS RESULTS

Romans 11:7–24

While Israel's failure does not derail God's ultimate plan for the nation, the apostle is not blind to that failure. In fact, he presents a lengthy explanation of Israel's failure and its results. Verses 7–24 form a bridge between the promise of God presented in verses 1–6 and the fulfillment of that promise described in verses 24–27. While the emphasis in this middle section is more on Israel's present circumstances and God's reason for them, there are several statements that reinforce God's future plan for the people.

Consequences for Israel (Romans 11:7-10)

[7] What then? Israel failed to obtain what it was seeking. The elect obtained it, but the rest were hardened, [8] as it is written, "God gave them a spirit of stupor, eyes that would not see and ears that would not hear, down to this very day." [9] And David says, "Let their table become a snare and a trap, a stumbling block and a retribution for them; [10] let their eyes be darkened so that they cannot see, and bend their backs forever" (Rom 11:7-10).

The Prognosis

The last word in verse 7 points to the condition of Israel's heart, as a nation. The Greek word translated "hardened" is *poroō* (πωρόω), which means to cover with a thick skin, to harden by covering with a callous.[4] The Greek word gives us our English medical word, *porosis* as in *osteoporosis*—the formation of bone around joints. In the Greek culture, it was used of a callous, a growth on the skin on some part of the body that is hardened or roughened up with use. A callous causes a part of the body to lose feeling and become insensitive. The divine Physician determined that the nation of Israel, among other things, has a *porosis* of the heart—a calloused heart. It is a terminal condition that will require a heart transplant if the nation is to survive.

The Symptoms

Symptom number one of the hardened heart is *"a spirit of stupor"* (v. 8). The quotation is taken from the prophet Isaiah, who writes, "For the Lord has poured out upon you a spirit of deep sleep, and has closed your eyes (the prophets), and covered your heads (the seers)" (Isa 29:10). In other words, Israel, "you do not know which way to turn. You are confused by your own spiritual wandering and speculation and disobedience." One of the marks of the unbelieving nation was a loss of spiritual direction and thus spiritual wandering. Isaiah spoke of the prophets and the seers of Israel losing their connection with the God of Israel, so that they began wandering around as if they were under the influence of wine and beer (Isa 29:9), staggering from one day to the next without any true spiritual direction.

---

[4] Cleon L. Rogers, Jr., and Cleon L. Rogers III, *The New Linguistic and Exegetical Key to the Greek New Testament* (Grand Rapids: Zondervan, 1998), 336.

Symptom number two of a hardened heart against the gospel of grace is *eyes that would not see*" (v. 8). This describes a loss of spiritual discernment. Paul quotes another Old Testament passage here, Deuteronomy 29:4, which refers to spiritual blindness, or the inability to discern truth from error. Other Scriptures speak clearly of the willful blindness of the Jewish nation.[5] In the New Testament, Christ referred to Israel's stubborn and tragic rebellion against Him and His kingdom: "O Jerusalem, Jerusalem, the city that kills the prophets and stones those who are sent to it! How often would I have gathered your children together as a hen gathers her brood under her wings, and you were not willing!" (Luke 13:34). The apostle John announced in the first chapter of his gospel, "The true light, which gives light to everyone, was coming into the world" (John 1:9). "Gives light" translates the Greek word *photizō* (φωτίζω), from which we get our word "photo." It means to shed light, either to reveal or to expose. So Christ, on the one hand, came to reveal God, for in Christ all the fullness of deity was embodied (Col 2:9). But sadly, the nation rejected the light. "He came to his own, and his own people did not receive him" (John 1:11). Thus, the light exposed the wickedness of the unbelief of the nation. "And this is the judgment: the light has come into the world, and people loved the darkness rather than the light because their works were evil. For everyone who does wicked things hates the light and does not come to the light, lest his works should be exposed" (John 3:19-20).

A third symptom of the callousness of the nation is a *loss of spiritual awareness*. Paul said of Israel that God had given them "ears that would not hear, down to this very day" (Rom 11:8). In a sermon Jesus preached to a Jewish audience, the Lord quoted from the same passages in Isaiah and Deuteronomy that Paul quotes in Romans 11, thus combining the ideas of loss of spiritual discernment and spiritual awareness.

"You will indeed hear but never understand, and you will indeed see but never perceive. For this people's heart has grown dull, and with their ears they can barely hear, and their eyes they have closed, lest they should see with their eyes and hear with their ears and understand with their heart and turn, and I would heal them. But blessed are your eyes, for they see, and your ears, for they hear" (Matt 13:14-16).

---

[5] This is the condition of all the unbelieving world, not just Israel (cf. 1 Cor 2:14).

In other words, unbelievers want to stay in the dark. Since their deeds are evil, they do not want them exposed to the light. They do not want to hear the truth or see the truth.

The Jews felt secure because they had the Law, the Prophets, and the Writings. But Paul quotes from all three in this paragraph. He quotes from the *prophet* Isaiah in Romans 11:8*a*. He quotes from the *law* book of Deuteronomy in verse 8*b*. And he quotes from the *writings* of one of David's psalms in verse 9. All three parts of the Jewish sacred Scriptures condemn Israel's decision to reject the grace of God through Jesus Christ.

The Warnings

Paul next quotes another Old Testament passage, again from the Psalms:

> And David says, "Let their table become a snare and a trap, a stumbling block and a retribution for them; let their eyes be darkened so that they cannot see, and bend their backs forever" (Rom 11:9-10; cf. Ps 69:22-23).

These verses give strong words of warning: snare—trap—stumbling block—retribution. The people trusted in their "table." This is perhaps a reference to their sacred feasts—their rituals, their Passover, their table of showbread, and their confidence that God would continue to "prepare a table before me in the presence of my enemies" (Ps 23:5). But the table had become a stumbling block, keeping them from seeing the truth of Jesus Christ. And the warnings take us from eyes that will not see (v. 8) to eyes that "cannot see" (v. 10). That's the condition of a hardened heart. It moves from "I will not believe" to "I cannot believe." The consequences of Israel's disobedience are grave. We might think that the story of Israel ended. But there is still hope, and that hope rests in the gracious promise of God.

God's Purposes for Israel (Romans 11:11–15)

Paul's argument takes a turn in this section of his analysis. Paul makes it clear that though the nation of Israel is being spiritually judged, the fall of Israel is not final.

> [11] So I ask, did they stumble in order that they might fall? By no means! Rather, through their trespass salvation has come to the Gentiles, so as to make Israel

jealous. [12] Now if their trespass means riches for the world, and if their failure means riches for the Gentiles, how much more will their full inclusion mean! [13] Now I am speaking to you Gentiles. Inasmuch then as I am an apostle to the Gentiles, I magnify my ministry [14] in order somehow to make my fellow Jews jealous, and thus save some of them. [15] For if their rejection means the reconciliation of the world, what will their acceptance mean but life from the dead? (Rom 11:11-15).

Paul's point is stated clearly in verse 11: "So I ask, did they stumble in order that they might fall? By no means!" Here, as in verse 1, Paul makes it clear the fall of Israel is not *final*. Their disobedience does not destroy their covenant with God, and all the literal promises to them are not transferred to the church. These literal promises still belong to a literal Israel. The present hardening of Israel is temporary, as verse 25 will assert.

But before he comes to this conclusion, Paul explains what God intends to do during this temporary setting aside of Israel in the dispensation of the church age (11-15). When Israel returns to God, it will be like the prodigal son who returned to his father, and the father said, "For this my son was dead, and is alive again" (Luke 15:24; cf. Ezek 37:11-14). Until then, however, through the current, temporary setting aside of Israel, God is accomplishing two purposes.

First, *salvation is being proclaimed to Gentile nations by means of the church.* The church, composed of Jews and Gentiles on equal status, is now the conduit of God's redemption for the nations. Second, *jealousy is being provoked in the Israelite nation because of the church.* The concept of jealousy, or desire, is not always negative. While it can mean a form of envy in wanting something that others have, it can also refer to desire for the good. Paul used another form of this word to encourage believers to earnestly long for spiritual gifts that will edify the body of Christ (1 Cor 12:31; 14:1). So the Jew will earnestly long for what he sees in the lives of believers—things like personal communion with God, freedom from the guilt of sin, and assurance of eternal heaven, just to name a few of our riches that Paul implies in Romans 11:12.

We know that during the Tribulation period millions of Jews will be saved, and the leading evangelists will be 144,000 Jews who blaze a trail for the gospel with a fruitful ministry that will reap an amazing harvest among the nations (Rev 7; Zech 13:9). As in the early church, Jews will be leading Jews and Gentiles to Christ. It is little wonder why Satan and his kingdom continue to launch violent attacks on the Jewish people. The Jews are clearly part of

God's future kingdom plan. The Middle East continues to produce violent and unending anti-Semitism. And there is a rising tide of anti-Semitism in Europe and America. It is all satanically inspired.

Yet, why would Satan bother with the Jews if God has set them aside permanently because they rejected their Messiah and transferred all their blessings to the church in some spiritual way? Why bother persecuting the Jews? Why the worldwide revulsion for this people group? The devil evidently understands *literally* God's promise of the land to the Jewish people; thus, he has fought it for centuries and continues to do so to this day. He evidently takes seriously Christ's promise to the Jews to one day rule in a future, literal kingdom. We know from Scripture that the devil will mount a worldwide attempt to keep it from happening during the Tribulation (Rev 19:19).

One of the greatest proofs God is not finished with Israel as a nation is the unnatural hatred for the Jewish people and the demonically inspired attempts throughout modern history to wipe them from the face of the earth. But God will keep His word to Israel.

The Family Tree (Romans 11:16–24)

An extended metaphor further explains his rationale.

[16] If the dough offered as firstfruits is holy, so is the whole lump, and if the root is holy, so are the branches. [17] But if some of the branches were broken off, and you, although a wild olive shoot, were grafted in among the others and now share in the nourishing root of the olive tree, [18] do not be arrogant toward the branches. If you are, remember it is not you who support the root, but the root that supports you. [19] Then you will say, "Branches were broken off so that I might be grafted in." [20] That is true. They were broken off because of their unbelief, but you stand fast through faith. So do not become proud, but fear. [21] For if God did not spare the natural branches, neither will he spare you. [22] Note then the kindness and the severity of God: severity toward those who have fallen, but God's kindness to you, provided you continue in his kindness. Otherwise you too will be cut off. [23] And even they, if they do not continue in their unbelief, will be grafted in, for God has the power to graft them in again. [24] For if you were cut from what is by nature a wild olive tree, and grafted, contrary to nature, into a cultivated olive tree, how much more will these, the natural branches, be grafted back into their own olive tree (Rom 11:16–24).

Paul employs four metaphors from nature in this section of the chapter to explain the relationship between Israel and the church.

1. The first fruits, or first piece of dough, and the root of the tree are Abraham.

In verse 16 Paul refers to the lump of dough, or the first fruits, as holy. The Jews immediately would have recognized this as a reference to the offering of first fruits in which the priest took some of the dough from the larger lump and offered it to God. Paul was making the point that if the lump offered to God was acceptable, the rest would naturally be accepted as well. The first fruit was Abraham, the father of the Jewish nation, and he was accepted before God by grace. Thus it was natural to consider his descendants to be accepted before God as well.[6] Unfortunately, the metaphor also delivers the news that some of Abraham's descendants were cut off by their unbelief. Still, God promised that Abraham's descendants would bring forth the Redeemer—the One in whom all the nations of the world would be blessed (Gen 12:1–3; 22:17–18). So, the first fruits, or dough, and the root of the tree spell the beginning of that redemptive purpose.

2. The lump from which the dough came and the olive tree, which came from the root, represent the blessing of God.

Israel experienced this divine blessing in the former dispensation. In the present church-age, the divine blessing is experienced primarily by Gentiles (though also by many Jews who are in Christ). The olive tree is not the church, and it is not salvation. It represents the blessing of God through Abraham, which first went to the Jewish nation.[7] However, when the religious leaders led the nation to reject her Messiah, God judged Israel by setting her aside temporarily.

Throughout this passage Paul is addressing the Gentiles as a whole. He asserts:

- "[The offer of] salvation has come to the Gentiles" (v. 11*b*);
- "[There are] riches for the Gentiles" (v. 12*b*);
- "I am speaking to you Gentiles" (v. 13*a*).

---

[6] R. Kent Hughes, *Romans: Righteousness from Heaven*, Preaching the Word, vol. 6 (Wheaton, IL: Crossway, 1991), 191.

[7] Alva J. McClain, *Romans: The Gospel of God's Grace* (Winona Lake, IN: BMH Books, 1973), 201.

In effect, Paul is saying, "If the Gentiles, to whom the offer of the gospel is now being advanced, refuse to believe, they will miss their opportunity for divine blessing, just as Israel, as a whole, missed theirs. And they too will be cut off."

3. The cultivated branches represent Israelites in general.

4. The grafted wild olive branches represent Gentiles in general.

How does this metaphor relate to Israel's future? It teaches that the Jewish nation was cut off the tree but ultimately will be grafted back into it. Paul thus has made three clear explanatory points: First, some Israelites have been cut off the tree because of unbelief (vv. 17, 20). In other words, they were removed from experiencing God's blessing.

Second, Gentiles have been grafted into a position of blessing. Paul uses the illustration of grafting to picture Gentiles being placed in a position of blessing. Paul writes in verse 17: "But if some of the branches were broken off, and you [Gentiles], although a wild olive shoot, were grafted in among the others and now share in the nourishing root of the olive tree...." Normally, the farmer took a healthy olive branch and grafted it into the wild olive tree. He never took a wild olive branch and grafted it into a healthy olive tree because that would ruin the tree from the graft upward. However, that is what Paul said happens. God does something *unnatural,* so to speak; He goes against nature (v. 24). God takes the wild Gentile branch and puts it into the root of Abraham—not so the Gentiles could become Jews, but rather so they might become partakers of the rich root of God's blessing. Instead of ruining the tree (God's place of divine blessing), this graft provides blessing to the believing Gentiles.

Third, Israel will be grafted back in later (v. 23). As God moves to restore Israel, He plans to reconnect them to divine blessing. This anticipates a time during the tribulation when God is both severe with Israel (about 66 percent of the nation is judged—Zech 13:8) and kind to them (as the nation is restored—Zech 13:9). Then, as they see the Messiah coming in the clouds as the Tribulation comes to a close, they will believe in Him and enter the millennial kingdom. The prophet Zechariah explains that this forthcoming national revival will be inaugurated by God's grace which results in national repentance: "And I will pour out on the house of David and the inhabitants of Jerusalem a spirit of grace and pleas for mercy, so that, when they look on me, on him whom they have pierced, they shall mourn for him, as one mourns for an only child, and weep bitterly over him, as one weeps over a firstborn." (Zech 12:10). We even know the substance of this sad prayer of repentance:

> Who has believed what he has heard from us? And to whom has the arm of the LORD been revealed? ² For he grew up before him like a young plant, and like a root out of dry ground; he had no form or majesty that we should look at him, and no beauty that we should desire him. ³ He was despised and rejected by men, a man of sorrows, and acquainted with grief; and as one from whom men hide their faces he was despised, and we esteemed him not.
>
> ⁴ Surely he has borne our griefs and carried our sorrows; yet we esteemed him stricken, smitten by God, and afflicted. ⁵ But he was pierced for our transgressions; he was crushed for our iniquities; upon him was the chastisement that brought us peace, and with his wounds we are healed. ⁶ All we like sheep have gone astray; we have turned—every one—to his own way; and the LORD has laid on him the iniquity of us all (Isa 53:1-6).

This is exactly what Paul is describing in 11:26 as he informs us that "all Israel will be saved."

THE FUTURE OF THE GENTILES AND THE NATION OF ISRAEL
Romans 11:25–32

We should remember that this entire passage in Romans is basically answering our primary question: "What happens to Israel in the future?" (vv. 1, 15, 25). The present time of divine blessing for Gentiles is also a record of unbelief. Verse 25 informs us that the time of the Gentiles will end as the bride of Christ is completed. At that time, only a minority of Gentile peoples will have believed. However, there is coming a time when "all Israel will be saved" (v. 26). So Paul looks into the future of both Gentiles and Jews in this section of his analysis.

> ²⁵ Lest you be wise in your own sight, I do not want you to be unaware of this mystery, brothers: a partial hardening has come upon Israel, until the fullness of the Gentiles has come in. ²⁶ And in this way all Israel will be saved, as it is written, "The Deliverer will come from Zion, he will banish ungodliness from Jacob"; ²⁷ "and this will be my covenant with them when I take away their sins." ²⁸ As regards the

gospel, they are enemies for your sake. But as regards election, they are beloved for the sake of their forefathers. [29] For the gifts and the calling of God are irrevocable. [30] For just as you were at one time disobedient to God but now have received mercy because of their disobedience, [31] so they too have now been disobedient in order that by the mercy shown to you they also may now receive mercy. [32] For God has consigned all to disobedience, that he may have mercy on all (Rom 11:25-32).

God's Plan for the Gentiles (Romans 11:25)

With regard to the Gentiles, the focus of God's plan is on an *ongoing gathering,* as a mystery is played out in world history. "Mystery" (μυστήριον, *musterion*) refers to the plan and purpose of God that was hidden in the past and impossible for human beings to discover apart from further revelation from God.[8] In other words, prior to Paul's writing about this mystery, it was a secret. The word is used several times in the New Testament to refer to truth that was previously not known.

- The mystery of the kingdom of heaven (Matt 13)
- The mystery of the union of Jews and Gentiles in one body (Eph 3:3)
- The mystery of Christ and His bride, the church (Eph 5:32)
- The mystery of the rapture (1 Cor 15:51)
- The mystery of lawlessness and the Antichrist (2 Thess 2:7)

And the mystery that Paul intends to explain here is the mystery of the temporary setting aside of the nation of Israel—"that a partial hardening has come upon Israel, until the fullness of the Gentiles has come in" v.25). God's plan for Gentiles centers on the ongoing ingathering of believers until the "fullness of the Gentiles" is accomplished. The completion of the bride of Christ, largely a Gentile bride, initiates the returned focus of God on Israel. And the salvation of Israel—when the remnant that survives the tribulation sees Christ coming in the clouds—will inaugurate the literal thousand-years kingdom.

The New Testament refers to both the *times* of the Gentiles (Luke 21:24) and the *fullness* of the Gentiles (Rom 11:25). These are two different eras, though they overlap. The *times of the Gentiles* refers to the period that began

---

[8] Rogers and Rogers, *The New Linguistic and Exegetical Key to the Greek New Testament,* 337.

with Egypt ruling the Jews, and will end with the return of Christ to defeat His enemies and assume the throne of David (Ezek 30:3; Dan 2:31–45; Rev 11:2; 17:10-11). In other words, *times of the Gentiles* refers to the Gentile political domination over Israel.

The *fullness of the Gentiles* refers to this present dispensation during which God's Spirit is calling primarily a Gentile bride for God's Son. James addressed this at the beginning of the church era when he said, "Simeon has related how God first visited the Gentiles, to take from them a people for his name" (Acts 15:14; cf. Acts 10-11).[9] So, the *times of the Gentiles* refers to political domination. But the *fullness of the Gentiles* refers to spiritual deliverance—the calling of Gentiles chosen by God to make up the bride of Christ, the church.[10]

Thus, the hardening of Israel will last "*until* the fullness of the Gentiles has come in." In other words, when the bride of Christ is completed, the principal focus on Gentiles ends, and the focus returns to the nation of Israel. This present age is a period of Gentile ingathering. But Paul clearly says it is going to end; namely, when "the fullness of the Gentiles has come in." The hardening of Israel to the gospel will remain until Christ's church is completed and the New Testament saints are raptured to heaven. We await this next event on the prophetic calendar: the rapture of this completed bride of Christ. Paul himself wrote about it elsewhere:

[15] For this we declare to you by a word from the Lord, that we who are alive, who are left until the coming of the Lord, will not precede those who have fallen asleep. [16] For the Lord himself will descend from heaven with a cry of command, with the voice of an archangel, and with the sound of the trumpet of God. And the dead in Christ will rise first. [17] Then we who are alive, who are left, will be caught up together with them in the clouds to meet the Lord in the air, and so we will always be with the Lord (1 Thess 4:15-17).

The end of the Gentile ingathering is marked by the trumpet call from the bridegroom and a shout that He is on His way. The church is taken up to

---

[9] See further, John Phillips, *Exploring Romans*, John Phillips Commentary Series, Vol. 12 (Grand Rapids: Kregel, 2002), 175-76.

[10] When the church was formed on the Day of Pentecost, it was made up of Jewish believers. Gradually other ethnic groups were added in—the Samaritans (Acts 8), and the Gentiles (Acts 10-11), and eventually the church became mostly Gentile. But we cannot forget that the essence of the church is Jew and Gentile together in one body on equal footing (Ephesians 3:4-6).

the Father's house, and the judgment of God on planet earth, which results in Israel's redemption, begins.

God's Plan for Israel (Romans 11:25–29)

[25] Lest you be wise in your own sight, I do not want you to be unaware of this mystery, brothers: a partial hardening has come upon Israel, until the fullness of the Gentiles has come in. [26] And in this way all Israel will be saved, as it is written, "The Deliverer will come from Zion, he will banish ungodliness from Jacob"; [27] "and this will be my covenant with them when I take away their sins." [28] As regards the gospel, they are enemies for your sake. But as regards election, they are beloved for the sake of their forefathers. [29] For the gifts and the calling of God are irrevocable (Rom 11:25-29).

While at times a Gentile believer is called a son of Abraham, these expressions relate to the fact that we Gentile believers are related to the God of Abraham by being in Christ. The Abrahamic covenant, the root of God's blessings, included this provision for the Gentiles: "in you [Abraham] all the families of the earth shall be blessed" (Gen 12:3, cf. Gal 3:7-8). The Gentiles too are people of God through faith. Nowhere, however, does this mean Israel is now dissolved. In fact, Paul warns against this very thing that non-dispensational systems approve in nullifying Israel's future. He says we should not "be wise in [our] own estimation" but understand "that a partial hardening has happened to Israel until the fullness of the Gentiles." It is only temporary! The Gentiles are not to become presumptuous or proud in believing they have permanently replaced Israel. The people of Israel will have their land, their throne, their temple, and their King. Clearly Israel has not and will not be discarded.

The hardening of Israel's heart in the current dispensation is *partial,* not total. Individual Jews can, and millions have, come to faith in Christ, even now in the church age. Furthermore, this hardening is only *temporary,* not eternal. It will end after the "fullness of the Gentiles" occurs. After God redeems Gentiles from every nation, tongue, and tribe, Israel will have the blinders removed, and the hardening of their hearts will be replaced with faith when they see the Son, the One they pierced, coming in the clouds at the end of the Tribulation. And Israel as a nation will be saved. The Old Testament prophets proclaimed that a separation between believers and unbelievers in Israel would take place in the Tribulation. Ezekiel wrote:

> [33] "As I live, declares the LORD GOD, surely with a mighty hand and an outstretched arm and with wrath poured out I will be king over you. [34] I will bring you out from the peoples and gather you out of the countries where you are scattered, with a mighty hand and an outstretched arm, and with wrath poured out. [37] I will make you pass under the rod, and I will bring you into the bond of the covenant. [38] I will purge out the rebels from among you, and those who transgress against me. I will bring them out of the land where they sojourn, but they shall not enter the land of Israel. Then you will know that I am the LORD" (Ezek 20:33-34; 37-38).

As we noted above, the prophet Zechariah even explained the percentages of believing and unbelieving Jews by the end of the Tribulation:

> [8] "In the whole land, declares the LORD, two thirds shall be cut off and perish, and one third shall be left alive. [9] And I will put this third into the fire, and refine them as one refines silver, and test them as gold is tested. They will call upon my name, and I will answer them. I will say, 'They are my people'; and they will say, 'The LORD is my God'" (Zech 13:8-9).

So when the long promised kingdom of Christ begins, every Israelite (as well as Gentile) entering into the kingdom will have accepted Jesus Christ as his or her Savior and been born again (John 3:3). The kingdom that believing Jews (and Gentiles) enter will last one thousand years (Rev 14:1–5; 20:5–6), before the eternal kingdom begins. During this millennium, the Jewish remnant saved during the Tribulation will comprise the nation of Israel, and the remnant will be a testimony to God's faithfulness in keeping His covenant and giving Israel her promised land forever (vv. 27-29). In this way, God's name will be uniquely glorified.

God's Plan for the World at Large (Romans 11:30-32)

God's plan for the unbelieving world in general is an oft-repeated *invitation*.

> [30] For just as you were at one time disobedient to God but now have received mercy because of their disobedience, [31] so they too have now been disobedient in order that by the mercy shown to you they also may now receive mercy. [32] For God has consigned all to disobedience, that he may have mercy on all (Rom 11:30-32).

Paul points out a wonderful paradox in God's plan of salvation for the world. God providentially uses the Gentiles to make the Jews jealous and come to Christ (Rom. 11:14). On the other hand, God will use redeemed Israel to be the conduit of salvation to the Gentile nations. Through the Old Testament prophet, Yahweh asserts: "And I will vindicate the holiness of my great name, which has been profaned among the nations, and which you have profaned among them. And the nations will know that I am the Lord, declares the Lord God, when *through you* I vindicate my holiness before their eyes" (Ezek 36:23, emphasis added).

Clearly, there is no racial prejudice in God. We find the word *mercy* several times in verses 30–32. God offers mercy to all—Jew and Gentile. His plan for Israel is unique, but to all who have been disobedient—and that means every human being—He graciously offers mercy and eternal life through His Son, Jesus Christ.

We can summarize Romans 11 with these three statements:

- The Aim of God is unstoppable.
- The Assurances from God are irrevocable.
- An Appointment with God is inescapable.

Eventually every living human being of all time will have his or her appointment with God. The Bible tells us, "And just as it is appointed for man to die once, and after that comes judgment" (Heb 9:27). For the believer this will come at the judgment seat of Christ, where Christ will reward the believer's righteous deeds (2 Cor 5:10). For the unbeliever, it will come at the great white throne judgment, where God will condemn him for his unbelief. He witnessed the testimony of God's creation, and he ignored it. He felt the pull of his own conscience, and he violated it. He worshiped tangible gods and refused to acknowledge the Creator God (Rom 1:18–23; Rev 20:11–15).

CONCLUSION
Romans 11:33–36

In summary, Paul has delivered to us in Romans 11 the truth regarding Israel's past, present, and future:

1. God has promised Israel a glorious, eternal future. Their disobedience has not annulled God's promise. He has not finally rejected His disobedient people because His promise was made based on His grace, not Israel's faithfulness. God's promise is evidenced by a continuing remnant of believing Jews, including Paul.

2. Israel's failure has had grave consequences for the nation. Their hearts have been hardened, and in God's plan they have been temporarily set aside.

3. This hardening of Israel has resulted in the salvation of Gentiles, which has prepared the way for Israel's return to the Lord.

4. Israel's hardening is only partial and temporary. When Christ returns at the end of the tribulation period, the nation of Israel as a whole will repent and turn to Him in faith and enter His millennial kingdom.

In the closing verses of Romans 11, the apostle Paul raises his voice in praise:

[33] Oh, the depth of the riches and wisdom and knowledge of God! How unsearchable are his judgments and how inscrutable his ways! [34] "For who has known the mind of the Lord, or who has been his counselor?" [35] "Or who has given a gift to him that he might be repaid?" [36] For from him and through him and to him are all things. To him be glory forever. Amen (Rom 11:33-36).

In response to the great truths of God that he has presented to this point in the letter, including God's plan for Israel, the Apostle Paul praises the One whose wisdom and knowledge are immeasurable and whose ways are unsearchable and inscrutable (v. 33). He praises God as the One who does not need the counsel of man and is not indebted to humanity in any way (vv. 34–35). And he concludes by acknowledging the Lord as the source of all things, the channel through whom all things come, and the goal and glory of all things (v. 36). God is perfectly capable of setting forth His eternal plan for Israel and the nations and bringing that plan to completion in every detail. And He will do precisely that—because He is a God who keeps His promises. It is not surprising, then, that Paul ends his closing doxology of praise by saying, "To Him be the glory forever. Amen."

POSTLUDE

Then he said to me, "Son of man, these bones are the whole house of Israel. Behold, they say, 'Our bones are dried up, and our hope is lost; we are indeed cut off.' Therefore prophesy, and say to them, Thus says the LORD GOD: Behold, I will open your graves and raise you from your graves, O my people. And I will bring you into the land of Israel. And you shall know that I am the Lord, when I open your graves, and raise you from your graves, O my people. And I will put my Spirit within you, and you shall live, and I will place you in your own land. Then you shall know that I am the LORD; I have spoken, and I will do it, declares the LORD."
(Ezekiel 37:11-14)

APPENDIX A:
THE NATURE OF THE OLD
TESTAMENT THEOCRACY[1]

Douglas D. Bookman

The theocracy[2] is well defined as the "form of government under the sole, *accessible Headship* of God Himself," who was "the Supreme Lawgiver in *civil and religious* affairs ... and when difficult cases required it ... the Divine Arbiter or Judge." In sum, "the *legislative, executive, and judicial* power was vested in Him, and partially delegated to others to be exercised under a restricted form."[3] Gleig emphasizes that in this arrangement, God "assumed not merely a religious, but a political, superiority, over the descendants of Abraham; He constituted Himself, in the strictest sense of the phrase, King of Israel, and the government of Israel became, in consequence, strictly and literally, a Theocracy."[4] Again, Oehler summarizes the relationship: "*In Him, as King, all political powers are united* (their earthly bearers are only Jehovah's organs);... As King, He is the *Lawgiver* and *Judge* of His people,... Legal and civil regulations are but an efflux of the divine will.... as King, God is also the *leader of His people's army* (comp. Num xxiii.21); Israel forms the hosts of

---

[1] This brief essay is excerpted from "The Urim and Thummim In Relation to the Old Testament Theocracy," a dissertation written by Doug Bookman in completion of the PhD requirements at Dallas Theological Seminary (2001).

[2] G. F. Oehler, *Theology of the Old Testament*, trans. George E. Day (New York: Funk & Wagnalls, 1889), 199, who credits Josephus with inventing the term "theocracy," defines it briefly as "the government of God," and characterizes the concept as "the form of government in the commonwealth founded by Moses."

[3] George N. H. Peters, *The Theocratic Kingdom*, 3 vols. (New York: Funk & Wagnalls, 1884; repr. Grand Rapids: Kregel, 1972), 1:216 [emphasis original]. Cf. J. H. Kurtz, *Manual of Sacred History*, trans. Charles H. Schaeffer (Philadelphia: Lindsay & Blakiston, 1855), 113, who states, "Theocracy is a government of the State by the immediate direction of God; Jehovah condescended to reign over Israel in the same direct manner in which an earthly king reigns over his people."

[4] G. R. Gleig, *The History of the Bible*, 2 vols. (New York: Harper & Brothers, 1857), 1:218.

Jehovah, Ex. xii. 41 (כל־צבאות יהוה). He goes before them as leader in the combat, Num x. 35; Israel's battles are מלחמת יהוה["the wars of Yahweh"], Num 21:14."[5]

That theocratic relationship, formed by Yahweh with Israel, was unique to human history.[6] Thus, the term should not be taken as descriptive of God's perpetual rule over all creation; as Oehler insists, "The Old Testament idea of the divine kingship expresses, not God's general relation of power toward the world (as being its creator and supporter), but the special relation of His government toward His elect people."[7] Indeed, there has never been another people who knew God as their King in this immediate and actual sense (Deut 4:7). Peters makes this point carefully: "The simple fact is, that since the overthrow of the Hebrew Theocracy, God has not acted in the capacity of *earthly Ruler*, with a set form of government, *for any nation or people on earth....* the application of the word to any nation or people, or organization since then, *is a perversion and prostitution of its plain meaning*"[8]

Thus, the remarkable enthronement scene in Exod 40:34-38; King Yahweh, majestically manifested in the Glory-cloud which represents His very real and special covenant presence with Israel, takes up His regal place above the Ark of the Covenant in the Holy of Holies. In so doing He formally initiates His direct and genuine rule over a newly formed "holy nation" which He has made His "own possession" in order that this people might function as a "kingdom of priests" (Exod 19:5,6). Briggs summarizes: "As holy, the Israelites are the

---

[5] Oehler, *Theology of the Old Testament*, 200 [emphasis original]. Cf. Josephus *Antiquities of the Jews* (trans. Wm. Whiston) 4.8.41, who speaks of God as the "supreme commander" in Israel's battles, "ordaining for a lieutenant under him, one that is of the greatest courage."

[6] The character of the theocracy in Israel is not universally recognized as distinct. For instance, Roland de Vaux, *The Bible and the Ancient Near East*, trans. Damian McHugh (Garden City, NY: Doubleday & Company, 1971), 154, describes that governing arrangement in some detail (which he takes as the tradition preserved by the "Deuteronomist editor"), but then insists that "there is nothing in all this which really sets Israel apart from her neighbors in the Ancient East." He then surveys various contemporary cultures (Mesopotamia, Egypt, Syria, Babylon) in which the kings represented themselves as serving on behalf of their gods. The issue at this point, however, becomes presuppositional, and as such goes beyond the scope of this study. It will suffice to say that to the degree that one acknowledges the supernatural character of Israel's religion and of the Old Testament record, he has the capacity to acknowledge the absolute qualitative distinction between the actual theocracy administered by the living God of Israel and the politically motivated and deliberately manipulative claims of pagan monarchs to rule in the name of their gods.

[7] Oehler, *Theology of the Old Testament*, 199. The term is sometimes used too broadly, as for any situation in which God rules. Peters, *The Theocratic Kingdom*, 217, insists that "the word is abundantly perverted; Romanists apply it to their church; Protestants, to the Christian Church; Unbelievers, to priestly rule; writers, to Christian states, ... thus violating the fundamental and essential idea involved in its meaning." He then affirms, "The Theocracy is something then *very different* from the Divine Sovereignty, and must not be confounded with the same" [emphasis his].

[8] Peters, *The Theocratic Kingdom*, 1:217, [emphasis original].

subjects of their holy King, and as priests they represent Him and mediate for Him with the nations."[9]

Nor should the presence of human mediators of the rule of Yahweh be taken as an indication that the governing arrangement established at Sinai was anything less than a true theocracy. Given the majesty of King Yahweh and the essentially unapproachable character of His holiness, it was essential that He minister His daily rule of the nation through such mediators. As Peters observes, "the institution of such subordinate rulers is *an integral part of a pure Theocracy*, leaving the *Supremacy* untouched and fully acknowledged. The purest Theocracy, adapted to the government of nations, that reason can suggest, must *necessarily*, as a means of honoring the Supreme Ruler and advancing His authority, etc., have its subordinate rulers."[10]

As part of the theocratic arrangement, King Yahweh provided a very special ministry of the Spirit by which those human mediators might be enabled to function as His personal representatives. The ruling arrangement developed in the course of the theocracy, from leaders who were personally selected by Yahweh (Moses, Joshua, the Judges) to a series of kings who rose to leadership by reason of dynastic succession. But throughout the years when the Glory-cloud was resident in the tabernacle/temple, every individual in that succession of human leaders was obligated to acknowledge that he was in fact ruling only as the proxy of King Yahweh.

As to its duration, the theocracy is properly understood as formally beginning with the ratification ceremony of Exod 24:1-8; that ceremony occurred as a result of Israel's acceptance of the covenant relationship initially offered them in Exod 19:3-6 and then reoffered (after more careful explication of the relationship) in 24:1-3.[11] Bush says that as a result of the series of events recorded in Exod 19-24,

---

[9] Charles Augustus Briggs, *Messianic Prophecy* (New York: Charles Scribner's Sons, 1889), 102. Cf. Walter C. Kaiser Jr., *Toward An Old Testament Theology* (Grand Rapids: Zondervan, 1978), 108-109, who concludes concerning the phrase "kingdom of priests" that "it was to be true of everyone in the nation," but then posits that the nation "declined the privilege of being a national priesthood in preference to representation under Moses and Aaron (Exod 19:16-25; 20:18-21)." This seems to vitiate the point of Exod 19:5-6. The terms of the covenant included Israel's service as the mediator of God's truth to the nations; this the nation did regardless of the willingness of that first generation to approach Yahweh individually and personally on the Mount.

[10] Peters, *The Theocratic Kingdom*, 1:217 [emphasis original].

[11] Oehler, *Theology of the Old Testament*, 199, corrects those who regard the theocracy as antedating Mt. Sinai: "The patriarchs called Him *Lord* and *Shepherd*, and it is not until He has formed a people for Himself by bringing Israel up out of Egypt that He is called, Ex. xv. 18, 'He who is *King* for ever and ever.' But the real beginning of His kingly rule was on that day on which He bound the tribes of Israel into a community by the promulgation of the law and the forming of a legal covenant: 'Then He became King in Jeshurun,'" Deut xxxiii.5" [emphasis original].

a peculiar constitution was adopted, familiarly known as the *Theocracy*; according to which God became *the temporal king and supreme civil magistrate of the nation*. Not that it was possible for Jehovah to sink his character of Lord and Master of the universe in his capacity as civil ruler of the Hebrews. He was still, as Creator and Judge, the God of each individual Israelite, as he is the God of each individual Christian; but he moreover sustained, both to every *individual* Israelite, and to the whole *collective body* of the Israelitish nation, the additional relation of *temporal sovereign*. In this character he solemnly proffered himself to the people at Mount Sinai, and in this character he was, with equal solemnity, accepted by their united voice.[12]

By the same token, the theocratic relationship was abandoned in 592 BC[13] when the Glory-cloud departed the temple in the final days before the Babylonians sacked the city of Jerusalem and carried Judah into captivity. Feinberg summarizes the solemn scene depicted in Ezekiel 9-11.

> Ezekiel set forth the fulfillment of the warning uttered by Moses (Deut 31:17) and later by Hosea (Hosea 9:12). God had determined to forsake His sanctuary. There are several steps in His action, showing the Lord's great reluctance to abandon the abode of His own choosing. First He removed the cherub to the threshold of the temple (9:3); next, He lifted His throne over the temple's threshold (10:1); with the cherubim remaining on the right side of the house (10:3), He mounted up and sat on the throne (10:4); finally, He and the cherubim, after lingering at the door of the east gate (10:18-19), left the house (11:22-23) and did not return until the time of 43:2…. God was about to desert the temple, and soon there would be written over the entire structure, as well as their entire religious life, "Ichabod" ("the glory has departed").[14]

To be sure, Yahweh's covenant relationship with Israel did not terminate at the departure of the Glory-cloud; it is not until the coming of Messiah Jesus that

---

[12] George Bush, *Exodus*, 2 vols. in one, (New York: Newman & Ivison, 1852; repr. Minneapolis: Klock & Klock, 1981), 2:3 [emphasis original]. See also his discussion of the appropriateness of the tabernacle prominently placed in the center of the nation, "where the pavilions of all kings and chiefs were usually erected" (2:6). Cf. Num 23:21; Isa 41:21; 43:15; 44:6; Ps 44:4[5]; 68:24[25].

[13] Charles H. Dyer, "Ezekiel," *Bible Knowledge Commentary: Old Testament*, ed. John F. Walvoord and Roy B. Zuck (Wheaton, IL: Victor Books, 1985), 1242. Ezekiel 8-11 constitute a single vision, and the date of the vision is given in 8:1. For a reaction to critical discussions of the date, see Hobart E. Freeman, *An Introduction to the Old Testament Prophets* (Chicago: Moody Press, 1968), 299-302.

[14] Charles Lee Feinberg, *The Prophecy of Ezekiel* (Chicago: Moody Press, 1969), 61.

the covenant ratified at Mt. Sinai "is ready to disappear" (Heb 8:13; Rom 10:4; Gal 3:19, 24).[15] As Andrews states, "This departure of Jehovah from His temple and land ... marked a change in His theocratic relation to His people—a change that continues even to this day. They did not cease to be His covenant people (Lev 26:44). His purpose in them was still unfulfilled, His promises respecting the Messiah and His kingdom were not withdrawn, and He continued to accept their worship."[16] But the relationship of immediate rule by a divine King who manifested His special presence via the Glory-cloud does come to an end at that point.[17]

---

[15] It is the persuasion of this researcher that the book of Esther is intended to teach Israel how Yahweh would administer His rule in the days following the dissolution of the theocracy proper: via providential oversight rather than direct intervention. Thus, after that time God continues to send prophets according to His will, but there are no miraculous interventions on the part of the nation (compare the deliverance from Egypt with the return from Babylon) and God is not available for oracular consultation. This latter point is discussed below.

[16] Samuel J. Andrews, *God's Revelations of Himself to Men* (New York: Scribner's Sons, 1886), 112-13. Andrews goes on to acknowledge this; he states that after the event seen in vision by Ezekiel, "[God] Himself was no more reigning at Jerusalem; the Visible Glory no more dwelt between the cherubim; the Ark was not in the Most Holy Place; the holy fire no longer burned upon the brazen altar; there was no response by Urim and Thummim."

[17] Cf. McClain, *Greatness of the Kingdom*, 126, who says that "the Mediatorial Kingdom of Israel was officially terminated by the departure of the Shekinah-Glory." He relates this to Jeremiah's pronouncement of doom upon the Solomonic line in Jer 22:29-30. "Since the kingdom of the Old Testament was finished, in the mind of the prophet there could be no king in Jerusalem until the kingdom would be re-established in Millennial glory."

APPENDIX B:
WORLDVIEW DISSONANCE

Douglas D. Bookman

Introduction: There are two very different theological and hermeneutical **worldviews** at stake in the debate between the two schools of thought discussed here. The charts on the following pages are an attempt to summarize the distinctions between those two.

The Ultimate Design and Strategy of God

Literalism/Dispensationalism/Premillennialism	Non-Literal/Supersessionism/Covenantal/Amillennialism/Historic Premillennialism
God's ultimate and controlling purpose in all He does in human history is the display of His own glory; the greatest expression of that display will be the culminating stage of world history.	God's ultimate and controlling purpose in all He does in human history is the display of His own glory; that glory will be known and appreciated only in an age and a world to come, rather than in the sequence of world history itself.
• Perhaps the most remarkable single element of God's design is the plan of personal redemption ultimately wrought through Jesus Christ, specifically as it is played out in fulfillment of a covenant God made with the people, Israel.	• The central and controlling element of God's doxological design is the plan of personal redemption ultimately wrought through Jesus Christ, specifically as it is played out in the salvation of the elect from every nation.
• That splendid plan of redemption has in this age been expanded to include Gentiles as Gentiles (as opposed to Abraham to Jesus, when Gentiles could be accepted by Yahweh as they, to one degree or another, surrendered their "gentile-ness" and identified with Israel—John 4:22).	• Although, in the ages before Messiah Jesus, that plan of individual redemption was revealed to and through Israel in shadowy and uncertain form, God's grand and superior revelation of a Gospel for all nations has been made in this age.
• It is in this sense that Gentiles are in this age given "the crumbs that fall from the table" (Mark 7:28). But God's ultimate doxological purpose of demonstrating His covenant faithfulness by redeeming a generation of Israelites awaits fulfillment. Indeed, Gentile acceptance in this age is an important part of God's ultimate scheme to glorify Himself in keeping covenant with the people, Israel.	• Thus, this present age is to be understood as that in which God's redemptive purpose (and thus His doxological purpose in human history) has been finally and completely revealed and is in the process of being fully accomplished.

Literalism/Dispensationalism/Premillennialism	Non-Literal/Supersessionism/Covenantal/Amillennialism/Historic Premillennialism
The Role of Israel in the Design of God	
As above, the most important strategy conceived by God to accomplish His glory is His dealings with the *people/nation*, Israel • Israel was chosen and given the covenant relationship not because of some special merit or goodness on her part (Deut 7:7) • In the days before the coming of Messiah Jesus, in order to be personally saved, individual Israelites were to trust in the promises of God regarding a coming Deliverer and in the provision of a blood-covering offered them by God. • However, God's purpose to display His character to the nations by means of His dealings with His covenant *nation*, Israel, was effective regardless of the number (or percentage) of individual Israelites who were genuine believers at any given time.	Israel was chosen as the *temporary* and *anticipatory* vehicle through which, in a preparatory age (i.e., the OT), God would make known the Gospel of individual redemption by means of types and shadows. • In the days before the coming of Messiah Jesus, God's requirement was that men would discern in those pre-figurements (types and shadows provided in the OT) the truth of the coming sacrifice of Messiah Jesus and trust specifically in that future sacrifice in order to be saved. • Israel's responsibility was to spread the message of God's offer of individual redemption – made known in veiled fashion in the manifold types given to them as a people – to the world.

Literalism/Dispensationalism/Premillennialism	Non-Literal/Supersessionism/ Covenantal/Amillennialism/ Historic Premillennialism
The Design of God in History Before Messiah Jesus	
In the Old Testament era, in successive stages, God utilized first the family of Abraham (Abraham—Moses) and then the nation of Israel (Moses—Christ) as the *primary* vehicle through whom He would display His glory. • The distinctive strategy used by God in the OT involved the placement of the land of Israel on the map of the world, and the shape and contour of that land itself. By reason (in part) of those factors, the dealings of Yahweh with His covenant nation—blessing their obedience and punishing their rebellion (Deut 11:26-28)—and thus His covenant-keeping character, was in fact made known to the nations (Exod 19:5, 6; 1 Sam 4:8; 6:6; Esth 3:16). • One important element of that strategy – the very real, physical Theocracy. At Sinai, Yahweh offered a covenant by which He would become King in Israel. Yahweh ruled as King from 1446 (Exod 40:34-38) through 592 BC (Ezek 11:22-25), though with a punitive hiatus in the days of the Judges (Ps 78:60). • Notice that this strategy involved God's dealings with Israel *as a people/ nation*; as above, the strategy was effective regardless of how many individual Israelites were personally regenerate. • During this era, the offer of individual redemption, first introduced with the promise of a Deliverer who would be the "seed of woman" (Gen 3:15), was always operative; further, continuing revelation (e.g. the Abrahamic covenant) was on occasion given to enhance man's understanding of the dynamics and details of that Gospel plan. • Most basically, however, God's purpose in Israel was the display of His own glory; that glory was on display through King Yahweh's interaction with the *nation* of Israel.	• Throughout the OT, Israel's role was simply to be the stewards and channel of God's growing but veiled plan of individual redemption, to believingly await the Messiah promised through her, and—one day—to receive that promised Deliverer.

Literalism/Dispensationalism/Premillennialism	Non-Literal/Supersessionism/ Covenantal/Amillennialism/Historic Premillennialism
	The Significance of the Hardness of Israel
Pivotal to God's purpose with respect to Israel is the hardness and absolute ill desert of that people—a hardness very much on display in the record of Scripture. That recalcitrance was most dramatically demonstrated in the high-handed rejection of Messiah by one generation of that people. • God promised to accomplish His purpose in Israel both through their obedience and their disobedience (Deut 11:26-28; Rom 11:22-36), all for His own glory. God has remained and will remain faithful to fulfill His promises and His purposes. • Indeed, God's grace and covenant-keeping faithfulness is most compellingly and undeniably demonstrated against the backdrop of man's wickedness and faithlessness; thus is the recalcitrance of Israel not an *impediment* to God's doxological purposes, but an important element of those purposes.	Israel's manifest hardness, ultimately expressed in her rejection of the Messiah, finally exhausted the grace of God and led to her rejection in God's purposes and to her forfeiture of the covenant relationship He had explicitly formed with her. It was because of her hardness that God took the covenant relationship and blessings from Israel and gave them to the "new Israel"—the Church. (Punitive Supersessionism) OR In God's eternal economy He always intended Israel to be only a preliminary stage in the plan of redemption, and thus the covenant God made explicitly with Israel was always meant to be granted ultimately to a different body: the Church. The Church does not *replace* Israel; she *fulfills* God's promises to Israel, albeit in ways entirely contrary to the way those promises were and had to be understood when they were made by God to Israel. (Economic Supersessionism)

Literalism/Dispensationalism/Premillennialism	Non-Literal/Supersessionism/ Covenantal/Amillennialism/ Historic Premillennialism

The Reaction of God to the Hardness of Israel

Literalism/Dispensationalism/Premillennialism	Non-Literal/Supersessionism/ Covenantal/Amillennialism/ Historic Premillennialism
By reason of her rejection of Messiah, Israel was *temporarily* (i.e., she will be restored in fulfillment of God's eternal covenant) and *judicially* (i.e., God is entirely just and faithful to His covenant nature in thus judging that people) set aside as God's primary representative to the nations. • Thus, an unanticipated organism—the church—has been raised up to represent God on earth during this unanticipated era (i.e., the time between the first and the second coming of the Messiah). • None of this was unanticipated *by God*; indeed, it is pivotal to the accomplishment of His doxological purposes as they will be played out with Israel. But the concept of two comings, and thus the reality of the interregnum, was not revealed in the OT (1 Pet 1:10-12). It is in this sense that the present age and the organism of the church can be accurately regarded as "unanticipated"—by God's people, but not by God. • One important role of that organism (the [local] church) in this unanticipated age is to "provoke Israel to jealousy" (Rom 11:11)—i.e., to live out the blessings of the New Covenant which was, after all, promised to Israel and will one day be given to that people – Jer 31, but the blessings of which are enjoyed by believers in this age. Thus, when the nation is confronted once again by Messiah, by reason in part of that people's corporate remembrance of the difference the New Covenant Gospel made in the lives of believers throughout this age, they will "look upon Him whom once they pierced" and cry out in repentance (Zech 12:8ff.).	By reason of her rejection of her Messiah, God abandoned His covenant relationship with Israel. In her stead God raised up a people who would—by reason of God's enabling grace, to be sure—show themselves worthy of His redeeming love, viz. the elect Church. • Israel as a people/nation has no more role to play in the purposes of God; her role has been (re-)assigned to the Church. • God will "keep" His covenant (which is to be understood by NT lights to be only and entirely about personal redemption from sin) only to individual Israelites, many of whom will be saved toward the end of the age and will thereby be made part of the Church.

Literalism/Dispensationalism/Premillennialism	Non-Literal/Supersessionism/Covenantal/Amillennialism/Historic Premillennialism
	The Culminating Kingdom Design of God
In an age to come, in careful fulfillment of explicit promises made to Israel, God will bring a generation of Israelites to saving faith in Messiah Jesus.	In an age to come, all of the elect will be taken to a place of delight and glory in a dimension entirely unlike this world, and in that blessed place God will be glorified forever by those elect ones. There is no end-time Messianic kingdom age to come *on this earth* simply because the kingdom of Messiah Jesus *is already here!*
• Messiah Jesus will then reign with them on the earth for the 1000-year initial stage of the eternal kingdom of God, to the praise of His glory *within the scope of human history.*	• Jesus came to re-define and inaugurate an unanticipated (and unanticipatable) "spiritual" kingdom in the hearts of believing men and women. The OT hope of a physical kingdom was, after all, carnal and material, and was only necessary because of the relative spiritual immaturity, rebellion, and unreadiness of God's covenant people.
• That Messianic kingdom—in both in its initial 1000-yr and its eternal stage—is the exact fulfillment of all that God promised it would be throughout the eras of revelation (including OT promises)—thus demonstrating the covenant-keeping character of Yahweh in a way which will be considered (but never exhaustively comprehended) by the elect throughout eternity.	• The "spiritual" kingdom (i.e., immaterial, non-physical) as re-defined by Jesus and the apostles is entirely different from the one promised in the OT and anticipated by Israel; it is here *today* as God rules and reigns in the hearts of the redeemed elect.
	• It took the superior revelation of the NT to re(de)fine the immature and unworthy concept of the kingdom as comprehended by the OT saints, who came to that misperception because, absent the superior (re-)revelation of the NT, they read the promises of God in their age as meaning what they said. (That is, they understood those promises "intuitively," whereas the superior revelation of the NT teaches that those passages should be understood "non-intuitively"; they mean something other than what the OT reader/hearer would have necessarily understood them to mean.)
	• God's glory will be displayed and appreciated by the elect in a world to come, but there will be no "triumphalist" season of divine glory on display within the scope of human history itself.

WORKS REFERENCED

Abelard, Peter. *Yes and No.* Translated by Priscilla Throop. Charlotte, VT: Medieval MS, 2007.

Allen, David L. "The Identity of Luke and the Jewish Background of Luke-Acts." *Lucan Authorship of Hebrews.* NAC Studies in Bible and Theology, vol. 8. Edited by E. Ray Clendenen. Nashville: B & H Academic, 2010.

Allen, Michael. *Sanctification.* Grand Rapids: Zondervan, 2017.

Allison, Greg. *Historical Theology.* Grand Rapids: Zondervan, 2011.

Ames, William. *The Marrow of Theology.* Edited and Translated by John D. Eusden. Boston: Pilgrim Press, 1968.

Andrews, Samuel J. *God's Revelations of Himself to Men.* New York: Scribner's Sons, 1886.

Arminius, James. "A Declaration of the Sentiments of James Arminius." *Arminius Speaks.* Edited by John D. Wagner. Eugene, OR: Wipf & Stock, 2011, 36-47.

_____. *The Works of James Arminius* (3 vols.). Translated by James and William Nichols. Nashville: Randall House, 2007.

Armstrong, Brian G. *Calvinism and the Amyraut Heresy.* Madison, WI: The University of Wisconsin Press, 1969.

Augustine. *On Christian Doctrine.* Translated by J. F. Shaw. *Nicene and Post-Nicene Fathers,* vol. 2. Grand Rapids: Eerdmans, 1956.

_____. *The City of God.* Nicene and Post-Nicene Fathers, vol. 2. Edited by Philip Schaff. Grand Rapids: Eerdmans, 1979. Also reprint, first series, Peabody: MA: Hendrickson, 1999.

_____. *The Retractions*. The Fathers of the Church, vol. 60. Translated by Mary Inez Bogan. Washington, D. C.: The Catholic University Press, 1999.

Babcock, William. "Augustine and Tyconius: A Study in the Latin Appropriation of Paul," *Studia Patristica* 17 (1978).

Bainton, Roland. *Christian Attitudes toward War Peace: A Historical Survey and Critical Reevaluation*. Nashville: Abingdon Press, 1960.

Bangs, Carl. "Arminius and the Reformation." *Church History*, 30:2 (June 1961), 155-170.

_____. *Arminius, A Study in the Dutch Reformation*. Grand Rapids: Francis Asbury Press, 1985.

Barnabas. "The Epistle of Barnabas." *Apostolic Fathers*. Edited by J. B. Lightfoot. London: Macmillan and Co., 1891; reprint, Grand Rapids: Baker, 1973.

Barth, Karl. "The Doctrine of Reconciliation." *Church Dogmatics*, vol. 4. Edited by G. W. Bromiley and T. F. Torrance. Peabody, MA: Hendrickson Publishers, 2010.

Bauer, Walter, W. F. Arndt, F. W. Gingrich, and F. W. Danker, *Greek-English Lexicon of the New Testament and other Early Christian Literature*, 3rd ed. Chicago: University of Chicago, 2000.

Bavinck, Herman. *Reformed Dogmatics*, vol.1. Translated by John Vriend. Grand Rapids: Baker Academic, 2003.

Baynes, Norman H. "The Political Ideas of St. Augustine's *De Civitate Dei*." *Byzantine Studies and Other Essays*. Edited by Norman H. Baynes. London: University of London, 1955.

Beale, David O. *In Pursuit of Purity*. Greenville, SC: Unusual Publications, 1986.

Bebbington, David W. *The Dominance of Evangelicalism*, vol. 3. A History of Evangelicalism. Downers Grove, IL: InterVarsity, 2005.

Beeke, Joel R. *Gisbertus Voetius, Toward a Reformed Marriage of Knowledge and Piety*. Grand Rapids: Reformation Heritage Books, 1999.

_____, and Paul M. Smalley, *Prepared by Grace, for Grace: The Puritans on God's Way of Leading Sinners to Christ*. Grand Rapids: Reformation Heritage Books, 2013.

Benware, Paul N. *Understanding End Times Prophecy.* Chicago: Moody, 1995.

Berkhof, Louis. *Systematic Theology.* Grand Rapids: Eerdmans, 1959.

Beza, Theodore. *A Brief Declaration of the Chiefe Poyntes of the Christian Religion.* www.covenanter.org/Beza/besas-table.html.

Bierma, Lyle D. *German Calvinism in the Confessional Age, The Covenant Theology of Caspar Olevianus.* Grand Rapids: Baker, 1996.

Bird, Michael. *The Saving Righteousness of God.* Milton Keynes, Great Britain: Paternoster; Wipf and Stock edition, 2007.

Blaising, Craig A. "A Case for the Pretribulation Rapture." *The Rapture, Pretribulation, Prewrath, or Posttribulation.* Edited by Stanley N, Gundry and Alan Hultberg. Grand Rapids: Zondervan, 2010.

_____. "Biblical Hermeneutics: How Are We to Interpret the Relation Between the Tanak and the New Testament on This Question." *The New Christian Zionism.* Edited by Gerald R. McDermott. Downers Grove, IL: IVP Academic, 2016.

Blaising, Craig A., and Darrell L. Bock, *Progressive Dispensationalism.* Wheaton, IL: BridgePoint, 1993.

Blaurock, George. "The Beginnings of the Anabaptist Reformation Reminiscences of George Blaurock." *Spiritual and Anabaptist Writers.* Edited by George H. Williams and Angel M. Merga. Philadelphia: Westminster Press, 1957.

Bock, Darrell. *Acts.* Grand Rapids: Baker Academic, 2007.

_____. *Luke,* The IVP New Testament Series. Edited by Grant R. Osborne. Downers Grove, IL: InterVarsity Press, 1994.

_____. "The Kingdom of God in New Testament Theology." *Looking Into The Future: Evangelical Studies in Eschatology.* Edited by David W. Baker. Grand Rapids: Baker Academic, 2001.

_____. *Acts.* Grand Rapids: Baker Academic, 2007.

Boettner, Loraine. *The Meaning of the Millennium: Four Views.* Edited by Robert G. Clouse. Downers Grove, IL: InterVarsity Press, 1977.

Bonner, Gerald. "Augustine as Biblical Scholar." *The Cambridge History of the Bible*. Edited by P. R. Ackroyd and C. F. Evans. New York: Cambridge University Press, 1989.

Boughton, Lynne Courter. "Supralapsarianism and the Role of Metaphysics in Sixteenth-Century Reformed Theology." *Westminster Theological Journal* 48 (1986): 63-96.

Bray, Gerald. *Augustine on the Christian Life*. Wheaton: Crossway, 2015.

Bredero, Adriann H. *Christendom and Christianity in the Middle Ages*. Grand Rapids: Eerdmans, 1986.

Breytenbach, Cilliers. "'Charis' and 'eleos' in Paul's Letter to the Romans." *The Letter to the Romans*. Edited by U. Schnelle. Walpole, MA: Peeters, 2009.

Briggs, Charles Augustus. *Messianic Prophecy*. New York: Charles Scribner's Sons, 1889.

Bright, Pamela *The Book of Rules of Tyconius*. Notre Dame, Indiana: U of ND Press, 1988.

Bromiley, Geoffrey W. *Historical Theology, An Introduction*. Grand Rapids: Eerdmans, 1978.

Brookes, James Hall. "Believers' Meeting at Clifton Springs." *The Truth*, IV (1878), 402-05.

_____. "Bible Schools." *The Truth*, XIV (1888).

_____. "How I Became a Premillennialist." *The Truth*, XXII (1896), 331-36.

_____. "Meeting for Bible Study." *The Truth*, VII (1881).

_____. *Present Truth*. Springfield, IL: Edwin A. Wilson, 1887.

Brown, Colin. *Christianity and Western Thought*, vol. 1. Downers Grove, IL: Intervarsity Press, 1990.

Brown, Michael, and Zach Keele. *Sacred Bond, Covenant Theology Explored*. Grandville, MI: Reformed Fellowship, 2012.

Brown, Peter. *Augustine of Hippo*. Berkeley, CA: University of California Press, 1969.

_____. *Religion and Society in the Age of Saint Augustine*. London: Faber, 1971.

Bullinger, Heinrich. "One and Eternal Testament," *Fountainhead of Federalism.* Edited by Charles S. McCoy and J. Wayne Baker. Louisville: Westminster/ John Knox Press, 1991.

————. *The Decades of Henry Bullinger.* Edited by Thomas Harding. Cambridge: The University Press, 1850.

Bunyan, John. *Grace Abounding to the Chief of Sinners.* Auburn, MA: Evangelical Press, 2000.

Burkitt, F. C. *The Book of Rules of Tyconius (Liber Regularum).* Cambridge: Univ Press, 1894; reprint, 1967.

Bush, George. *Exodus,* 2 vols. in one. New York: Newman & Ivison, 1852; reprint, Minneapolis: Klock & Klock, 1981.

"Call for the Conference." *Premillennial Essays of the Prophetic Conference.* Edited by Nathaniel West. Chicago: F. H. Revell, 1879; reprint, Bryant Baptist Publications of Minneapolis: Klock and Klock, 1981.

Callahan, James Patrick. *The Clarity of Scripture.* Downers Grove, IL: InterVarsity, 2001.

Calvin, John. *Institutes of the Christian Religion.* Edited by John T. McNeill. Translated by Ford Lewis Battles. Philadelphia: Westminster Press.

Campos, Heber Carlos de Jr. "Johannes Piscator (1546-1625) and the Consequent Development of the Doctrine of the Imputation of Christ's Active Obedience." Ph. D. diss., Calvin Theological Seminary, 2011.

————. *Doctrine in Development.* Grand Rapids: Reformation Heritage Books, 2017.

Canlis, Julie. "The Fatherhood of God and Union with Christ in Calvin, in *"In Christ" in Paul,* ed. Michael J. Thate, Kevin J. Vanhoozer, and Constantine R. Campbell. Grand Rapids: Eerdmans, 2014.

"Canons and Decrees of the Council of Trent." *The Creeds of Christendom*, vol. II. Edited by Philip Schaff. New York: Harper and Brothers, 1877; reprint, Grand Rapids: Baker, 1977.

"The Canons of Dort." *The Creeds of Christendom*, vol. I. Edited by Philip Schaff. New York: Harper and Brothers, 1877; reprint, Grand Rapids: Baker, 1977.

Carpenter, Joel A. *Revive Us Again*. New York: Oxford University Press, 1997.

Carson, D. A. "The Vindication of Imputation: On Fields of Discourse and Semantic Fields." *Justification, What's at State in the Current Debates*. Edited by Mark Husbands and Daniel J. Treier. Downers Grove, IL: IVP Academic, 2004.

Chadwick, Henry. "Augustine," *A Dictionary of Biblical Interpretation*. Edited by R.J. Coggins and J. L. Houlden. London: SCM Press, 1990.

Chafer, Lewis Sperry. "Dispensationalism." *Bibliotheca Sacra* 93 (October-December 1936): 390-449.

Clement. "First Epistle to the Corinthians." *The Apostolic Fathers*. Edited by J. B. Lightfoot. London: Macmillan and Co., 1891; reprint, Grand Rapids: Baker, 1973.

Clouse, Robert G. Introduction to *The Meaning of the Millennium: Four Views*. Edited by Robert G. Clouse. Downers Grove, IL: InterVarsity, 1977.

Cocceius, Johannes. *The Doctrine of the Covenant and Testament of God*, volume 3 of Classic Reformed Theology. Translated by Casey Carmichael. Grand Rapids: Reformation Heritage Books, 2016.

Cohen, Jeremy. *Living Letters of the Law*. Los Angeles: University of California Press, 1999.

Cole, Stewart G. *The History of Fundamentalism*. Westport, CT: Greenwood Press, 1931.

Compton, R. Bruce. "Dispensationalism, The Church, and The New Covenant," *Detroit Baptist Seminary Journal*, 8 (Fall 2003): 3–48.

Cowan, Steven B., and James S. Spiegel. *The Love of Wisdom*. Nashville: B&H Academic, 2009.

Cranfield, C. E. B. *Romans*. International Critical Commentary. Edinburgh: Clark, 1975-79.

Cranz, F. C. "The Development of Augustine's Ideas on Society before the Donatist Controversy." *Augustine: a Collection of Critical Essays.* Edited by R.A. Markus. NY: Doubleday, 1950.

Crowe, Brandon D. *The Last Adam.* Grand Rapids: Baker Academic, 2017

Crutchfield, Larry V. "Ages and Dispensations in the Ante-Nicene Fathers," part two of "Rudiments of Dispensationalism in the Ante-Nicene Period," *Bibliotheca Sacra* 144 (Oct-Dec 1987)377-401.

Daley, Brian E. *The Hope of the Early Church: A Handbook of Patristic Eschatology.* Cambridge: Cambridge University Press, 1991.

Davenant, John. "On the Death of Christ" (1627). *Life, Letters and Writings of John Davenant.* Edited by Morris Fuller. London: Methuen & Co., 1897.

Dawson, Christopher. "St. Augustine and His Age." *A Monument to St. Augustine.* Edited by Thomas F. Burns. New York: The Dial Press, 1930.

Deane, A. *The Political and Social Ideas of St. Augustine.* New York: Columbia University Press, 1963.

Deibler, Edwin C. "The Chief Characteristic of Early English Puritanism." *Bibliotheca Sacra,* 129:516 (October-December 1972): 326-335.

Dekker, Erf. "Was Arminius a Molinist?" *Sixteenth Century Journal* XXVII/2 (1996): 337-351.

DeMar, Gary, and Francis X. Gumerlock. *The Early Church and the End of the World.* Powder Springs, GA: American Vision, 2006.

Dermer, Scott. "'Vellet' or 'Vellent'? A Textual Variant in Augustine's Enchiridion." *The Use of Textual Criticism for the Interpretation of Patristic Texts.* Edited by Kenneth B. Steinhauser and Scott Dermer. Lewiston, NY: Edwin Mellen Press, 2013.

De Vaux, Roland. *The Bible and the Ancient Near East.* Translated by Damian McHugh. Garden City, NY: Doubleday & Company, 1971.

Djaballah, Amar. "Controversy on Universal Grace." *From Heaven He Came and Sought Her.* Edited by David Gibson and Jonathan Gibson. Wheaton, IL: Crossway, 2013.

Dockery, David S. "The Doctrine of the Future: Millennialism in Contemporary Evangelical Theology." *Eschatology: Biblical, Historical, and Practical Approaches*. Edited by D. Jeffrey Bingham and Glenn R. Kreider. Grand Rapids: Kregel, 2016.

Doriani, Daniel M. *Matthew*, vol. 2. *Reformed Expository Commentary*. Edited by Richard D. Phillips and Philip Graham Ryken. Phillipsburg, NJ: P&R Publishing, 2008.

Dunn, James D. G. *The Parting of the Ways*, 2nd ed. London: SCM Press, 2005.

Dyer, Charles H. "Ezekiel." *Bible Knowledge Commentary: Old Testament*. Edited by John F. Walvoord and Roy B. Zuck. Wheaton, IL: Victor Books, 1985.

Erdman, W. J. "Believers' Meeting for Bible Study." *The Truth*, XV (1889).

Estep, William R. *The Anabaptist Story*, 3rd ed. Grand Rapids: Eerdmans, 1996.

Eusebius—The Church History: A New Translation with Commentary. Translated by Paul L. Maier. Grand Rapids: Kregel, 1999.

Evans, Craig A. "Root Causes of the Jewish-Christian Rift from Jesus to Justin." *Christian-Jewish Relations Through the Centuries*. Edited by Alexander Roberts and James Donaldson. Grand Rapids: Eerdmans, n. d

Evans, William B. *Imputation and Impartation, Union with Christ in American Reformed Theology*. Milton Keynes, Great Britain: Paternoster; reprint, Eugene, OR: Wipf and Stock edition, 2009.

Faber, George S. *The Primitive Doctrine of Election*. San Bernardino, CA: Ulan Press, 2012.

Fairbairn, Donald. "Contemporary Millennial/TribulationalDebates: Whose Side Was the Early Church On?" *A Case for Historic Premillennialism*. Edited by Craig L. Blomberg and Sung Wook Chung. Grand Rapids: Baker Academic, 2009.

Feinberg, Charles Lee. *The Prophecy of Ezekiel*. Chicago: Moody Press, 1969.

Feinberg, John S. "Arguing for the Rapture: Who Must Prove What and How?" *When the Trumpet Sounds*. Edited by Thomas Ice and Timothy Demy. Eugene, OR: Harvest House, 1995.

————. "Systems of Discontinuity." *Continuity and Discontinuity*. Edited by John S. Feinberg. Westchester, IL: Crossway Books, 1988.

Fesko, J. V. *Death in Adam, Life in Christ*. Geanies, Fearn, Ross-shire, UK: Christian Focus, 2016.

————. *The Trinity and the Covenant of Redemption*. Geanies, Geanies, Fearn, Ross-shire, UK: Christian Focus, 2016.

Figgis, John Neville. *The Political Aspects of St. Augustine's "City of God."* London: Longmans, Green, and Co., 1921.

Fisher, G. P. *A History of Christian Doctrine*. New York: Charles Scribner's Son, 1896.

Foakes-Jackson, F. J. *The Rise of Gentile Christianity*. New York: George H. Doran Co., 1927.

Fredriksen, Paula. "Tyconius and Augustine on the Apocalypse." *The Apocalypse in the Middle Ages*. Edited by Richard K. Emmerson and Bernard McGinn. Ithaca, NY: Cornell University Press, 1992.

Fredriksen [Landes], Paula. "Tyconius and the End of the World." *Revue des etudes Augustiniennes* 28 (1982).

Freeman, Hobart E. *An Introduction to the Old Testament Prophets*. Chicago: Moody Press, 1968.

Frend, W. H. C. *The Donatist Church: A Movement of Protest in Roman North Africa*, 2nd ed. New York: Oxford, 1985.

Fuller, Morris. *The Life, Letters and Writings of John Davenant*. London: Methuen & Co., 1897.

Gaffin, R. B., Jr., "Glory, Glorification" in *Dictionary of Paul and His Letters*. Downers Grove, IL: InterVarsity Press, 1993.

Gager, John. *Kingdom and Community: The Social World of Early Christianity*. Englewood Cliffs, NJ: Prentice Hall, 1975.

Garcia, Mark A. *Life in Christ*. Milton Keynes, Great Britain: Paternoster; Eugene, OR: Wipf and Stock edition, 2007.

Garner, David B. *Sons in the Son*. Phillipsburg, NJ: P&R, 2016.

Gatiss, Lee. "The Synod of Dort and Definite Atonement." *From Heaven He Came and Sought Her.* Edited by David Gibson and Jonathan Gibson. Wheaton, IL: Crossway, 2013.

Gentry, Kenneth. *He Shall Have Dominion,* 3rd edition. Draper, VA: Apologetics Group, 2009.

Gentry, Peter J., and Stephen J. Wellum. *Kingdom Through Covenant.* Wheaton, IL: Crossway, 2012.

Gilson, Etienne. *God and Philosophy.* New Haven, CT: Yale University Press, 1941.

_____. *The Christian Philosophy of Saint Augustine.* New York: Knopf, 1960.

Gleig, G. R. *The History of the Bible,* 2 vols. New York: Harper & Brothers, 1857.

Glenny, W. Edward. "The Divine Meaning of Scripture: Explanations and Limitations," *Journal of the Evangelical Theological Society* 38:4 (Dec 1995): 481-500.

_____. "The Israelite Imagery of 1 Peter 2." *Dispensationalism, Israel and the Church.* Edited by Craig A. Blaising and Darrel L. Bock. Grand Rapids: Zondervan, 1992.

Gordon, A. J. "The Prophetic Conference." *The Watchword,* I (Dec 1878).

Green, Michael. *The Second Epistle of Peter and the Epistle of Jude.* Tyndale New Testament Commentaries. Edited by R. V. G. Tasker. Grand Rapids: Eerdmans, 1980.

Grisanti, Michael A. "Israel's Mission to the Nations in Isaiah 40-55: An Update," *The Master's Seminary Journal* 9:1 (Spring, 1998): 39-61.

Guindon, Ken. *History Is Not Enough!* n. p.: Xulon Press, 2007.

Gumerlock, Francis X. "The Rapture in an Eleventh-Century Text," *Bibliotheca Sacra* 176 (January-March 2019): 81-91.

Gundry, Robert. *The Church and the Tribulation.* Grand Rapids: Zondervan, 1973.

Hall, David D. *The Antinomian Controversy, 1636-1638.* Middletown, CT: Wesleyan University Press, 1968.

Harinck, Cor. "Preparationism As Taught By the Puritans." *Puritan Reformed Journal* 02:2 (July 2010): 159-171.

Harvey, Chadwick. *God's Prophetic Timeline.* Washington D.C.: WND, 2016.

Harvey, Paul B., Jr., "Approaching the Apocalypse: Augustine, Tyconius, and John's Revelation." *Augustinian Studies* 30:2 (1999).

Hauser, Charles August, Jr. "The Eschatology of the Early Church Fathers." Th.D. diss., Grace Theological Seminary, May, 1961.

Haynes, Stephen R. *Reluctant Witnesses: Jews and the Christian Imagination.* Louisville, KY: Westminster John Knox Press, 1995.

Helm, Paul. "Calvin, Indefinite Language, and Definite Atonement." *From Heaven He Came and Sought Her.* Edited by David Gibson and Jonathan Gibson. Wheaton, IL: Crossway, 2013.

Hesselgrave, David J. "Saving the Future of Evangelical Missions: How to Survive a Tsunami." Unpublished paper, n.d.

Hill, Charles. *Regnum Caelorum*, 2nd ed. Grand Rapids: Eerdmans, 2001.

Hill, Jonathan. *The History of Christian Thought.* Downers Grove: InterVarsity Press, 2003.

Hoch, Carl. "The Significance of the SYN-Compounds," *Journal of the Evangelical Theological Society* 25:2 (June 1982): 175-183.

Hodge, A. A. *Outlines of Theology.* Carlisle, PA: The Banner of Truth Trust, reprint, 1999; rewritten and enlarged edition originally published in 1878.

Hodge, Charles. *Systematic Theology*, vol. III. Grand Rapids: Eerdmans, 1871-73.

Hoekema, Anthony. *Created in God's Image.* Grand Rapids: Eerdmans, 1986.

Holifield, E. Brooks. *The Covenant Sealed: The Development of Puritan Sacramental Theology in Old and New England, 1570-1720.* New Haven: Yale University Press, 1974.

Hollett, Brock David. *Debunking Preterism* (Kearney, NE: Morris Publishing, 2018).

Hooker, Thomas. *The Soul's Preparation for Christ, Being a Treatise of Contrition*; reprint, Ames, IA: International Outreach, Inc., 1994.

Horner, Barry E. *Eternal Israel.* Nashville: Wordsearch Academic, 2018.

Horton, Michael. *The Christian Faith*. Grand Rapids: Baker, 2006.

_____. *God of Promise*. Grand Rapids: Baker, 2006.

House, H. Wayne "Premillennialism in the Ante-Nicene Church." *Bibliotheca Sacra* 169 (Jul.-Sept. 2012): 271-282.

Hughes, R. Kent. *Romans: Righteousness from Heaven*. Preaching the Word, vol. 6. Wheaton, IL: Crossway, 1991.

Hultberg, Alan. "A Case for the Prewrath Rapture." *The Rapture, Pretribulation, Prewrath, or Posttribulation*. Edited by Stanley N, Gundry and Alan Hultberg. Grand Rapids: Zondervan, 2010.

Hyde, Daniel. Web article, Sep 26, 2014, at http://www.ligonier.org/blog/what-covenant-grace.Hippolytus. *Christ and Antichrist*. Ante-Nicene Fathers, vol. 5. Edited by Alexander Roberts and James Donaldson; reprint, Peabody, MA: Hendrickson, 1999.

_____. *The Expository Treatise Against* Jews. Ante-Nicene Fathers, vol. 5. Edited by Alexander Roberts and James Donaldson; reprint, Peabody, MA: Hendrickson, 1999.

Ice, Thomas. "Did Edward Irving Invent the Pre-Trib Rapture View?" *The Master's Seminary Journal* 27:1 (Spring, 2016): 57-73.

_____. Introduction. *The Great Tribulation, Past or Future?* Grand Rapids: Kregel, 1999.

Ignatius. "Epistle to the Magnesians," *Apostolic Fathers*. Edited by J. B. Lightfoot. London: Macmillan; reprint, Grand Rapids: Baker, 1973.

Irenaeus. *Against Heresies*. The Ante-Nicene Fathers, vol. 1. Edited by A. Cleveland Coxe; reprint, Peabody, MA: Hendrickson, 1999.

"Is Evangelical Theology Changing?" *Christian Life* (March 1956), 16-19.

Jacobs, Andrew S. "Jews and Christians." *The Oxford Handbook of Early Christian Studies*. Edited by Susan Ashbrook Harvey and David G. Hunter. New York: Oxford University Press, 2008, 169-185.

Johnson, James T. *The Quest for Peace*. Princeton, NJ: Princeton University Press, 1987.

Johnson, S. Lewis Jr. "Paul and the 'Israel of God': An Exegetical and Eschatological Case-Study." *Essays in Honor of J. Dwight Pentecost*. Chicago: Moody Press, 1986.

Jones, Mark. *Antinomianism, Reformed Theology's Unwelcome Guest*. Phillipsburg, NJ: Presbyterian and Reformed, 2013.

Josephus. *The Works of Josephus*, trans. William Whitson. Peabody, MA: Hendrickson, 2007.

Julius (Africanus). *Fragments of the Five Books of the Chronography of Julius Africanus*. Ante-Nicene Fathers, vol. 6. Edited by A. Cleveland Coxe; reprint, Peabody, MA: Hendrickson, 1999.

Justin (Martyr). *Dialogue with Trypho*. Ante-Nicene Fathers, vol. 1. Edited by Alexander Roberts and James Donaldson; reprint, Peabody, MA: Hendrickson, 1999.

Kaiser, Walter C. Jr., "An Assessment of 'Replacement Theology,'" *Mishkan* 71 (2013), 41-51.

_____. *The Messiah in the Old* Testament. Grand Rapids: Zondervan, 1995,

_____. *Toward An Old Testament Theology*. Grand Rapids: Zondervan, 1978.

Kannengiesser, Charles. *Handbook of Patristic Exegesis: The Bible in Ancient Christianity*. Leiden: Brill, 2004.

Karleen, Paul S. *The Pre-Wrath Rapture of the Church: Is It Biblical?* Langhorne, PA: BF Press, 1991.

Kelly, Douglas F. *Systematic Theology*, vol. 2. Geanies, Fearn, Ross-shire, UK: Christian Focus, 2014.

Kirwan, Christopher. *Augustine*. New York: Routledge, 1989.

Kistler, Don, ed. *The Puritans on Conversion*. Morgan, PA: Soli Deo Gloria Publications, 1990.

Kittel, Gerhard, and Gerhard Friedrich, eds. *Theological Dictionary of the New Testament*. Translated by Geoffey W. Bromiley. 10 vols. Grand Rapids: Eerdmans, 1964–1976.

Koetting, Bernard. "Enzeitprognosen zwischen Lactantius und Augustinus," *Historisches Jahrbuch* 77 (1958).

Kromminga, D. H. *The Millennium in the Church*. Grand Rapids: Eerdmans, 1945.

Kurtz, J. H. *Manual of Sacred History*. Translated by Charles H. Schaeffer. Philadelphia: Lindsay & Blakiston, 1855.

Kuyper, Abraham. *The Work of the Holy Spirit*. Translated by Henri de Vries; reprint, Grand Rapids: Eerdmans, 1956.

Lactantius. *Divine Institutiones*. Ante-Nicene Fathers, vol. 7. Translated by William Fletcher; reprint, Peabody, MA: Hendrickson, 1999.

Ladd, George Eldon. *The Blessed Hope*. Grand Rapids: Eerdmans, 1956.

Landes, Richard. "Lest the Millennium Be Fulfilled: Apocalyptic Expectations and the Pattern of Western Chronography, 100-800 CE." *The Use and Abuse of Eschatology in the Middle Ages*. Edited by Werner Verbeche, Daniel Verhelst, and Andries Welkenhuysen. Leuven, 1988.

LaRondelle, Hans K. *The Israel of God in Prophecy*. Berrien Springs, MI: Andrews University Press, 1983.

Lehrer, Steve. *New Covenant Theology: Questions Answered*. Self-Published, 2006.

Lillback, Peter A. *The Binding of God*. Grand Rapids: Baker, 2001.

Lumpkin, William L., ed. *Baptist Confessions of Faith*. Philadelphia: Judson Press, 1959.

Luther, Martin. *On the Jews and Their Lies*. Translated by Martin Bertram. Luther's Works, Vol. 47. Edited by Franklin Sherman. Philadelphia: Fortress Press; reprint 1971.

_____. *The Magnificat*. Luther's Works, vol. 21. Edited by Jaroslav Pelikan. St. Louis: Concordia, 1956.

Lyons, George. "Eschatology in the Early Church." *The Second Coming: A Wesleyan Approach to the Doctrine of Last Things*. Edited by H. Ray Dunning. Kansas City, Mo: Beacon Hill, 1995.

MacArthur, John F. *The Second Coming*. Wheaton: Crossway Books, 1999.

_____. *Romans*, vol. 2. Chicago: Moody, 1994.

MacArthur, John, and Richard Mayhue, eds. *Christ's Prophetic Plans.* Chicago: Moody, 2012.

Mangum, R. Todd. *The Dispensational-Covenant Rift.* Waynesboro, GA: Paternoster, 2007.

Markus, R. A. "Saint Augustine's Views on the Just War," *The Church and War.* Edited by W. J. Sheils. London: Basil Blackwell, 1983.

_____. *Saeculum: History and Society in the Theology of St. Augustine.* Cambridge: Cambridge University Press, 1970; reprint, 1988.

Martin, Rex. "The Two Cities in Augustine's Political Philosophy," *Journal of the History of Ideas* 33 (April 1972).

McClain, Alva J. *Romans: The Gospel of God's Grace.* Winona Lake, IN: BMH Books, 1973.

McCoy, Charles S., and J. Wayne Baker. *Fountainhead of Federalism, Heinrich Bullinger and the Covenantal Tradition.* Louisville: Westminster/John Knox Press, 1991.

McDermott, Gerald R. "A History of Supersessionism: Is Christian Zionism Rooted Primarily in Premillennial Dispensationalism?" *The New Christian Zionism.* Edited by Gerald R. McDermott. Downers Grove, IL: IVP Academic, 2016.

McGeown, Martyn. "The Notion of Preparatory Grace in the Puritans," (http://www.cprf.co.uk/articles/preparationism.htm).

Melito of Sardis. *On Pascha.* Crestwood, NY: St. Vladimir's Seminary Press, 2000.

Miller, Perry. "The Marrow of Puritan Divinity. *Errand into the Wilderness.* Cambridge, MA: Belknap Press, 1956; reprint, New York: Harper and Row, 1964.

Miller, Timothy. "The Debate Over the *Ordo Salutis* in American Reformed Theology." *Detroit Baptist Seminary Journal* 18 (2013): 41-66.

Minns, Denis. *Irenaeus.* New York: T & T Clark, 2010.

Moo, Douglas J. "The Case for the Posttribulation Rapture Position." *The Rapture, Pre-, Mid-, or Post-Tribulational?* Grand Rapids: Zondervan, 1984.

Moore, Jonathan D. *English Hypothetical Universalism.* Grand Rapids: Eerdmans, 2007.

Moorhead, Jonathan. "The Father of Zionism: William E. Blackstone?" *Journal of the Evangelical Society* 53/4 (Dec. 2000): 787-800.

Morgan, Edmund S. *The Puritan Dilemma.* Boston: Little, Brown and Co., 1958.

Mounce, Robert H. *Romans,* The New American Commentary, vol. 27. Nashville: Broadman & Holman Publishers.

Muller, Richard A. *After Calvin, Studies in the Development of a Theological Tradition.* New York: Oxford University Press, 2003.

_____. "Arminius and the Reformed Tradition," *Westminster Theological Journal* 70.1 (2008): 19-48.

_____. "Divine Covenants, Absolute and Conditional: John Cameron and the Early Orthodox Development of Reformed Covenant Theology," *Mid-America Journal of Theology* 17 (2006): 11-56.

_____. "The Federal Motif in Seventeenth Century Arminian Theology," *Dutch Review of Church History* 62, No. 1 (1982): 102-122.

_____. *God, Creation, and Providence in the Thought of Jacob* Arminius. Grand Rapids: Baker: 1991.

_____. "How Many Points?" *Calvin Theological Journal* 28:2 (November 1993): 425-33.

_____. "Toward the *Pactum Salutis*: Locating the Origins of a Concept," *Mid-America Journal of Theology* 18 (2007): 11-65.

Murray, John. *Collected Writings of John Murray,* vol.2. Carlisle, PA: Banner of Truth, 1977.

_____. *The Imputation of Adam's Sin.* Grand Rapids: Eerdmans, 1959.

"The Mystic Baptist," *Christianity Today,* 56:10 (Nov. 2012), 52-55.

Needham, George C. "Bible Conferences." *The Watchword,* XIX (March 1897.

_____. "Introduction," James H. Brookes. *Present Truth.* Springfield, IL: Edwin A. Wilson, 1887.

_____. *The Life and Labors of Charles H. Spurgeon*. Boston: D. L. Buernsey, 1881.

_____. *The Spiritual Life*. Philadelphia: American Baptist Publication Society, 1895.

Nelson, Neil D., Jr. "'This Generation' in Mat. 24:34: A Literary Critical Perspective." *Journal of the Evangelical Theological Society* 38/3 (Sept. 1996): 369-85.

Newell, William R. *Romans*. Chicago: Moody, 1938.

Nicholson, William R. "The Gathering of Israel." *Premillennial Essays*. Edited by Nathaniel West. Chicago: F. H. Revell, 1879; reprint, Bryant Baptist Publications of Minneapolis: Klock and Klock, 1981, originally 1878.

Nixon, R. E. "Glory." *New Bible Dictionary*. Leicester, England: Downers Grove, IL: IVP, 1996, 415.

Noe, John. *Beyond the End Times*. Bradford, PA: International Preterist Association, 1999.

_____. *Shattering the "Left Behind" Delusion*. Bradford, PA: International Preterist Association, 2000.

O'Keefe, John J., and R. R. Reno. *Sanctified Vision*. Baltimore: Johns Hopkins University Press, 2005.

Oehler, G. F. *Theology of the Old Testament*. Translated by George E. Day. New York: Funk & Wagnalls, 1889.

Olson, Roger E. *The Story of Christian Theology*. Downers Grove, IL.: InterVarsity, 1999.

_____. "943 כָּבֵד." *Theological Wordbook of the Old Testament*. Chicago: Moody, 1999, 426–427.

Origen. *Commentary on John*. Ante-Nicene Fathers, vol. 9. Edited by Allan Menzies; reprint, Peabody, MA: Hendrickson, 1999.

_____. Origen, *Contra Celsum*. Ante-Nicene Fathers, vol.4. Edited by Alexander Roberts and James Donaldson; reprint, Peabody, MA: Hendrickson, 1999.

Oswalt, John. *The Book of Isaiah Chapters 40-66.* The New International Commentary on the Old Testament. Edited by R. K. Harrison and Robert L. Hubbard, Jr. Grand Rapids: Eerdmans, 1993.

Owen, John. *The Works of John Owen*, vol. 3. Edited by William H. Goold; reprint, Edinburgh: Banner of Truth, 1966.

Packer, J. I. "Regeneration." *Evangelical Dictionary of Theology*, 3rd ed. Edited by Daniel J. Treier and Walter A. Elwell. Grand Rapids: Baker, 2017.

_____. *A Quest for Godliness.* Wheaton, IL: Crossway Books, 1990.

Parker, Brent E. "The Israel-Christ-Church Relationship." *Progressive Covenantalism.* Edited by Stephen J. Wellum and Brent E. Parker. Nashville: B&H Academic, 2016.

Payne, Don J. "The Theological Method of Premillennialism." *A Case for Historic Premillennialism.* Edited by Craig L. Blomberg and Sung Wook Chung. Grand Rapids: Baker Academic.

Payne, J. Barton. *The Imminent Appearance of Christ.* Grand Rapids: Eerdmans, 1962.

Perkins, William. *A Golden Chain.* Cambridge: John Legate, 1597; reprint Puritan Reprints, 2010. Edited by Greg Fox. www.lulu.com/spotlight/puritanreprints.

_____. *The Whole Treatise of the Cases of Conscience.* London: John Legatt, 1642; reprint, Early English Books Online, n. d. https://quod.lib.umich.edu/e/eebo/A09365.0001.001?view=toc.

Peters, George N. H. *The Theocratic Kingdom*, 3 vols. New York: Funk & Wagnalls, 1884; reprint, Grand Rapids: Kregel, 1972.

Peura, Simo, "Christ as Favor and Gift (donum): The Challenge of Luther's Understanding of Justification," in *Union with Christ*, ed. Carl E. Braaten and Robert W. Jensen. Grand Rapids: Eerdmans, 1998, 42-75.

Pettegrew, Larry D. "The Historical and Theological Contributions of the Niagara Bible Conference to American Fundamentalism." Th.D. diss., Dallas Theological Seminary, 1976.

_____. "The Perspicuity of Scripture." *The Master's Seminary Journal* 15:2 (Fall 2004): 216-225.

_____. "The New Covenant and New Covenant Theology." *The Master's Seminary Journal 118:2* (Fall 2007): 181-199.

_____. "The New Covenant and New Covenant Theology." *The Master's Seminary Journal* 18:2 (Fall 2007): 181-189.

Pettit, Norman. *The Heart Prepared.* Middletown, CT: Wesleyan University Press, 1989.

Phillips, John. *Exploring Romans.* John Phillips Commentary Series, vol. 12. Grand Rapids: Kregel, 2002.

_____. *Exploring Romans.* Chicago: Moody, 1969.

Picirilli, Robert E. "Foreword." *Arminius Speaks.* Edited by John D. Wagner. Eugene, OR: Wipf & Stock, 2011.

Pietsch, B. M. *Dispensationalism Modernism.* New York: Oxford University Press, 2015.

Piper, John. "Biblical Texts to Show God's Zeal for His Own Glory," Nov 24, 2007, http://www.desiringgod.org/articles/biblical-texts-to-show-gods-zeal-for-his-own-glory.

Piscator, Johannes. *A Learned and Profitable Treatise of Man's Justification.* London: Thomas Creede, 1599. Reproduction by Early English Books Online.

Pocock, Michael. "The Influence of Premillennial Eschatology on Evangelical Missionary Theory and Praxis from the Late Nineteenth Century to the Present." *International Bulletin of Missionary Research*, 33:3 (July, 2009).

Pollman, K "Molding the Present: Apocalyptic as Hermeneutics in *City of God. History, Apocalypse, and the Secular Imagination: New Essays on Augustine's City of God.* Edited by M. Vessy, K. Pollman, and A. Fitzgerald. Bowling Green, OH: Philosophy Document Center. 1999.

Pond, Eugene W. "The Background and Timing of the Judgment of the Sheep and Goats." *Bibliotheca Sacra* 159 (April-June 2002): 201-20; "Who Are the Sheep and Goats in Matthew 25:31-46?" *Bibliotheca Sacra*

159 (July-September 2002): 288-301; and "Who Are 'the Least of My Brethren'?" *Bibliotheca Sacra* 159 (October-December 2002), 426-448.

Portalie, Eugene. *A Guide to the Thought of St. Augustine*. Chicago: Regency, 1960.

Porter, Stanley E., and Brook W. R. Pearson, "Ancient Understandings of the Christian-Jewish Split." *Christian-Jewish Relations through the Centuries*. Edited by Stanley E. Porter and Brook W. R. Pearson. New York: T & T Clark, 2004.

Preus, James. *From Shadow to Promise*. Cambridge, MA: Harvard University Press, 1969.

Preus, Robert. *The Theology of Post-Reformation Lutheranism*, 2 vols. St. Louis: Concordia, 1972.

Quenstedt, Johann Andreas. *The Nature and Character of Theology: An Introduction to the Thought of J. A. Quenstedt from Theologia Didactico-Polemica Sive Systema Theologicum*. Edited, translated, and abridged by Luther Poellot. St. Louis: Concordia, 1986.

Reymond, Robert. *A New Systematic Theology of the Christian Faith*. Nashville: Thomas Nelson Publishers, 1998.

"The Remonstrance." *The Creeds of Christendom*, vol. I. Edited by Philip Schaff. New York: Harper and Brothers; reprint, Grand Rapids: Baker, 1977.

Richardson, Joel. *Mideast Beast*. Washington, D.C.: WND, 2012.

Richardson, Peter. *Israel in the Apostolic Church*. Society for New Testament Studies, Monograph Series 10. New York: Cambridge University Press, 1969.

Riddlebarger, Kim. *A Case for Amillennialism*. Grand Rapids: Baker, 2003.

Rist, John. *Augustine*. Cambridge: Cambridge University Press, 1994.

Roberts, Alexander and James Donaldson, ed. *The Ante-Nicene Fathers*. 1885-1887. 10 vols; reprint, Peabody, MA: Hendrickson, 1994.

Rogers, Cleon L., Jr., and Cleon L. Rogers III. *The New Linguistic and Exegetical Key to the Greek New Testament*. Grand Rapids: Zondervan, 1998.

Rollock, Robert. *Select Works of Robert Rollock*. Edited by William M. Gunn. Edinburgh: Woodrow Society, 1844-1849; reprint, Grand Rapids: Reformation Heritage Books, 2008.

Rosenthal, Marvin. *The Pre-Wrath Rapture of the Church*. Nashville: Nelson, 1990.

Rowley, H. H. *The Unity of the Bible*. New York: Meridian Books, 1957.

Ryrie, Charles C. *Dispensationalism Today*. Chicago: Moody, 1965.

Sandeen, Ernest. *The Roots of Fundamentalism*. Chicago: University of Chicago, 1970; reprint, Baker, 1978.

Saucy, Robert L. *The Case for Progressive Dispensationalism*. Grand Rapids: Zondervan, 1993.

_____. "Is Christ the Fulfillment of National Israel's Prophecy? Yes and No!" *The Master's Seminary Journal* 28:1 (Spring 2017): 17-39.

Schaff, Philip. *History of the Christian Church*, vol. 2, *Ante-Nicene Christianity from the Death of John the Apostle to Constantine the Great, A.D. 100-325*, 5th ed. New York: Scribner's Sons, 1889; reprint, Peabody, MA: Hendrickson, 1996.

_____, ed. "The Westminster Shorter Catechism, 1647." *Creeds of Christendom*, vol. 3. New York: Harper and Brothers, 1877; reprint, Grand Rapids: Baker, 1977.

"Second Clement." Edited by J. B. Lightfoot. London: Macmillan and Co., 1891; reprint, Grand Rapids: Baker, 1973.

Shaw, Mark R. "William Perkins and the New Pelagians: Another Look at the Cambridge Predestination Controversy of the 1590's." *Westminster Theological Journal* 58 (1996):267-301.

Shedd, Russell Phillip. *Man in Community*. Grand Rapids: Eerdmans, 1964.

"Shepherd of Hermas." *The Apostolic Fathers*. Edited by J. B. Lightfoot. Grand Rapids: Baker, n.d.

Showers, Renald E. *The Pre-Wrath Rapture View*. Grand Rapids: Kregel, 2001.

Simon, Marcel. *Versus Israel*. Translated by H. McKeating. Portland: The Litman Library of Jewish Civilization, 1986.

Snider, Andrew. "Justification and the Active Obedience of Christ: Toward a Biblical Understanding of Imputed Righteousness." Th.M. Thesis, The Master's Seminary, 2002.

Stallard, Mike. "Literal Hermeneutics, Theological Method, and the Essence of Dispensationalism," Unpublished paper, Pre-Trib Research Center, 1995, 13-16.

_____. "A Review of R. C. Sproul's *The Last Days According to Jesus*: An Analysis of Moderate Preterism, Part I. *The Conservative Journal* 6/17 (March 2002): 45-71.

Strachan, R. H. "The Second Epistle General of Peter," *The Expositor's Greek Testament*, vol. V. Edited by W Robertson Nicoll. Grand Rapids: Eerdmans, 1970.

Stanglin, Kenneth D. and Thomas H. McCall. *Jacob Arminius, Theologian of Grace*. New York: Oxford University Press, 2012.

Steinhauser, Kenneth. *The Apocalypse Commentary of Tyconius: A History of Its Reception and Influence*. Frankfurt: Peter Lang, 1987.

Stewart-Sykes, Alistair. "Introduction to Melito of Sardis." *On Pascha*. Crestwood, NY: St. Vladimir's Seminary Press, 2000.

Storm, Sam. *Kingdom Come, The Amillennial Alternative*. Fearn, Tain, Ross-shire, UK: Christian Focus, 2013.

Strong, Augustus Hopkins. *Systematic Theology*. Valley Forge, PA: The Judson Press, 1907.

Tertullian. *Against Marcion*. Ante-Nicene Fathers, vol. 3. Edited by A. Cleveland Coxe; reprint, Peabody, MA: Hendrickson, 1999.

_____. *An Answer to the Jews*, vol. 3. Edited by A. Cleveland Coxe; reprint, Peabody, MA: Hendrickson, 1999.

TeSelle, Eugene. *Augustine the Theologian*. New York: Herder and Herder, 1970.

Thuesen, Peter J. *Predestination, The American Career of a Contentious Doctrine*. New York: Oxford, 2009.

Toussaint, Stanley D. "Are the Church and the Rapture in Matthew 24?" *The Return*. Edited by Thomas Ice and Timothy J. Demy. Grand Rapids: Kregel, 1999.

Trueman, Carl R. "Atonement and the Covenant of Redemption." *From Heaven He Came and Sought Her*. Edited by David Gibson and Jonathan Gibson. Wheaton, IL: Crossway, 2013.

_____. "Foreword." Jonathan D. Moore. *English Hypothetical Universalism*. Grand Rapids: Eerdmans, 2007.

Turner, David L. "The Structure and Sequence of Matthew 24:1-41: Interaction with Evangelical Treatments." *Grace Theological Journal* 10.1 (1989): 3-27.

Ursinus, Zacharias. "Larger Catechism." *An Introduction to the Heidelberg Catechism*. Edited by Lyle Bierma, et. al. Grand Rapids: Baker Academic, 2005.

_____. *The Commentary of Zacharias Ursinus on the Heidelberg Catechism*. Translated by G. W. Willard. www.forgottenbooks.com.

van Asselt, Willem J. "Expromissio Or Fideiussio?" *Mid-America Journal of Theology* 14 (2003): 37-57.

_____. Introduction to *The Doctrine of the Covenant and Testament of God*, volume 3 of Classic Reformed Theology. Translated by Casey Carmichael. Grand Rapids: Reformation Heritage Books, 2016.

_____. *The Federal Theology of Johannes Cocceius*. Translated by Raymond A. Blacketer. Boston: Brill, 2001.

van Asselt, Willem J. and Pieter L. Rouwendal. "Introduction: What is Reformed Scholasticism?" *Introduction to Reformed Scholasticism*. Translated by Albert Gootjes. Grand Rapids: Reformation Heritage Books, 2011.

Van der Meer, Frederick *Augustine the Bishop*. New York: Sheed and Ward, 1961.

Van Kampen, Robert D. *The Rapture Question Answered*. Grand Rapids: Fleming H. Revell, 1997.

_____. *The Sign*. Wheaton: Crossway, 1992.

Vercruysse, Jean-Marc. "Tyconius' Hermeneutics." Edited by Tarmo Toom. *Patristic Theories of Biblical Interpretation: The Latin Fathers*. New York: Cambridge University Press, 2016.

Verduin, Leonard. *The Reformers and Their Stepchildren*. Grand Rapids: Eerdmans, 1964.

Vlach, Michael J. "What Does Christ as 'True Israel' Mean for the Nation Israel? Critique of the Non-Dispensational Understanding." *The Master's Seminary Journal* 23:1 (Spring 2012): 43-54.

_____. *Has the Church Replaced Israel, A Theological Evaluation*. Nashville: B&H Publishing, 2010.

_____. *He Will Reign Forever*. Silverton, OR: Lampion, 2017.

_____. "A Non-Typological Future-Mass-Conversion View," in *Three Views on Israel and the Church*. Edited by Jared Compton and Andrew David Naselli. Grand Rapids: Kregel Academic, 2018.

_____. "Rejection Then Hope: The Church's Doctrine of Israel in the Patristic Era." *The Master's Seminary Journal* 19/1 (Spring 2008): 51-70.

_____. "What Dispensationalism Is Not" *Christ's Prophetic Plan*. Edited by John MacArthur and Richard Mayhue. Chicago: Moody, 2012.

Vos, Geerhardus. *Biblical Theology, Old and New Testaments*. Grand Rapids: Eerdmans, 1948.

Walvoord, John. *The Blessed Hope and the Tribulation*. Grand Rapids: Zondervan, 1976.

_____. *The Millennial Kingdom*. Grand Rapids: Zondervan, 1959.

Ware, Bruce A. "Is the Church in View in Matthew 24-25?" *Bibliotheca Sacra* 138 (April-June 1981):158-72.

Watson, Thomas. *A Body of Divinity*. London: Banner of Truth, 1974.

Watson, William C. *Dispensationalism before Darby: Seventeenth-Century and Eighteenth-Century English Apocalypticism*. Silverton, OR: Lampion Press, 2015.

Waymeyer, Matt. *Amillennialism and the Age to Come*. The Woodland, TX: Kress, 2016.

Weber, Timothy. "Dispensational and Historic Premillennialism as Popular Millennialist Movements." *A Case for Historic Premillennialism*. Edited by Craig L. Blomberg and Sung Wook Chung. Grand Rapids: Baker Academic, 2009.

Weir, David A. *The Origins of the Federal Theology in Sixteenth-Century Reformation Thought*. Oxford: Clarendon Press, 1990.

Wells, Tom, and Fred Zaspel. *New Covenant Theology*. Frederick, MD: New Covenant Media, 2002.

Wellum, Stephen J. "Baptism and the Relationship Between the Covenants." *Believer's Baptism*. Edited by Thomas R. Schreiner and Shawn D. Wright. Nashville: B&H Academic, 2006.

Wellum, Stephen J., and Brent E. Parker, ed. *Progressive Covenantalism*. Nashville: B&H Academic, 2016.

Williams, David Riddle. *James H. Brookes: A Memoir*. St. Louis: Presbyterian Board of Publication, 1897.

Williams, George Huntston. *The Radical Reformation*, 3rd edition. Kirksville, MO: Truman State University Press, 2000.

Willis, Geoffrey. *St. Augustine and the Donatist Controversy*. London: S.P.C.K., 1950.

Windass, Stanley. *Christianity versus Violence: A Social and Historical Study of War and Christianity*. London: Sheed and Ward, 1964.

Witsius, Herman. *The Economy of the Covenants Between God and Man*. London: R. Baynes, 1822; original Latin version, 1677; reprint, Kingsburg, CA: den Dulk Christian Foundation, 1990.

Woolsey, Andrew A. *Unity and Continuity in Covenantal Thought*. Grand Rapids: Reformation Heritage, 2012.

Wright, D. F. "Tyconius." *The New International Dictionary of the Christian Church*. Edited by J. D. Douglas. Grand Rapids: Zondervan, 1975.

Yates, Jonathan P. "The Doctrine of the Future in Augustine." *Eschatology*. Edited by D. Jeffrey Bingham and Glenn R. Kreider. Grand Rapids: Kregel, 2016.

Zwingli, Ulrich. *Selected Works of Huldreich Zwingli*. Edited by Samuel Macauley Jackson. Translated by Lawrence A. McLouth, Henry Preble, and George W. Gilmore. Philadelphia: University of Pennsylvania, 1901.

http://creeds.net/Westminster/shortercatechism.html.

http://www.desiringgod.org/interviews/what-is-gods-glory.

INDEXES

BIBLICAL AND OTHER HISTORICAL PERSONS INDEX

SUBJECT INDEX

SCRIPTURAL INDEX
Old Testament

SCRIPTURAL INDEX
New Testament